BφφφφCNO4M

THE INSPIRED WORD

THE INSPIRED WORD

Scripture in the Light of Language and Literature

LUIS ALONSO SCHÖKEL, S.J.

Translated by
Francis Martin, O.C.S.O.

BURNS & OATES/HERDER AND HERDER

BURNS & OATES LIMITED
25 Ashley Place, London, S.W.1

First published in Great Britain 1967

This translation made from the original manuscript,
La Palabra Inspirada,
published by Editorial Herder S.A., Barcelona, 1966.

Nihil obstat: Rt. Rev. Msgr. William J. Collins, S.T.L.
Censor Librorum

Imprimatur: ✠ Ernest J. Primeau
Bishop of Manchester
July 23, 1965

Disc No.: 78293
© 1965 by Herder and Herder, Incorporated
Reproduced and printed in Great Britain by
Billing & Sons Limited
Guildford and London

General Table of Contents

Abbreviations

AAS	*Acta Apostolicae Sedis*
Ang	*Angelicum*
Bib	*Biblica*
BJRylL	*Bulletin of the John Rylands Library*
CB	*Cultura Bíblica*
CBQ	*Catholic Biblical Quarterly*
CCL	*Corpus Christianorum*, Series Latina
Const.	*Constitution on the Sacred Liturgy*, Latin and English Texts, Liturgical Press, 1964
CTSA	Papers read at the annual meeting of the Catholic Theological Society of America
DBS	*Dictionnaire de la Bible, Supplement*, ed. by L. Pirot, A. Robert, H. Cazelles, Paris, 1928–
D-S	*Enchiridion Symbolorum Definitionum et Declarationum*, last edited by Schönmetzer (22nd ed.), Herder and Herder, 1963
DivTh	*Divus Thomas*
EB	*Enchiridion Biblicum*
EstBíb	*Estudios Bíblicos*
EstEc	*Estudios Eclesiásticos*
ETL	*Ephemerides Theologicae Lovanienses*
GCS	*Griechische christliche Schriftsteller*, ed. by the Kirchenväter-Kommission der Preussischen Akademie, Berlin
Gnom	*Gnomon*
IPQ	*International Philosophical Quarterly*
JTS	*Journal of Theological Studies*
LumVi	*Lumière et Vie*

Mansi	Mansi, *Sacrorum Conciliorum*
NRT	*Nouvelle Revue Théologique*
Pesch	Christian Pesch, *De Inspiratione Sacrae Scripturae*, Freiburg, 1905
PG	Migne, *Patrologia Graeca*
PL	Migne, *Patrologia Latina*
PT	*Philosophy Today*
RB	*Revue Biblique*
RevScPhTh	*Revue des Sciences Philosophiques et Théologiques*
RSS	*Rome and the Study of Scripture*, 6th ed., Grail, 1958
Schol	*Scholastik*
SZ	*Stimmen der Zeit*
TD	*Theology Digest*
TLZ	*Theologische Literaturzeitung*
TRu	*Theologische Rundschau*
TS	*Theological Studies*
VD	*Verbum Domini*
VT	*Vetus Testamentum*
ZAW	*Zeitschrift für die Alttestamentliche Wissenschaft*
ZKT	*Zeitschrift für Katholische Theologie*

ACKNOWLEDGMENTS

The translations of the Old Testament, when they are not original, are taken from the Confraternity of Christian Doctrine version. The New Testament translations, when they are not original, are taken from the New English Bible. Spellings of biblical names and places, however, are those of the King James version. Numbering of the psalms is likewise that used in the King James version. Whenever patristic and other texts are not my own translation, credit is given in the footnotes. Thanks are here expressed to the following publishers for permission to reprint: New Directions, for the two selections from "Requiem for Wolf Graf von Kalckreuth," in *Rainer Maria Rilke. Selected Works*, volume 2, translated by J. B. Leishman, 1960, p. 209; to the same publisher for the selection from *The Literary Essays of Ezra Pound*, edited by T. S. Eliot, 1960, p. 25; and to Penquin Books for the selection from *Poems of St. John of the Cross*, translated by Roy Campbell, 1951, pp. 42–43.

Preface

This book is not meant to be a treatise on inspiration, as can be seen from its theme, the categories in which it moves, and its manner of exposition.

Rather than inspiration, its theme is the word. That is, it centers on that article of faith which declares that God "spoke through the prophets." In my consideration of a mystery which is broad and unfathomable, I have attempted to approach it from a precisely determined viewpoint. Christian Pesch introduced me to the centuries-old tradition of the Church in regard to this mystery, and beginning from that position, I have attempted to bring to it the categories and acquisitions of the philosophy of language and literary analysis. These represent a limited aspect, but one that embraces many more particular aspects in a unifying synthesis.

This approach determines the general lines of our essay. The radical human capacity to speak is realized in various languages and actualized in the individual speech act. This individual act may be given form in a literary work which is then actualized by being re-presented and repeated, and then finally consummated in the act by which it is received. God also descends to speak to us, taking hold of the human capacity to speak (Logos, condescension) which is realized in two languages concretely (election in history, language in society). These chosen languages are given literary form by means of a divine impulse given to certain men (inspiration, psychology of literary creation), and this results in a series of works which go to make up one work (the inspired work, the Scriptures) which is in turn actualized by being proclaimed and read in the Church wherein it is received and given its consummation. Thus, God speaks to man, and man listens and responds.

13

This book is not a strictly scientific study: there is no vast accumulation of erudition or profound and exclusive penetration into one problem. It is rather the result of frequent reflection on the mystery of the word of God in the Church.

I have sought in these reflections to achieve breadth rather than depth. And, in a certain sense, this book is more or less a review of these reflections, ordering them and examining them so as to prepare the way for future reflection. I hope to profit from the criticism and interest of others, for in these matters monologue is less fruitful than dialogue.

I have preferred the expositive tone of an essay in order to be more conversational and accessible, and thus I have put the more technical matters in footnotes. The essay form has allowed me to express my reflections in terms that are imaginative and symbolic, without always bringing them to the last stage of conceptual refinement.

As I was writing this book, I kept in mind the educated Christian public who have become aware of the modern biblical movement. The study which follows seeks to preserve contact with those who were already actively present as it was being written.

Jerusalem, Easter 1964
Rome, All Saints Day 1964

I
THE WORD
HUMAN AND DIVINE

Locutus Est per Prophetas

1. An Article of Faith

During Mass on Sunday, the people stand and, led by the priest, make profession of their faith. In this solemn liturgical act, the community is assembled and arrayed in readiness—not for war, but to declare its belief. The people stand firm and united, showing forth the strength of the Spirit which inspires them and the unanimity of their convictions. Yet they stand humbly, for an act of faith is an act of humility and a gift of grace. At this moment in the liturgy, a flood tide of grace levels all other differences by raising those present to the level of the priest-mediator, to the level of the supernatural. The community is activated by a force more than human, because within it there flows the power of grace.

Do all understand what they profess? Yes, at least in a rudimentary fashion; for to believe is already to understand, in the sense that faith means an opening out of oneself and a surrendering to an insight. Do all understand in the same way? Do all believe with the same awareness, depth, clarity, and fullness? No, for these perfections of faith vary and can increase with meditation and study. Intellectual effort which has as its object a reality of faith enables us to grow in knowledge. This is what we mean by theology; it is faith seeking to understand.

This increase in understanding the faith we profess can take place in the liturgy itself. The structure of the liturgical office for a feast day, its various components: Scripture readings, prayers, hymns, and actions, are designed to shed light on the mystery being commemorated. Then, too, during the service, a preacher may explain the meaning of the feast and its mystery and thereby increase our understanding. This growth in understanding which is effected by the liturgy tends to be living and spontaneous rather *than reflexive or systematic. Thus, the Christian inspired by the liturgy may continue his search for understanding outside of it in a science which is called theology.*

Our profession of faith as expressed in the Creed is divided into articles. In the third section, which treats of the Holy Spirit, we declare of Him that He "spoke through the prophets" . . . "qui locutus est per prophetas." These words express the substance of our faith regarding sacred Scripture, our inspired books. Does everyone grasp the meaning of what they are professing to believe? Again, yes—they do. It is quite easy to understand what it means to speak, and not too difficult to have some notion of what a prophet is, while we all know in general what it means to speak through another. It is precisely this rudimentary understanding of the activity of the Holy Spirit and of the word of God which can be enriched by theological study. We can reflect on the movement of the Holy Spirit which we call inspiration, or on the historical context of the inspired authors. We can consider the presence of the inspired books within the Church, and see the consequences implied by such a reality for our own lives as Christians. These are some of the directions in which we can turn our gaze in order to enlarge our view and understanding of what it means when we say "Who spoke through the prophets."

THE SPIRIT

Before descending to particulars, let us first examine the context in which we are going to move—the context of the Spirit.[1] The Spirit is a "divine wind" (Gn 1), an elemental force. The Spirit hovered over the abyss at the beginning of creation; the Spirit swooped down on the warrior Samson and drove him on to great exploits for the salvation of his people. The same Spirit gathered from the four winds gave life to dry bones, while Ezekiel the prophet looked on; just as it was this Spirit which God breathed into Adam to give him life. The Spirit was a soft breeze relieving the anguish of Elijah, and a fourfold docile wind, resting on the shoot of Jesse. The Spirit is a hurricane and tongues of Pentecostal fire, the secret prompter of our cry to God as "Father," prodigal of His gifts and graces in the early Church and throughout all time.

[1] We will treat of the context of the Trinity later on: cf. chs. 14 and 15.

It is thus that we should think of the Spirit; mighty, sovereignly free, restless and many-sided, present and yet unseen. It is within this context of vitality and freedom that we must consider the inspiration of the sacred books. We search for neat precision, but the Spirit eludes the pigeonholes of our thinking. We attempt to focus our concepts, but the Wind will not be contained; we make airtight distinctions, yet the Spirit renders them porous. The Spirit breathes where He will; we hear His voice but we know not whence He comes or where He goes. This is the context in which to situate the charism of inspiration. It finds actual and living existence only in intimate connection with the many other charisms conferred on Israel and the Church.

With such suppleness of mind, sensitive to these dynamic realities, and humble enough to see ourselves baffled, we approach the study of the inspired authors and their inspired books. We are undertaking an investigation of what is radically a mystery of faith. May the Spirit Himself give us the gift of understanding that we may penetrate a little into this mystery of His action.

When we call inspiration a charism, we are describing one of the characteristics of the Church. The sacred books pertain to the institution of the Church, to her structure. They are something institutional and constitutive. Yet, in the Church, what is institutional remains open to charismatic activity, since without charisms, the Church could not endure. All of her institutions, the papacy, episcapacy, priesthood, dogmatic definitions, and the rest, are permeated with the charismatic, that is to say, they are activated by the presence of the Spirit Who guarantees to the Church the possession of supernatural realities such as infallibility and holiness. But even these recognized and established institutions must leave room for charismatic activity which is unforeseen and irresistible. The Spirit Who acts within the Church will not be bound.

When we say, then, that inspiration is a charism, there are important consequences. The presence of the Scriptures within the Church is a presence of the Spirit, and that means the presence of activity. The Bible is one of the institutional channels for the working of the Holy Spirit, and at the same time it lies open and ready at hand for any new and unexpected activity on His part. The very reading and interpreting of the sacred text pertain to the realm of the charismatic. There is an infallible and authoritative interpretation as well as one that is inspired and free. And at the service of both of these is the more modest, human effort of the scholar, who may also receive the Spirit's touch.[2]

By designating inspiration as a charism, we are not led to think of it as something apart from the other charisms which give life to the Church: the charisms of sanctity, of inspiration, of miracles and healing, of wisdom, counsel, and preaching, are as so many interwoven threads forming the design of a unique and beautiful tapestry.

Pierre Benoit[3] has attempted to extend the range covered by the term "inspiration," distinguishing and organizing its application by means of "analogies." Thus, he speaks of a "cognitive inspiration," conferring knowledge; an "oratorical inspiration," which can be subdivided into "prophetic" and "apostolic"; a "hagiographical inspiration," conferring the power to write; and a "dramatic inspiration," conferring the power to act. This last can be operative either within the people of God as a whole or conferred on specially chosen individuals, and is realized today in ecclesiastical inspiration or in the assistance given to the magisterium.

This schema of Benoit, by indicating the mutual relations and common source in the Spirit of the various charisms, restores to the inspiration of sacred Scripture a context which is full, more complex, and "analogous." One could cite in its favor the etymology of the word "in-spiration" itself (breathe into), as well as the free use made of the word by early writers who applied the term "inspired" to councils and to some ecclesiastical authors.

However, all things considered, we cannot accept Benoit's terminology. Nowadays, usage has consecrated the term "inspiration" and given it a specific significance. To use it now, and ignore this specification, could easily cause us to slide from analogy to ambiguity. A much more traditional and less risky procedure would be to use the term "charism" to indicate this common context and intimate interconnection, keeping "inspiration" as a technical term. This would not prevent us from distinguishing within the over-all process of inspiration itself various stages or aspects. In such a line

2 During the third session of Vatican II (October 5th, 1964), Bishop Edelby gave a very forceful presentation of this theme of the Spirit in Scriptures.

3 P. Benoit, "Les Analogies de l'inspiration," in *Sacra Pagina*, Gembloux, 1959, vol. 1, pp. 86–99.

of investigation, the studies of Benoit can be seen to have contributed greatly to the speculative clarification of the mystery.

St. Thomas has taught us to situate the gift of "prophecy" (not, strictly speaking, inspiration) among the charisms, or *gratiae gratis datae*.[4] With his predilection for the sapiential ordering of things he divides the charisms into three groups. There are gifts pertaining to knowledge, namely prophecy and ecstasy; gifts pertaining to speech, namely the gift of tongues, and of eloquence; and gifts pertaining to action, that is, the gift of miracles. Rigid adherence to this division has brought with it unnecessary problems in the neo-scholastic tracts *"de inspiratione sacrae Scripturae."* Later, we shall have occasion to return to this idea. For the present, without entering into "disputed questions," we simply assert the fact that inspiration is a charism pertaining to language— "Who spoke through the prophets."

The Word

In the charism of inspiration, the activity of the Spirit is characterized by language. There is assertion, communication, and knowledge. Now all of these pertain to the realm of Logos which means precisely knowledge and its communication in words, and they constitute the elements of revelation which involves thinking, speaking, communication, and understanding.

Let us take the word "revelation" in a very wide sense; then we shall be able to begin our consideration on the level of strictly human experience. For example, we say that the image made by light on a sensitive film is "revealed" during the developing process. Or we say that the atom or heredity "reveal" their secrets to a mathematical or experimental investigation. Then there is a higher, or deeper, meaning to the term. I might say that a landscape, tempest, or a tropical sky at night has been a revelation to me because it led me to see something behind or beyond it. Is it that things reveal themselves, or is it that something which is not a mere object, is discovered in them?

But we need not go so far or so deep. The most insignificant thing in the world lies open, manifesting itself to man. Its being is a presence, a manifestation; its being is knowable, and yet we

[4] *Summa Theol.* II–II, 171–178.

would not say of it that it lays aside its veil or reveals itself. When a man takes possession of such a manifestation and contemplates a being which manifests itself to his understanding, he names it in an act of his spirit; he gives to it a power to be manifest, and confers on it a new kind of presence and openness; he reveals it to himself and to others.

Already we can see the radical connection which binds "revelation" and "language" together. If we wish to proceed, cautious in our terminology, we might reserve the term "revelation" to a more exalted sphere. But since everyday language knows no such scruples, we think it better to begin at this level, so rich in suggestive possibilities, which comes before any strict terminological precisions. The child is the great explorer of a "new world" because all the world is new to him. Everything is for him a revelation, and to bestow names on objects and use them is for a child sheer delight.

Actually, the word "revelation" is more often used in connection with persons, or subjects. Two characteristics serve to describe a person: intellectual self-possession, or consciousness; and volitional self-possession, or liberty. A dog also has knowledge in a sensory way, but it does not know that it is knowing; it possesses tendencies, but not freely. I, on the contrary, when I know an object, am aware of myself as a knower in the act of knowing. I can store up knowledge and bring it to bear on new situations, aware of it as past and as mine. I possess my knowledge, and, in it, myself. In a way still more radical, I possess my will. For I make decisions, and suspend them or revoke them. I direct my activity to a goal I have determined; I reflect and ponder before deciding, and after having acted, I know that I am master of these acts and responsible for them. This possession is something interior to itself, it is enclosed on itself. Thus, I can keep this activity as my own exclusive possession; I can veil it from other eyes, or again, I may reveal it. Because I possess myself, I am able to hide myself and cut myself off, no matter what pressure or violence is brought to bear. Because I possess myself, I am able to open myself in communication with another person, revealing myself in a gift freely given. Here, in acts which are fully personal, do we find completely justified the use of the term "revelation."

It is true, of course, that even without wishing it, we reveal ourselves by our actions and spontaneous reactions. There are sciences and methods which interpret such symptoms. But in a full and free self-revelation, one which is desired and realized, there is no need to interpret symptoms; there is a mutual knowledge and penetration. This personal revelation, both conscious and free, can be expressed through some deliberate action such as the giving of a bouquet of flowers ("say it with flowers"), or by a handshake, or it can be expressed in words. By personal revelation, we make another person a sharer in our own intimate possession, and he in his turn makes us a sharer in his.

Once again our analysis has brought us to language as the ideal medium for personal revelation. What is more, our theme of mutual revelation, consummated in dialogue, has been struck. This theme will recur again. For the moment, however, let us be content only with having enunciated it.

And what about God? Is He a Person? May He, too, veil Himself or reveal Himself? Here faith comes to our aid, and tells us that God subsists in three Persons; indeed, this faith itself already implies a revelation. The Augustinian speculations on the Trinity, which rely on data taken from the Scriptures, will be our guide here.

No one possesses himself by knowledge and liberty as God does. The plenitude of God can be possessed only by God. The Father possesses the fullness of God, which means He possesses Himself; but He does not keep this possession for Himself. Rather, in a Word, mysterious and all-embracing, He communicates the divine plenitude to the Person of the Son in such a way that the Son possesses the whole of divinity just as the Father does. He is the Son, the Image, the Word of the Father. This fullness of divinity, which the Father and the Son possess as shared, is communicated by them to the Holy Spirit, again in such a way that He, too, possesses the whole of divinity. If we stretch the term "revelation" to its limits, we could say that within God there is a sort of revelation. Or better, we might say that the divine life is an interior revelation of the Father to the Son, of the Father in the Son. But this is to speculate on a truth which must remain a mystery.

We have not yet left the interior of the divinity; rather, we have followed the bold speculations of St. Augustine into the very center of the divine life. If, however, we limit the term "revelation" to a narrower sense, then the inner life of God does not meet its requirements. We have need of some action on the part of God, by which He would open Himself, "externalize" Himself in actions or words. But is such a revelation compatible with the nature of God? Again, relying on the authority of St. Augustine, who is, in turn, basing his writings on Scripture, we can say that it is precisely because there is within God a Word Who is the adequate expression of the divinity, that there can be some act external to God which is a partial, many-sided reflection of what He is. The reason why St. John and St. Paul say that all things were made by the Word and in the Word is that any external manifestation of God is rooted in this inner manifestation, in the Son, the Image, the Word. All revelation of God outside Himself is an imitation of the mysterious manifestation within.

If we know anything or are able to say anything about the inner life of God, it is because this life has been given external expression in a revelation, and has provided us with a means of entering dimly into the very source of its mystery.

THE THREE MEDIA OF REVELATION

The Epistle to the Hebrews opens with a solemn, closely worded introduction: "When in former times God spoke to our forefathers, he spoke in fragmentary and varied fashion through the prophets. But in this, the final age, he has spoken to us in the Son, Whom he has made heir to the whole universe, and through whom he created all orders of existence: the Son who is the effulgence of God's splendour and the stamp of God's very Being, and sustains the universe by his word of power. When he had brought about the purgation of sins, he took his seat at the right hand of majesty on high, raised as far above the angels, as the title he has inherited is superior to theirs." [5]

In the above theological synthesis, all that is lacking for completeness is some reference to God's revelation in history. This we find in Chapter 11, and even here in Chapter 1 it is implied in the verbal forms which are used. Christ is referred to as the effulgence of God's splendor and the stamp of God's very Being. Strictly speaking, these words refer to the Incarnate Christ. But since, in

[5] Heb 1:1–4.

the Incarnation, the substantial image of the divinity enters into the world, these words may be referred also to the intimate life of the Trinity. We learn further that the world, the first revelation of God outside Himself, was created through Christ, the Word. Prior to His historical coming, and by way of preparation for this final stage of salvation history, there was a "fragmentary and varied" revelation made through the prophets. We have the final and definitive revelation in Christ, Who in His Person is the splendor and the Image of the Father, Who in His acts has "brought about the purgation of sins," and Who in His words has pronounced the message of the Father. The creation, the Scriptures, and redemption in Christ are all intimately related to one another and constitute for us the revelation of God.

REVELATION IN CREATION

Expressions such as "nature," "universe," and "cosmos," are poor substitutes for the word "creation." For the true substance of all nature is found in the fact that it is a creature and as such it is a revelation, or, if we wish to be more precise, a manifestation of God. Everything that God works outside Himself makes Him known and is a sort of language. "The heavens declare the glory of God" by their very existence and motion. When men's eyes are not closed to it, they understand this language of nature which speaks as a creature of its Creator. Indeed, it is a literary commonplace to speak of "the book of creation."

> Everything in this creation
> is to us a book or painting
> or, indeed, a looking glass.[6]

Or, as St. Bonaventure observes in his *Breviloquium*,[7] "The world is like some book in which there appears . . . the Trinity, its Maker."

[6] "*Omnis mundi creatura*
Quasi liber, et pictura
Nobis est, et speculum." Alan of Lille, "Poem," PL 210, 579.
[7] "*Creatura mundi est quasi quidam liber in quo relucet . . . Trinitas fabricatrix.*" Brevil. II, 12.
E. R. Curtius dedicates a chapter to this theme in his study of European literature, *European Literature and the Latin Middle Ages*, New York, 1963, ch. 16, "The Book as a Symbol." There he traces the idea from Greek litera-

St. Paul tells us that "all that may be known of God by men lies plain before their eyes; indeed, God Himself has disclosed it to them. His invisible attributes, that is to say, His everlasting power and deity, have been visible ever since the world began, to the eye of reason, in the things He has made." [8] In other words, for a mind that knows how to reflect, things visible are a revelation of God. St. Paul does not specify exactly what he means by this process of reflection, though he does employ a technical philosophical term, "*nooúmena*," which ought to be translated more or less as "thought out." One form of reflection would be by means of syllogisms which, based on the principle of causality, rise step by step to God and His attributes and perfection. The different "ways" or methods proving the existence of God are more or less various realizations of the principle of sufficient reason. For the Greeks of St. Paul's time and for the men of an age of science, the "ways" of syllogistic thought lie always accessible, and all such roads terminate in God. And fundamentally, given the fact that rationality is of the essence of man, the capacity to reason, as this is actuated by man, can lead him to God. We speak here of possibility in the sense in which the notion is used by Vatican I.[9]

For primitive people of a pre-philosophical culture, there seems to be another "way," and this is usually called the way of symbolic thought. I do not mean to imply that we have here another "demonstration." To demonstrate something is to proceed by precise philosophical method, whereas symbolic thought leads us to God without this strict use of syllogisms. There is, for example, the feeling of some transcendent power within a storm. The storm is somehow greater than itself. It bears the revelation of something transcendent and majestic, something sacred and divine; and this is communicated not through any reasoning process, but in a deep emotional experience. The same can be said about a jet-black sky, all covered with stars; the roar of a volcano; the vast silence of the sea; or the imperious stillness of a forest. Such a "way" is open to

---

ture to Shakespeare, and clearly shows the constant recurrence of the theme. This is of particular interest in the study of Scripture, especially in view of the medieval notion of the three "books" of nature, the soul, and the Scriptures (cf. H. de Lubac, *Exégèse Médiévale*, Paris, 1959–1961, vol. 1, pp. 121–125).

[8] Rom 1:19–20.

[9] D-S 3004. Cf. R. Latourelle, *Théologie de la Révélation*, Bruges, 1963, p. 356.

innumerable vagaries, as the study of comparative religion can well attest. Nevertheless, this same study demonstrates quite clearly that such an approach is deeply religious, and that for many peoples it is a sincere expression of religion. Granted that this be the way of the imagination, one freighted with emotion, still, this does not exclude its fundamentally intellectual character. All symbolic perception has an intellectual content, and is rooted in the subconscious structures of the soul. Afterward, this same perception is transmitted in myths and in powerful poetic images which are of great value both for their intelligible content and their communicative efficacy.[10]

If among the Psalms we find one which is taken and adapted from the cult of Canaan, this only serves as proof that the sacred author saw in this poem an authentic religious experience, expressed correctly enough to be taken over bodily and inserted into a Yahwistic context. This is, in fact, the case with Psalm 29, which honors God present in a storm. It is authentic poetry, intuitive, and free of any trace of a strict reasoning process. A surging, commanding event in nature is contemplated and becomes the object of a symbolic reflection—nooúmena—in which thunder becomes the voice of God. In a similar way, the Hebrew religious poets never hesitated to borrow the classical images of Canaanite poetry in order to express some aspect of God. Thus, the restless ocean appears as a rebellion or confusion on which God victoriously imposes His rule:

> The floods lift up, O Lord
> the floods lift up their voice;
> the floods lift up their tumult.
> More powerful than the roar of many waters,
> more powerful than the breakers of the sea—
> powerful on high is the Lord.[11]

We should not think of the images, symbols, and myths of these Oriental religions as though they were so many illusions or errors, suddenly become holy and true by being incorporated in the Israelite religion, The transmutation process at work within the biblical tradition is not of this order. It would be even more ridiculous to

[10] Cf. R. Guardini, *Religion und Offenbarung*, Würzburg, 1958, ch. 1.
[11] Ps 93.

imagine the biblical authors as men who, though they themselves thought syllogistically, still couched their thought in images because of the rude culture of their people. Poetry is not the art of dressing up syllogisms.

In these and many other biblical examples which could be cited, there is an obvious point of contact with the religions of the ancient Near East. This means that, at least with regard to these points of contact, better still these interchanges of contact, the extra-biblical religions bear witness to an authentic experience of God, even though this may have become contaminated and twisted by other elements.

This is the view commonly held today, and admitted by those who still persist in thinking of myths in categories drawn from rationalism or the Enlightenment. Scholars may discuss the advantages of these ways of approaching God. Here we are only concerned with the fact, creation shows forth God.

Is this manifestation of God a sort of divine language, or must there be some addition made by human language to the data provided by nature? It would seem that the word *nooúmena* in the Epistle to the Romans implies some kind of interior speech; such activity seems to involve a symbolic synthesis or process of reasoning by which propositions are linked together. While it is certainly true that in these processes there is always some sort of rudimentary interior language, for the present we would prefer not to speak of such intellectual activity as an act of language in the formal sense. We have yet to clarify and become familiar with the various shades of meaning in the term "language."

In the Logos, the Father expresses Himself to Himself and communicates to His Son the whole of the divinity. The nature of this vital expressive act itself entitles us to call it analogically a Word— "Logos." The Word is unique and all-sufficient. It is simple, not divided or composed; it is a natural subsisting image, rather than one which is conventional and passing. But when God begins to act outside Himself through the Son, the case is different. God cannot exhaust the infinite virtualities of His image in just one creature. He must now divide and spell out, as it were, this unique image in a well-ordered series of images. These, indeed, make up a sort of language, for they are an ordered system of substitute forms. God cannot communicate to anything outside Himself His own subsisting Being, but only gives to it an existence which is contingent. The necessary loss of a subsistent mode of being is one more factor which makes a creature resemble a language. Every being, though it be on a lesser scale of existence and deprived of the subsistent Being of that for which it stands, represents some interior perfection within God. It is like some immense vocabulary of meaningful words. Created things, by their mutual relationship to one another within a certain order, show forth something of the unity and the relations in God, and go to make up well-formed sentences: while the whole of creation is an ordered system, like some perfect literary masterpiece. As we have seen, this image of the book of creation is not a new one. Fray Luis of Granada, ranging himself in this tradition, speaks of the creatures of this world as so many letters—"beautiful in their consummate perfection, resembling illuminated initial letters which bespeak the handicraft and wisdom of their Fashioner," while Dante compares the world to sheaves of paper *elegantly* bound:

> Within its depths I saw assembled,
> bound by love in one great volume,
> the scattered sheaves of all the world.[12]

The Old Testament employs the idea of language in describing the very moment of creation. The author draws a fine distinction in relating these first creative acts of God. There is first a command, then its execution, and then a naming. This is seen clearly when the call into existence is distinct from the imposition of the name: "Let there be light, and there was light . . . and God called the light Day." We can speak of a "vocation" to exist; and then afterward a "nomination" of a thing in its being. The call to existence is a "saying" on the part of God: "And God said . . ."—and it presents itself as a great and invincible act of language, couched in the form of an imperative, and followed by a series of nouns: light, water, land. As the name of each successive thing is called out by God, its individual reality, its intelligible presence, is established. Things are named at the beginning and remain forever capable of receiving a name. In the creative acts which follow, the

12 "*Nel suo profundo vidi che s'interna,
  legato con amore in un volume,
  ciò che per l'universo si squaderna.*" *Paradiso* 33, 83.

31

author maintains his sublime economy of description, and renounces any attempt to convey the world's objective multiplicity.
Thus, on the fourth day God called the "lights" into existence and
distinguished between the two more important lights. One is for
the day and the other for the night, and they are named respectively "sun" and "moon." But it would be quite foreign to the
simple hieratic style of our author to continue his enumeration by
naming all the stars. He says simply: ". . . and the stars." Yet, we
read in Psalm 147 that God calls all the stars by name, implying at
least that at the beginning He had conferred names on them in the
same way as He had named the sun and the moon. Something
similar happens in the creative acts which follow. The author insists that everything was made "according to its kind" and given
powers "according to its kind," but he never stops to tell us what
name God gave to each of these many creatures.

In the Bible as we have it, where Chapter 2 seems to continue
the story of Chapter 1, it appears that God ceded to Adam the
right of naming all the animals. But since man is the image and
likeness of God, his naming of things in no way excludes a prior
constitutive naming by God. The redactor who joined these first
two chapters did not broach every theological problem. We may
consider the "saying" of God as the cause of a thing's existence,
and the "naming" by God as the reason why it can receive a name.
For to name things means to differentiate them and place them in
order. We may recall in this connection that the first attempts at
science on the part of the Sumerians and Babylonians consisted in
drawing up lists of things, grouped according to some similarity,
plants, animals, atmospheric phenomena, etc. Indeed, this practice
continues into our own time, in the classifying work done by Lin-
naeus or Mendeleev, as well as in the textbooks of descriptive anat-
omy, and linguistic dictionaries.[13]

God creates with His Word, placing things outside Himself
which share in His wisdom and power. This action of His can be
considered a manifestation made through an articulated language
which in its turn is able to divide and order. The result of this
activity is a well-ordered system of things which may be compared

[13] For a treatment of this "Listenwissenschaft," cf. G. von Rad, Old Testament Theology, New York, 1962, p. 425, and the bibliographical material
in n. 23.

to a language system in that it contains a differentiated yet ordered body of reality, capable of being named, and which, in fact, is named and becomes formally language with the advent of man.

This may seem to some people to be a vicious circle. We started from our common experience of language in order to explain by analogy the creative activity of God. Then we saw a similarity to language in this activity itself as described in the Scriptures and by theology. However, the constant practice of the Bible in describing creation as an act of language, the theological formulas of St. John and their subsequent use by the Fathers, assure us of the validity of our explanation. If we are able to take our experience of language as the analogical basis for explaining the divine activity, it is because in a real sense our language imitates this activity. Later, we will see how this is so.

Thus, the first manifestation of God, which is revelation in the broad sense, is accomplished by the works of creation, by creatures themselves. We see in these an image and an analogy of formal language in which revelation in the strict sense will be found.

REVELATION IN HISTORY

Nature is but the stage for history. Absolutely speaking, only man can possess a history, a continual process of irreversible events. Evolutionist thought, even in its acceptable version, tends to transpose this historical dimension of man to the order of a process of nature. Man's history is a revelation of man. Is it also a revelation of God? One hastens to answer in the affirmative, since history makes manifest the providence of God. But in many respects, human history is more a scandal than a manifestation of God, and it is no easy accomplishment to see always and in every event of our lives, whether adverse, humiliating, senseless, or boring, the providence of God.

Psalm 136 is an admirable synthesis of nature and history. It chooses from among creatures a stage-setting of three levels: heaven, the abode of God; earth, the dwelling place of man; and the waters under the earth, which house dark and contrary forces. Then there is mention of the two "lights" which rule the day and night. Even if this veiled reference to time and history is not fully intended, it still remains a fortunate intuition. Nature tends toward history, and shares already in the dimension of the historical.

Leaving aside for the moment the discussion of providence which could seem too remote and general for our consideration, we wish to ask another question more immediate and concrete. Can God take a personal role in history and reveal Himself in this activity?

A scholar who would wish to write a genuine history of a town called Lourdes would have to take into account a person who often plays a leading role in the life of that town. That person is God. Of course, in order to explain correctly these historical facts, a special light would be needed, namely faith. An agnostic would be inclined to list a series of enigmatic happenings which have undoubtedly affected the history of the town. He would finally confront this series of facts with a negative conclusion that they are "at present inexplicable." A believer would have the same facts, but he could give them their true interpretation. But in order to convey this deep meaning which lies revealed, yet hidden, he would have to use narrative techniques which, according to Bernheim, are not allowed in modern historiography. Again, only readers who were also believers would be able to understand the true history of Lourdes.

What we say of Lourdes can be applied also to other times and places in which the presence and power of the Church demand an explanation exceeding that of mere history. But even further afield, we are confronted with a people whose name and deeds are recorded by the chroniclers of this world, but whose history is only explicable when God is seen to be its protagonist. Their history, recounted by those who made it, does not conform to the norms of our modern critical historical writing. This is due not only to their cultural and temporal distance from us, but also to the particular type of history they wish to tell. For they wish to present a true picture of the events they are recounting, one whose depths can only be sounded by faith, and this history is a story whose hero is God.

When God comes down from His transcendence in order to intervene in human history, He manifests His presence and His action. If these interventions are repeated often enough to form a continuity of action, then the individual manifestations, which are as so many points, join to form a line, and this line begins to trace a pattern. This pattern is one of constancy and faithfulness. God's activity reveals His "constants," and man comes to know Him as a loving friend seeking a response, all-seeing, all-powerful, and concerned. God reveals Himself in history.

History is to a people what biography is to an individual. For an individual is also able to reflect on his own life and see there a series of special divine interventions, which make up a line and finally a pattern which reveals God. This revelation is of the same nature that discussed above, though, of course, it remains private. But even as private, we must not forget that this revelation can be communicated to others and shared with them, and can become a center from which radiates the light of God to many persons, and these individuals make up a people.

Theoretically, the action of God, by its power and uniqueness, can suffice of itself to make itself known. Thus, when the third plague fell upon Egypt, the magicians exclaimed: "The finger of God is here." But ordinarily, we require that words be joined to actions, in order that the real meaning of these latter be understood.

In the movie "The End of the Affair" (adapted from the novel by Graham Greene), the director Dmytryk has us look upon a scene in which no word is spoken. The house of Maurice Bendrix is bombed during the London Blitz, and we see the terror of it: actions, gestures, the roar and the din, yet not a word. The story continues, but Sarah, the heroine, begins to act in a strange, incoherent way which neither Bendrix nor the audience is able to understand. Then, at one point, Bendrix begins to read Sarah's diary out loud, and he (and the audience) begins to understand. As he reads, his voice conjures up the scene once again, and we see the same incidents and images which now become intelligible because of the spoken word.

This example, borrowed from the cinema, suggests to us a question. "Isn't God's action in history a sort of language?" Insofar as it is an expression outside Himself, one which is characterized by differentiation and order, we may say that it is a language. It pertains to that type of language which, if we accept the term, may be called "cinematographic." Eisenstein among the creators of this language, and Renato among its analysts, may have discussed its qualities and described its formal elements and their semantic and expressive functions, as well as questions of syntax and style. The analogy is quite sound and not at all fanciful, and it helps us to a real understanding of this new medium.[14] Though sound is important, a movie substantially consists of images. These images succeed one another, uniting and dividing, to present a story. They portray a series of actions which sketch some intelligible pattern by which persons and their histories are made known. We have only to think of the unforgettable achievements of the silent movies: "The Battleship Potemkin" of Eisenstein, "Mother" by Pudovkin, "The Passion of Joan of Arc" by Dreyer, and we will see how true it is that action is a language—provided, of course, that its "vocabulary" be carefully chosen and artistically handled.

It is in this sense that we are entitled to call God's activity in history a sort of language, made up of actions chosen and arranged by Himself in such a way that they "speak" to us. Then, too, God uses language itself as a means of acting in history. The prophet not only foresees what is to happen and predicts it, his very words help to bring it about.[15] The people of God began to exist when they were called together by God. They were assembled as the people of God and began to exist as such when they were called "My people," "the Lord's people," by the imposition of a name which not only defined them, but also established them in their existence. The people received a divine ordinance of a religious and ethical nature which was framed in a series of commandments, called "the ten words."

The story of any love can only be told by introducing elements of dialogue. A child becomes aware of his own personal existence because of the actions and dialogue of his father, just as the people of God achieved self-consciousness because of a relationship with God, in which He both acted in their behalf and spoke with them. We cannot separate, except logically, God's revelation in history and His revelation in words.

We should note in passing that God acts in history using nature as His instrument. That is what characterizes the theophanies, the

14 Cf. S. Eisenstein, *Film Form. Film Sense*, New York, 1957; and R. May, *L'avventura del film; immagini, suono, colore*, Rome, 1952, and *Civiltà della immagini; la TV e il cinema*, Rome, 1957.

15 Von Rad, *op. cit.* (n. 13), treats of the power of the prophetic word in ch. C. Cf. esp. pp. 340ff.

action of God on the "day of the Lord," and the presence of the cosmos as a witness to the justice of God's judgments.

And now we return to the example of a film, in order to draw some conclusions. History usually needs to be explained by word in order to achieve full intelligibility and to make its meaning known. In a film, events, be they real or fictional, are transformed into a series of well-organized images, and in this process they both receive and transmit an interpretation. Mediocre indeed is the director who has to provide, either by a narrator or through one of his characters, a commentary on the scenes he has created. God acts in history, creating and directing it, and then sends His word to "cast the scenes," and convey its deepest meaning. This is the task of the prophet, of the inspired author; they give a meaning to history in the way that they tell it. It is not as though they first related the facts, like some voice off stage, and then interpreted them. No, it is in their very manner of relating the facts that they give to them an interpretation. Their selection and arrangement of events convey in the telling their true interpretation, and give evidence of the deep significance of these events, revealing God as the protagonist. Of course, the sacred author maintains his right to use other facets of language in order to interpret events: speeches placed in the mouth of the principal actors, introductions to his stories, reflections on them, and the rest. By means of the message of Moses and the prophets, the people of God are led to an understanding of the history which they are living. This understanding has been bequeathed to us in writings which might be called "the memoirs of God." St. Paul says that "all these things happened to them by way of symbol, and were written down for our instruction." [16] Events become the narrated word, and thus receive their authentic interpretation through this word which raises them to the level of formal revelation.

Again we see in this second form of revelation, which is through history, that it has its own specific character, and yet it, too, is intimately linked to language and inseparable from word, both acting and interpreting.

[16] 1 Cor 10:11.

37

REVELATION THROUGH THE WORD

God also has especially chosen this way of communicating Himself, of revealing Himself to us.

Let us take any intense human experience—love, pain, beauty, discovery. Its vitality is something total and all-engaging, and it appears to us that the "I" sails on, swept along by the force of the current, and that we behold all this, completely surrounded by the waves, unable to speak, hardly able to understand. Then we are free from the rush of the waters and we retreat some quiet distance, to confront ourselves reflectively with our new experience. First, we divide the continuous whole into various segments. Then we form these segments into some meaningful unity, some structured totality. Thus, our experience becomes language.[17]

> My chest, my chest, —the pain!
> The house of my heart, inside my heart is surging,
> I cannot be still!
>
> My soul hears the trumpet, the cry of war—
> Ruin calls upon ruin, the whole land is asunder.
> Suddenly my tents, quickly my coverings are torn open.
> How long must I see that banner, must I hear that trumpet?
>
> How stupid my people, they know me not.
> Degenerate children, unable to think,
> Wise enough for evil, to do good they know not.
>
> I look at the earth, behold
> waste and emptiness,
> at the heavens—
> there is no light.
> I look at the mountains, behold
> they are shaking,
> at the hills—
> and they quake.
> I look, behold
> there is no one,

[17] For a good treatment of these aspects of poetic language, see Amado Alonso, *Materia y forma en poesía*, Madrid, 1955, esp. the first chapter, "Sentimiento e intuición en la lírica," pp. 11–20.

the birds of the heavens have flown away.
I look, behold
the garden is desert,
all the cities are ravaged and charred
before Yahweh,
before his scowling flame.[18]

Once I have given form to my experience, I dominate it and possess it. Later, I can make it live again with freshness and communicate it. I have described the movement by which we divide the continuum of our experience into elements, which we then order by language. The natural unit of this movement of articulation is the sentence. There are two other movements also possible within language; the first of these complements the one just described, while the other tends in just the opposite direction. The complementary movement occurs when, in place of an intense emotional experience, I am faced with a great multiplicity or a whole series of impressions which seem about to overwhelm me with their abundance. Such realities may be likened to the totality and indivisibility of a vivid experience; and then again language comes to my aid to divide, order, articulate, and compose.

But more important than that activity which is complementary to the movement of articulation is that movement which goes in the opposite direction. It begins with an act of naming. A being actually and concretely existing, manifests itself in its intelligible presence, and is grasped by the mind which gives a name to this presence. It is an elemental and spiritual act in which, by naming a thing, possession is gained both of it and of the self. The name designates the actually existing thing in a total way, without further precisions or distinctions. Distinction pertains to the movement of articulation. The name is co-extensive with the thing for which it stands, since its whole nature is to signify, though in a global and concrete manner. From the act of naming, we pass to the sentence. This is an act by which two names, designations, or significations are joined because of some perceived relation and mutual influence. This relation and influence once understood are possessed by the sentence, which on the one hand renders more precise the global significance of the two names it uses, and on the other raises these designations to a new level of meaning. Once

[18] Jer 4:19–26.

again, this meaning is co-extensive with the sentence, and is also global and concrete. However, the sentence can receive a further significance from its context within life, or action, or thought. Thus, in forming a sentence, man takes possession in a greater measure both of things and of himself in a spiritual act which rises to a unity amid diversity.

This third ascending movement has the same structural character as the two which we have discussed previously. There is differentiation and order, the capacity for division and composition, and both possession and communicability are involved.

But why do I name things and form sentences at all? Is it for my own benefit, my own possession of reality and of myself? Or does my need to communicate with others impel me to articulate my experience, to name and to enunciate in order to share my possession with someone else in a desire for mutual and personal exchange? Man was created social. "Male and female He created them," and this has reference not only to that first and fundamental community of two persons, but also envisages these two as the origin of all society: "increase and multiply." Man lives socially, reaches his perfection in society, and in society achieves his vocation as ruler of the earth. Now, the natural means of establishing a social existence is language, or, if one prefers, dialogue. It seems, then, that the question of deciding whether or not language is primarily a personal or social act is not only difficult, but somewhat pointless. Given the social environment in which I grew up, it is possible either that I conform my expressions of experience to my environment, or that I name things for my own benefit, though even this is consequent on a social situation.[19] Within a diversified community, there will always be these two types, the communicative and the reserved, but this does not lessen the social nature of language and its natural expression in dialogue.

The world becomes human by entering into our life; we change it, conferring on it a new order in which we reveal ourselves. Language is a creation of man, made in his image and likeness. It is manifold and systematic, abundant and ordered. But language, even in the greatest works of literature, never has the subsistent

---

[19] The monological functions of language are usually considered to be consequent on its dialogical functions; cf. Fr. Kainz, *Psychologie der Sprache*, Stuttgart, 1954, vol. 1, part 3, A. 1, 2.

quality of a human person. Man reveals himself by breaking down what is within himself as he places it outside himself, where it lacks something of his own subsistence. In the act of language, man is true to his role as the image and likeness of God. He, too, must create an order of reality in which to reveal himself.

Language embodies the apex of human revelation, and therefore God has chosen this means of communicating and revealing Himself to men, overcoming the anonymity of nature and history. This is, in the strict sense, formal revelation.

All supernatural revelation is immediate in comparison with the natural revelation of God. For in natural revelation, God makes and governs creatures which man can use as a means of knowing God by analogy. That is, God manifests Himself as an *object*, knowable but mediately. In supernatural revelation, however, God reveals His interior, the way one *person* communicates his thoughts to another person, in speech properly so called. This personal and subjective manifestation is of its nature more direct and immediate than the purely objective manifestation of a cause in its effect. Therefore, we may say that *in the Scriptures God speaks to us immediately* because Scripture is the word of God in a formal and proper sense.[20]

We have thus established the context of our act of faith. God's speaking pertains to the realm of Logos, of revelation. And this in the formal sense and in the concrete means that God has spoken, using words. God opens Himself out and reveals Himself to us as one person to another, using the personal, or interpersonal, means of communicating. It is interesting to observe that in the text of the letter to the Hebrews, the verb "to speak" takes no direct object; only the speakers are mentioned. "Of old God spoke to our fathers. . . . now . . . He has spoken to us."

We must now proceed to render this context more precise, following the lead of the article of faith in which we say: "Who spoke

[20] *Omnis revelatio supernaturalis est immediata, prout opponitur revelationi Dei naturali. Nam in revelatione naturali Deus producit et gubernat creaturas, quibus homo uti possit ut mediis ad Deum secundum earum analogiam cognoscendum, seu Deus se exhibet ut* OBJECTUM *mediate cognoscibile. In revelatione vero supernaturali Deus mentem suam manifestat eo modo, quo* PERSONA *cum persona communicat cogitationes suas, seu locutione proprie dicta. Haec personalis et subiectiva manifestatio ex genere suo est magis immediata quam manifestatio pure obiectiva causae per effectum, Eatenus igitur* DEUS NOBIS IN SCRIPTURA IMMEDIATE LOQUITUR, *quia Scriptura est verbum Dei formale et proprie dictum.* Pesch, no. 411.

through the prophets." God spoke to us in human language and through human beings. It is here that this mystery of faith begins to reveal its hiddenness.

Human Words

But does God really speak to us in human words? Well, if He wishes to address us as men, He must. Words can only be a vehicle of interpersonal communication when both persons share their meaning; the two beings who wish to communicate must have a common medium.

But there still remains the question whether God could ever have a language in common with men. Suppose a missionary attempted to translate our elaborate theological science, or some part of it, into a primitive language. Between a sophisticated occidental language and this hypothetical primitive language there will be a considerable difference in the linguistic material available, especially in the area of intellectual concepts and relations. In order to remedy this difference, the missionary will take some elements of his teaching and suit them to the capacity of a less well-wrought language. If he continues, his effort to adapt and translate will inevitably result in raising the level of the primitive language. Even here in the West, such interchanges of adaptation and translation have served to level off, in the good sense of the term, many of our languages. But in all these examples there is a common basis, since all languages result from the common human capacity for articulate communication, and have an essential common likeness.

But this cannot apply to the language of God, for here the differences are infinite. The divine transcendence must be taken seriously. It can only be by some special act of self-abasement, of condescension, that God could direct His speech to us in human words. It is necessarily a completely free and gratuitous act by which God opens Himself to us, and does so in a language truly human. It may be that this divine abasement has left our language touched by the Godhead, raising it to a new level, giving it a new capacity for meaning. Still, it will always be a human language. When we speak of the language of God, it is an analogous predication.

This act by which God lowered Himself to our level was called by the Greek Fathers "*Sunkatabasis*," which the Latin rendered as "*condescendentia*." [21] St. John Chrysostom invokes this principle when he comes on some biblical passage that cannot be taken too literally, as for example the statement that "God walked in the garden in the cool of day." He says in this connection:

We should not take these words too lightly, but neither should we interpret them as they stand. We ought rather to reflect that such simple speech is used because of our weakness, and in order that our salvation be brought about in a manner worthy of God. For if we wish to take words just as they are, and not explain them in a way which befits God, will not the result be utter absurdity? [22]

We should note in the above passage the twofold theme of our weakness and the divine dignity. It is for our salvation that God uses human words, and it is in this sense that they are to be interpreted. The principle of our weakness, and of a salvation worthy of God, is operative throughout all Scripture, and, indeed, certain passages demand its intelligent application. Thus, with regard to the creation of Adam, Chrysostom says:

Do not take these words too humanly, but attribute their style to our weakness. For unless such words were used, how could we ever understand ineffable mysteries? We ought not, therefore, to adhere to the words alone, but should rather understand all things in a way worthy of God.[23]

Here, in addition to the themes mentioned above, we have the notion of a mystery which is to be revealed, but which cannot be revealed except through poor, human language. This principle is also valid throughout all Scripture.

St. Thomas enunciates the same principle in his commentary on

[21] Cf. F. Fabbi, "La condiscendenza divina nell'ispirazione biblica secondo S. Giovanni Crisostomo," *Bib* 14, 1933, pp. 330–347.

[22] Μὴ ἁπλῶς παραδράμωμεν, ἀγαπητοί, τὰ εἰρημένα παρὰ τῆς Θείας Γραφῆς, μήδε ταῖς λέξεσιν ἐναπομείνωμεν, ἀλλ'εννοῶμεν, ὅτι διὰ τὴν ἀσθένειαν τὴν ἡμετέραν ἡ ταπεινότης τῶν λέξεων ἔγκειται, καὶ Θεοπρεπῶς ἅπαντα γίγνεται διὰ τὴν σωτηρίαν τὴν ἡμετέραν. Εἰπὲ γάρ μοι, εἰ βουληθείημεν τῇ προφορᾷ τῶν ῥημάτων κατακολου-Θῆσαι, καὶ μὴ Θεοπρεπῶς ἐκλαβεῖν τὰ λεγόμενα, πῶς οὐ πολλὰ ἕψεται τὰ ἄτοπα. St. John Chrys., "Homily 17 on Gn 3," *PG* 53, 135.

[23] Μὴ ἀνθρωπίνως δέχου τὰ λεγόμενα, ἀλλὰ παχύτητα τῶν λέξεων τῇ ἀσθενείᾳ λογίζου τῇ ἀνθρωπίνῃ. Εἰ γὰρ μὴ τούτοις τοῖς ῥήμασιν ἐχρήσατο, πῶς ἄν μαθεῖν ἐδυνήθημεν ταῦτα τὰ ἀπόρρετα μυστήρια; μὴ τοῖς ῥήμασιν οὖν μόνοις ἐναπομίνωμεν, ἀλλὰ Θεοπρεπῶς ἅπαντα νοῶμεν ὡς ἐπὶ Θεοῦ. St. John Chrys., "Homily 15 on Gn 2," *PG* 53, 121.

the Epistle to the Hebrews, when he says: "In the Scriptures, divine things are communicated to us in the way usually employed among men." [24]

THE WORDS OF MEN

If God were to cause the air to vibrate according to certain frequencies, He could form a sentence, and the man who heard this sentence would hear human words. But they would not be spoken through men. In a similar way, God could have an angel speak, or He could act directly on the nervous system to produce an effect equivalent to speech, or He could form images in the imagination. All this might be called human language, but it would not have been spoken by men. Some seem to think that this would be the ideal manner for God to communicate Himself; it should be through angels, or through some interior word. But such an opinion has little appreciation for the mystery of the Incarnation.

God has wished to speak to us in words which are fully human, and which are spoken by men—"through the prophets." And this means that He has selected a determined language, either Hebrew or Greek, and has chosen certain men: Jeremiah or Paul. In these words, in Hebrew or Greek, written by these authors, God is speaking to me.

But how is that possible? Jeremiah speaks, pouring out his soul, and it is God Who is speaking. St. Paul speaks with all his vibrant emotion, and it is God Who is speaking. Something mysterious must happen within St. Paul or Jeremiah, so that when they speak, God speaks. In reality, what happens is that a mysterious force is at work, one well-described in the Second Epistle of Peter:

But first note this: no one can interpret any prophecy of Scripture by himself. For it was not through any human whim that men prophesied of old; men they were, but, impelled by the Holy Spirit, they spoke the words of God.[25]

Like some ship, impelled by the wind which marks out the wake of its passage, so the biblical writers spoke in the name of God,

---

[24] *In scriptura autem divina traduntur nobis per modum quo homines solent uti.* "Comm. on Heb, ch. 1, L. 4" (Marietti ed., no. 64).

[25] 2 Pt. 1:20–21.

under the action of the Spirit. We call this action "inspiration." It is a work of the Spirit in the realm of language. The effect of this action is described in the Second Epistle to Timothy: "All Scripture is divinely inspired and useful . . ." [26] Scripture comes about by the Breath of God, by the action of the Spirit.

The two passages quoted above, the one from Second Peter and the other from the Second Epistle to Timothy, are the classical statements on the fact of biblical inspiration. With them, we have come full circle, and have fitted the context of the Logos with that of the Spirit or Pneuma. God reveals Himself; He does so in words, and these words are human words, spoken by men. Yet, it is the Spirit Who moves these men to speak and directs them. It is He Whom we profess to have spoken through the prophets.

We have thus completed the circle of our inquiry, and now another, perhaps still more challenging, opens out before us. How exactly does the Spirit act? We wish to penetrate more deeply into the *manner* in which inspiration takes place, in order to appreciate more fully the mystery, though we are aware that our question brings us face to face with problems that are, ultimately, insoluble.

Bibliography for Chapter 1

The Context of the Spirit. For a study of the charismatic gifts, in addition to the commentaries on Romans and First Corinthians (Allo is especially good here), one may consult the theologies of the New Testament: J. Bonsirven, *Theology of the New Testament*, Westminster, 1963; M. Meinertz, *Theologie des Neuen Testaments*, Bonn, 1950. Also the articles in the various theological and biblical dictionaries: *Encyclopedic Dictionary of the Bible* (EDB), a translation and adaptation of *Bijbels Woordenboek*, 2nd ed., by Louis Hartman, New York, 1963; *Dictionary of the Bible*, rev. ed., ed. by J. Hastings, New York, 1963, under "Spiritual Gifts"; *The Interpreter's Dictionary of the Bible*, Nashville, 1962, under "Spiritual Gifts"; and, of course,

[26] 2 Tim 3:16. For a discussion of these texts, cf. A. Bea, *De inspiratione et inerrantia Sacrae Scripturae. Notae historicae et dogmaticae*, Rome, 1947, pp. 2–6.

G. Kittel's *Theologisches Wörterbuch zum Neuen Testament*, Stuttgart, 1933–/, *Theological Dictionary of the Bible*, Grand Rapids 1964–/, ed. by G. W. Bromiley: the first two volumes are available. The finest monograph is that by Karl Rahner, *The Dynamic Element in the Church*, New York, 1964. There are also some good pages in F. Prat, *The Theology of St. Paul*, New York, 1952.

The Context of the Word. Karl Rahner begins his first essay in "Toward a Theology of the Word" (in *The Word*, "Readings in Theology" series, ed. by the Canisianum, New York, 1964) with the remark: "To the poet is entrusted the word. Alas that there is no theology of the word! Why has no one yet begun, like an Ezekiel, to collect the limbs strewn about upon the fields of philosophy and theology, and then to speak the word of the spirit over them so that they rise up a living body?" (p. 3). The renewal of interest can also be seen in the excellent study by R. Latourelle, *Théologie de la Révélation*, Bruges, 1963. In his historical section, he presents us with a clear and concise résumé of the opinions and controversies. The speculative part begins with three chapters entitled "Revelation as Word, Witness and Encounter," "Revelation and Creation," and "History and Revelation." Each is treated briefly and there is not much development of the interrelation of these realities (cf. the review by A. Dulles in *TS* 25, 1964, pp. 43–58). In addition to the bibliography at the end of the book, each chapter is provided with a special bibliography at the beginning of each chapter.

Hans Urs von Balthasar now has *Word and Revelation. Essays in Theology 1*, New York, 1964, and *Word and Redemption. Essays in Theology 2*, New York, 1965; and there is still the excellent study of R. Guardini, *Religion und Offenbarung*, Würzburg, 1958: this latter is less scholastic than Latourelle and approaches the problem more phenomenologically. The first section describes the fact or the phenomenon of religious experience. The second section discusses certain concrete patterns of this experience, while the third section treats of the articulation and formulation of the experience in concepts and images. The work of H. Fries, *Glauben-Wissen. Wege zu einer Lösung des Problems*, Berlin, 1960, is marked by great clarity and is especially valuable for the discussion of faith as directed to a person and faith directed toward propositions. Just recently J. L. McKenzie has collected some of his essays under the title *Myths and Realities*, Milwaukee, 1964; chapter 3, "The Word of God in the Old Testament" (*TS* 21, 1960, pp. 183–206), is very valuable, as is *The Old Testament as Word of God* by S. Mowinckel, New York, 1959. More bibliographical information on this aspect will be given in Chapter 13.

Creation. In addition to the chapter in Latourelle's book, we should mention here the problem of myth and mythopoeic thought. The bibliographical material is immense, much of it is assembled by J. L. McKenzie in his article, "Myth and the Old Testament" (above and *CBQ* 21, 1959, pp. 265–82). The most important single investigator in this field is undoubtedly Mircea Eliade; the works most relevant to our theme are: *Patterns in Comparative Religion*, New York, 1963; *Images and Symbols. Studies in Religious Symbolism*, New York, 1961; *Cosmos and History*, New York, 1959. A more philosophical approach can be found in the works of Ernst Cassirer; cf. esp. *The Philosophy of Symbolic Forms*, vol. 2, *Mythical Thought*, New Haven, 1955; *Language and Myth*, New York, 1946. There are some valuable intuitions in G. van der Leeuw, *Religion. Its Essence and Manifestation*, New York, 1963. A form-critical approach to the problem of myth in the Old Testament can be found in Brevard Childs' *Myth and Reality in the Old Testament*, Studies in Biblical Theology, no. 27, Naperville, 1960. This problem also brings us into the question of the "demythologizing" of the New Testament; the *Elenchus Bibliographicus* compiled by Father Nober in *Biblica* is obliged to accord this question a special section. Some preliminary discussion of the problem can be found in M. Bourke's "Rudolf Bultmann's Demythologizing of the New Testament," *CTSA* 12, 1957, pp. 103–33. A good introduction to Bultmann's thought can be found in L. Malevez, *The Christian Message and Myth. The Theology of Rudolph Bultmann*, Westminster, 1960. Cf. also H. Noack, *Sprache und Offenbarung*, Gütersloh, 1960 (though the language is hard to follow), and J. Pépin, *Mythe et Allégorie*, Paris, 1958 (but only the first chapter: his explanation of Christian allegory is equivocal, as H. de Lubac points out in his *Exégèse Médiévale*).

History. The theme of God's revelation in history is very prominent today. A bibliography relating to the techniques of history writing will be found in Chapter 3. In relation to the Old Testament, there is a fine summary of present thought on the question (though with some misunderstanding of the role of systematic theology) in G. E. Wright, *God Who Acts*, Studies in Biblical Theology no. 8, Naperville, 1952. There is some excellent material in R. A. F. MacKenzie, *Faith and History*, Minneapolis, 1963. W. Pannenberg dedicates a book to the theme of revelation and history (*Offenbarung als Geschichte*, Göttingen, 1961) and returns to the idea in *Essays in Old Testament Hermeneutics*, ed. by C. Westermann, Richmond, 1963; (cf. "Redemption Event and History"). G. von Rad's two-volume *Theologie des Alten Testaments* is extremely helpful (though controversial because of the

47

epistemological views inherent in his view of history); both volumes are available in German, Munich, 1961; the first volume is available in English, *Old Testament Theology*, New York, 1962. The English edition of W. Eichrodt's first volume of his *Theologie des Alten Testaments*, Stuttgart, 1933–1939, Philadelphia, 1961, contains an appendix in which the author vigorously discusses von Rad's historical minimalism. A popular treatment of some of these aspects can be found in J. L. McKenzie, *The Two-Edged Sword*, Milwaukee, 1955. The transposition of historical revelation to the realm of the Christ fact is often mentioned but seldom treated specifically. Studies dealing with the mysteries of the life of Christ are rare. St. Thomas includes thirty-three questions in the third part of the Summa (27–59), and there is a helpful commentary by I. M. Voste, *Commentarius in Summam Theologicam S. Thomae. De Mysteriis Vitae Christi*, Rome, 1940. The continuing revelation in history effected through the sacraments can be studied with the aid of the books by Rahner and Schillebeeckx mentioned in Chapter 15.

2. The Word Divine and Human

THE ACTION OF THE SPIRIT

Once Jesus Christ was describing for an intellectual of His time the mystery of the Spirit—"It blows where it will; you hear its sound, but you know not whence it comes or where it goes."

The Spirit is like that. Is it not then rash to try to seek out His paths? Will He not turn and confound our human speculations, as God once did to Job? Then, too, sometimes His voice is but the whispering of a breeze, and there are times when not even the one inspired hears the noise of the wind astir within him, which moves him.

And so, once again, we are called on to believe in the suppleness and power of the Spirit, able to work in many ways and to traverse untrammeled both the heavens and the earth, able to move men, without forcing their freedom, their personality, or their style.

How ought we to think of this action of the Spirit, so soft that at times no man is aware of it, yet so effective that to Him is attributed whatever is achieved? The activity of the Spirit by which the word of men is also the word of God is quite simply a mystery. In His presence, we ought first to make an act of faith and to confess ourselves too ignorant and weak to understand it. Then we must go on, with humility, to seek understanding.

INSPIRATION AND THE INCARNATION

We are seeking some understanding of a mystery. Well, then, the first thing we must do with any mystery of our redemption is to refer it to the central mystery of this redemption, the Incarnation.

This is not an attempt to explain the obscure by what is more

49

obscure. For, given the unity of the work of our salvation and the unity of revelation, to refer a mystery to this center is already to shed light on it and make it more intelligible. It is especially true of the mystery of inspiration, that in making such a reference there is no artificiality. The movement is already well established by Scripture and tradition, and the famous passage in the letter to the Hebrews has given it classical expression.

". . . God spoke to our forefathers in fragmentary and varied fashion through the prophets. But in this the final age he has spoken to us in the Son. . . ."

The "fragmentary and varied" utterances of the prophets all culminate in God's message delivered "in the Son." We find often in the early Fathers of the Church the notion that Christ was speaking in the Old Testament, preparing for His coming, and foretelling it Himself. I do not refer to that theory which attributes to the Word, or Logos, as the Second Person of the Blessed Trinity, all the words of Scripture; I refer rather to Christ as incarnate. But, actually, it is not easy to distinguish these two aspects in the writings of the Fathers, especially since for some of them "Word" is practically equivalent to "Word Incarnate." Here are some examples of their way of speaking:

St. Hippolytus wrote an essay refuting the errors of a certain Noetus, who held that the Father and the Son were identical. When speaking of the prophets, St. Hippolytus said:

The Word dwelt in these men and spoke of Himself. He was His own herald, pointing out that the Word would appear among men. . . .

By the Word of the Lord the heavens were made: and this is the Word which has been openly made manifest. Thus we behold the Word made flesh and we know the Father through Him. . . .

Only the Word of God is visible, man's word is audible.[1]

St. Ambrose implies the same comparison, putting it in a Eucharistic context:

---

[1] Ἐν τούτοις τοίνυν πολιτευόμενος ὁ Λόγος ἐφθέγγετο περὶ ἑαυτοῦ. Ἤδη γὰρ αὐτὸς ἑαυτοῦ κῆρυξ ἐγένετο, δεικνύων μέλλοντα Λόγον φαίνεσθαι ἐν ἀνθρώποις. . . . τῷ λόγῳ Κυρίου οἱ οὐρανοὶ ἐστερεώθησαν ἄρα οὗτός ἐστιν ὁ λόγος ὁ καὶ ἐμφανὴς δεικνύμενος. Οὐκοῦν ἔνσαρκον λόγον θεωροῦμεν, Πατέρα δ'αὐτοῦ νοοῦμεν. . . . Λόγος δὲ Θεοῦ μόνος ὁρατὸς, ἀνθρώπων δὲ ἀκουστός. St. Hippolytus, "Against Noetus, ch. 12," PG 10, 820.

Drink of Christ that you may drink His words. His word is the Old Testament, His word is the New Testament. The divine Scriptures are taken as drink and consumed as food when the sweetness of the eternal Word sinks into the very marrow and powers of the soul.[2]

St. Cyril of Jerusalem, stressing the unity of the two testaments, the work of one Spirit, concludes with this Trinitarian formula borrowed from St. Paul:

One God, the Father, the Lord of the Old Testament and the New; One Lord, Jesus Christ, Who was foretold in the Old Testament and came in the New; and One Holy Spirit, Who through the prophets preached concerning Christ, and when Christ had come descended on Him and made Him known.[3]

The comparison between the Word Incarnate and the word of the Scriptures was dear to many medieval theologians, whose reflections on the *"verbum dei abbreviatum"* gave rise to many passages of real beauty. Rupert of Deutz, for instance, in his treatise on the Holy Spirit says:

What do we believe the Scriptures to be if not the Word of God? . . . The whole of the Scriptures is but the One Word of God. . . . Therefore, when we read the holy Scriptures, we are dealing with the Word of God, we behold the Son of God through a mirror, darkly.[4]

When Moses and the prophets composed the Scriptures, which are the word of God, what did they do but conceive Christ spiritually in their hearts by the spirit of prophecy, and bring Him to birth with their mouth? [5]

2 "Bibe Christum, ut bibas sermones eius; sermo eius Testamentum est Vetus, sermo eius Testamentum est Novum. Bibitur Scriptura divina et devoratur Scriptura divina, cum in venas mentis ac vires animae succus Verbi descendat aeterni." St. Ambrose, "Comm. on Ps 1:33," PL 14, 984.

3 Εἰς Θεὸς, ὁ Πατὴρ, παλαιᾶς και Καινῆς Διαθήκης Δεσπότης; καὶ (εἰς) Κύριος Ἰησοῦς Χριστὸς, ὁ ἐν Παλαιᾷ προφητευθεὶς καὶ ἐν Καινῇ παραγενόμενος; καὶ ἕν Πνεῦμα ἅγιον, διὰ προφητῶν μὲν περὶ τοῦ Χριστοῦ κηρύξαν, ἐλθόντος δὲ τοῦ Χριστοῦ καταβὰν, καὶ ἐπιδείξαν αὐτόν. St. Cyril of Jer., "Catech. 16, On the Holy Spirit," PG 33, 920.

4 "Quid autem Scripturam sanctam nisi verbum Dei esse credimus? —sed unum est Dei Verbum universitas Scripturarum. Cum igitur Scripturam sanctam legimus, Verbum Dei tractamus Filium Dei per speculum et in aenigmate prae oculis habemus." "On the Works of the Holy Spirit," PL 167, 1575.

5 "Quid, inquam, fuit Moysi et prophetis sanctam Scripturam quae verbum

51

Thus the Scriptures, the law, and the prophets were in existence before God concentrated the whole of the Scriptures, His Word, in the womb of the virgin. This virgin conceived first in her mind and then in her flesh; first prophesying with her tongue before bringing to birth from her womb. Therefore, it is false to say that Christ did not exist before Mary was. Since, before His flesh was born, Sion, the Blessed, had brought forth the self-same Christ, the self-same Word.[6]

Then Garnier has the following words in one of his Christmas sermons:

Of old, God wrote a book by which in many words one Word was uttered; today He has opened a book for us in which by One Word many words are said. . . . This is the book which has for its pages the flesh of man and for writing the Word of the Father. . . . The greatest of all books is the Incarnate Son, because just as through writing words are joined to a page, so by assuming a human nature the Word of God is joined to flesh.[7]

Finally, Pius XII applied this traditional comparison to the domain of inspiration and hermeneutics:

For as the substantial Word of God became like to men in all things "except sin," so the words of God expressed in human language are made like to human speech in every respect, except error.[8]

Dei est, contexere, nisi Christum et corde per spiritum propheticum concipere et ore parere?" "Comm. on the Book of Kings," PL 167, 1175.

[6] "Sic omnis Scriptura legalis et prophetica condita est, antequam omnis Scripturae universitatem, omne Verbum suum Deus in utero Virginis coadunaret. Ipsa Virgo prius mente quam carne concepit, prius ore prophetando quam ventre parturiendo. Igitur falsum est ante Mariam non exstitisse Christum. Nam antequam carnem ejus parturiret, peperit ore prophetarum, beata Sion unum eumdemque Christum, unum idemque Dei Verbum." "Comm. on Isaiah," PL 167, 1362.

[7] "Olim librum scripsit nobis Deus, in quo sub multis verbis unum comprehendit: hodie librum nobis aperuit, in quo multa sub uno verbo conclusit . . . Ipse enim liber est, qui pro pelle carnem habuit, et pro scriptura Verbum Patris . . . Liber maximus est Filius incarnatus, quia per scripturam verbum unitur pelli, ita per assumpsionem hominis Verbum Patris unitum est carni." "Sixth Sermon for Christmas," PL 205, 609–610.

[8] "Sicut enim substantiale Dei Verbum hominibus simile factum est quoad omnia 'absque peccato,' ita etiam Dei verba, humanis linguis expressa, quoad omnia humano sermoni assimilia facta sunt, excepto errore. . . ." EB 559; RSS, p. 98.

For a discussion on the patristic use of this analogy, see J. H. Crehan, "The Analogy between *Verbum Dei Incarnatum* and *Verbum Dei scriptum*

The texts adduced above both enable and entitle us to conclude that the inspiration of sacred Scripture is ordered to the mystery of the Incarnation; it prepares for it, prolongs it, and explains it. It follows that the resemblance between these two mysteries establishes a basis, in virtue of which they mutually shed light on one another. Most important of all, we see now clearly the twofold nature of the inspired word. It, too, is both divine and human. Just as the Christological heresies veer from one extreme to the other, so in this mystery, too, there are analogous exaggerations. There can be a sort of Docetism or Monophysitism which denies or diminishes the human quality of the inspired word; there can be a Nestorianism which denies its divine character.

Another result of this confrontation between the two mysteries is that we constantly look to the mystery of the Incarnation when particular questions arise, and profit from the light shed thereby on our investigation. We will be following this method throughout these pages.

Finally, we should remember that just as the Incarnation is a transcendent mystery to be adored in grateful silence, so, too, inspiration pertains to the realm of this same mystery. Thus, when we inquire into the fundamental problem in the mystery of inspiration and ask: "How can words be at once both divine and human?", the answer is spontaneous: in a way similar to that by which Christ is both man and God. Beginning with this basic insight, we will go on to investigate a few other aspects, both negative and positive.

First Negative Aspect

The First Vatican Council, in its decree on revelation, eliminated two explanations which were then currently being given of the dignity of the sacred Scriptures:

---

in the Fathers," *JTS* 6, 1955, pp. 87–90; and P. Bellet, "El sentido de la analogía 'Verbum Dei Incarnatum—Verbum Dei Scriptum,' " *EstBíb* 14, 1955, pp. 415–428. The first author begins by citing modern authors who are in favor or opposed to the analogy, and then goes on to invoke the authority of the Fathers. The second author replies by showing that the analogy, as used by the Fathers, was inspired by the desire to interpret the Old Testament allegorically and to draw out the full meaning of the New Testament.

The Church regards the books of the Old and New Testaments as sacred and canonical, not because, after having been composed by purely human effort, they were then approved by her authority, nor because they contain revelation without error. . . .[9]

Let us suppose, for example, that the Church were to give official approval of some spiritual book, say *The Imitation of Christ* or *The Spiritual Exercises* of St. Ignatius. Such approbation would not make these books the word of God. The Church cannot change mere human words into words that are divine, nor can the Holy Spirit wait until a human work is completed, and then take possession of it. This is not how He makes it a work of His own. In the same way, Jesus Christ is not God because of an apotheosis which took place within the bosom of the early Church, nor because of some great divine action which took hold of a man already complete in his own right. There was never a moment in the life of Jesus when He was not True God. The action of the Holy Spirit took place at the moment of conception—"The Holy Spirit will come upon you, and the Power of the Most High will overshadow you; and for that reason the Holy Child to be born will be called 'Son of God.' "

But in denying that a completed reality was subsequently assumed by God in the case either of the Incarnation or the inspiration of the Scriptures, we are not denying the presence of preexisting material. The Holy Spirit did not create the matter for the body of Jesus out of nothing, but used the sanctified body and life processes of a virgin. So, too, the biblical authors overshadowed by the Spirit utilized preëxisting material: language, literary themes, stylistic devices, citations, etc., and it is not necessary that this material be also the direct result of the Spirit's activity. There is one important difference in our comparison, however. In the realm of literature, a piece can be transposed bodily into a new context and receive thereby an entirely new literary existence. Such an act would be a true literary creation, and we cannot, *a priori*, exclude such procedures from the Bible.[10]

[9] "*Eos vero Ecclesia pro sacris et canonicis habet, non ideo, quod sola humana industria concinnati, sua deinde auctoritate sint approbati; nec ideo dumtaxat, quod revelationem sine errore contineant; . . .*" D–S 3006.

[10] That is, if we take inspiration in the strict sense as we are doing here. It is not impossible that the Holy Spirit was active in the composition of

SECOND NEGATIVE ASPECT

". . . nor because they contain revelation without error." Theoretically, we could imagine some book, composed by purely human effort, which would collect and formulate revelation.[11] It is possible that such a book would contain no errors, but, in the strict sense, it would not be inspired or the word of God. The matter would be from God, as would be the theme and the facts. But the activity which conferred on such matter a literary existence would still be human, not divine. In the same way, a book which collected all the infallible pronouncements of the Church would contain and correctly formulate revelation, but it would not, for all that, be the word of God.

The statement of Vatican I implies a distinction which is very important for our consideration. It is that between revelation and inspiration. Oversimplifying for the moment, we could say that revelation affects the materials out of which the literary work is formed, while inspiration affects rather the literary process which brings the work into existence. But have we not already agreed that inspiration pertains to the realm of revelation? Yes, but recall that we said this while considering the mystery of human speech. We should make a distinction here between a revelation which precedes the act of literary composition, and one which follows it. Thus the sacred author, while being moved by the Spirit, could be busily engaged in drawing up court documents or in composing a song in imitation of some model, and not receive any revelation from God either before or during his work. In this case, there would be inspiration without any revelation preceding. But so long as our author has written under the motion of the Spirit, his words are the words of God, and the words of God reveal Him. These words would constitute a revelation in our regard, and would constitute what may be termed "subsequent revelation." The whole Bible is revelation for us, because it is the word of God; but not all the Bible was composed as a result of some previous revelation made to its authors.

---

some material before the moment when it was transposed to an inspired work within the life of the Chosen People.

[11] N. Lohfink calls this a "hagiographical act." Cf. Über die Irrtumslosigkeit und Einheit der Schrift," SZ 84, 1964, pp. 161–181.

The distinction between revelation and inspiration has already been elaborated on by St. Thomas[12] as well as his distinction between the act by which reality is received into the mind and that by which it is judged. We dare say that this distinction constitutes one of the keys to an understanding of the whole treatise on inspiration. It will appear often in these pages. Yet, there is danger of an oversimplification. We must not consider revelation which precedes literary composition too exclusively in terms derived from the notion of a fully formed proposition, meant only to be handed on.

We would like to add another negative aspect to the two given by Vatican I. In order that human words be also the words of God, there must be more than moral activity, such as a counsel or command from God. For such an activity would make God the moral source of the work, but it would leave intact its totally human character. The action of the Spirit must be physical; it must reach the author in his act of eliciting language. This motion is not moral, but physical; it pertains to the supernatural order; we call it, using our terms strictly now, the charism of inspiration.

There are other negative aspects of this mystery, but most of them will become apparent in our study of the analogies used in a positive elucidation.

FOUR ANALOGIES

In order to arrive at some understanding of the mystery of words which are at once divine and human, the Church's theologians have from the earliest times made use of various analogies. These are instruments leading us to knowledge; they are illustrations, valid though limited, pointing to a reality which is transcendent. We should note, however, that there is no question here of some purely abstract intellectual process, which then looks for apt images in which to convey its thought. Most often, an analogy is the result of an intuition which precedes conceptual elaboration. This is what is meant by a "theology in symbols." It is a type of thinking which historically preceded a more conceptualized theology, and which must complement this latter under pain of sterility at every stage of its development. The Fathers spoke of St. John as "the Theologian," and St. John's theology is often in symbols.

[12] II–II, 173.

It is certainly true that when we speak of "the Word of God" or of the "verbal" nature of the world, we are using metaphors. But these are more than pretty comparisons; they are metaphors of weighty metaphysical import. We speak in images, but not figuratively. Or better, we speak using imagery, but it is proper. A theologian or a philosopher begins to be such, when first he sees what is metaphysical in metaphors, and the metaphors in metaphysics. There is a metaphysics of the schools which is oblivious of metaphor and which renounces thereby that without which no great and original metaphysics has ever been formed. Metaphysics does not spell the end of metaphor. Thus, such expressions as "the Word of God," "the Word of the Creator," and "the Word in God" are for the human mind metaphors. But they are not purely imaginative language. They are rather analogous expressions, not purely metaphorical analogies, but essential predications in the order of being and operation.[13]

Thus does Söhngen, the theologian and philosopher, express himself. Theology cannot dispense with symbols or images, since all creation is an image of God, and man himself is created in God's image and likeness. Analogy is not the exclusive possession of abstract reasoning; it belongs also to the realm of the concrete and sensory, and this is the secret of all great literary metaphors.

We see, then, that language is something deeply human. We have already borrowed its images, in order to ascend by means of analogy to the mystery of divine words in human language. It is in this spirit of serious inquiry that we now approach the more classical images of traditional theology, even adding to their number a contribution of our own.

---

13 "Gewiss reden wir, wenn wir vom Worten Gottes und vom Gewortetsein der Welt reden, in Metaphern, aber nicht in bloss schönen Vergleichen, sondern in Metaphern von metaphysischen Schwergewicht; wir reden bildlich, aber nicht uneigentlich, oder vielmehr wir reden bildhaft, und gerade so auch eigentlich. Theologe und Philosoph sind es beide doch erst, wenn sie das Metaphysische im Metaphorischen und das Metaphorische im Metaphysischen zusammenschauend sehen. Es mag Schulmetaphysik geben, die auf die Metaphern vergisst (verzichtet), ohne die keine grosse, ursprüngliche Metaphysik gestaltet ist. Metaphysik besagt also nicht den Ausschluss der Metaphorik. So sind für den Menschenverstand "Wort Gottes" und "Wort des Schöpfers" und "das Wort in Gott" Metaphern; es sind aber keine bloss bildlichen, sondern analoge Ausdrücke, und zwar eben keine bloss metaphorischen Analogien, sondern überwesentliche Aussagen in der Wesens- und Tätigkeitsordnung." G. Söhngen, Analogie und Metaphern. Kleine Philosophie und Theologie der Sprache, Munich, 1962, p. 104.

Instrument

Without doubt, the image which has met with the greatest success in this field is that of an instrument. In some scholastic treatises, it is the only one employed.[14] There was a time when scholars discussed whether the tract should take as its foundation the concept (not the image) of instrument or that of author. This discussion is no longer relevant. A single image is able to provide us with more light than a whole sheaf of them bound together.

Neither nature nor human devising can enable men to know things so great and so divine. This is accomplished by the gift which came down from above on holy men who had no need of the craft of words, or of speaking anything contentiously, or with a love of argument. Rather, they offered themselves up pure to the energy of the divine Spirit, so that the divine Plectrum itself, coming down from heaven and using just men as some instrument, such as a harp or lyre, might reveal to us a knowledge of things divine and heavenly.[15]

For having begun by expounding minutely the principle that the inspired writer, in composing the sacred book, is the living and reasonable instrument of the Holy Spirit, they rightly observe that, impelled by the divine motion, he so uses his faculties and powers, that from the book composed by him all may easily infer "the special character of each one and, as it were, his personal traits." [16]

Seventeen centuries elapsed between the two statements given above, yet they evince a remarkable continuity of thought. Chris-

---

14 Grelot is quite frankly optimistic about the value of this notion in its philosophical conceptualization: "*Bref, la notion philosophique d'instrument est assez souple pour pouvoir épouser tous les contours d'une réalité complexe où la nature est assumée par le surnaturel.*" "L'inspiration scripturaire," RSR 51, 1963, p. 368.

15 Οὔτε γὰρ φύσει οὔτε ἀνφρωπίνῃ ἐννοίᾳ οὕτω μεγάλα καὶ Θεῖα γινώσκειν ἀνφρώποις δυνατόν, ἀλλὰ τῇ ἄνωϑεν ἐπὶ τοὺς ἁγίους ἄνδρας τηνκαῦτα κατελϑούσῃ δωρεᾷ, οἷς οὐ λόγων ἐδέησε τέχνης, οὐδὲ τοῦ ἐριστικῶς τι καὶ φιλονείκως εἰπεῖν, ἀλλὰ καϑαροὺς ἑαυτοὺς τῇ τοῦ Θείου Πνεύματος παρασχεῖν ἐνεργείᾳ, ἵν' αὐτὸ τὸ Θεῖον ἐξ οὐρανοῦ κατιὸν πλῆκτρον, ὥσπερ ὀργάνῳ κιϑάρας τινὸς ἢ λύρας, τοῖς δικαίοις ἀνδράσι χρώμενον, τὴν τῶν Θείων ἡμῖν καὶ οὐρανίων ἀποκαλύψῃ γνῶσιν. "Exhortation to the Greeks" (second or third century), PG 6, 256.

16 "*Ex eo enim edisserendo profecti, quod hagiographus in sacro conficiendo libro est Spiritus Sancti* ORGANON *seu instrumentum, idque vivum ac ratione praeditum, recte animadvertunt illum, divina motione actum, ita suis uti facultatibus et viribus, 'ut propriam uniuscuiusque indolem et veluti singulares notas ac lineamenta.'*" EB 556; RSS, p. 96.

tian Pesch[17] has collected twenty-four different theological texts representing all ages, which employ the image of instrument in their study of this mystery of inspiration. It is worth a little trouble to read some of these texts and appreciate for ourselves their consistency and variations.

St. Athenagoras:

For those things which we know and believe, we have the prophets as witnesses. Those men who, possessed by the Spirit, spoke out concerning God and the things of God . . . The Holy Spirit Who moved the mouths of the prophets like some instrument . . . The Spirit used them as a flute player blows through his flute.[18]

St. Hippolytus:

These Fathers were endowed with a prophetic spirit, and were worthily honored by the Word Himself. Just like musical instruments, they had the Word with them as a plectrum, so that when they were touched by Him, these prophets announced the things that God had willed.[19]

Theophilus of Antioch:

Moses, . . . or rather the Word of God, through Moses as an instrument, said: "In the beginning God created heaven and earth." [20]

St. Jerome (on the verse, "my tongue is quick like the pen of a scribe"—Ps 45:2):

I ought therefore to prepare my tongue as a quill or pen, so that by means of it the Holy Spirit can write in the heart and hearing of my audience. My role is to offer my tongue as an instrument, His to make it sound with His composition. . . . If the law which came through a

[17] De Inspiratione Sacrae Scripturae, Freiburg, 1906.

[18] Ἡμεῖς δὲ ὧν νοοῦμεν καὶ πεπιστεύκαμεν, ἔχομεν προφήτας μάρτυρας, οἱ Πνεύματι ἐνθέῳ ἐκπεφωνήκασι καὶ περὶ τοῦ Θεοῦ καὶ των τοῦ Θεου. Εἴποιτε δ' ἄν καὶ ὑμεῖς, συνέσι καὶ τῇ περὶ ὄντως θεῖον εὐσεβίᾳ τοὺς ἄλλος προύχοντες, ὡς ἔστιν ἄλογον, παραλιπόντας πιστεύειν τῷ παρὰ τοῦ Θεοῦ Πνεύματι, ὡς ὄργανα κεκινηκότι τὰ προφητῶν στόματα, προσέχειν δόξαις ἀνθρωπίναις. . . . συγχρησαμένου τοῦ Πνεύματος, ὡσεὶ καὶ αὐλτῆς αὐλὸν ἐμπνεῦσαι. St. Athenagoras, "Supplication for the Christians, 7 and 9," PG 6, 904, 908.

[19] Οὗτοι γὰρ πνεύματι προφητικῷ δι πατέρες κατηρτισμένοι, καὶ ὑπ' αὐτοῦ τοῦ Λόγου ἀξίως τετιμημένοι, ὀργάνων δίκην ἑαυτοῖς ἀεὶ τὸν Λόγον ὡς πλήκτρον. δι' οὗ κινούμενοι ἀπήγελλον ταῦτα, ἅπερ ἤθελεν ὁ Θεός, οἱ προφῆται. St. Hippolytus, "On the Antichrist, 1," PG 10, 728–729.

[20] Μωυσῆς δὲ ὁ καὶ Σολομῶνος πρὸ πολλῶν ἐτῶν γενόμενος, μᾶλλον δὲ ὁ Λόγος ὁ τοῦ Θεοῦ ὡς δι' ὀργάνου δι' αὐτοῦ φησίν. Ἐν ἀρχῇ ἐποίσεν ὁ θεὸς τὸν οὐρανὸν καὶ τὴν γῆν. Theophilus of Antioch, "To Autolycus, bk. 2, 10," PG 6, 1065.

mediator was written by the finger of God, if what was abolished was so glorified, then the good news, which abides, is written by the Holy Spirit through means of my tongue.[21]

St. Gregory the Great (while discussing the problem as to who the writer of the Book of Job might be, he declares it to be a useless question):

Suppose we were to receive a letter from some eminent man, and after having read it, were to inquire as to what pen actually wrote the letter; it would be ridiculous, along with our knowledge of the author and our understanding of his meaning, were we to insist on knowing just which pen made the marks on the paper. So, when we possess the message and know that the Holy Spirit is its author, and then go on to try to find out who the writer is, what are we doing but reading a letter and wondering about the pen? [22]

St. Augustine:

He is the Head of all His disciples, who are as members of His body through that human nature which He has assumed. Thus, when they write what He has taught and said, it should not be asserted that He did not write it, since the members only put down what they had come to know at the dictation of the Head. Therefore, whatever He wanted us to read concerning His words and deeds, He commanded the disciples, His hands, to write. Whoever understands this shared unity and the convergence in divine functions of many members under one Head, cannot but receive what he reads in the Gospels, though written by the disciples, as though it were written by the very hand of the Lord Himself.[23]

21 "*Debeo ergo et linguam meam quasi stilum et calamum praeparare ut per illam in corde et auribus audientium scribat Sanctus Spiritus. Meum enim est organum praebere linguam: illius quasi per organum sonare quae sunt. . . . Si enim Lex per manum Mediatoris digito scripta est, et quod destructum est, glorificatum est: quanto magis Evangelium; quod mansurum est, per meam linguam scribetur a Spiritu Sancto.*" "Letter 65," PL 22, 627.
Note that St. Jerome puts these words on the lips of the Psalmist, whom he considers to be an evangelist because he foretold Christ.

22 "*Si magnicujusdam viri susceptis epistolis legeremus verba, sed quo calamo fuissent scripta quaereremus, ridiculum profecto esset epistolarum auctorem scire sensumque cognoscere, sed quali calamo earum verba impressa fuerint indagare. Cum ergo rem cognoscimus ejusque rei Spiritum Sanctum auctorem tenemus, quia scriptorem quaerimus, quid aliud agimus nisi legentes literas, de calamo percontamur?*" "Moralia on Job, Preface," PL 75, 517.

23 "*Omnibus autem discipulis suis per hominem quem assumpsit, tanquam membris sui corporis caput est. Itaque cum illi scripserunt quae ille ostendit*

We have here three series of texts, which show interesting variations. The first and oldest group employs the image of a musical instrument, the second does not specify any particular instrument or refers to a pen, etc., while St. Augustine speaks of the organs of the body.

Instrument pertains to fundamental human experience. Man, either as *homo faber* or as *homo ludens*, either as a workman or at play, is prone to avail himself of instruments in order to realize his activity. Chapter 4 of Genesis describing the origins of culture tells us of Jubal, who was the ancestor of all those who "play the lyre and the flute," and of Tubal-Cain, "the forger of bronze and iron utensils." [24] The description is of a semi-nomadic culture which followed the neolithic era. The making of tools is the sign of *homo faber*. From the stone axes of paleolithic man to our immense mechanized factories there runs a deep underlying continuity. Of course, the experience of primitive man with his plow or spear was deeper, more intimate, and more vivid. He was conscious of his instrument as some part of himself, as an extension, needed and docile, of his own activity. An instrument depends on man, and man on his instrument. Early man's experience was a complex awareness of the mysterious union between a man and his tool, a union in which, by an intimate interchange, man's activity was given new dimensions. The mass production of tools has helped to diminish the intensity of such experiences, and we would need to relive the feeling of being without tools in order to appreciate once again our dependence on them.

Let us take the example of a musical instrument. Man has sung with no instrument; but he has invented the art of accompaniment, and has made for himself instruments distinct from his voice which he calls "musical instruments." The musician dominates his instrument and at the same time is subject to it. Factors, such as

---

et dixit, nequaquam dicendum est quod ipse non scripserit; quandoquidem membra ejus id operata sunt, quod dictante capite cognoverunt. Quidquid enim ille de suis factis et dictis nos legere voluit, hoc scribendum illis tanquam suis manibus imperavit. Hoc unitatis consortium et in diversis officiis concordium membrorum sub uno capite ministerium quisquis intellexerit, non aliter accipiet quod narrantibus discipulis Christi in Evangelio legerit, quam si ipsam manum Domini, quam in proprio corpore gestabat, scribentem conspexerit." "De Consensu Evangelistarum," PL 34, 1070.

[24] Gn 4:21–22.

timber, range, and expression, are conditioned by the instrument which thus vitally influences the total musical effect. When a harpsichord is well tempered, it can render a harmonious system; when it is sensitive to touch, it yields new possibilities of expression, and if it were fitted with a series of quartertone strings, it would acquire still further dimensions of musical expression. Electronic instruments, theoretically at least, could broaden the range of possibilities. Think, for instance, of the regard a soloist has for his instrument. There are pianists who take their own piano with them when they tour. Think of the care a flutist gives to the reed which receives his breath and the touch of his fingers. Or take some personal experience: what a difference between an instrument which is out of tune or broken and one that is of real quality! Now we see what an instrument means to man at play, to *homo ludens*.

The Spirit has a similar relationship to the human instruments which He has taken up in order to produce His work in language. He breathes into them, and each human author has his unique timber and key, language and style. The melody results from them both. There is but one song, perfectly human, yet somehow divine.

The comparison with a pen is much less suggestive and also less frequent in the early documents, even though it fits in the context of Scripture so very well. In the final analysis, the writing down of language is a much more artificial and extrinsic type of operation, and the role of the instrument is scarcely noticed, except, of course, when it is a question of expert calligraphy.[25]

The third example has reference to the organs of the body. It is difficult to determine whether or not primitive man ever experienced the quasi-instrumentality of bodily limbs. It is a fact that the Greek word for instrument is *"organon,"* which has developed semantically in two different directions in our language; we give the name "organ" to a musical instrument, and we also speak of bodily organs, the organs of public opinion, etc. If, by a certain reflection on myself, I consider the difference between my intention and the

[25] Theodore of Mopsuestia utilizes this image in a curious way, dividing it into three elements: writer, ink, and pen; and by transposition these become: the Holy Spirit, revelation, and the sacred writer. There is another transposition effected with regard to speech, since the text commented on has, "my tongue is the pen of a scribe." Cf. R. Devreesse, *Essai sur Théodore de Mopsueste*, Studi e Testi, no. 141, Rome, 1948.

hand which carries it out, or between my thought and the tongue which gives it expression, I experience the fact of instrumentality under its most vital and intimate aspect. The work done is mine, and it belongs to my hand; the words spoken pertain to me and to the tongue which uttered them; they are both material and spiritual. An impulse goes from the brain through the nervous system to the hand or tongue, which execute the order. We could picture to ourselves the relationship between the Holy Spirit and the sacred authors in much the same way. St. Augustine applies it rather to Christ and the disciples. We could perhaps introduce a new factor into his speculations. The impulse given by Christ, the Head, is in fact the Holy Spirit.

There is another interesting facet to St. Augustine's example. By invoking the image of the Mystical Body, he highlights the social and ecclesiastical roles played by the hagiographers of the New Testament, who wrote as organs of a great mystical body, which is the Church. In the Old Testament, the prophet often called himself "the mouth of God." In Isaiah 30:2, God charges His people: ". . . you did not consult My mouth"; in Jeremiah He promises: "If you repent, so that I restore you, in My presence you shall stand; if you bring forth the precious without the vile, you shall be My mouth" (15:19). Frequent also is the expression that God carries out something *"beyad,"* "by the hand," of his prophet. Etymologically, *"beyad"* signifies "in" or "by the hand of," but semantically it became an ordinary expression with the meaning "by," "by means of," etc. Thus, we find such phrases as "the precept of the Lord [delivered] by means of Moses" (Nm 36:13); "the Word of the Lord through the prophet Haggai" (Hag 1:1; 1:3; 2:2); "the words which the Lord proclaimed through the prophets of old" (Za 7:7, 12).

Thus we find two images: one generic, referring to some indetermined relationship of instrumentality, the other more specific and employing the notion of bodily organ. By a similar thought process, the enemy ruler is often pictured as an instrument of chastisement in the hand of Yahweh, a rod, a hammer, etc.

The scholastics took up the image of instrument, and gave it a conceptual elaboration according to the Aristotelian system of the four causes: efficient, material, formal, and final. An efficient cause can be either principal or instrumental.[26] An instrumental cause, which is in the order of efficient cause, has a secondary and subordinate role and is elevated by the principal cause to produce an effect which exceeds its own power. The result is brought about by both causes, and bears a resemblance to each. Thus, for example, the pen is raised by the human hand to produce a series of marks on paper, which have a spiritual significance; or a flute produces sound which, because of the artist, is music. The sacred writer receives from the Spirit, Who is the principal cause, an impulse, in virtue of which the human instrument is raised above itself to produce effects exceeding its innate capacities, either of knowledge or of communication. There is a difference, however; in our examples, the instrument is an inert object, while the sacred writer is a person, living, intelligent, and free.

Benoit observes that St. Thomas is very sparing in his use of the term "instrument" when explaining the charism of prophecy. He speaks rather of a "quasi-instrument," of an instrument in the wide sense of the term, or else he avoids the term altogether.[27]

In our neo-scholastic theology manuals, the notion of instrumental cause and its application to the mystery of inspiration plays a preponderant role. Tromp, for example, has this to say:

Inspiration is that act by which God becomes the primary Author of a sacred book and man its secondary author. In this activity, God, in his writing of a sacred book, uses man as an instrumental cause which has been raised by a supernatural power.[28]

Tromp goes on to divide instrument according to whether or not it can move itself and whether its action is one of receiving or of performing; then he describes instruments as either adequate or inadequate, separate or joined, inanimate or animate; and finally, he notes that the activity of an instrument can be considered either

26 Grelot has distinguished well between the pre-philosophical use of this notion by the Fathers and the philosophical elaboration of the scholastics; he prefers the latter. Art. cit., n.14.

27 Cf. P. Synave and P. Benoit, *Prophecy and Inspiration*, New York, 1961, esp. pp. 40, 77–83.

28 "*Inspiratio, qua Deus est vere auctor principalis libri sacri, homo autem vere auctor secundarius, in eo est, quod Deus in ordine ad librum sacrum conficiendum homine utitur tamquam causa instrumentali, supernaturali virtute elevata.*" *De Sacrae Scripturae Inspiratione*, 3rd ed., Rome, 1936.

as proper to it or as pertaining to its nature as instrument. He then applies these distinctions to biblical inspiration.

In the index of Pesch's book, under the entry *"Instrumentum,"* we are referred to *"causa instrumentalis."* In his text itself, we read: "In these and other sayings, the holy Fathers clearly teach that the sacred writers are the instrumental causes, and that God is the principal cause." [29]

Pesch thus attributes to the Fathers a metaphysical elaboration of the doctrine more proper to scholasticism. For if we compare the conceptual formulations of the mystery given by medieval and modern authors with the symbolic expressions of the ancients, we see that we have gained in precision, but that we have lost something of the vitality and rich intuitive power of those early theological symbols. The encyclical *Divino afflante Spiritu* simply uses the term "instrument" in Greek or in Latin, and refers to a "divine motion" without making any explicit mention of the metaphysical doctrine of the four causes.[30]

The notion of instrument, both as a symbol on the anthropological level, and as a concept on the metaphysical level of instrumental cause, has helped us somewhat to understand the twofold nature of the sacred writings. We say "somewhat," because the analogy, though positive and enlightening, demands that we remain always conscious of its limits. The danger of forgetting these limits tragically illustrated in the crisis of Montanism.[31]

Montanus, who lived in the middle of the second century, availed himself of the image of a plectrum and a lyre, in order to conclude that a man who was inspired was possessed by the power of God. Such a person acted without consciousness, being moved completely by the Holy Spirit while in an ecstasy or *"mania,"* as the Greeks called it. This theory, which leans heavily on some Platonic doctrines, tries to eliminate any specifically human activity and ends up in a sort of Monophysite heresy in regard to the Scriptures. The Church quickly saw the danger, and Montanus was vig-

[29] No. 403.
[30] EB 556. On the question of instrumental cause, cf. G. Mortari, *La nozione di causa istrumentale e le sue applicazione alla questione dell'inspirazione verbale*, Verona, 1928.
[31] Cf. P. de Labriolle, *La crise montaniste*, Paris, 1913.

orously attacked by the theologians of the age, among whom St. Epiphanius was prominent.

Montanism had carried the analogy beyond its limits, and the final result was that its adherents proclaimed a new age of revelation inaugurated by the Holy Spirit through two "prophetesses" of the sect—Prisca and Maximilla.

Since a man is a person endowed with freedom, he can be moved by moral influence, command, persuasion, or threats. If a man is moved by physical violence or by drugs, his action is not human. Thus, if he were forced to sign a document or to fire a pistol, he would not be held responsible for the results of the action. Now, the influence of the Holy Spirit cannot be classified as physical violence, in which He would use a man as though he were some machine; but then, moral causality would not suffice to make the Holy Spirit the author of a book written by a man. We must try to conceive of some physical action which does no violence and which is effective but not mechanical. Such is the nature of the mysterious movement of the Spirit Who breathes where He will.

The scholastics were also aware that their conceptual equipment had its limitations. These were made explicit by Pius XII in his use of two qualifying adjectives. ". . . the inspired writer . . . is the living and reasonable instrument of the Holy Spirit." [32]

Dictation

Among the Latin Fathers, we find the term *"dictare"* also used to describe that action of the Spirit present in the writing of the Scriptures. Thus, St. Jerome could say:

The whole of the Epistle to the Romans requires an interpretation, and is so fraught with difficulties that in order to understand it, we need the grace of the Holy Spirit Who dictated all this through the apostle.[33]

[32] Text quoted above, n. 16. St. Thomas also elaborates the doctrine of the humanity of Christ as an instrument of the Divinity (of the Divine Nature) in the work of salvation. The humanity, full of grace dynamically, was an instrument during the whole of Christ's life here on earth, and is so now in His active presence in the Church. Cf. T. Tschipke, *Die Menschheit Christi als Heilsorgan der Gottheit, unter besonderer Berücksichtigung der Lehre des hl. Thomas von Aquin*, Freiburger Theologische Studien, no. 55, Freiburg, 1940.

[33] "Omnis quidem ad Romanos Epistula interpretatione indigit, et tantis obscuritatibus involuta est, ut ad intelligendam eam, Spiritus Sancti indigeamus auxilio, qui per Apostolum haec ipsa dictavit." "Letter 120," PL 22, 997.

And we have seen already that phrase of St. Augustine in which he says:

The members put down what they know at the dictation of the Head.[34]

St. Gregory the Great says simply:

He wrote these things, Who dictated what was to be written.[35]

And the Council of Trent uses the formula:

At the dictation of the Holy Spirit . . .[36]

to describe tradition.

The words "dictate" and "dictation" are familiar in our culture, and it would seem that an analogy based on them would be easy for us to understand. But there is a danger of misunderstanding precisely because of this familiarity. Today, as a result of dictaphones and tape recorders, we have achieved a scientific exactitude in dictating which even shorthand (a method known also to the ancients) must emulate. When we hear the word "dictation," we think immediately of some executive with his secretary, or of some prompter in his box below stage, or even, as the Egyptian statutes picture it, a bird perched on the shoulder of a man whispering to him what to write. But this image is false. The Holy Spirit does not come down as a dove on the shoulder of the sacred author and act as some sort of prompter, dictating His lines to him. In the traditional context, the word has another meaning.

If we look back, for instance, at the patristic texts just cited, we will see that St. Jerome does not say that the Holy Spirit dictated to the apostles, but that he dictated *through* them. St. Augustine says that the members put down what they *knew* at the dictation of the Head. The phrase of St. Gregory and St. Isidore is even more explicit: "He *wrote* these things, Who dictated to his prophets what was to be written."

Since the Council of Trent, the way was opened for a concept of the term "dictation" in our modern sense, one which reduced the sacred writer to the role of a junior secretary. For such a role, one

---

[34] Text quoted above, n. 23.

[35] "*Ipse igitur haec scripsit, qui scribenda dictavit.*" "Moralia on Job, Preface," PL 75, 517.

[36] "*Spiritu Sancto dictante . . .*" D-S 1501.

need only understand the words materially and be able to write them correctly, nothing more. But is this the proper understanding of the Council of Trent? Some theologians seem to have thought so.

In 1584, Dominic Bañez published at Rome his *Scholastic Commentary on the first Part of the Summa of the Angelic Doctor, St. Thomas, as far as Question 64.* There we read:

The second conclusion. The Holy Spirit not only inspired the matter contained in the Scriptures, but also dictated and suggested every word in which it was written. . . . To dictate means to determine every word.

The third conclusion (which is not of faith, but is the safer opinion). Since God disposes all things sweetly, He enlightens the mind of each individual sacred author and dictates to him words which well befit his state and condition.[37]

In the middle of the eighteenth century, C. R. Billuart published his *Summa Theologica*, which has had a very great influence. Speaking of the norms of faith, he says:

I presuppose that all the phrases of Scripture are inspired and dictated by the Holy Spirit. . . . It seems more probable that the nature of sacred Scripture would require that not only the general sense and the phrases of Scripture be dictated by the Holy Spirit, but even every single word. It is the more common opinion . . . that the Holy Spirit accommodated Himself to the way of thinking, the style, and the temperament of each of the sacred writers, and concurred with them as He dictated every word, just as though the author had written from his own resources.[38]

---

[37] "*Spiritus Sanctus non solum res in Scriptura contentas inspiravit, sed etiam singula verba, quibus scriberentur, dictavit atque suggessit. . . . Dictare autem verba ipsa determinare significat. . . . Cum Deus omnia suaviter disponat, ita uniuscuiusque scriptoris sacri mentem illuminabat eidemque verba dictabat quae maxime illorum statum et condicionem decebant.*" As cited by Pesch, no. 278.

[38] "*Suppono omnes Scripturae sententias esse a Spiritu Sancto inspiratas. . . . Probabilius videtur ad rationem Scripturae Sacrae requiri, quod non solum sensus et sententiae, sed etiam singula verba sint a Spiritu Sancto dictata. Est communior . . . Spiritus Sanctus se accomodavit genio, stilo et affectionibus cuiusque scriptoris sacri sicque concurrit dictando singula, ac ipse scriptor de suo scripsisset.*" Cited by Pesch, no. 280.

The "orthodox" Protestants proceeded in much the same manner. In the profession of faith known as the *Formula Consensus Helvetica*, we read that the text of the Old Testament is inspired "with regard both to the consonants and to the vowel points, both the punctuation and its equivalent." Among the classical Protestant authors, we find Johann Gerhard (*Loci communes theologici*, 1610–1622) holding as a theological conclusion that God inspired the Hebrew text, including its vowel points and punctuation, just as we have it today. Quenstedt, in his *Theologia Didactica-Polemica* (1657), calls the sacred writers the "amanuenses" and notaries of the Holy Spirit, who are only authors in the improper sense of the term. The Holy Spirit "supplied, inspired, and dictated every single word and phrase to each of the sacred writers." The differences in style are explained by the fact that the Holy Spirit accommodated Himself to the temperament of each author, dictating those words which the author would have used, had he been drawing on his own resources.

These parallel positions, adopted by both Catholics and Protestants, smack of a certain Monophysitism and provoked a variety of reactions. Among the Protestants, there arose a rationalism which went to the other extreme and denied to God any activity in the composition of the Scriptures, while among Catholics there arose the famous controversy over "verbal inspiration."

The statement of the problem among Catholics went something like this: Inspiration cannot be dictation, since dictation eliminates any properly human activity. Therefore, in order to understand the formula, "God is the author of Scripture, and man is the author of Scripture," we have to make a distinction. The distinction is not difficult. God provides the matter or the content, and man provides the form; God gives the ideas, and man elaborates the style. In the last century, the great champion of this position was Cardinal Franzelin, who was simply developing the ideas of some theologians who came immediately after the Council of Trent, such as Lessius, Suarez, Cornelius à Lapide, and others. Pesch wrote his book while under the burden of this controversy, and he often has the Fathers of the Church employing his distinction.[39]

---

[39] Obviously, the "form" had some influence on the "matter" or the choice of words, and this was admitted by all. The theme which God willed to be treated already restricted the area of language, and the exposition of

At the present moment, we have gone beyond such a statement of the problem. Not only is it no longer solved by the distinction, "God—the ideas, man—the words," but the whole view of literature which thinks in terms of "either the ideas or the words" has been abandoned. Such a distinction has no basis in reality; it is a product of the laboratory, suffering from an intellectualism which values only "ideas." As a matter of fact, such an approach was vitiated by the way it first posed the problem: "Either God dictated the words, or the words are solely from the sacred writer." There is a third possibility, namely that of a divine motion permeating every phase of the literary production, making it a work of God, and all the while enshrining and elevating man's freedom and creativity. Today, most theologians accept the literary work in the concrete as inspired, without distinguishing content and form. A piece of literature is an organized complex of words whose meaning is inseparable from its medium. The term "dictate" is still applicable, but not in its modern connotation.

A related problem is that discussed by the Council Fathers during Vatican I: "Is sacred Scripture the word of God, or does it contain the word of God?" The distinction was prompted by the phrases often found in the prophets, which seemed to set apart certain divine oracles as they introduced them: "Thus does God speak," "an oracle of Yahweh," "the Word of the Lord." [40] Tradition has always considered all the Scripture as the word of God. St. John Chrysostom has this to say about one of St. Paul's phrases in his first letter to the Thessalonians: "Paul said all these things by the Spirit, but what he says now, he heard literally from God." [41]

A third problem, one which is much discussed today, concerns the "ipsissima verba" of the prophets or of Our Lord. We hear such questions as: "Does the prophet give us the very words of

---

the theme demanded apt formulation. According to this theory, God moved the author immediately in regard to the ideas, and mediately in regard to their formulation. In the words of Tromp: "*Rerum conceptio est simpliciter ex illustratione divina; verba sunt etiam ex illustratione divina, attamen non necessario quatenus sunt haec verba simpliciter, sed quatenus sunt haec verba apta.*" *Op. cit.*, no. 28, p. 91.

[40] For a discussion of this question at the First Vatican Council, cf. N. I. Weyns, "De notione inspirationis biblicae iuxta Concilium Vaticanum," *Ang* 30, 1953, pp. 315–336.

[41] Ἐκεῖνα μὲν οὖν πνεύματι πάντα ἐφθέγγετο, τοῦτο δὲ, ὃ λέγει νῦν, καὶ ῥητῶς ἤκουσε παρὰ τοῦ Θεοῦ. "On 1 Th 4:15," PG 62, 439.

God, or does he elaborate the message?"; "Can we discern in a prophetic oracle one part which is the direct message of God, and another which is the explanation given by the prophet?" [42] In regard to the New Testament, the question takes the form: "Did the evangelists give us the very words which Christ spoke, or is their message only the word of Christ, in the sense that it comes from the Spirit of Christ?" Later on, we will come back to this question; for the moment, however, we must continue our analysis of the term "dictate."

The semantic evolution of the Latin word *"dictare"* is extremely interesting. On the one hand, it has given rise to such words as the German *"dichten"* ("compose as an author or poet"), *"Gedicht"* ("poem"), etc., while on the other hand we have such words as "dictation" and even "dictator." The first line of thought appears in medieval treatises on the "art of composition" (*"ars dictaminis"*). These were simply manuals which taught the art of writing and composing poetically. *"Dictare"* in the medieval world implied real intellectual and even poetic activity. We see its origin in the administrative bureaus of the government or Church, where men were employed who could draw up, in the appropriate style, the decrees and correspondence of the ruler. They called their profession the "art of dictation." The term was then transferred from the realm of prose and rhetoric to that of poetic composition, and finally gave rise to the maxim, "Whoever wishes to be a poet [*dictator*] must study the art of composing well [*ars dictaminis*]." Dante even calls the poets the *"dictatores illustres."* The second line of development refers more to the realm of volition, and is concerned with command, legislation, etc. In this sense, we speak of the will of the ruler dictating norms of conduct for the nation, and also of the "dictate" of our conscience.

The twofold possibility of the word should make us cautious in our attempt to understand this second traditional analogy. In a modern context, we should think of a good secretary who knows how to take the notes jotted down by the executive, and expand them into a letter; or we should think of a manner in which some of our modern heads of government use speech writers. In these cases, there is a close collaboration, a union of mind and will, in

[42] Cf. H. Wildberger, *Jahwewort und prophetische Rede bei Jeremia,* Zurich, 1942.

order to produce the end result. The executive gives the general theme, sketches its development and some of its leading ideas, and perhaps proposes one or two good phrases which ought to be incorporated. The secretary draws up the document, which is then corrected and written once again in its final form. To whom do we attribute authorship? In one sense, both are authors; in another sense, there is a principal author and a secondary author, since both worked together intelligently. In the case of a speech of the president, for example, the juridical effects of what he says are due to his authorship, while their literary form is due mostly to his secretary who knows the *"ars dictaminis."*

It does not seem that a modern ghost writer or the editor of a magazine is a good example of this type of joint authorship, since the original "author" merely provides the material and is not a true literary author.

Understood in the sense described above, the analogy based on the notion of dictation can help us to penetrate more deeply into the mystery. But while we appreciate its light, we must not forget its limitations. Even in the example we just gave, of an executive and his secretary, we can apportion to each his share in the final result. We know when one worked on the document, and at what stage the other made his contribution, and on this basis we can distinguish what part was played by each. Again, we suppose that the contribution of the secretary was more in the order of literary composition, while that of the executive was more in the realm of creative thought. To one we attribute the knowledge, to the other the style. But this type of "division of labor" is inapplicable to a work produced by the Holy Spirit through the inspired writer.

In Christ, there are two wills and two principles of operation which are neither confused nor opposed, since the will of Christ is completely submissive to the divine. So also in the mystery of inspiration there is a human literary effort which is submissive and in no way opposed to the operation of the Holy Spirit. To diminish the human reality of this effort, and to make of it the mere activity of an amanuensis, does nothing to increase the glory of God's causality.[43]

[43] Cf. *D-S* 550–559.

A Messenger

The image of a man bearing a message from another is one whose echoes are found throughout the Bible. The prophets are the envoys of God, the messengers and heralds of Yahweh—just as the apostles are later to be called the envoys and heralds of Christ. In a culture without telegraph, telephone, or airplane, the messenger played an important role. Sometimes, all that was required of him was that he deliver written documents and carry back written replies; then it sufficed if he could ride a horse. However, since writing was not as common as it is today, he was often obliged to memorize a message and then carry back an oral reply, in which case he needed also to have mastered the techniques then in use for the memorization of long passages. There were also messengers who, after having received the general tenor of the instructions, were empowered to deliver and explain them according to circumstances. These latter were much like our modern special envoys or ambassadors. They had very precise instructions, but were expected to adapt them to the exigencies of the moment. The duty of such people is to make known the will of those who sent them, but we would not say that their words are the words of the president or king.

The prophets presented themselves as envoys from God, and used the words and formulas which characterized the messenger's style of the age: "Thus says Yahweh to . . . N"). They overcame the distance between God and man by means of their word.

As can be seen, this third analogy adds very little to the second. In one case, the messenger need not even speak, in another he memorized and delivered the message as dictated. In the third case, he is the "secondary author" of what he says, and in a certain sense through his own activity he allows the one who sent him to speak.

An Author and the Characters He Creates

We find this analogy, taken from the world of literary creation, very attractive. Admittedly, it lacks noble lineage and a long history, at least in the tract on inspiration. St. Justin, who seems to be one of the few ancients ever to have made this comparison (other aspects of the passage are more difficult to understand), has noted:

When you hear the words of the prophets, spoken as it were in their own person, do not consider that they were uttered by these inspired people, but rather by the divine Word who moves them. For sometimes he declares things that are yet to happen, as one foretelling the future; sometimes he speaks as if in the role of the Lord of all, God the Father; sometimes as Christ; sometimes as if in the role of the people, answering to the Lord or to his Father. You find a similar thing among your own writers: one man writes the whole work introducing the roles of the various people who speak.[44]

A second-rate novelist cannot create real people in his work. He takes up puppets and has them perform in the interest of some preconceived theory or plot. Nothing must interfere, everything must conspire to the achievement of the end foreseen. The characters in the novel speak and act as they cross the pages, yet their words and actions do not ring true. Our author provides them with words which seem unfelt or unsuited.

Great writers, however, can truly create people whose action determines the plot, and whose words well up from some depth within themselves. We need only think, for instance, of Don Quixote, Hamlet, the Brothers Karamazov, or Anna Karenina. If we hear the words of these personalities read out loud, we have little trouble in determining who is speaking. No one can confuse Ivan with Aloysha, Don Quixote with his Squire. But then, suppose we push the question further, and ask: "Whose words are these?" "Do they belong to Aloysha or Dostoevski?" "Are they from Sancho or Cervantes; from Laertes or Shakespeare?" The question makes us think.

These people in a novel are the creation of their authors; they depend on him for their existence, life, and movement, yet he depends on them, too, and must respect them.

Some writers tell us how they hear within themselves the conversation of their characters, as though they themselves were specta-

---

44 "Ὅταν δὲ τὰς λέξεις τῶν προφητῶν λεγομένας ὡς ἀπὸ προσώπου ἀκούητε, μὴ ἀπ᾽ αὐτῶν τῶν ἐμπεπνευσμένων λέγεσθαι νομίσητε, ἀλλ᾽ ἀπὸ τοῦ κινοῦντος αὐτοὺς θείου λόγου. Ποτὲ μὲν γὰρ ὡς προαγγελτικῶς τὰ μέλλοντα γενήσεσθαι λέγει, ποτὲ δ᾽ ὡς ἀπὸ προσώπου τοῦ Δεσπότου πάντων κὰι Πατρὸς Θεοῦ φθέγγεται, ποτὲ δὲ ὡς ἀπὸ προσώπου τοῦ Χριστοῦ, ποτὲ δὲ ὡς ἀπὸ προσώπου λαῶν ἀποκρινομένων τῷ Κυρίῳ, ἢ τῷ Πατρὶ αὐτοῦ. ὁποῖον κὰι ἐπὶ τῶν παρ᾽ὑμῖν συγγραφέων ἰδεῖν ἔστιν, ἕνα μὲν τὸν τὰ πάντα συγγράφοντα ὄντα, πρόσωπα δὲ τὰ διαλεγόμενα παραφέροντα. "First Apology for the Christians, ch. 36," PG 6, 385,

tors rather than authors, though, paradoxically, they more than we hear only a figment of the imagination. A novelist once admitted to me that he was forced to make one of his characters die, because this person was becoming so strong that he threatened to absorb the whole novel. Trollope tells us how he lived with his characters, how he knew the tone of their voice and what each would say in a given situation; he tried to introduce his readers to these people. But no one has equaled Pirandello in his description of the process by which life is conferred on these literary personalities within the mind of their author. It is not the author who seeks out his characters, but rather there are *Six Characters in Search of an Author*, in order to live and act and speak.

It is interesting to see how some of these "people" acquire an independent existence and solidity. We need only think of the life of Sherlock Holmes (with the subsequent discussion as to whether he studied at Oxford or Cambridge), or the *Vida de Don Quijote y Sancho* by Unamuno, or the *Memoirs of Maigret* by Simenon. Anthropology and psychology alike study such great figures as Don Juan, Hamlet, and Richard III.

All this indicates the power of these personalities of fancy, and the respect they claim for the words they have uttered. None of us can forget the soliloquies of Hamlet or Henry IV, the anguish of Ivan Karamazov, the bitter reveries of Segismund.

Yet we have only said half the truth. The words of these characters belong to them and come somehow from within them, yet, and this is the other half of the truth, they are also the words of the author. There is no doubt that Calderón is reflecting on life's dream as Segismund speaks, or that Ivan gives voice to the fullness of suffering experienced by Dostoevski, and we hear Shakespeare musing in the monologue of Henry IV. Shakespeare, Cervantes, or Dostoevski can lay claim to every word spoken by the characters they have created. Even when these people confront one another and are diametrically opposed, Cervantes speaks in Don Quixote and Sancho, as does Shakespeare in Othello and Iago, or Dostoevski in Ivan and Smeryakov.

Guy de Maupassant, contrasting the "objective" novel with one based on psychological analysis, defends the latter on the ground that it provides the subjectivity of the author diverse facets of self-expression by enabling him to assume different personalities. "How should I act if I were a king, an assassin, a thief, a prostitute, a nun, a young boy, or a street vendor?" It is only by this means that the author is able to "transfer his own view of the world, his knowledge of it, and his ideas about life." This reminds us of the famous remark of Flaubert: "*Madame Bovary, c'est moi.*"

A novelist speaks in his works, not only when he recounts his autobiography or when he relates facts, but also when his characters express their ideas; and a dramatist is on the stage speaking in the personalities he has created. But then a special problem arises when an author creates two characters who are opposed to one another. In which of these is the author really speaking? It depends somewhat on the author and on the situation he has created. It may be that the thought of the writer arises within him in a dialectical movement that demands such opposition, or perhaps one of the antagonists is subtly condemned by the context in which he speaks. Then, too, there are cases in which an author creates someone whom he hates, even though he speaks through him. Care must be taken in such a case, however, since dislike for a character can easily give rise to a lack of authenticity. One novelist recommended to her colleagues "a love which is universal like that of Christ."

It is hard for us to understand this manifold unfolding, this union in word between an author and the character he creates. It is only made possible by the depth and richness of the human experience granted to the geniuses of literature. This is captured and expressed by his intuitive penetration which extends to the smallest detail, appreciating its every shade of meaning and able to enlarge and adapt it to a variety of contexts. But, above all, there is within a great writer a capacity to live with his characters, to enter into them and incarnate himself in them.

We have just used the term "incarnate"; it is a sort of metaphor in reverse, taking its concept and terminology from a mystery, and then extending itself to the world of men. We say that God has become incarnate in man or in human words, just as an artist incarnates himself in his literary creation. This is the point of our analogy.

As an analogy, this image shares with its predecessors the fact of limitation. A literary character is not a real person with a body and soul, rights and duties. Even the richest and most complete of these personalities, those which E. M. Forster calls "round characters," are at best stylized simplifications. As Somerset Maugham puts it: "The writer does not copy his originals; he takes what he wants from them, a few traits that have caught his attention, a turn of mind that has fired his imagination, and therefrom constructs his characters." To speak of the existence, liberty, and responsibility of a literary character is ultimately only figurative language. In a real human being, the personality exists and acts continually, and his speech gives expression to this subsistence. A literary personality, on the other hand, only exists when he speaks, when he is on the stage, or when someone else speaks of him. To move and live within an assumed character who is made of language is a very different thing from moving a real person within his own liberty and literary activity.

This is the obvious limitation of our analogy. Nevertheless, we would presume to close our discussion of it with these words of St. Augustine: "If He is the head, then we are the body; one man is speaking. Whether the head speaks or the members speak, it is the One Christ Who speaks." [45]

GOD THE AUTHOR OF SCRIPTURE

The use of this term "author" to describe the activity of God gives rise to many questions. First of all, do we mean it to be but one more illustrative image? If so, why not include it along with the others in the section above? Or do we consider that we have here a concept which needs further scientific precision, in order to be applicable to God? The discussion ought to begin with the observation that this term already forms part of a definition of faith. The Council of Florence declared in 1442:

[The Roman Church] professes that one and the same God is the author of both the Old and New Testaments, that is, the law, the prophets, and the Gospel, since the holy men of both testaments have spoken under the inspiration of the same Holy Spirit.[46]

---

[45] "Si ergo ille caput, nos corpus, unus homo loquitur; sive caput loquatur, sive membra, unus Christus loquitur." "Comm. on Ps 140," CCL 40, 2027.

[46] "Unum atque eundem Deum Veteris et Novi Testamenti, hoc est, Legis et Prophetarum atque Evangelii profitetur auctorem: quoniam eodem Spiritu Sancto inspirante utriusque Testamenti Sancti locuti sunt." D-S 1334.

77

About one hundred years later, the Council of Trent, describing its acceptance and veneration of Scripture and tradition, said:

[The Council] follows the example of the orthodox Fathers . . . accepts and venerates the books of both the Old and New Testaments since one God is the author of both. . . .[47]

The Vatican Council (1870) said:

The Church holds the books [of both the Old and New Testaments] to be sacred and canonical . . . because, written under the inspiration of the Holy Spirit, they have God for their author.[48]

In the first two formulas, the accent falls on the word "one." The intention of these definitions is to assert first and foremost the unity of the two testaments or economies of salvation against the errors once proposed by Marcion and the Manichaeans, who attributed the Old Testament to some evil spirit or some other god. The One True God is the author of both testaments. This is the reason why they are so closely bound in unity. Intimately linked with this declaration is the assertion of the indisputable fact that God is the author of sacred Scripture.

The formula of Vatican I goes further and enters into a discussion of the nature of inspiration. It first considers two negative aspects, as we have seen. It then goes on to describe the mystery positively in a sentence which syntactically links "inspired" with "author," and whose principle verb is in the phrase, "have God for their author."

We cannot draw from the simple fact that the definition was made any clear indication of the sense in which we ought to understand its key word. Should we consider that the Council is using the word "author" as an image, somewhat like the symbolic terms "ascended" and "heavens" of other formulas describing the glorious Christ, or should we give it its modern conceptual content? In

---

[47] ". . . orthodoxorum Patrum exempla secuta, omnes libros tam Veteris quam Novi Testamenti, cum utriusque unus Deus sit auctor, nec non traditiones ipsas, tum ad fidem, tum ad mores pertinentes, tamquam vel oretenus a Christo, vel Spiritu Sancto dictatas et continua successione in Ecclesia catholica conservatas, pari pietatis affectu ac reverentia suscipit et veneratur." D-S 1501.

[48] "Eos vero Ecclesia pro sacris et canonicis habet . . . propterea quod Spiritu Sancto inspirante conscripti Deum habent auctorem, atque ut tales ipsi Ecclesiae traditi sunt." D-S 3006.

our culture, the meaning attached to the word "author" derives principally from the world of literature, and its concept is quite precise. When a history of literature speaks of authors, there is no doubt as to what is intended, and such expressions as "authors' club," "author's copyright," etc., refer to well-defined aspects of our culture. But is this the meaning of the term as applied to the Scriptures?

We should remember first of all that, in ancient times, and especially in the biblical world, an author was something very different from what we conceive of him as today. Works were very often anonymous or pseudonymous, and nearly everything literary underwent a process of collaboration, reëlaboration, corruption, borrowing, and addition simply unknown in our world of the printed book. However, our discussion at the moment has to do with the authorship of God. Can we take the term "author" and apply it in exactly the same sense to God and to some human writer? Once again, this question places us in the world of literary creation, and the meaning we give to the term "author" is one which is specifically literary. This is the context familiar to the passage we read of St. Gregory the Great, in which he speaks of the recipient of a letter who makes inquiries about the pen which wrote it. He compares such inquiries to the action of someone who would seek to know the human author of sacred Scripture when he knows that the author is God. Here, obviously, we have an analogous use of the term, and it this use which introduces us to the *fifth* analogy in our consideration.

But we should ask first of all whether or not the strict literary interpretation of the word "author" is actually demanded by the conciliar use of "*auctor*." Is it a *dogma* that God is the literary author of the Scriptures? Could the word "author" have no other sense in the early ecclesiastical documents?

The Greek language makes a distinction between *sungrapheus* and *archegos*, or *aitios*, which corresponds rather closely with our "writer" and "originator" ("author" has both meanings), and the German "*Verfasser*" and "*Urheber*." For example, some prominent man may ask a writer to compose the biography of one of his family, the general of a religious order may commission one of his subjects to write the life of the order's founder, or a government may appoint some professor to publish a history of the country during the early nineteenth century. In all these cases, the literary author of the work is the man who is enlisted to do the work and does it, be he paid, commanded, or appointed, while the cause or originator of the book is the one who commissioned him. The celebrity, the general of an order, or the appointing government official would not be called the "author" of the work in a literary context.

Now, we have said that the action of God in inspiration does not pertain merely to the order of moral cause, but rather that God's action is real or physical. The question then arises: "Does this activity of God make Him the writer or simply the originator of the Scriptures?" "Should we say that He is the literary author, or that He is the cause in a more general sense?" This distinction brings us face to face with two differing schools of opinion. We are in the presence here of an open and "disputed question."

N. I. Weyns,[49] after an analysis of the conciliar acts of Vatican I, proceeds to a study of the meaning of the definition given by this Council on the sacred Scriptures. We have just seen the principal phrases of this definition on a preceding page. In the profession of faith, proposed to Michael VIII Palaeologus (1274), God is called "author" (*"auctor"*) of both the Old and New Testaments. The Greek text has at this point not *"sungrapheus"* ("writer or literary author"), but *"archegos"* ("originator"). It is interesting to note that in the formulas from the Councils of Florence and Trent, which we have seen, the term *"auctor"* does not receive any further specification and is used in connection with the words "Old and New Testaments" (or "dispositions"). In the schema proposed at Vatican I in December, 1869, the word "author" was clearly defined by the phrase, "they have God for their author and thus contain in a true and proper sense the word of God." The explanation of these words was as follows:

God is the author of the books, that is, the author of the writing, in such a way that the actual committing of things to paper [*consignatio*] or writing ought to be attributed principally to the divine operation acting in and through man.

A new schema corrected the phrase, "contain the word of God," to read: "are the word of God." Finally, after discussion, the

[49] *Op. cit.*, n. 40.

Council decided to omit this last phrase altogether. It thus defined nothing new in this regard, and left open the discussion as to the manner and extension of inspiration. Weyns concludes his study by interpreting the decree to mean: ". . . the Scriptures were written under some positive influence of the Holy Spirit, they have a divine origin." [50]

Karl Rahner also prefers the term "originator" ("*Urheber*") to "writer" or "literary author" ("*Verfasser*"). God is the originator or source of the Scriptures, because He "pre-defined" that the Church in the act of constituting herself should express herself to herself. The literary authors of that expression are men. God and man are both causes of the same effect, namely the Scriptures, under different formalities. The formality under which God is the cause, is that act by which the Church confers on herself her act of self-expression. The formality under which man is the cause, is that by which a man gives this expression literary existence. According to Rahner, it is not exact to say that God wrote a letter to Philemon. Therefore, we do not think that he would accept this phrase of St. John Chrysostom:

When Paul writes, or better, not Paul but the Holy Spirit dictates a letter to a whole city or to such a people and through them to the whole world . . .[51]

The other line of thought is best represented by the writings of Augustin Cardinal Bea. While recognizing that the question is open, he prefers to take the word "author" in its more usual ac-

---

[50] *Ibid.*: " . . . *sub influxu quodam positivo Spiritus Sancti conscripti sunt, divinam habent originem.*" Desroches implicitly accepts this opinion when he writes: "*On sera étonné, sans doute, de nous voir revenir à la notion d'auteur, pour éclairer la phénomène surnaturel de l'inspiration. Il semblerait que le Père Lagrange ait fait justice de cette méthode surannée, comme nous l'avons souligné dans la première partie de ce travail. Nous admettons sans difficultés après lui et son éminent disciple, le Père Benoit, que la formule Dieu-auteur ne puisse servir de point de départ a notre explication. Mais avec eux encore, il nous faut affirmer avec autant de force que cette formule doit se rencontrer au point d'arrivée.*" A. Desroches, *Jugement pratique et Jugement spéculatif chez l'Ecrivain inspiré*, Ottawa, 1958, p. 107. (However, the formula which Desroches avoids is found in the Vatican definition.)

[51] Παύλου δὲ γράφοντος, μᾶλλον δὲ οὐ τοῦ Παύλου, ἀλλὰ τῆς τοῦ Πνεύματος χάριτος τὴν ἐπιστολὴν ὑπαγορευούσης ὁλοκλήρῳ πόλει καὶ δήμῳ τοσούτῳ καὶ δι' ἐκείνων τῇ οἰκουμένῃ πάσῃ. . . . "Homily on Rom 16:3," PG 51, 187.

ceptance, as the ancients did.[52] The formula, *"Deus Auctor,"* appears for the first time in the so-called "Ancient Statutes of the Church" (*Statuta Ecclesiae Antiqua*), in which it is laid down that before a man be consecrated a bishop, it should be determined if he believe ". . . that there be one and the same author of the Old and New Testaments, that is, the law, the prophets, and the apostles." [53] This text was already known at the beginning of the sixth century, and its intention is clearly anti-Manichaean. St. Augustine, in his controversy with the Manichaeans, cites Faustus to the effect that the Manichaean Church "finds distasteful the gifts of the Old Testament and of its author. A most jealous guardian of its own prestige, it receives letters only if they are from its Spouse." [54] However, neither of these two texts which we have just seen are absolutely clear, and neither relates the word "author" to any body of writings. In fact, the text of St. Augustine is of a decidedly metaphorical character. However, in other anti-Manichaean writers, the application of the term "author" is clearly made to the written documents, and not only to the covenants or dispositions of God. The "Acts of Archelaus" describes the Manichaean doctrine as maintaining that "what is written in the law and the prophets should be attributed to Satan . . . who willed to write some truths, so that moved by these, people would accept the errors also." And Serapion of Thmuis presents the Manichaeans with this argument: "If the evil one, who possesses no splendor but is all darkness, wrote the law, how did he know about the coming of the Son?" Bea thus concludes his historical investigation by interpreting the word "author" in its strict sense of "literary author."

These, then, are the two lines of thought in this disputed question. It would seem that the formula in the Credo, "Who spoke through the prophets," as well as frequent patristic allusions to this aspect of the mystery favor the opinion that the term "author"

[52] Cf. A. Bea, "Deus Auctor Sacrae Scripturae: Herkunft und Bedeutung der Formel," Ang 20, 1943, pp. 16–31.

[53] "Quaerendum etiam ab eo, si novi et veteris testamenti, id est, legis et prophetarum, et apostolorum unum eundumque credat auctorem et Deum." EB 30.

[54] ". . . sordent ei Testamenti Veteris et ejus auctoris munera, famaeque suae custos diligentissima, nisi sponsi sui non accipit litteras." "Contra Faustum," PL 42, 303.

should be interpreted as literary author, and be used in this sense in constructing an analogy. Though, of course, the Fathers did not consider explicitly the problem with which we are faced today, still their spontaneous recourse to such words as "pronounced," "spoke," "wrote," etc., seem to fit best in this context of "literary author."

Eusebius:

They either do not believe that the divine writings were pronounced by the Holy Spirit, in which case they are heretics, or . . .[55]

St. Irenaeus:

. . . the Scriptures are perfect, because they were uttered by the Word of God and His Spirit.[56]

St. Clement of Alexandria:

The Lord speaks in person through Isaiah, through Elijah, through the mouth of the prophets.[57]

Origen:

The Holy Spirit relates this.[58]

St. Cyril of Alexandria:

All of Scripture is but one book, uttered by the One Holy Spirit.[59]

St. Cyril of Jerusalem:

Who else knows the deep things of God, but the Holy Spirit alone Who has spoken the divine writings? . . . Why are you so preoccu-

---

[55] Ἡ γὰρ οὐ πιστεύουσιν ἁγίῳ Πνεύματι λελέχθαι τὰς Θείας Γραφὰς, καὶ εἰσὶν ἄπιστοι, ἢ ἑαυτοὺς ἡγοῦνται σοφωτέρους τοῦ ἁγίου Πνεύματος ὑπάρχειν. Eusebius, "Ecclesiastical History, 5," PG 20, 517.

[56] "Scripturae quidem perfectae sunt, quippe a Verbo Dei et Spiritu ejus dictae." "Adversus Haereses, 5," PG 7, 805.

[57] Αὐτὸς ἐν Ἡσαΐᾳ ὁ Κύριος λαλῶν, αὐτὸς ἐν Ἠλίᾳ, ἐν στόματι προφητῶν αὐτός. "Exhortation to the Gentiles, 1," PG 8, 64.

[58] "Qui haec gesta narrat quae legimus, neque puer est, qualem supra descripsimus, neque vir talis aliquis, neque senior, nec omnino aliquis homo est: et ut amplius aliquid dicam, nec angelorum aliquis, aut virtutum coelestium est, sed sicut traditio majorum tenet, Spiritus sanctus haec narrat." "Homily 26 on the Book of Numbers," PG 12, 774.

[59] Ἐν γὰρ ἡ πᾶσα ἐστι καὶ λελάληται δι᾽ ἑνὸς τοῦ ἁγίου Πνεύματος. "On Is 29:12," PG 70, 656.

pied about things which even the Holy Spirit did not write in the Scriptures? [60]

The Holy Spirit Himself pronounced the Scriptures. . . . Let those things be said which He has said, and what He has not said neither let us dare to say.[61]

The above list could be extended without great difficulty, but this sampling of patristic texts is sufficient to give us an idea of their orientation. They all seem to favor a conception of God's activity in inspiration which is better described as "literary author" than as "origin." We will conclude with this passage from St. Isidore, which synthesizes both aspects:

These are the writers of the sacred books. . . . But the author of these same Scriptures is believed to be the Holy Spirit. For He Himself wrote those things which He dictated to the prophets to be written.[62]

Once we have decided to take the term "author" in the sense of "literary author," we are, of course, in the realm of analogy, since the authorship of the Holy Spirit is necessarily unique. He is an author who writes by means of others who are also truly authors. This analogy, then, also has its limitations.

Conclusion

In our effort to shed some light on the mystery of inspiration, we have considered some of the images used to describe it. The image latent in the term itself, *"in-spirare"* ("breathe into") evokes the picture of an all-pervading wind or breath. Drawn from this most elemental experience of the cosmos, it accentuates the notion of vitality and dynamism, and since it is an analogy whose origin is completely biblical, its privileged position is assured. Its conceptual

---

60 Τί ἐστιν ἕτερον γινῶσκον τὰ βάθη τοῦ Θεοῦ, εἰ μὴ μόνον τὸ Πνεῦμα τὸ ἅγιον, τὸ λαλῆσαν τὰς θείας Γραφάς; . . . Τί τοίνυν πολυπραγμονεῖς, ἃ μηδὲ τὸ Πνεῦμα τὸ ἅγιον ἔγραψεν ἐν ταῖς Γραφαῖς; . . . "Catech. 12, On the Only Begotten," PG 33, 705.

61 Αὐτὸ τὸ Πνεῦμα τὸ ἅγιον ἐλάλησε τὰς Γραφάς. . . . Λεγέσθω οὖν ἃ εἴρηκεν. ὅσα γὰρ οὐκ εἴρηκεν, ἡμεῖς οὐ τολμῶμεν. "Catech. 16, On the Holy Spirit," PG 33, 920.

62 "Hi sunt scriptorum librorum. . . . Auctor autem earumdem Scripturarum Spiritus Sanctus esse creditur. Ipse enim scripsit, qui prophetas suos scribenda dictavit." "De Eccl. Officiis," PL 83, 750.

elaboration in theology, however, has tended to empty it of any imaginative content.

The image of instrument comes from the world of man and human culture, from work and music. It rests on the two qualities of man—*homo faber* and *homo ludens*. Though scanty biblical support can be found for the image, its symbolic value is unchallenged, and it has lent itself readily to a metaphysical transposition. Even today, its possibilities as a symbol are quite rich, while its use in metaphysics has not dulled its human resources.

The image evoked by the word "dictation" comes from the world of chancelleries and curiae and is at home in the realm of literature. It has a firm biblical basis in some of the phrases used by the prophets, but its subsequent conceptual elaboration has often tended to a rigidity which obliges us to be cautious in its application. At the same time, the progress made in overcoming the dangers in such conceptualization is a good indication of the advancement made in our understanding of the doctrine.

The image of a messenger derives also from the world of the court and the curia. It is a well-established biblical frame of reference, but has received hardly any conceptual refinement. Perhaps this is because it adds but little to the two preceding images.

The image of an author and the literary personalities he fashions, proceeds directly from the world of literary creation. It has no biblical roots, since formerly men gave little reflective consideration to the nature of literary activity. In its application to the Scriptures, there has not been as yet any process of conceptual analysis.

If the term "author" is used as an image when it is predicated of God's activity in regard to the Scriptures, then it clearly derives from the world of literature and can be shown to have its roots in the Bible itself. Its use in the tract on inspiration has occasioned many discussions, but as yet there is no commonly accepted view as to its area of meaning.

Everyone of these analogies can offer us some positive understanding of the fact of inspiration. By making the contribution in the full consciousness of their limitations, they enlighten us while yet affirming the transcendence of the mystery.

We should note however, that if we are to place this whole study in its proper context, we must distinguish clearly between two different ways of considering and comparing realities in their relation to the Incarnation. They are called, respectively, "communication of idiom" and "analogy."

Because of the Incarnation it is possible to speak of Christ, using a communication of idiom or interchange of predicate in the following way: with Christ as the subject of the sentence, I may say that God died for us, or that this man is omnipotent. However, I cannot interchange predicates when speaking of the separate natures as such, because they exist "without commingling or confusion."

When I consider Christ as a concrete totality, I am obliged to refer to many human factors in order to understand and describe Him. But if I want to know what God is in Himself, or what the Word is as a Divine Person, then I cannot avail myself of the human factors in Christ except by way of analogy. I am able to say and to know something of God by taking man as my starting point because man is the image of God, and not solely because God has become man. Thus in the case of Christ, when it is a question of an analogy, we must be conscious of its limits and be aware of the nature of these limits. In order to know and say something about the Trinity, I use the analogy of human filiation while remaining aware of its limitations: generation in the Trinity is a true generation but it is not like human generation which involves the union of a man and woman, a body, succession in time, etc. On the other hand, the human generation of Christ is unlike other human generations in that it was virginal. If in my effort to understand something of the Trinity, I take as the basis for my analogy the mental conception of a word, I must also remember the limitations imposed by the fact of the infinity of God, the fact that the "Word" in the Trinity is a Person, etc.

Nevertheless, in this matter of analogy, since Christ is truly man, truly the son of Mary, his human nature is an especially privileged analogue by which God, the Trinity, can be known analogically.

As we pass now to a consideration of the inspired word, we should bear the foregoing considerations in mind. There is here also, a sort of "communication of idiom" when we consider the Bible in the concrete: an oracle, a story, a psalm, etc. We may say that we hear the word of God which bears the power of God. Then if I wish to describe this concrete divine-human reality, I am obliged to employ a whole series of human qualities which are present because it is truly human language, and literature.

But if I wish to understand the divine aspect of this concrete reality, its divine quality as such, then I no longer use a "communication of idiom" but analogy, aware of course of its limitations. I can arrive at a partial understanding of this word of God outside Himself by making an analogy with human speech. Since it is an analogy, there will not be correspondence at every point, and I must recognize this if I am not to slip into equivocation. Nevertheless, the inspired language, the biblical word, occupies a privileged position in our attempt to understand the divine Word.

We could put it this way: If we wish to understand or say anything with regard to the divine aspect of the inspired word, which is the divine word addressed to man, then we cannot use a communication of idiom, but analogy. We must consider human language in general, then more particularly, and finally the language of the Bible as an especially valuable analogue. If we wish to know or say anything about the divine-human word, then we must use the way of interchange of predicates as applied to the concrete fact of language; and we must describe the human reality assumed by God.

The first consideration, that of the divine aspect of the inspired word, was treated briefly in Chapter 1, using the analogy of human language in general and employing as common point of reference the notion of "manifestation." In this chapter we have reflected upon the mystery of the union of the divine and the human. As our study progresses, we will speak of the concrete reality giving to it the name, "the inspired word" and concentrating especially on the fact of its being a human word and human literature.

If we wish to avoid the danger of equivocation, we must bear these distinctions in mind. Whatever of revelation and grace is contained in the inspired word, accrues to it because it has been assumed by the divine word to man become incarnate in a word truly human. If we concentrate our attention here on describing the wealth of meaning and power contained in the human word, that is only because it is the verbal body in which divine revelation and grace has become incarnate. That is why we have entitled our study *The Inspired Word*, putting the accent on the concrete fact of the Bible as a reality both divine and human.

Bibliography for Chapter 2

The Action of the Spirit. The question of word and its relation to human thought and divine revelation has not received sufficient study. We have already given a bibliography for the biblical background of the concept, and there will be a bibliography in Chapter 4 in regard to the linguistic aspects. Here it will suffice to mention the short article by H. Krings, "Wort," in *Handbuch Theologischer Grundbegriffe*, ed. by H. Volk and H. Fries, Munich, 1963, also the articles in the biblical dictionaries mentioned in Chapter 1. There are two studies of the concept of the word in Origen: von Balthasar, *Parole et Mystère chez Origene*, Paris, 1957; R. Gögler, *Zur Theologie des Biblischen Wortes bei Origenes*, Düsseldorf, 1963.

Inspiration and the Incarnation. For a discussion of the comparison incarnate Word—inspired word, the fundamental study is that by H. de Lubac in his *Exégèse Médiévale*, vol. 2, pp. 181–197, "Verbum Abbreviatum." There is an article in *JTS* 6, 1955, pp. 87–90, by J. Crehan entitled "The Analogy between *Verbum Dei Incarnatum* and *Verbum scriptum* in the Fathers" (cf. the discussion concerning this work in Chapter 2, n. 8). Origen's views have exerted a great influence in Christian thought in this regard, as the works by von Balthasar and Gögler mentioned above witness. There is an interesting article by H. Schelkle, "Sacred Scripture and Word of God," in *Dogmatic vs. Biblical Theology*, ed. by H. Vorgrimler, Baltimore, 1964; and the work by Mowinckel, *The Old Testament as the Word of God*, mentioned in Chapter 1, is also helpful. A good résumé of present thought on this question may be found in C. Charlier, "Le Christ, Parole de Dieu," in *La Parole de Dieu en Jésus Christ*, Cahiers de l'actualité religieuse, no. 15, Paris, 1961, while a profound analysis of the philosophical basis for our analogous predication of the term "word" of the Son of God may be found in B. Lonergan's articles in *TS* 7, 1964, pp. 349–392; 8, 1947, pp. 35–79, 404–444; 10, 1949, pp. 3–40, 359–393; and also *De Deo Trino*, vol. 2, *Pars Systematica*, Rome, 1964.

Negative Aspects. The best treatment is that of C. Pesch (cf. Appendix).

Four Analogies. For a discussion of the cognitive function of symbol there is, in addition to the work of Söhngen cited in the text (*Analogie und Metaphern*), the work of W. Stählin, *Symbolon. Vom gleichnishaften Denken*, Stuttgart, 1958. A more general work, but in English, is that by E. Cassirer mentioned in Chapter 1 (*The Philosophy of Symbolic Forms*, esp. vol. 1). The function of symbols in religion is studied by A. Brunner in *Die Religion. Eine Philosophische Untersuchung auf geschichtlicher Grundlage*, Freiburg, 1956 (cf. the remarks of G. McCool in *IPQ* 1, 1961, pp. 671–81). There have been some interesting articles on the question of symbol, analogy, and religious language in recent philosophical periodicals. Since there is little work in English in book form, some of the more important articles will be listed here: M. J. Charlesworth, "Linguistic Analysis and Language About God," *IPQ* 1, 1961, pp. 193–167, and J. Ross, in the same volume of *IPQ* (pp. 633–662), where there is an interesting discussion of R. McInerny's *The Logic of Analogy*, The Hague, 1961, carried on by D. Burrell and J. Ross; another aspect can be seen in the same volume of *IPQ* (pp. 191–218) in the article by P. Ricoeur, "The Hermeneutics of Symbols and Philosophical Reflection," which is extremely helpful; earlier ideas of the same author can be seen in the translation of his article (*Espirit*, 1959) found in *PT* 4, 1960, pp. 192–207, "The Symbol, Food for Thought." Finally, there are some very enlightening (though difficult) pages in B. Lonergan's *Insight*, 2nd ed., New York, 1958 (consult the index under "Symbol" and "Analogy," as well as Chapter 20, "Special Transcendent Knowledge."

Instrument. Since these concepts are more familiar, there is less need for bibliographical material in this book. The fundamental work for the division of the tract on inspiration into an analysis of the analogies is A. Bea, *De Inspiratione et Inerrantia Sacrae Scripturae*, Rome, 1947; the analogies that he uses are: *theopneustos*, instrument, dictation, and author. There is a select bibliography up until 1946. On the notion of instrument, cf. R. Krumholtz, "Instrumentality and the *Sensus Plenior*," *CBQ* 20, 1958, pp. 200–205. In Chapter 2, we insisted more on the image aspect of these analogies, putting the emphasis on their concrete, cultural realizations.

Dictation. A. Bea, "Libri sacri Deo dictante conscripti," *EstEc* 34, 1960, pp. 329–337, and in the book of E. R. Curtius, *European Literature in the Latin Middle Ages*, New York, 1963, p. 75ff., "Ars dictaminis."

A Messenger. There is a good historical résumé and bibliography in the article by James Ross, "The Prophet as Yahweh's Messenger," in *Israel's Prophetic Heritage*, Essays in Honor of James Muilenburg, ed. by B. W. Anderson and W. Harrelson, New York, 1962, pp. 98–107. Ross briefly discusses the work of C. Westermann, *Grundformen prophetischer Rede*, Munich, 1962, which is very thorough in its historical analysis of the history of this idea in biblical research and somewhat unique in its conclusions.

An Author and the Characters He Creates. Generally, works which deal with the art of writing fiction touch on this aspect in one way or another. The fundamental work from the aspect of literary criticism is that by R. Wellek and A. Warren, *Theory of Literature,* New York, 1956; the bibliographical material there is quite complete. There is a selection of statements by authors themselves in *Writers on Writing,* ed. by W. Allen, New York, 1948, Chapter 13 "Characters," and F. Fergusson has some very penetrating remarks in his *The Human Image in Dramatic Literature,* New York, 1957. There is a wealth of insight to be gained by reading E. Auerbach, *Mimesis,* New York, 1953, even though his line of investigation is slightly different.

God the Author of Scripture. The two fundamental articles are A. Bea, "Deus Auctor Scripturae: Herkunft und Bedeutung der Formel," *Ang* 20, 1943, pp. 16-31, and N. I. Weyns, "De notione inspirationis biblicae iuxta Concilium Vaticanum," *Ang* 30, 1953, pp. 315–336. There is a further discussion of this analogy and reference to the work of K. Rahner in Chapter 8.

3. The Witness of the Scriptures

We are about to embark on a new journey, through the realm of the Scriptures, in order to enrich our idea of the meaning of inspiration. We will begin this trip by repeating once again the words of the Creed, "Who spoke through the prophets," and then we will visit the sacred text itself, not with the idea of finding proofs and arguments, but simply to allow what we meet there to form in us a more realistic idea of the mystery. We will base ourselves on the facts as they are available to us. It would be hazardous, indeed, to try to form some clear, precise idea of inspiration without ever consulting the inspired text. We would be running the risk of finding ourselves forced to leave out of our brilliantly constructed system some information or even some books of the Bible. Our idea of inspiration must be spacious enough to allow room for all its concrete expressions and all the varieties of the inspired books. It is not up to us to set boundaries for the Spirit.

The Old Testament

The Prophets

The Creed itself invites us to begin our study with a consideration of the prophets. St. Thomas never wrote a tract on inspiration. Rather, what he has to say on the subject is to be found in his tract on "prophecy," and it is from there that many modern authors have drawn much of what they have to say on inspiration. The prophets were not the only men who had the gift of inspiration, but in them we are able to see this reality in its most dynamic form, and to derive therefrom a clearer idea of the action of the

Spirit. The prophets are the "prime analogates" of our study, and so it will be well to begin with them.

Vocation. Three of the prophets have left us a rather detailed description of their vocation. Once, when Isaiah[1] was in the Temple, he beheld Yahweh on His throne, "and the train of his garment filled the Temple." He heard the song of the Seraphim, "and the threshold of the entrance shook, and the whole place was filled with smoke." He cried out, "Woe is me, I am doomed! For I am a man of unclean lips, living among a people of unclean lips." The first reaction of the future prophet was the painful awareness, not of any incapacity or inelegance in his speech, but of the fact that his language, that of his whole people, was profane and utterly unequal to the holiness which he experienced so overwhelmingly. A sacred fire borne by one of the seraphim touched and sanctified his lips. He spoke the same language, and had acquired no new style or talent for expression, but now his lips had been made holy and consecrated; somehow, they had been transferred to the realm of the divine holiness or transcendence. He then received his mission. He heard the voice of Yahweh saying, " 'Whom shall I send? Who will go for us?' 'Here I am,' I said; 'send me!' And He replied, 'Go and say to this people . . .' " His whole mission consisted in speaking in behalf of God to the people of God. If we were to express this mission in our well-defined modern categories, we would say that the prophet had received a commission and corresponding charism in the order of speech or language. Nothing is said about committing anything to writing. Many other particular commissions were to be given to Isaiah, specifying this initial calling, yet these, too, were always in the realm of speech and proclamation.

The Book of Jeremiah[2] begins with an account of his vocation. Even before he was born, God had chosen him, sanctified or set him apart, and made him a prophet. Jeremiah well understood the role that God was giving him, and he objected: "Ah, Lord God, I know not how to speak, I am too young." Many commentators have wanted to see in these words an attempt, inspired by fear, to

[1] Cf. Is 6.

[2] Jer 1. Von Reventlow, in an extreme reaction against the psychological preoccupations of a former generation, has tried to reduce everything to a set of prophetic formulas. Cf. H. von Reventlow, *Das Amt des Propheten bei Amos*, Göttingen, 1962.

avoid the inevitable consequences of the prophetic vocation. But, in fact, the objection makes its plea by pointing to an incapacity in the realm of language. Obviously, Jeremiah knew how to speak; he had just framed his objection to God. His reluctance is based on his inability to speak as a prophet; perhaps he felt a lack of literary training. God responds by asserting the efficacy of the mission on which He has determined to send Jeremiah: "Wherever I send you, you will go; and whatever I command you, you will declare." The commission is then sealed by a ritual, sacramental gesture. "Then the Lord extended His hand and touched my mouth saying, "See, I place My words in your mouth! This day I set you over nations and over kingdoms, to root up and to tear down, to destroy and to demolish, to build and to plant." Jeremiah's mission was to speak; he was to declare the message of God in words of power. This is what characterizes his vocation; no mention is made here of any obligation to write. God had conferred on him the charism of speech, in order to make known and effect His will.

Ezekiel, though he tells his story with less restraint and clarity, conveys the same fundamental notions. He is commissioned: "I send you to them" (2:4). He receives the word of the Lord: ". . . Open your mouth and eat what I shall give you. It was then I saw a hand stretched out to me, in which was a written scroll which He unrolled before me. It was covered with writing, front and back, and written on it there were words of lamentation, mourning, and woe. He said to me: Son of man, eat what is before you; eat this scroll, then go, speak to the house of Israel. So I opened my mouth and He gave me the scroll to eat. Son of man, He then said to me, feed your belly and fill your stomach with this scroll I am giving you. I ate it, and it was as sweet as honey in my mouth. He said: Son of man, go now to the house of Israel and speak My words to them" (2:8—3:4). The predominant theme here is also one of speaking. The scroll already contained writing; the prophet was able to make out the various literary types that were written there. But his task was not to take the scroll in his hands and, unrolling it, read out its burden to the people. He was obliged, rather, to eat the scroll, assimilate what it held, and then from this interior fullness utter his message. There is nothing mechanistic about the prophetic activity; it is vital, dynamic, and interior. In the same section as that which we quoted above, we read that God said to Ezekiel: "Son of man, . . . take into your heart all My words that I speak to you; hear them well. Now go to the exiles, to your countrymen and say to them . . ." The phrase "take into your heart" could also be translated "take by heart," or "memorize," but if this is the correct interpretation, it is a unique realization of the messenger aspect of the prophetic role.

The elements of prophetic vocation are thus seen to be three: mission, consecration, and speech. There is no hint here of dictaphones or school-boy repetition, but of a living and deeply personal activity. The lips of Isaiah were consecrated; Jeremiah received the word of God in his mouth, while Ezekiel had it penetrate his entrails.

Autobiography. The objective accounts of vocation which we have just seen, can be completed with some intimate autobiographical passages found in the prophets. Jeremiah's comments are the most explicit, and his work is particularly rich in these "modern" self-reflections. The task that God had laid on Jeremiah was not only difficult, but positively dangerous. Men either laughed at him or tried to kill him, and it finally occurred to Jeremiah that his only chance of avoiding persecution was to keep silent. He has left us an account of his subsequent prayer:

> You led me on, O Yahweh,
> and I let myself be led.
> You forced me, and you won.
> And I? —a laughingstock all day,
> sport for every passer-by.
>
> Whenever I speak, I shout Violence!
> Plunder is my cry.
>
> For Yahweh's word to me—
> scorn and derision all the day long.
> I said:
> I will not remember it,
> No more will I speak in his name.
> Then in my heart it turned to fire
> burning, imprisoned in my bones.
> I am weary holding it in,
> I can no longer.[3]

[3] Jer 20:7–9.

The prophet feels the word of God within his soul. It is like fire, burning in his very bones, or like molten lava, ready to erupt and spill out along the path of least resistance. This is a description which has much in common with that experience of creative compulsion attested to by many geniuses. But in Jeremiah's case, the deep source of the drive is the word of Yahweh. It does not take away liberty—Jeremiah had decided to keep silent, yet it is a force within him which demands realization. Ezekiel saw the problem of his liberty as a "case of conscience." He was a sentinel whose duty it was to cry "Danger!" If he shouted his warning, then he was not answerable for the lives of those who refused to take refuge; but if he kept silent, the guilt was his own.[4]

Prophetic Formulas. It is interesting to note that the phrases used in the prophetic messages all have reference to speech:

"The word of the Lord came to me."
"The word which was received by . . ."
"Listen to the word of the Lord."
"Thus says Yahweh."
"An oracle of Yahweh."

This word of the Lord is not distinct from the word of the prophet:

The House of Israel will refuse to listen to you, since they will not listen to Me (Ez 3:7).

I have sent them my servants, the prophets, morning and night, night and morning, yet they have not listened to Me or paid heed (Jer 7:25).

Confronted with such texts, it seems that the efforts of some moderns to separate within the oracles words that are God's from words that are the prophet's, are simply futile. There is a "communication of idiom" in these messages which recalls the relation established between an author and the characters he has created (the words of Hamlet and the words of Shakespeare). The prophet is the man of God (1 K 2:27), the man of the Spirit (Hos 9:7), the very mouth of God (Jer 15:19).

Literary Effort. Such descriptions of the prophet and the insistence on the identity of his message with that of God, might lead one to conclude that his role is that of a secretary or messenger, commissioned to record the dictation or memorize the message to

4 Ez 33:1–9.

95

be delivered. But a close analysis of the actual writings of the prophets leads us to a very different conclusion. It is true that not every prophet has a fully developed personal style. Still, anyone can recognize the characteristics of a classical writter such as Isaiah and distinguish them from the romanticism of Jeremiah or the baroque of Ezekiel. If we approach these texts with the tools of literary criticism, we begin to appreciate how well some of these men both knew and practiced the writer's craft. We see them searching for onomatopoeia, assembling assonance, laying out a chiastic phrase of six or more members, subtly changing a rhythmic formula, constructing an oracle piece by piece, exploiting the possibility of a topical image or formula, sometimes changing it and sometimes consciously modelling themselves on a predecessor. We come to know these men in their toil, and we can almost reach out and wipe the sweat from their brow as their poem or oracle takes shape, chiselled from the quarry of language. When our analysis has allowed us to share and appreciate this effort, we are prepared to offer the prophet a medal for his honest and capable craftsmanship. But he pushes it away: "It is the word of God." Strange dictation which costs its literary fashioner so dearly. The fact of the matter is that it is not dictation at all.

If we wish to reconcile these two facts, that of the obvious literary effort of the prophet, and his repeated phrase, "the word of the Lord," we will have to follow another path than that indicated by the term "dictation." The Spirit's action is not one of dictating a message word by word, it is not something mechanical at all. It is found deep within the wellsprings of the act of language, and more precisely at the sources of literary effort.

This much we can learn from the prophets, our "prime analogates." If anyone would be expected to have received his words immediately from God, if anyone should merely receive and repeat the divine message, it is the prophet. Yet precisely here, in the obvious tension between the conscious toil of the literary craft and the oft-repeated "word of the Lord," we begin to appreciate the dimensions of the mystery of inspiration. It is something that transpires deep inside one; it is marvellous yet hidden.

The divine and the human are both present; the divine elevates the human, it does not suppress it. God's call elevates the personality of the prophet rather than destroys it; literary sensibilities are polarized, creativity is delivered not chained. A prophet belongs to his society, pertains to a certain school of prophecy or literary tradition, and may have a function within some religious institution. The prophets are the most forceful personalities of the Old Testament. For the Spirit knows how to awaken and sustain the forces of true greatness. A writer of any stature does not reveal his talent in creating literary puppets; his greatness does not make his characters puny, but just the contrary. So, too, the action of the Spirit reveals its power in raising up great men, endowed with literary gifts of a high order. But there are also lesser lights in the literary world of the Bible, craftsmen of a more modest achievement, "minor prophets" according to the standards of literary excellence.

Sapiential Literature

The conclusions of the preceding analysis can be strengthened by studying another group of men who have contributed to the composition of the Scriptures. By way of example, we will choose out one of these writers, a fascinating personality who calls himself "the Preacher." He is a confirmed non-conformist who turns his disenchantment into challenge and makes his attack by way of suggestion. Let us take a few of the phrases he uses to introduce his observations, and compare them with the formulas of the prophets:

I applied my mind to search and investigate in wisdom all things that are done under the sun (Eccl 1:13).

And I said to myself . . . (1:16) ("Thus says the Lord").

. . . yet when I applied my mind to know wisdom and knowledge . . . (1:17).

I said to myself (2:1) ("Listen to the word of the Lord").

I have considered the task which God has appointed for men (3:10).

I turned and looked at all the oppression that take place under the sun (4:1) ("The word of the Lord came to me").

I have seen all manner of things in my vain days . . . (7:15).

97

I turned my thoughts toward knowledge; I sought and pursued wisdom and reason (7:25).

All this I took to heart . . . (9:1).

I said: "Better wisdom than power . . ." (9:16) ("What I have heard from the Lord, I pass on to you").

And so it goes throughout his work. Never once does he say that he received the word of the Lord; never is there any pretension to a divine oracle. On the contrary, we hear constantly of his observation, study, and reflection, all reported in the first person, yet in a way that never strikes us as heavy. We never get the impression of pedantic self-sufficiency, but rather of disillusionment and resignation.[5]

But though our author tells us quite frankly of his efforts and their results, the Church tells us that his work is part of the sacred Scripture, the word of God. The writer felt no fire or breeze of the Spirit, yet the Church says that his book is inspired.

Certainly, in this case we cannot think of inspiration as some process of dictation. Inspiration did not eliminate the man's personality, but rather enshrined it. If these words, so pathetically human, are also the words of God, it is because somewhere deep within the act which gave them existence, there was the action of the Holy Spirit, mysterious yet effective. This motion from God must have something in common with the motion we discerned in the prophets, if we are able to use the same term, "inspiration," of both of them. Yet the great difference between these two extreme instances of the same divine action seems to recommend the suggestion of Benoit, that we take the term "inspiration" as representing an analogous concept.

There is another author in the sapiential tradition who has left us a somewhat different account of his literary activity. This man, Jesus Ben Sirach, the last in the series of Hebrew wisdom writers, is fully aware of and quite content with his literary talents and effort.

---

[5] O. Loretz interprets the use of the first person as a literary device of the author. This does not invalidate what we have said, but only highlights the literary self-consciousness of the author, who certainly then is making no pretensions at passing on a revelation received. Nevertheless, we do not think that the "I" is a literary device (cf. O. Loretz, "Zur Darbietungsform 'ich-Erzählung' im Buche Qohelet," CBQ 25, 1963, pp. 46–59.

He tells us that his travels have taught him much (34:9–12), and he often appeals to his experience. In his view, "when an intelligent man hears words of wisdom, he approves them and adds to them" (21:14), and he hints modestly that he knows more than he is saying (34:11). The prophet called out: "Hear the word of the Lord"; Ben Sirach says: "Listen to me, O princes."

In Chapter 39 of his work, Ben Sirach gives us a sketch of the ideal wise man. It is a poem of four strophes in which the first speaks of his studies, the second of his activities at court, his journeys and his prayer, the third of wisdom as the fruit of study and prayer, and the fourth of the glory accruing to a man of these attainments:

> How different the man who devotes himself
> to the study of the Law of the Most High:
> He explores the wisdom of the men of old
> and occupies himself with the prophecies;
> He treasures the discourses of famous men,
> and goes to the heart of involved sayings;
> He studies obscure parables,
> and is busied with the hidden meanings of the sages.
>
> He is in attendance on the great
> and has entrance to the ruler.
> He travels among the peoples of foreign lands
> to learn what is good and evil among men.
> His care is to seek the Lord, his Maker,
> to petition the Most High,
> To open his lips in prayer,
> to ask pardon for his sins.
>
> Then, if it pleases the Lord Almighty,
> he will be filled with the spirit of understanding;
> He will pour forth his words of wisdom
> and in prayer give thanks to the Lord,
> Who will direct his knowledge and his counsel,
> as he meditates upon his mysteries.
> He will show the wisdom of what he has learned
> and glory in the Law of the Lord's covenant.
>
> Many will praise his understanding;
> his fame can never be effaced;

D

> Unfading will be his memory,
> through all generations his name will live;
> Peoples will speak of his wisdom,
> and in assembly sing his praises.
> While he lives he is one out of a thousand,
> and when he dies his renown will not cease.[6]

The wise man has recourse to God in prayer, and receives from Him the spirit of wisdom, not that of prophecy; he goes to the Scriptures and meditates on the prophecies and the sayings of famous men. But even this act is a purely human effort.

Once again, we see the same two aspects of the mystery. The fruit of this human reflection and literary effort is the word of God; the man who has applied himself so earnestly has received the gift of inspiration. Our idea of inspiration, then, must be supple enough to adapt itself to these undeniable facts presented by the Scriptures. There is a passage in Ben Sirach which, in fleeting glance, seems to give evidence that our professional wise man himself had some inkling of the mystery at work within him. At any rate, his comparison is interesting, especially in the light of his obvious regard for the inspired books which he knew so well: "I pour out instruction like prophecy and bestow it on generations to come" (24:31).

It is significant to observe in this connection that the prophetic formula "the word of God" has its exact equivalent in the description given of the sayings of the ancient scholars, "the words of the wise men." [7] This wisdom is a human achievement, an international possession characterized by a free exchange of ideas whose basic theme is man—which is not to say that it is irreligious—and whose methods consist in the thoroughly human procedure of observation and experimentation.[8] A comparison of this literature with that of the prophets indicates to us how deep and subtle the action of the Spirit can sometimes be. These scholars and well-travelled men of letters have written and published works which we receive as the word of God.

This, we feel, is what Theodore of Mopsuestia intended to say in

[6] Sir 39:1–11.
[7] Cf. Prv 22:17; 24:23.
[8] Cf. W. Zimmerli, "Zur Struktur der alttestamentlichen Weisheit," ZAW 51, 1933, pp. 177-204.

one of those passages which have unjustly earned him the reputation for a certain biblical rationalism and a desire to restrict the extent of inspiration:

Among works written for human instruction are to be counted the writings of Solomon, that is, the Book of Proverbs and Ecclesiastes. These he composed on his own initiative as a service to others. He did not receive the grace of prophecy but that of prudence, which is a different gift, as Paul has indicated.[9]

Theodore does not use the term "inspiration," but he does accord to Solomon a charism which we would call part of the charism of prophecy. His purpose is not to deny or limit the gift of inspiration, but to point out an objective difference between the sapiential writings and those of the prophets. Ben Sirach claimed for himself a "spirit of wisdom," not prophecy. A man such as Theodore, writing at the beginning of the fifth century, does not view the question of inspiration exactly as we do.[10]

Other Writers

The greater part of the writings of the Old Testament lie somewhere between the two extremes we have just considered. Many times it is very difficult to determine exactly to which group a certain work belongs, or which type of literature it approximates. Should we, for instance, classify the narrators of history, Genesis, Exodus, Josuah, Samuel, and Kings as prophets or wise men? Jewish tradition has always called the "historic" books outside of the Torah "*nebi'im*," or "prophets," while Moses, whose name is linked with the Torah, is called the greatest of the prophets.

The technical name for the Decalogue is "The words of Yahweh," and the term seems to have been extended to cover other legal presciptions. *The narrators* of history, insofar as they interpret events with the aid of a special light, share in the charism of

---

[9] "*His quae pro doctrina hominum scripta sunt et Salomonis libri connumerandi sunt, id est Proverbia et Ecclesiastes, quae ipse ex sua persona ad aliorum utilitatem composuit, cum prophetiae quidem gratiam non accepisset, prudentiae vero gratiam quae evidenter altera est praeter illa secundum beati Pauli vocem.*" Mansi 9, 223.

[10] For an evaluation of the text we have just cited, and for a more complete study of acts of the Council of Constantinople where the text is cited, cf. R. Devreesse, *Essai sur Théodore de Mopsueste*, Studi e Testi, no. 141, Rome, 1948, esp. pp. 34–35, 243–258, 283–285.

prophecy, yet in their method of proceeding they bear a closer resemblance to the sapiential tradition. They collect material, consult court archives, and preserve and elaborate ancient poems. They make no appeal to a special revelation, and they never speak of their work as the "word of God." In some cases, the account of Paradise and the Fall for instance, we find clear traces of that type of intellectual reflection characteristic of the wise men.[11] The author of the Book of Deuteronomy poses theological questions to himself and seeks the explanation for certain facts of sacred history. His activity is a kind of "faith seeking understanding" which brings him close to the outlook of the wise men. For just as the author of Deuteronomy reflects on sacred history, so Ben Sirach reflects on the sacred text. In *apocalyptic literature*, the writer seeks the meaning of history, organizes the past according to a schema of periods, and transposes his reflections into a series of elaborate intellectual allegories. If he prefaces his work by appealing to a divine revelation, it is because such is the literary convention for this type of writing. Those who wrote the Psalms never think to call their poems the word of God, since they are the words in which the people are to make answer to God.

Then, to this list of authors, we must add an indeterminate number of those who contributed to the inspired text as we have it today. There were editors, compilers of anthologies, and men who inserted glosses or explanatory notes to bring the text "up to date." All of these shared in the gift of inspiration. They may have been prophets of a sort, pointing out the relevance of ancient texts, or, as was most often the case, scholars whose activity resembled that of the wise men.

We may sum up our considerations, then, by saying that the greater part of the Old Testament does not contain that type of literature which we call prophetic in the strict sense of the term, but represents rather a type of activity approximating that of the wisdom tradition. Nevertheless, we accept the whole of the Old Testament as the word of God. If the Letter to the Hebrews mentions only the prophets when it says, "God spoke to our fathers through the prophets," and if the Creed employs the same phrase, "Who spoke through the prophets," we know that all the Old Tes-

---

[11] Cf. L. Alonso Schökel, "Motivos sapienciales y de alianza en Gn 2–3, *Bib* 43, 1962, pp. 295–316.

tament is prophetic, because it looks forward to the New. We know, too, that all of sacred Scripture, Old and New Testament, is the word of God. The councils apply the term "inspiration" to the whole of the Bible. From this it follows that we cannot possibly conceive of inspiration as some kind of standardized mechanical dictation. It is an action of the Holy Spirit which moves a man mysteriously yet unfailingly from within the very wellspring of his free activity. Given the distance which separates the two extreme instances of inspiration, prophetic and sapiential, it seems quite reasonable to accept the term "inspiration" as analogous predication, and thereby to acknowledge the great range of the Spirit's power, moving men who were so different, who lived in social and political milieux so varied, and who wrote a literature so prolific in types, in order to reveal God to us in His word.

For the needs of the present investigation into the nature of inspiration, the division of Hebrew literature which we have already made is quite sufficient. It is possible to apply the norms of literary criticism to the contents of Scripture, and to differentiate the various modes of inspiration according to the work produced. But such a classification would occupy too much space, and would not perhaps be of very great use. The variety of literary types or genera employed by the authors of the Old Testament witnesses to the vibrant religious life and rich literary activity of the people of God. It testifies also to the virtuosity of the Spirit, Who awakened and sustained this many-sided activity in order to address us, using the whole range of human language. "God spoke to our forefathers in fragmentary and varied fashion." [12]

The scholastic theologians were quite appreciative of this rich variation, and they often discussed the various "modes" of sacred Scripture. They held that the science of theology was based on sacred Scripture, but that the text itself did not proceed by way of science. The mode of science includes *definition* (defining the terms), *division* (refining the concepts by distinguishing), and *argument* (deduction and syllogism), whereas the mode of Scripture

[12] A description and classification of the various literary genera can be found in most introductions to the Old Testament: A. Robert and A. Tricot, *Guide to the Bible*, 2 vols., New York, 1955–1960; A. Robert and A. Feuillet, *Introduction à la Bible*, Bruges, 1959, vol. 1; O. Eissfeldt, *Einleitung in das Alte Testament*, 3rd. ed., Tübingen, 1963; also the articles by L. Alonso Schökel on Hebrew poetry in *DBS* and the New Catholic Encyclopedia.

is characterized by "narration, commandment, prohibition, exhortation, instruction, commination, promise, supplication, and praise." This variety is explained by the end which Scripture has in view; it must reach all men, for to them is it directed.

For instance, were a man to remain unmoved by a command or a prohibition, he might perhaps be moved by a concrete example; were this to fail, he might be moved by the favors shown him; were this again to fail, he might be moved by wise admonitions, trustworthy promises, or terrifying threats, and thus be stirred, if not in one way, then in another, to devotion and praise of God.[13]

Alexander of Hales enumerates five "modes" of sacred Scripture:

Command, as in the law and the Gospel; example, as in the historical books; exhortation, as in the books of Solomon and the letters of the Apostle; revelation in the prophecies; prayer in the Psalms.[14]

He goes on, in true scholastic style, to justify this multiplicity by an analysis of the four causes of Scripture:

The modes of Scripture ought to be manifold, both by reason of their efficient cause, as well as by reason of their final and material cause . . . . The first is by reason of efficient cause, that is the Holy Spirit Who is (according to Wis 7:22) a Spirit of understanding, manifold and unique. Therefore, in order that the mode of its efficient cause should be apparent, sacred science ought to be complex and manysided. The second is by reason of material cause, which is the manifold wisdom of God. And therefore [sacred science] ought to be manysided in order to correspond to the mode of its material cause. The third is by reason of final cause, which is instruction in those things which pertain to salvation.[15]

13 ". . . narrativus, praeceptorius, prohibitivus, comminatorius, prommissivus, deprecatorius, et laudativus . . . ut si quis non movetur ad praecepta et prohibita, saltem moveatur per exempla narrata; si quis non per haec movetur, moveatur per beneficia sibi ostensa; si quis nec per haec movetur, moveatur per monitiones sagaces, per promissiones veraces, per comminationes terribiles, ut sic saltem excitetur ad devotionem et laudem Dei." St. Bonaventure, The Works of St. Bonaventure, vol. 2, The Breviloquium, tr. by José de Vinck, Paterson, 1963.
14 ". . . modus dicitur esse praeceptivus (in lege et evangelio), exemplificativus (in historicis libris), exhortativus (in libris Salomonis et epistulis apostolicis), revelativus (in prophetis), orativus (in psalmis), quia huiusmodi affectui pietatis." Cited by Pesch, no. 157, Summa I, 1.
15 "Sacrae Scripturae modum ratione efficientiae et ratione finis ac materiae

Not only were the medieval scholastics sensitive to these various literary types in the scriptures, but they applied themselves to finding a theological reason to explain them.[16]

Pesch allows that there were various degrees of intensity in the graces of inspiration given to the writers of the sacred text, but he will not concede that there are various degrees of inspiration in the books themselves, as though one book could be more inspired than another.[17] However, in the following article[18] he does add a very nuanced treatment, explaining how the various statements in the Bible are the word of God. His point of view is too cerebral and tends toward a certain atomism, but still, he opens up a very interesting line of approach.

Conclusion

Our trip through the Old Testament, rather than provide us with a precise, easily managed concept of inspiration, has imposed even greater flexibility and openness on our thinking. Our concept or idea might be less precise, but at least it corresponds to reality, and allows a place to all the facts. Later, we will have occasion to study more closely some aspects of the mystery which we have discovered in our investigation.[19]

THE INSPIRATION OF THE NEW TESTAMENT

In the New Testament, something new and definitive takes place. The various words have been spoken, now the Word resounds. It is a Word which can be heard and seen and touched;[20] a Word which

---

multiformem esse decuit. . . . Prima est ratio efficientis, id est Spiritus Sancti, qui est (ut dicitur Sap 7:22) Spiritus intellegentiae multiplex unicus. Propterea, ut in scientia sacra modus efficientis appareat, debet esse multiplex seu multiformis. Secunda est ratio materiae, quae est multiformis sapientia Dei. Propterea, ut materiae modus respondeat, debet esse multiformis. Tertia est ratio finis, qui est instructio in iis, quae pertinent ad salutem." Summa I, 3, Pesch, *ibid.*

[16] Curtius describes how this theory of the "modes" reached as far as the poetic theories of Dante. *European Literature and the Latin Middle Ages,* p. 222ff.

[17] No. 429.

[18] Nos. 436–450.

[19] Cf. ch. 7.

[20] 1 Jn 1:1.

justifies all that has gone before: their summation (*verbum abbre-viatum*) and explanation. This Word is complete and definitive, addressed to all men, because He is the true Light. In order to reach all men, this Word, Who is Jesus Christ, must continue to resound, to be present and alive to all generations. "For this deliverance was first announced through the lips of the Lord Himself; those who heard Him confirmed it to us . . ." [21]

In order that His word, He Himself as Word, might continue to resound, Christ sent His apostles and sends them still, and to them He gives His Spirit. The apostles, both by name (*apo-stello*) and by function are the "sent ones"; their mission is precisely their "mission" from Christ. It is with this theme that the Gospel closes —and yet remains open. [22]

The Apostles and Prophets

The fact that the vocation of the apostles is to be sent, established a relationship between them and the prophets of the Old Testament who were also sent to proclaim the word of God. St. Augustine has said it briefly:

He, Who before He descended to us sent the prophets, is the same Who sent the apostles after His ascension. [23]

He repeats the same thing elsewhere:

God spoke first by the prophets, then by Himself, and then by the apostles, what He judged sufficient . . . [24]

The comparison between the apostles and the prophets is frequent in the New Testament. The passage in the Epistle to the Ephesians which describes the Church as "built on the foundation of the apostles and prophets, with Christ Jesus Himself as the cornerstone" (2:20), seems to intend a reference to the prophets of the New Testament as other passages in the same letter indicate (3:5; 4:11). However, it would be difficult to exclude completely any reference to the prophets of the Old Testament.

[21] Heb 2:3.
[22] Cf. Mt 28:18–20; Mk 16:15–16; Lk 24:47–49; Jn 20:21.
[23] *Proinde qui Prophetas ante descensionem suam praemisit, ipse et Apostolos post ascensionem suam misit.*" "De Consensu Evangelistarum," PL 34, 1070.
[24] "*Hic prius per Prophetas, deinde per seipsum, postea per Apostolos, quantum satis esse judicavit. . . .*" "City of God, bk. 11," PL 41, 318.

In this same line of thought, we find a very significant statement in the First Epistle of Peter (1:10–12)

This salvation was the theme which the prophets pondered and explored, those who prophesied about the grace of God awaiting you. They tried to find out what was the time, and what the circumstances, to which the spirit of Christ in them pointed, foretelling the sufferings in store for Christ and the splendours to follow; and it was disclosed to them that the matter they treated of was not for their time, but for yours. And now it has been openly announced to you through preachers who brought you the Gospel in the power of the Holy Spirit sent from heaven. These are things that angels long to see into.

This somewhat difficult text compresses in a few lines the whole synthesis of what we have been saying. At the core of the mystery of inspiration lies the mystery of Christ, which is a mystery of "salvation" and "grace," and whose very life-center is found in His "sufferings" and "splendors to follow." This mystery was glimpsed and announced by the prophets, who had "the Spirit of Christ in them." Here we see the inspiration of the prophets described as an interior possession of a Spirit Who is the Spirit of Christ, enlightening them as to the mystery yet leaving them ignorant of the "time and circumstances" of its realization. "Now," that is, in this definitive era of salvation, the "preachers" have received the "Holy Spirit sent from heaven," from the glorified Christ. Their inspiration consists in possessing this Spirit, and in virtue of His power announcing the Gospel, the good news of salvation in Christ.

That which the apostles announced is the "word of God," and they do not hesitate to use the same prophetic formula:

This is why we thank God continually, because when we handed on God's message, you received it, not as the word of men, but as what it truly is, the very word of God at work in you who hold the faith.[25]

There are other formulas which indicate a very interesting transition in which the activity of God is predicated of Christ:

. . . When I come this time, I will show no leniency. Then you will have the proof you seek of the Christ who speaks through me, the Christ who, far from being weak with you, makes his power felt among you.[26]

[25] 1 Th 2:13–14.
[26] 2 Cor 13:3.

It is interesting to observe that the words translated as "speaks through me" are literally "speaks *in* me." The Greek construction here is identical with that in the Epistle to the Hebrews: "God has spoken to us *in* the Son" (Heb 1:2). Christ speaks *in* St. Paul (2 Cor 13:3). The Greek preposition *"en"* establishes an intimate and immediate relationships whose theological importance is stressed elsewhere in the text: "as the Father sent me, so I send you" (Jn 20:21). There is another text in the same Second Epistle to the Corinthians (2:17) which echoes this same theme: "We are not like many others, peddlers of God's word; rather, commissioned by God and in God's presence, we speak in Christ." This second formula, "in Christ," recalls the prophetic "in the Spirit" (inspiration). This phrase is also represented in the New Testament:

Our Gospel came to you not in words alone, but in power and *in the Holy Spirit*" (1 Th 1:5).

[The mystery of Christ] was not made known to the men of former generations, but now it has been revealed to His holy apostles and prophets, *in the Spirit*" (Eph 3:5).

The same words are applied in St. Matthew's Gospel to a writer of the Old Testament:

Then how does David *in the Spirit* call Him Lord?" (22:43).

Distinctions and Unity

Can we divide the New Testament according to literary types as we did in the Old Testament? There would certainly seem to be some basis for division in the fact that there are Gospels, Acts, Epistles, and an Apocalypse. The divisions are not as clearly marked as in the Old Testament, but the same types seem to be represented.

But before distinguishing, we must appreciate the unity. The New Testament is one in Christ in a way that could never be said of the manifold variety found in the writings of the Old Testament. St. Paul, in his epistles, refers to his "Gospel," and considers that his activity either of preaching or writing is one of "evangelization."

When Paul writes: "according to my Gospel," we can use these words to show that all of the New Testament is Gospel, for among the writings of Paul there is none which is usually called a Gospel. What he preached and said was Gospel. However, he wrote those things which he preached and said, and therefore his writings are Gospel. If, then, the writings of Paul are Gospel, it follows that the same can be said of Peter, and, more generally, of those writings which treat of Christ's sojourn among us, or prepare for His Parousia, or which produce it in the souls of those who desire to receive Him Who stands at the door knocking and wishing to come into them: the Word of God.[27]

We might answer that, before the visit of Christ, the law and the prophets, since He Who was to make plain their mysteries had not yet come, did not contain the message according to the terms of the Gospel. But when the Savior came and gave body to the Gospel, by means of the Gospel He made all these a sort of Gospel too.[28]

The reason for this profound inner unity lies in the fact that no one can add anything to the word of Christ. Christ as the Word, the expression and revelation of the Father, is infinitely complete. No one can add to the Father's self-expression. This is not to say that nothing can be added to the words that Christ spoke. These were limited in number, and many things that St. Paul says, Our Lord had not pronounced before him. But Christ did not only speak words; He is a Word, an expression, in His very being and in His acts and speech. Therefore, since Christ is the ultimate revelation of God, any new knowledge of God must consist in penetrating ever deeper into the fullness which dwells in Him. All of the New Testament is one, since it derives from and speaks of this mystery.

But is it not the role of the Spirit to teach us many things? Yes,

---

[27] Ἔστι δὲ προσαχθῆναι ἀπὸ τῶν ὑπὸ Παύλου λεγομένων περὶ τοῦ πᾶσαν τὴν καινὴν εἶναι εὐαγγέλια, ὅταν γράφῃ Κατὰ τὸ εὐαγγέλιόν μου. Ἐν γράμματι ὑπὸ Παύλου οὐκ ἔχομεν βιβλίον εὐαγγέλιον συνήθως καλούμενον. Ἀλλὰ πᾶν ὃ ἐκήρυσσε καὶ ἔλεγε τὸ εὐαγγέλιον ἦν. ἃ καὶ ἐκήρυσσε καὶ ἔλεγε, ταῦτα καὶ ἔγραφε. καὶ ἃ ἔγραφε ἄρα εὐαγγέλιον ἦν. Εἰ δὲ τὰ Παύλου εὐαγγέλιον ἦν, ἀκόλουϑον λέγειν ὅτι καὶ τὰ Πέτρου εὐαγγέλιον ἦν, καὶ ἀπαξαπλῶς τὰ συνιστάντα τοῦ Χριστοῦ ἐπιδημίαν, καὶ κατασκευάζοντα τὴν παρουσίαν αὐτοῦ, ἐμποιοῦντά τε αὐτὴν ταῖς ψυχαῖς τῶν βουλομένων παραδέξεσϑαι τὸν ἑστῶτα ἐπὶ τὴν ϑύραν, καὶ κρούοντα, καὶ εἰσελϑεῖν βουλόμενον εἰς τὰς ψυχὰς λόγον Θεοῦ. Origen, "Comm. on Jn 1:6," PG 14, 32.

[28] Λεχϑείη δ'ἂν πρὸς τοῦτο ὅτι πρὸ τῆς Χριστοῦ ἐπιδημίας ὁ νόμος καὶ οἱ προφῆται, ἅτε μηδέπω ἐληλυϑότος τοῦ τὰ ἐν αὐτοῖς μυστήρια σαφηνίζοντος, οὐκ εἶχον τὸ ἐπάγγελμα τοῦ περὶ τοῦ εὐαγγελίου ὅρου. Ὁ δὲ Σωτὴρ ἐπιδημήσας καὶ τὸ εὐαγγέλιον σωματοποιηϑῆναι ποιήσας, τῷ εὐαγγελίῳ πάντα ὡσεὶ εὐαγγέλιον πεποίηκεν. Ibid., "Jn 1:8," PG 14, 33.

but whatever He teaches, and whatever He taught the apostles, is contained in the mystery of Christ: "He will glorify me, for everything that he makes known to you he will draw from what is mine" (Jn 16:15). The Spirit adds nothing to the Word which is Christ and which stands revealed in His actions and speech. "All that the Father has is mine, and that is why I said, 'Everything that he makes known to you he will draw from what is mine'" (Jn 16:16). The letters and preaching of St. Paul are Gospel, and the same can be said of the other letters; the Book of Acts is specifically called part two of St. Luke's Gospel, and the Apocalypse is described as "the revelation of Jesus Christ, which God has given to Him to make known to His servants . . ." From this it follows that when we read the epistles of St. Paul, we are reading the word of Christ, even though these words were never pronounced by Christ.

With this unity firmly in mind, we can now go on to consider the variety present in the New Testament. St. Paul said in his letter to the Thessalonians (1 Th 4:15): "This I say on the word of the Lord." St. John Chrysostom comments: "Everything that Paul says is inspired, but what he says here he heard literally from God." [29] Interestingly enough, modern commentators prefer to see in the phrase "the word of the Lord" an instance of early tradition rather than a direct revelation. Nevertheless, the distinction indicated by St. John Chrysostom does represent a real difference in the way St. Paul acquired his knowledge about Christ. St. Paul had undoubtedly received many special revelations from God, and he knew many words of Christ from the oral tradition, but to these he added a profound and enlightened theological reflection which we might compare to the activity of the Hebrew wise men. St. Paul's way of using the Old Testament stems from the same tradition which gave us Ben Sirach, while on at least one occasion he expressly says that the doctrine he is giving is his own: "To the married I give this ruling, which is not mine but the Lord's . . . To the rest I say this, as my own word, not the Lord's . . . About virgins I have no ordinance of the Lord, but I give my judgment as one who by God's mercy is fit to be trusted" (1 Cor 7:10, 12, 25). At other times, we can trace the development of St. Paul's thought, as it grows in depth and clarity, as can be seen, for instance, in a com-

[29] "On 1 Th." Cf. ch. 2, n. 41.

parison of the Epistle to the Galatians with the more mature treatment of the same themes in the Epistle to the Romans. Inspiration did not mean for St. Paul the simple recording of what the Holy Spirit dictated or what he received as the words and statements of Christ. His charism did not dispense him from serious work, both theological and literary. There is a great difference between the theological treatise to the Romans and the "postcard" recommending Onesimus to Philemon; yet both these extremes and the whole New Testament range of literature which lies between them are the inspired word of God.[30]

The Gospels

The Word of God resounds in a unique way in the Gospels, which represent for us the words and deeds of Jesus, and this accounts for the special reverence and recognition which has always been accorded to them. But when we say that they hand on to us the words of Christ, what meaning does this phrase have?

Suppose that Christ decided to transmit His words in the most authentic way possible to all generations of men, and that He asked our advice on how best to do this. What would we answer? Probably our first suggestion would be a tape recorder. The preservation would be uniquely faithful, even down to the original tone of voice, and we would hear Jesus just as now we can listen to the address John XXIII gave at the opening of Vatican II. What better remembrance could we have? Why, we would even want to study Aramaic in order to understand for ourselves just what Our Lord had said. The fact that there were no electric means of preserving sound back in those days is not really an objection. God could have arranged things so that these machines would have

[30] "*Qui nolunt inter epistulas Pauli eam recipere, quae ad Philemonem scribitur, aiunt non apostolum nec omnia Christo in se loquente dixisse, quia nec humana imbecillitas unum tenorem Spiritus Sancti ferre potuisset nec huius corpusculi necessitates sub praesentia Domini semper complerentur, velut disponere prandium, cibum capere. . . . His et ceteris eiusmodi volunt aut epistulam non esse Pauli, quae ad Philemonem scribitur, aut etiam, si Pauli sit, nihil habere quod aedificare possit, et a plerisque veteribus repudiatam, dum commendandi tantum scribatur officio, non docendi. . . . Sed mihi videtur, dum epistulam simplicitatis arguunt, suam imperitiam prodere, non intelligentes, quid in singulis sermonibus virtutis ac sapientiae lateat.*" St. Jerome, "Prologue to Phil," PL 26, 637–638.

been in existence when Christ came. It would have sufficed to turn the clock ahead a few centuries and everything would have been in readiness.

But God did not choose this method. We are often surprised when we think over the plans of God and imagine ways of improving them. We think that we could have done things a little more efficiently and simply. But God smiles at our childish pretensions. "Who is this that obscures divine plans with words of ignorance?" (Jb 38:2). A roll of tape is lifeless and mechanical, whereas God has chosen the path of the Incarnation, making use of living men.

Well, then, we have another solution, not as safe as the first, of course, but sufficiently reliable. Choose out the man with the best memory in the world. Someone who can retain and repeat exactly whole paragraphs and speeches after he has heard them only once. Or better, hire four of them or even a dozen and have them listen to everything that is said. Then, if one of them makes a mistake, the others will be able to act as a control. Now we have a system that is not mechanical, but human, consisting of a select group of collaborators. This will be more in keeping with the plan of the Incarnation.

Again, God only shakes His head at our brilliant scheme. "Who has directed the Spirit of the Lord, or has instructed Him as his counselor? Whom did he consult to gain knowledge? Who taught him the path of judgment, or showed him the way of understanding?" (Is 40:13-14). God did not seek out professional memory men, completely passive and quasi-automatic. It is not through such that the word of God will resound in authentic tones throughout the ages.

Christ chose a way which was more subtle and unexpected. And, let us have the humility to admit it, He has shown that His grasp of what was needed far exceeds our own. He ascended into heaven and from there He sent his Spirit with the task of teaching the apostles about the mystery of Christ. He brought to their minds whatever Jesus had said to them, and guided them in their mission of spreading and preserving Christ's message. Between His own words and the ever attentive ears of the Church, Christ has placed the mystery of inspiration. The New Testament, and in particular the four Gospels, are the word of Christ, not because they mechanically reproduce everything that Christ has said, but because they are written under the impulse of the Spirit Whom Christ has sent.

I have told you all this while I am still here with you; that your Advocate, the Holy Spirit Whom the Father will send in My name, will teach you everything, and will call to mind all that I have told you.[31]

But when your Advocate has come, Whom I will send you from the Father—the Spirit of Truth that issues from the Father—he will bear witness to me. And you also are my witnesses, because you have been with me from the first.[32]

However, when he comes Who is the Spirit of truth, he will guide you into all truth; for he will not speak on his own authority, but will tell only what he hears; and he will make known to you the things that are coming.[33]

Faced with such realities, some people feel a sort of disillusionment, as though someone had just proved that their favorite relic was a fake. "You mean to say, then, that the evangelists do not repeat word for word what Jesus said?" It is quite certain that many times they do not. They wrote in Greek, while Our Lord spoke Aramaic, and even the Greek words of one evangelist do not correspond to those of another, for example in the Our Father, or the words of consecration. "Well, then, the words really don't matter; all that counts is the sense." Absolutely false! These words are important because they are inspired, because they are written by God, and because they come to us still redolent of the words which Christ originally spoke.

Our expressions of disillusionment are just another way of trying to teach God how He should have arranged His plan of salvation. Such protestations might pass for the apex of piety, but at bottom they are not far from rebellion. There is in them no joyous acceptance of God's plan, and no admiring gratitude for His wisdom. Such people insist on treating the words of Scripture as though they were relics, precious but inert. But God's word is living, and the inspired text is meant to come alive for us and awaken in us the

[31] Jn 14:25–26.
[32] Jn 15:26–27.
[33] Jn 16:13–14.

same life that it awakened in its authors. Let us repeat again our conviction that the best plan is that of the Incarnation. And in the realm of the Scriptures, this means that by the inspiration of the Holy Spirit the words of Christ, and Christ as Word, take flesh in the human speech of the evangelists.

The gift of inspiration in the New Testament implies not only that the evangelists remembered well or were reminded of what they should write, but also that they thought about the words of Christ and listened anew to their message

After his resurrection, his disciples recalled what he had said, and they believed the Scripture and the words that Jesus had spoken.[34]

At the time, his disciples did not understand this, but after Jesus had been glorified they remembered that this had been written about him, and that this had happened to him.[35]

You do not understand now what I am doing, but one day you will.[36]

The glorification of Christ, which includes the mission of the Spirit Who was sent specifically to "glorify" Christ (Jn 16:14), enabled the apostles to recall and understand things that they never understood before. The Spirit stirred their memories and enlightened their minds, and they transmitted the revelation they had received in Christ.

But it was not only their memories and minds that were affected. Every step in the whole process of literary activity, composing, redacting, and organizing, was governed by the motion of the Spirit. St. Ambrose in his commentary on St. Luke's gospel remarks on the words of the prologue which mention that "many writers have attempted to draw up an account . . .":

Therefore, there were many who began but did not finish. We have sufficient testimony in Luke who says that "many have attempted." Whoever strives to set something in order strives to do so by his work, but he does not finish. However, the gifts and grace of God are without this striving. For wherever the grace of God is poured out, it flows so abundantly that the talents of the writer are not needed and are, in fact, superfluous. Matthew did not strive, Mark did not strive, John did

34 Jn 2:22.
35 Jn 12:16.
36 Jn 13:7.

not strive; rather, with the Spirit providing them with an abundance of words and all of the deeds, they brought their work to completion without effort.[37]

The explanation of St. Ambrose is not exactly correct. In the first place, "attempt" does not necessarily mean "fail," and in the second place St. Luke himself, rather than appeal to some motion of the Holy Spirit which dispensed him from effort, takes care to mention his diligent investigations and labor. The grace of God does not dispense from human effort; it raises it, directs it, and even makes it possible. Anyone who has studied the techniques of redaction employed by the evangelists can appreciate the conscious resolve and meticulous care exercised by these writers. These men worked in the sweat of their brow and by the breath of the Spirit.

St. Augustine showed a much greater capacity to reflect on the nature of literary activity. He was very interested in the problem of how the evangelists remembered all the things that they recorded about Christ, and this is how he explains the discrepancies in their accounts:

Of what great importance is it to notice where an evangelist places an incident, whether he puts an event in its proper order, or whether he inserts something he forgot, or inverses the order of events, so long as he does not contradict another evangelist who relates this same incident or some other, nor indeed contradict himself. No one has it in his power, no matter how well he knows the events, to remember exactly the order in which they occurred. (For the fact that one event comes to our mind before or after another does not depend on our will, but simply happens so.) Most probably, each evangelist wrote down the events in that order which he felt to be the best, and which God willed to recall to his mind in regard to those things whose order one way or the other does not lessen the truth of the Gospel. The Holy Spirit Who gives to each as He wills, for the sake of those books which were to be given such a preëminence, directed and controlled the minds of

[37] "Ergo multos coepisse, nec implevisse, etiam Sanctus Lucas testimonio locupletiore testatur, dicens plurimos esse conatos. Qui enim conatus est ordinare, suo labore conatus est, nec implevit. Sine conatu sunt enim donationes et gratia Dei, quae ubi se infuderit, rigare consuevit, ut non egeat, sed redundet scriptoris ingenium. Non conatus est Matthaeus, non conatus est Marcus, non conatus est Joannes, non conatus est Lucas, sed divino Spiritu ubertatem dictorum rerumque omnium ministrante, sine ullo molinine coepta complerunt." "Comm. on St. Luke, bk. 1," PL 15, 1613; CCL 14, 7–8.

the saints as He recalled to them that which they ought to write, allowing each one to dispose the events in his narration, one man this way, another that, as it was given to each to view things with the aid of the divine light.[38]

St. Augustine takes into account the techniques of composition and narration used by the evangelists, the action of the Spirit recalling things to their memory and directing their intelligence, the will of God, the end of the Scriptures which is to teach the truth, and their corresponding authority. He was preoccupied with the problem of the different order of events in each of the Gospels, but his solution and the principles he invokes are equally valid when applied to the whole of the literary activity of the evangelists. As a matter of fact, modern research has shown both the relevance and the solidity of this approach.

Conclusion

Our analysis of the New Testament has revealed to us its striking variety. The writers are dependent on a well established oral tradition; at times they utilize preëxisting documents, or repeat formulas from the liturgy and Christian preaching, all the while deftly weaving into their narrative words and texts from the Old Testament. There are other writings which seem to have been composed as the occasion presented itself, in order to answer some concrete need in the Church. Each of these writers had a personal style, evinced preferences for certain literary devices, and viewed his message in the context of a distinctive theological outlook.[39]

[38] "*Quid autem interest quis quo loco ponat, sive quod ex ordine inserit, sive quod omissum recolit, sive quod postea factum ante praeoccupat; dum tamen non adversetur eadem vel alia narranti, nec sibi, nec alteri? Quia enim nullius in potestate est, quamvis optime fideliterque res cognatas, quo quisque ordine recordetur (quid enim prius posteriusve homini veniat in mentem, non est ut volumus, sed ut datur); satis probabile est quod unusquisque Evangelistarum eo se ordine credidit debuisse narrare, quo voluisset Deus ea ipsa quae narrabat ejus recordationi suggere, in eis duntaxat rebus, quarum ordo, sive ille, sive ille sit, nihil minuit auctoritati veritatique evangelicae.*

"*Cur autem Spiritus sanctus dividens propria unicuique prout vult* (1 Cor 12:11), *et ideo mentes quoque sanctorum propter Libros in tanto auctoritatis culmine collocandos, in recolando quae scriberent sine dubio gubernans et regens, alium sic, alium vero sic narrationem suam ordinare permiserit, quisquis pia diligentia quaesiverit, divinitus adjutus poterit invenire.*" "De Consensu Evangelistarum," PL 34, 1102.

[39] Consult any introduction to the New Testament: A. Wikenhauser,

This great variety bears its own witness to the human nature of the divinely inspired writings, as well as to the vitality of the Church. We may apply to the New Testament the "modes" of the medieval scholastics, or, in this regard, the concept of analogy proposed by Benoit. For though we stopped to investigate some of the aspects peculiar to the New Testament, the differences in literary characteristics are of the same type within both the Old Testament and the New Testament.

Bibliography for Chapter 3

The Prophets. J. Lindblom, *Prophecy in Ancient Israel*, New York, 1962, is an excellent general study of this question (cf. the review by P. Beauchamp in *Bib* 45, 1964, pp. 433–438), as is the older work of A. Neher, *L'Essence de Prophétisme*, Paris, 1955. A complete résumé of the work done during the last ten years in this area can be found in *TRu* 28, 1962, pp. 1–75, 235–297, 301–415.

In regard to the prophetic formulas, the work of Cl. Westermann mentioned in Chapter 2 is the best single source of information (*Grundformen prophetischer Rede*).

The most complete work on the literary analysis of the Bible is L. Alonso Schökel, *Estudios de Poética Hebrea*, Barcelona, 1963, with an ample bibliography; among works in English, there is still the pioneering work of Robert Lowth, *The Sacred Poetry of the Hebrews*, in Latin, London, 1753, in English, London, 1754; R. Moulton, *The Literary Study of the Bible*, New York, 1899, and G. B. Gray, *The Forms of Hebrew Poetry*, Hodder New York, 1915. For an appreciation of some of the literary qualities of Job, cf. R. Sewall, *The Vision of Tragedy*, New Haven, 1959.

Sapiential Literature. There is a clear presentation combined with a sense of literature in A. M. Dubarle, *Les Sages d'Israel*, Lectio Divina, No. 1, Paris, 1946. The article of W. Baumgartner, "The Wisdom Literature," in *The Old Testament and Modern Study*, New York, 1956,

---

New Testament Introduction, New York, 1958; A. Robert and A. Feuillet, Introduction à la Bible, vol. 2, Bruges, 1959; E. C. Hoskyns and F. N. Davey, The Riddle of the New Testament, Naperville, 1957.

as well as his "Die israelitische Weisheitsliteratur," *TRu* 5, 1933, pp. 259–288, are very valuable though more technical than the work of Dubarle. There are some very helpful articles in *VT*, Suppl. III, 1955, "Wisdom in Israel and in the Ancient Near East." In a more popular vein, there is the excellent work of R. Murphy, *Seven Books of Wisdom*, Milwaukee, 1960. Volume one of von Rad's *Old Testament Theology* (pp. 418–459) treats of the wisdom tradition in Israel.

Other Writers. For an excellent study of Hebrew methods of history writing, cf. the article by C. R. North on "History" in *The Interpreter's Dictionary of the Bible*, ed. by G. A. Buttrick, 4 vols., Nashville, 1962, with the bibliography that he gives there. There is also the work edited by R. Denton, *The Idea of History in the Ancient Near East*, New Haven, 1955. The article by M. Noth, "History and the Word of God in the Old Testament," *BJrylL* 32, 1949–1950, pp. 194–206, is helpful, as well as Chapter 7, "The Deuteronomistic Theology of History in the Books of Kings," in G. von Rad's *Studies in Deuteronomy*, Studies in Biblical Theology, no. 9, Naperville, 1956. Cf. also Alan Richardson's *History, Sacred and Profane*, Westminster, 1964, as well as G. Hölscher, *Die Anfänge der hebräischen Geschichtsschreibung*, Heidelberg, 1942, and O. Eissfeldt, *Geschichtsschreibung im Alten Testament*, Berlin, 1948. For a wider approach to the question of history writing, cf. J. Shotwell, *The Story of Ancient History*, New York, 1961 (the early chapters are uneven).

Distinctions and Unity. The second part of Gögler's study on Origen, mentioned in Chapter 1, unifies revelation around the concept of word. The same can be said of the contributions to *La Parole de Dieu en Jésus-Christ*, mentioned in Chapter 2. None of the extant theologies of the New Testament attempts an explicit unifying perspective as does Eichrodt's *Theology of the Old Testament*.

The problem of the relationship between the Old and New Testaments is hotly discussed today. Different approaches can be found in J. Guillet, *Themes of the Bible*, Notre Dame, 1960, and C. Larcher, *L'actualité chrétienne de l'Ancien Testament d'après le Nouveau Testament*, Lectio Divina, no. 34, Paris, 1962. Cf. also P. Grelot, *Sens Chrétien de L'Ancien Testament*, Paris, 1962, and *The Old Testament and Christian Faith*, ed. by B. W. Anderson, New York, 1963.

ΠΟΛΥΜΕΡΩΣ ΚΑΙ ΠΟΛΥΤΡΟΠΩΣ
Ο ΘΕΟΣ ΛΑΛΗΣΑΣ

II
THE INSPIRED WORD

4. Inspiration and Language

IN THE CONTEXT OF LANGUAGE

The article of the Creed which we have been considering states that God *spoke* through the prophets, and the Fathers of the Church never tired of dwelling on this mystery, saying often that God has talked to us or that He has written to us. The Bible, as we have seen, is called the word of God. The conclusion of all this, to say it once again, is that inspiration pertains to the realm of language. This means that if we can acquire a deeper understanding of what language is, we shall by that very fact be better prepared to penetrate into the mystery of inspiration.

The Bible is the word of God, God speaks to us. But what is a word? And what does it really mean to speak? There is a danger that we will so accentuate the qualifying "of God" that we will obliterate the force of the analogy contained in the noun "word." We are tempted to think that God could not possibly allow Himself to be associated with our poor, earth-bound words, or at least that He would choose some special little part of them less unworthy of His majesty. It is indeed laudable to insist on the divine transcendence, but we do not make God greater by our minimal respect for what is human. Let us listen again to the words of Pope Pius XII: "For as the substantial Word of God became like to men in all things, 'except sin,' so the words of God, expressed in human language, are made like to human speech in every respect, except error." [1] The reference here to the Incarnation is of the

---

[1] *"Sicut enim substantiale Dei Verbum hominibus simile factum est quoad omnia 'absque peccato,' ita etiam Dei verba, humanis linguis expressa, quoad omnia humani sermoni assimilia facta sunt, excepto errore."* EB 559, RSS, p. 98.

greatest importance. God did not choose some elements of human nature, those most worthy of Him, and join Himself to these only. The mystery of the Incarnation lies precisely in the fact that God assumed a true and whole human nature. The Docetists thought that they were doing honor to God by denying that His body was real, and they were condemned as heretics. Christ's body was material and mortal, and our refusal to accept this fact gives Him no glory.

We may apply these same criteria to the Scriptures. God does not assume only ideas as the "soul" of language and disdain their human dimensions. "Pure ideas" are not language at all, and in the world of men ideas themselves can hardly exist without some form of language. We cannot restrict inspiration to the assertion of formulas completely purified of all images and emotions. Such restrictions have nothing in common with the patristic outlook or the statements of the encyclicals, and they savor somewhat of a certain Docetism or Monophysitism. God assumed human language as it is, in its total reality, in order to speak to us. "God speaks through a man, in a human way, because in thus speaking he is looking for us." [2] We are confronted with a mystery of divine condescension inspired by love. God's lowering of Himself to human language shares in the kenosis or "self-emptying" of the Incarnation.[3] But by this we do not mean to imply that God adopted a poor style, as some of the Fathers mistakenly thought, but simply that God has deigned to use human language in all its dimensions and limitations.

These are the principles that should govern our approach to an understanding of inspiration. We ought not to begin by trying so to purify and spiritualize human language that it resembles the speech of angels. Nor should we start by accentuating the distance between the human and the divine and arming ourselves with a catalogue of negations. We can make a better beginning, one freer of prejudice and more adequate to the truth, if we set out simply and humbly, taking our language as it is and expanding our study

[2] "*Sed per hominem more hominum loquitur; quia et sic loquendo nos quaerit.*" St. Augustine, "The City of God, bk. 17," *PL* 41, 537.
[3] Cf. R. Gögler, *Zur Theologie des biblischen Wortes bei Origenes*, Düsseldorf, 1963, part 2, ch. 6, pp. 307ff.

of it to include all the rich multiplicity of the thing as it actually exists. To understand what it means when we say that God has spoken to us, we need only accept the reality of the human language He has used, error alone excepted, just as we believe that Christ was like us in all things, but without sin.

Such will be the spirit of the study we are beginning now. It is traditional in that it attempts to arrive at understanding by the positive use of analogy, though there are some original contributions. Its newness lies in its orientation: The way the data are formally organized and reflected on.

But why has this type of approach never been used before? We believe that there are two principal reasons:

First, St. Thomas located the prophetic charism in the category of knowledge, and this has influenced theologians of a later age who undertook to treat explicitly of inspiration, which is closely related to prophecy.

Secondly, philosophical reflection on the nature of language is a fairly modern discipline. Plato discusses language in "Cratylus," it is true, and there were subsequent discussions concerning language as natural or conventional. Aristotle studied some aspects of literary language, but the scholastics added little to our knowledge of this branch of the human sciences.[4] It is with Wilhelm von Humboldt that our present philosophy of language assumed the form and importance which it has today. However, since modern treatises on inspiration pertain rather to the neo-scholastic movement, it is not surprising that they embody nothing of this aspect of the study of man. If here or there we find a slight exception to this rule, the procedure reveals an ingenuous realism or complete ignorance of the depths of the problem of language.[5]

In recent years, there has been a considerable movement toward re-thinking this question, and attempts have been made to integrate modern acquisitions with the thousand-year-old theological tradition of the West. Many of these efforts begin from a reëxami-

[4] R. Latourelle in *Théologie de la Révélation*, Bruges, 1963, credits de Lugo with having been the first among the scholastics to study this question at any length (cf. pp. 195–197).

[5] A selected bibliography can be found in our article, "Hermeneutics in the Light of Language and Literature," *CBQ* 25, 1963, pp. 371ff.

nation of the role of language in the economy of salvation, and it is in this line that we wish to place our study of inspiration and its relation to the language.[6]

The obvious lacunae in the neo-scholastic treatment of inspiration, and the renewed theological interest in revelation as word, explain the orientation of this present study, which is offered as a complement to the traditional approach, not as a supplement.

THE SCRIPTURES AS WORD

In the Old Testament, we find persons, events, and words, both of God and of men. We meet real human persons and God as a Person, we come to know real human events and see God as their protagonist, we hear real human words and we hear the word of God echoing throughout all history. All of these come to us as language, in the strict ontological sense of the term. For the events do not happen again, nor do men live again to speak and reënact their original existence. These men and their actions have passed, and they only reach us as language. This is, of course, not true of God, Who transcends time: but of the human actors in the drama of salvation we may repeat the words of St. Paul: "These things . . . happened to them . . . and were written for our instruction" (1 Cor 10:11); "Let these be written for generations to come" (Ps 102:19).

These same reflections are valid for the New Testament also. We meet many people, including the Person of Christ; and we possess many facts and words, again including the words and deeds of Christ. These men were mortal, they have passed from this life and what they said and did here comes to us only in language. Christ as glorified transcends this law of limitation, yet even He does not make the past present again precisely in its dimension as past.

Now, it is precisely this language with its mission of bringing to

---

[6] Indication of this interest can be found in a collection of articles published in the "Readings in Theology" series entitled *The Word*, New York, 1964. Contributions are taken from books and reviews, dating from 1939 (H. Rahner, S.J., *Eine Theologie der Verkündigung*) up to 1963 (L. Claussen, *Theologisches Jahrbuch*). Among the authors are A. Deissler, L. M. Dewailly, J. Giblet, D. Grasso, R. Latourelle, A. Léonard, K. Rahner, J. Ratzinger, E. Schillebeeckx, O. Semmelroth, Y. B. Trémel.

us the words and deeds in which our salvation was wrought, which is the word of God. As Tertullian expresses it:

In order that we might have access to God more fully and more swiftly, in His determinations and designs He has added the means of literature to aid those who might wish to seek God, to find Him Whom they seek, and once found, believe in Him, and believing serve Him. . . . The words [of the prophets] and the miracles which they performed in order to lead men to faith in the divinity, are now kept in the treasury of literature where they are available to us even now.[7]

The written text preserves the words and activities of the past, keeping them alive for each generation; it is a means helping us to draw nearer to God.[8] And if we want to understand the nature of this means, it seems logical to begin with a study of the nature of language. Thus, the themes of this study are clear enough; they would include the inspired word, the inspired authors, and their inspired books.

THE FOURFOLD MEANING OF THE WORD "LANGUAGE"

We have spoken a great deal about language and about its mystery. Before proceeding further with the study of language, we should discuss the four areas of meaning which are covered by the term.

(1) Language signifies, in the first place, the radical human capacity for self-expression. It includes the twofold movement of naming and joining, of articulating and differentiating. This capacity is the basis of social, interpersonal communication. It is the capacity to "humanize" the world, creating a new world in the image and likeness of man, and in which man reveals himself. We spoke of this aspect of language in the first chapter, when we considered inspiration in the context of Logos. This is the proper field for the philosophy of language.

---

[7] "Sed quo plenius et impressius tam ipsum quam dispositiones ejus et voluntates adiremus, instrumentum adjecit litteraturae, si qui velit de Deo inquirere, et inquisito invenire, et invento credere, et credito deservire. . . . Voces eorum itemque virtutes, quas ad fidem divinitatis edebant, in thesauris litterarum manent, nec ista nunc latent." Tertullian, "Apologeticum, 18," CCL 1, 118; PL 1, 434–435.

[8] Some ecclesiastical writers call Scripture simply "instrumentum," perhaps deriving its meaning from the legal and juridical usage. Cf. Tertullian, "Apol. 18, 19, 21," CCL 1.

(2) Secondly, when we say "language," we can be referring to any one of the various linguistic systems in which men actually do express themselves. In this sense, the word exists only in the plural. That is not to say that such was always the case, but simply that it is the fact with which we start. Humboldt began at this point as is clear from the title of his work, *The Heterogeneity of Language and its Influence on the Intellectual Development of Mankind*.[9]

There are two consequences following from the plurality of language. First, the simple fact of variety in which the identical language capacity of man is realized differently; and second, the reality of each language as a social unit. The first consequence is obvious and should cause no surprise. The multiplicity of language has given rise to many speculations, one of the earliest of which is to be found in Chapter 11 of the Book of Genesis.

Each language exists as a social reality, belonging to a group of related systems which is called a linguistic "family." As such, every language is the product of a society in its historical continuity. Generations have contributed to its richness and peculiar character as they met in spiritual interchange; and this was reflectively elevated and enriched by those who developed its literature, either oral or written. The reality is found already existing by the individual to whom it presents itself as a necessity and enrichment, and a condition. By means of it, the individual enters the realm of interpersonal communication, and the communal life of the group. Within its framework his personality unfolds.

As a social reality, language is more than a conglomeration of grammatical rules—with their exceptions—and a range of vocabulary. Many other elements, idioms, turns of phrase, literary formulas, cultural clichés, must be included in any consideration of language as a social fact. These are all preëxisting material offering a set of possibilities to be actualized in the vitality of the language and employed by him who would use it freely.[10]

---

[9] W. von Humboldt, *Über die Verschiedenheit des menschlichen Sprachbaues und ihren Einfluss auf die geistige Entwicklung des Menschengeschlects,* Berlin, 1830–1835.

[10] In relation to the liberty involved in the usage of language, cf. Ph. Lersch, *Sprache als Freiheit und Verhängnis,* Munich, 1947. For a more philosophic viewpoint, cf. H. G. Gadamer, *Wahrheit und Methode,* Tübingen, 1960, esp. pp. 419–420. H. Urs von Balthasar, in "God Speaks as Man," in *Word and Revelation,* treats especially of the first characteristic.

As a social reality which is learned and assimilated by the individual, language exercises a certain influence on intellectual formation. It is true, of course, that a genuine intellectual formation is conveyed not so much by the mere teaching of language, but rather by assimilating the works that are written in the language. Nevertheless, a language system conditions a man's way of thinking, his way of looking at the world and expressing himself. This is realized in a decided degree in someone of quite average attainments, who assimilates rather than creates his language. Such a person usually accepts the common meaning given to words with their overtones, their precision or lack of it, their clarity, or their power of suggestion. At the same time, he accepts the complex of categories and divisions inherent in the language as a means of shaping his own thought, and this thought itself is colored by the logical connections established by syntax. In this way, language collaborates in the education of a man's power of appreciation and thought. Though its role is subordinate to the principal factors of education —statements, theories and doctrines—nevertheless, the collaboration is real and the effect is unmistakable.

Now let us apply this notion to inspiration. The word of God in order to be incarnate must assume a concrete, specific language. The human capacity of self-expression exists only as a diversified series of concretely existing languages. A specific language, of a specific group, is the point at which the Transcendent enters time, and through which the divine message reaches human ears. The choice depends on the free decision of God, Who, as we know, has assumed for this purpose the languages of Hebrew and Greek, and to a lesser extent Aramaic.

In the case of Hebrew, as it received successive formulation by generations of inspired writers, it exercised in its turn a far-reaching influence on the formation of the language system. The speech of Israel and the land of Palestine are both criss-crossed by the footprints of God. The beginning was simple, the language already existed; it was a variety of Canaanite. But this speech was to develop, influenced by the preaching of the prophets, the prayer of the Psalms, and the sacred story of Israel's adventures. This process enriched, refined, and elevated the language, exploiting all its possibilities without destroying its nature. Of course, we should note that all the ancient Hebrew we possess is in the Bible; we have no examples of the everyday or at least the non-sacral language of Israel. Our judgment, then, must remain but partial since it is based on an acquaintance with Hebrew derived almost exclusively from a language already raised to the level of revelation.

The matter stands quite differently when we come to discuss Greek. In this case, the language which offered itself to the inspired writers was already quite sophisticated and habituated to its role as the medium for a rich literary and philosophical tradition. Its subsequent use by the Holy Spirit developed this language in the sphere of religion, initiating semantic evolutions, and appropriating common words to serve as technical terms. Hebrew, too, exercised its influence on the Greek language, obliging it to serve as the vehicle for Semitic ideas when the Old Testament was translated at Alexandria. It suffices to compare the Greek of the Book of Wisdom with that of some parts of the Old Testament as translated in the Septuagint to appreciate the nature of this influence.

The actual multiplicity of human languages imposes on the word of God the necessity of translation with all its concomitant problems, both theoretical and practical. We will discuss this problem more explicitly later on.[11]

The people of God when acting as such—and the people of God today is the Church in its Christ-life—also has a language which constitutes for it a social reality. This language was prepared by the action of the Holy Spirit, and it presents itself as a well-ordered system capable of forming both the individual and the community in a mentality open to God. The Hebrew child, and now the Christian child, are introduced to their relationship with God by the language peculiar to God's people; and this language is inspired. In order to learn this language, they have recourse to the treasures of literature which it contains, and then reciprocally, as they grow in a knowledge of these treasures, they acquire a mastery of the language. We cannot afford to take lightly this question of the language which the Christian learns to use in his relations with God—the language of the books about God that he hears, and in which he prays. Religious language collaborates in the development of a man's powers of appreciation and thought at the deepest level of his existence. We have only to think of the sentimentalism, the cloudy thinking, the loss of the true sense of mystery that oc-

[11] Cf. ch. 11.

curs whenever good formation in a religious language is lacking. The remedy is a return to the language of the Scriptures, and the most effective way of securing this return is the liturgy. "To bring once again the word of God to the people of God," is a watchword embodying an ideal of the greatest consequence. Of course, by far the greater part of the people of God will effect this return to the word of God through translations. Christ, when He became incarnate, entered into one race and became a citizen of one nation. Yet, because He is Lord, He has transcended the limits and obstacles inherent in such a situation in order to reach out to all peoples and races. So, too, the word of God of necessity assumed one language, but through the very fact of this incarnation it can now burst through the limits of that language, and by means of translation identify itself and express itself in all languages.

The various languages, in their social dimension, can constitute the object of a sociological investigation. Insofar as they are languages though, they are matter for linguistic disciplines: structural linguistics, comparative linguistics, or historical linguistics, and the allied branches of phonetics, syntax, semantics, etc.[12] This is the reason why the eruption of the word of God into human language has enlisted the service of all these linguistic sciences. Their positive method demands disciplined and even arid work, but when applied to the Bible, the results of such studies can be the means of securing great insight into the revealed message.[13] The protests raised against these investigations are simply not legitimate. No one claims that they are the principal or ultimate concern of exegetes, but refusal to approach the word of God with the tools by which we study human speech is tantamount to denying the very essence of the mystery of the divine condescension.

(3) We also use the term "language" in a third sense to indicate the use an individual actually makes of the social reality we have just described. Scholars are accustomed to call this individual use "speech." Language, as a system of significant forms providing possibilities for expression, exists only in the individual speech act. The whole process involved in this act is studied by the psychology

---

[12] Cf. F. Kainz, *Psychologie der Sprache*, vol. 1., part 1, A 6, "Die Sprachpsychologie im System der gesammten Sprachwissenschaft." Also, W. Porzig's book, *Das Wunder der Sprache*, Berne, 1950.
[13] Cf. EB 561.

of language. Normally, language is actualized in a series of reciprocal acts in which what is spoken is heard, and to which reply is made in kind. This is what we call dialogue.

As a means of communication, language has a whole range of functions, some of which are primary and others secondary. What is said may be recorded in a series of written signs which are then reinterpreted by the process we call "reading." This activity of reading and writing is also the field of the psychology of language.

An individual's use of language may acquire certain characteristics, certain constants of expression or preferences in phraseology, which in time constitute a personal style. These facets of language, especially as they are present in the great writers, form the object of a study known as "descriptive stylistics." [14] The methods of this discipline are not restricted only to the study of individual works, but can be extended to the classification and analysis of the stylistic procedures of an author, a period, or a school.

Then, too, an individual in his use of language may belong to one of three categories. There are those who take their language as they find it, using it and submitting to it without much reflection. Then there are those who dominate their language, and use it with great reflective awareness of its structure and possibilities. And finally, there are those whose genius makes them creators within the realm of the language at their disposal.[15]

Many of these aspects of language will occupy our attention in the chapters to follow. It suffices to note here that inspiration must move within the process of the individual actualization of language as a social reality. It should be possible to study a typical occurrence of this process and then go on from there to speculate on the nature of the Spirit's activity, taking into account, of course, the individual differences which will modify the realization of this activity.

Hermeneutics for its part cannot remain content with a grammatical analysis of the text before it, but must also institute a stylis-

---

[14] For an idea of the orientation and methods of stylistic analysis, see the adequate bibliography of H. Hatzfeld, *Bibliografia critica de la Nueva Estilistica*, Madrid, 1955. Also see various chapters of M. Wehrli's informative work, *Allgemeine Literaturwissenschaft*, Zurich, 1951. We have applied this method to the Old Testament in our book *Estudios de Poética Hebrea*, Barcelona, 1963, with complete bibliography.

[15] Cf. J. L. Weisgerber, *Das Gesetz der Sprache*, Heidelberg, 1951, pp. 137–147.

tic analysis of the individual work in order truly to interpret the message of the author.[16]

(4) In the fourth place, the term "language" can be used to designate the works themselves which embody the individual use of language. These include literary texts in the strict sense of the term, as well as all classes of written language. Such texts make up concrete intelligible systems composed of words, fixed by an oral tradition and often enough also by other written documents.

These literary realities, the texts and literary works of the language, form the object of philology which is the science or art of determining exactly the meaning of a given text. And since our human culture exists for the most part in written texts—except for that part of it which is actually being formed and lived at the moment—it has been justly said that philology is to the sciences of the mind what mathematics is to the natural sciences.[17]

The science of literature, or of literary criticism, also has for its object the actual text in which literature is contained, though some seem to have thought that its proper sphere was the personality or even the private life of the authors.[18]

The word "Bible" comes from the Greek "*biblia*," and indicates a plurality of books. This fact already informs us as to its nature. It is a collection of literary works, of linguistic expressions which are fixed once for all by the fact that they are written. The distinctions we have made before will have a great deal of relevance when we come to pose the question as to where we should place inspiration: in the author or in his work? These considerations are also quite relevant to the science of hermeneutics, which must avail itself of the precision instruments of philology, and of the instruments, less precise but often more apt, of literary criticism. Then, too, it is possible to apply phenomenological methods to the study of a work of literature in order to explain what meaning the work has within

[16] See the new series, "New Frontiers in Theology" esp. vol. 2, *The New Hermeneutic*, ed. by J. M. Robinson and J. B. Cobb, Jr., New York, 1964.

[17] ". . . I had to use the scientific technique which is the foundation of all historical investigation: philology. For the intellectual sciences it has the same significance as mathematics has for the natural sciences. . . . The accidental truths of fact can only be established by philology. Philology is the handmaid of the historical disciplines. . . . Geometry demonstrates with figures, philology with texts." Curtius, *op. cit.* p. x (cf. ch. 1, n. 7).

[18] The fundamental work in this regard is that by R. Wellek and A. Warren, *Theory of Literature*, New York, 1956.

E

the society in which it lives. In our case, this society is the Church.

Finally, the concrete realization of language in a work of literature highlights the problem of translation, since this is the ordinary means by which such a work is diffused and made accessible to a great number. This is especially true in our case, since the mastery of the original languages of the text is, for the greater part of the people of God, an extraordinary means of approach.

Conclusion

These four meanings given to the term "language" are progressively more and more concrete. There is first the radical human capacity for speech, which is actually realized in a whole series of diverse languages, each forming a social reality, which then becomes existing in the individual actualization of self-expression; and this in turn, as it is forged by constant use on the part of the community and individuals, can become fixed by assuming the new dimension of a written work.

The four aspects thus considered provide a broad avenue of approach in studying the mystery of the inspired word. Many facets of the problem have, of course, been studied before, but the full systematic investigation of what is contained in our outline is yet to be written. The pages which follow can only aspire to be an initial attempt in that direction.

Bibliography for Chapter 4

The Context of Language. There are three collections of essays which treat of biblical revelation in the context of language: the papers given at the Third National Congress of the Centre de Pastorale Liturgique, Strasbourg, 1958, *The Liturgy and the Word of God*, Collegeville, 1959, especially the paper by Hans Urs von Balthasar, "God Has Spoken in Human Language," center around this theme. The volume, *La Parole de Dieu en Jésus-Christ*, Paris, 1961, which we have mentioned before, concentrates more exclusively on the word as found in the Bible. There is an introduction by A. Léonard, "Vers une théologie de la Parole de Dieu"; an article by J. Giblet, "La théologie du Logos selon l'évangile de Jean"; another by E. Verdonc, "Phénoménologie de la parole" (more or less dependent on Merleau-Ponty); articles by Dupont, Holstein, von Balthasar, etc. and a conclusion by A. Léonard, "La Parole de Dieu, mystère et événement, vérité et présence." The Protestant viewpoint is well represented by *Das Problem der Sprache in Theologie und Kirche*, ed. by W. Schneemelcher, Berlin, 1959, and also *Worship in Scripture and Tradition*, ed. by Massey H. Shepherd, Jr., New York, 1963.

The Fourfold Meaning of the Word "Language." The basic study is that by F. Kainz, *Psychologie der Sprache*, Stuttgart, 1954, esp. vol. 1, A 5, "Die verschiedenen Seiten der Sprache." Humboldt's book, *Über die Verschiedenheit des menschlichen Sprachbaues und ihren Einfluss auf die geistige Entwicklung des Menschengeschlechts*, Berlin, 1830–1835, is still basic (though for some reason not yet translated into English). J. L. Weisgerber, *Das Gesetz der Sprache*, Heidelberg, 1951, follows in the line of Humboldt not without exaggerating some of his positions. A manageable one-volume work which is clear is W. Porzig, *Das Wunder der Sprache*, Berne, 1950. There is little in English which treats of language from this point of view. The articles mentioned in relation to symbol and analogy in Chapter 2 are useful here, and there is an excellent introduction to the whole field of semantics in *General Semantics and Contemporary Thomism*, by Mother Margaret Gorman, R.S.C.J., Lincoln, 1962. Also helpful but a bit too positivistic is the work by Samuel I. Hayakawa, *Language in Action*, New York, 1941; a nice summary of the field can be found in David Crystal's *Linguistics, Language and Religion*, Twentieth Century Encyclopedia, no. 126, New York, 1965.

5. The Three Functions of Language

According to the classical work of Karl Bühler,[1] language can be considered as an instrument or *"organon,"* and is to be designated according to its three principal functions: "statement" (*Darstellung*), "expression" (*Kundgabe*), and "address" (*Auslösung*), (Actually, this earlier work uses the terms *"Ausdruck"* and *"Appell,"* which were later changed to *"Kundgabe"* and *"Auslösung."*)

We make statements about facts, things, and events with a certain preference for the third person and the indicative mood. This function of language is objective; it regards the outside world and is the proper medium for history and didactic literature.

We also express our interior state, our emotions and feelings, our participation in the reality of things and events. For this purpose, we prefer language in the first person; it is a subjective function of language, one which regards the individual, and it is the proper medium for memoirs, confessions, and lyric.

We address an interlocutor, attempting to stir him to action by way of response. We want to influence him and impress upon him our sentiments, preferring for this purpose the second person and the imperative mood. This function of language is intersubjective; it has regard to society and is the proper medium for oratory.

It must be admitted that this schema, so clear and intelligible, is a product of the laboratory, not because these three functions of language do not exist, but rather because the schema tries to categorize them too neatly, and also because the "statement" in its quality of being a representation tends to dominate and polarize the other two factors. Rarely do we find in language as it actually

[1] *Sprachtheorie. Die Darstellungsfunktion der Sprache*, Jena, 1934.

exists any of these three functions in a pure state: Language is not the juxtaposition of clinical statements, pure interjections, and simple commands. In reality, these functions are operative conjointly, mutually affecting one another. If we wish to distinguish various aspects of language as it actually exists, we must speak of language as *symbolizing* (embodying statements and re-presentation) as *expressing* (indicating an interior state) and *beckoning* (addressing or calling another).

A statement is mine because I make it, and yours because you hear it. Already we are in the realm of the subjective and intersubjective. In a statement or act of declaring, I express myself and make an impression on you. You are "impressed" precisely because I have expressed myself; and your impression derives its nature and depth from the contents of my statement and my manner of enunciating it. And since the statement in which I express myself evokes a reaction in you, you answer me, thus initiating a reversal of the process which goes on, exploiting the possibilities and heightening the tension of language. It is a dialogue. In a dialogue, there are mutual statements, mutual expressions, and a mutual influence, all unfolding within the fullness of a single act of interpersonal communication. Statement or representation may continue to dominate and polarize, yet by itself it is unequal to the fullness of communication. The threefold actualization of language's functions gives to them a well-rounded richness, and restores to them their fundamental primacy.[2]

INSPIRED LANGUAGE

Which of these functions of language has God assumed in the sacred Scriptures?[3] Those who are accustomed to distinguish between words and ideas would be inclined to say that God only uses human language in its function as statement.

[2] That is, as a formal dynamic unity, it cannot be reduced to the mere sum of its parts or to the simple fact of their juxtaposition. The respect for the inner dynamism of an organic reality can be demonstrated by the "Gestalt Psychology" school of thought in another field, or by the phenomenological approach to the study of comparative religion.

[3] Cf. L. Alonso Schökel, "Preguntas nuevas de la inspiración," XVI Semana Bíblica Española, 1956; R. Latourelle, "La révélation comme parole, témoignage et rencontre" in *op. cit.* (ch. 1, n. 9); E. H. Schillebeeckx, "Parole et Sacrement dans l'Eglise," *LumVi* 9, 46, 1960, pp. 25–43.

The same conclusion is reached by those who view revelation as a collection of objective propositions. God proposes a series of revealed truths in which the expressive or evocative functions of language are accessory and peripheral, being merely the contribution of the human author.[4]

Faith, too, if it is considered a purely objective statement of "revealed truths," must prescind from all but the informative functions of language. Again, we must leave the expressive and evocative functions aside and restrict ourselves to language which is informative. If we wish the other aspects of language to play a role in faith, we must raise their content to the level of proposition and not care too much if in the process the immediacy of their original function is lost.

Now, it is certainly true that faith is an act of the mind, that its content can be formulated in proposition. Faith is by no means a vague sentiment completely devoid of intelligible content. It is a supernatural virtue by which "we believe that those things which God has revealed are true." However, this definition of faith given by Vatican I is an assertion, not an exclusion. In the same paragraph, we read that "we must offer to God, by faith, the full homage of our intellect and will." Faith includes an intellectual factor, but it cannot be reduced to this alone. It is a free act, "the beginning of our salvation," an act which engages the whole personality. Revelation can be defined as "a declaration made and attested by God"[5] (*locutio Dei attestans*), but again, while this definition is correct in what it asserts, it is not all inclusive. Revelation in its highest act is the manifestation of God as someone, as a person whose self-expression should evoke a response. We read in the Gospel of St. John:. "This is eternal life: to know You, the unique and true God, and Him Whom You have sent, Jesus Christ" (17:3). Notice how this formula concentrates entirely on *persons*: "To know You, to know Jesus Christ." No mention is

---

[4] Cf. Latourelle, *op. cit.*, pp. 336–337.

[5] "*Cum homo a Deo tamquam creatore et Domino suo totus dependeat et ratio creata increatae Veritati penitus subiecta sit, plenum revelanti Deo intellectus et voluntatis obsequium fide praestare tenemur. Hanc vero fidem quae, 'humanae satutis initium est,' Ecclesia catholica profitetur, virtutem esse supernaturalem, qua, Dei aspirante et adiuvante gratia, ab eo revelata vera esse credimus, non propter intrinsecam rerum veritatem naturali rationis lumine perspectam, sed propter auctoritatem ipsius Dei revelantis, qui nec falli nec fallere potest.*" D-S 3008.

made of propositions, but of a deeper knowledge, one that is personal, or better, interpersonal. (Recall, for instance, the mystical theology of St. Bernard, or the method by which St. Ignatius in his Exercises concentrates all the disciples' attention on the acts of knowing and loving Jesus Christ.)

True, a person refracts his inner unity in a series of "multicolored" statements, and it is by means of these statements that we are able to get an insight into the personality of the other who has revealed himself to us. Yet, this is not accomplished by some process in which we add up his statements or convert them into syllogisms. A person does not only use formal propositions in his self revelation; his medium is the totality of language.[6]

PRELIMINARY CONCLUSIONS

If God, in a personal exchange, wishes to reveal Himself to us as a Person, then He must use the medium of language in all of its functions. Or to look at it the other way, the very fact that God has chosen all of language as His medium of communication proves that He desires to make a personal revelation; ". . . the words of God, expressed in human language, are made like to human speech in every respect, except error."

The consequences of such a view, both for the reading and understanding of sacred Scripture, are quite extensive. Once such an outlook is adopted, it is no longer legitimate to approach the Bible with the object of dismantling it piece by piece in order to construct a few thousand propositions each one of which would contain an article of faith. It is no longer legitimate to suppress those facets of Scripture's language which fulfill the functions of expression or address. Scripture must be read as an integral literary work embodying all the functions of language and in which God speaks to me.

Let each one consider that through the tongue of the prophets, we hear God speaking to us.[7]

---

[6] There is a very clear exposition of these aspects of the problem in H. Fries, Glauben und Wissen. Wege zu einer Lösung des Problems, Berlin, 1960.

[7] ἀλλ'ἐννοῶν τῆς πνευματικῆς ταύτης συνόδου τὸ ἀξίωμα καὶ ὅτι διὰ τῆς προφητῶν γλώττης τοῦ Θεοῦ πρὸς ἡμᾶς διαλεγομένου ἀκούομεν. St. John Chrys., "Homily 15 on Gn," PG 53, 119.

In order that I might know You, You have, I believe, composed the sacred writings by means of Your servants Moses and the prophets.[8]

This treasure house in which all the treasures of wisdom and knowledge are hidden, is the Word of God, or the sacred Scriptures in which resides the knowledge of the Savior.[9]

To be ignorant of the Scriptures, is to know not Christ.[10]

SOME EXAMPLES

Suppose that we were to come upon a thesis in some theology manual which ran like this: "God loves His people." First, we would have the definitions: what "love" means, what "people" means, the meaning of the term "His people," etc. Then there would be the divisions: carnal love, emotional, spiritual; the people of Israel, the Church . . . Then we would have the proof from Scripture fortified with the text: "God so loved the world . . ." "God is love," etc. We do not know if there would be any proof from the councils. In the Index of Denzinger-Schönmetzer under "Love" and "Charity," we find only references pertaining to that virtue by which we love God. This would all conclude with a scholion: "consequences for the spiritual life." (In the theology manual that we studied, there was a thesis on the omnipresence of God, on His knowledge—including the distinction between His knowledge of possibles and His knowledge of futures—but there was no thesis on the love of God.)

Now let us compare this imaginary thesis composed of propositions of well-defined concepts, with a page from Hosea in which God speaks in the first person. We ask the reader to pause a moment and put himself in a different frame of mind in order to hear the word of God.

[8] "Ad cognitionem me tui sacris, ut arbitror, per servos tuos Moysen et prophetas voluminibus erudisti." St. Hilary, "On the Trinity, bk. 6," PL 10, 171.

[9] "Thesaurus iste in quo sunt omnes thesauri sapientiae et scientiae absconditi, aut Dei Verbum est, qui in carne Christi videtur absconditus, aut Sanctae Scripturae, in quibus reposita est notitia Salvatoris." St. Jerome, "Comm. on Mt," PL 26, 97.

[10] "Ignoratio Scripturarum ignoratio Christi est." St. Jerome, "Prol. to Comm. on Is," PL 24, 17.

When Israel was a child, I loved him;
Out of Egypt I called my son.

I call to them,
But they only walk away from me;
to the Baals they sacrifice
to idols they burn their incense.

Yet it was I who taught Ephraim to walk.
I took him up in my arms,
and they did not know
that I cared for them.
With human ties I tugged at them,
with cords of love.
I was to them
like one raising a suckling child
up close to his cheek.
I stooped to them
and fed them.

Now to Egypt he shall return;
Assur will be his king

Because they refused to return
to me.
The sword will whirl through their cities
and destroy their fields
and consume their plots completely.
My people hang back from returning
to God the Exalted; they call out together
but he will not raise them up.

How could I give you up O Ephraim—
give you away O Israel?
Can I give you up like Adamah—
or treat you like Zeboim?
My own heart turns against me—
within me, my pity is aflame;
I will not give rein to my anger,
I will not return to ruin Ephraim.
For I am God
not man;

In the midst of you
the Holy One;
I do not come to destroy.[11]

Now that we have read the text, let us reflect a bit. Is there any comparison between the well-constructed thesis and this vibrant passage? Which one is more "revealing"? The words of Hosea, which include a series of statements whose predominant function is informative, actuate the other two elemental functions of language. God expresses Himself and I am deeply impressed. After having read the propositions of the thesis, I can still remain cold or indifferent. If the passage from Hosea leaves me cold or indifferent, it is simply because I have never really read it.

Granted that the language of Hosea is symbolic and even anthropomorphic; still, it is an analogy which confers real understanding. As St. Gregory the Great says, "Come to know the heart of God in the words of God." [12]

We purposely selected an outstanding example in order to make our point with greater clarity. Our procedure may give rise to a whole series of objections all of which say in effect: "Not all of Scripture is like that." Our first answer would be that one instance suffices to prove our point that not all of Scripture can be reduced to propositions whose sole function is to simply state a truth.

Let us take another example in which not God but man speaks. St. Paul, in Chapter 7 of his Epistle to the Romans, movingly describes the internal conflict in the heart of man. His description moves in a series of powerful crescendos beset with repetitions and culminating in the climax of the concluding phrase.[13] In the Latin Vulgate, this concluding phrase has a syntax somewhat different from the original Greek. In order that we may have the experience of this difference for ourselves, we should read carefully first one text and then the other. We will first give a translation of the Latin, and then, after an interruption, we will present a translation of the Greek text. First, the Vulgate:

[11] Hos 11:1–9. For an excellent treatment of this passage and on the whole of Hosea, cf. H. W. Wolff, *Dodekapropheton 1. Hosea*, Neukirchen, 1961.

[12] *"Disce cor Dei in verbis Dei."* "Letter to Theodore," PL 77, 706.

[13] For an analysis of this passage (Rom 7:14–25), cf. M.-J. Lagrange, *Epitre aux Romains*, Paris, 1950 (written 1915), pp. 172ff.

We know that the Law is spiritual, but I am carnal, sold into the power of sin.

I do not understand what I do. For the good that I will, I do not do; but the evil that I hate, that I do.

If I do what I do not will, then I admit that the Law is good.

Now it is longer I who do it, but sin which dwells in me.

I know that good does not dwell in me, that is in my flesh: for to will is present to me, but to perform the good, that I do not find.

The good that I will, I do not, but the evil that I will not, that I do.

If what I do not will, I do, then it is not I who carry it out, but sin which dwells in me.

Therefore, I find that this is a law for me who want to do good: that evil is at hand.

I delight in the Law of God according to the inner man:

But I see another law in my members fighting against the law of my mind, and holding me captive in the law of sin, which is in my members.

Unhappy man am I. Who will free me from this body of death?

The grace of God, through Jesus Christ Our Lord.

Someone reading this text notices immediately a break between the last two lines. The crescendo that has been building up terminates in a dramatic question; and the answer is given in an exact proposition. This is not what we were expecting, and we feel that the result is somewhat jagged stylistically. Now let us see how the Greek text sounds (without skipping anything):

Yes, we know that the Law is spiritual; but I am carnal, sold in slavery to sin.

For the things that I accomplish, I do not understand: It is not what I want that I do, but what I hate, that I do.

If, then, what I do not want is what I do, I acknowledge that the Law is good.

Now it is no longer I who accomplish these things, but sin which dwells in me.

I know that good does not dwell in me, that is, in my flesh.

To want is close at hand, but to accomplish the good—no.

Not the good that I want to do, but the evil that I do not want, that I do.

If, then, what I do not want, I do, it is no longer I but sin that dwells in me that accomplishes it.

And so I, wanting to do good, find this the law: that evil is at hand.

Deep within myself I delight in the Law of God; but I see another law

141

in my members making war on the law of my mind and imprisoning
me in the law of sin which is in my members.
Wretched man that I am! Who will set me free from this deadly body?
Thanks to God through Jesus Christ Our Lord!

In the Greek text, the pathetic, nearly desperate question is answered by a shout of liberation. St. Paul debates with himself, recording in divergent movements the battle in which he is at once
onlooker, aggressor, and defender. He is simultaneously the battle-
ground, the disputed territory, and the two contenders. He calls, he
questions, he shouts; in his language, all three functions are intensely operative.

But where is the revelation of God in such a page? The answer is
that the Scriptures not only reveal God to us as He acts in regard to
men, but also reveals man's reaction when confronted with God.
In this passage from St. Paul, we recognize ourselves before God,
in our encounter with Him, and the description of our reactions
reveals God to us through the medium of His action within us. It is
always the word of God, and reveals God speaking to us and enlightening us.

Just as our eyes see the external world and do not see themselves unless
they fall on some hard and polished object in which they see themselves
reflected, . . . so our soul, which sees all things, in order to see itself
must behold itself reflected in the sacred Scriptures. The light which
they give forth is reflected and enables us to see ourselves.[14]

Here the analogy of an author and his literary creations can be very
useful. We wanted to use this example of St. Paul since it is a good
illustration of the functions of inspired language, and because we
have here a passage in which God, the author, does not speak in
the first person.

We could investigate many other ways in which God speaks and
communicates Himself, but for the moment it will suffice to have
appreciated the fundamental fact that inspired language utilizes all
three of language's functions. These three functions can be related

---

[14] Ὥσπερ γὰρ οἱ ὀφθαλμοὶ ἡμῶν τὰ ἔξω βλέποντες, ἑαυτοὺς οὐχ ὁρῶσιν, ἐάν
μή που λείου τινὸς ἄψωνται στερεοῦ, κἀκεῖθεν ἀνακλασθεῖσα ἡ ὄψις, ὥσπερ ἀπὸ
παλιρροίας, ὁρᾶν αὐτοὺς ποιήσῃ τὰ ἑαυτῶν κατόπιν. οὕτω καὶ ὁ νοῦς ὁ ἡμέτερος,
ἄλλα ὁρῶν, ἄλλως ἑαυτὸν οὐ βλέπει, ἐάν μὴ ταῖς Γραφαῖς ἐγκύψῃ. τὸ γὰρ ἐνταῦθα
φῶς, ἀνακλώμενον, τοῦ καθορᾶσθαι ἕκαστον αἴτιον ἡμῶν γίνεται. "On the Structure
of Man" (wrongly attributed to St. Basil), ". . . ," PG 30, 12.

to the three fundamental aspects of divine revelation. For revelation is objective, personal, and dynamic. This means that from now on we must always regard the inspired text under these three aspects: It is objective, in that it reveals facts and events; it is personal, in that it shows us God as personal in the act of revealing himself; and it is dynamic, calling forth and making possible a response on the part of man. The consequences of this three-dimensional view of the Scriptures will be continually unfolding in the pages which follow.

LANGUAGE AND MONOLOGUE

The three functions we have just described are called "dialogue functions," since they all have reference to an interlocutor and are meant for communication. There are three other functions, modeled on these which are called "monologue functions." Language serves an informative function even within me since I use it to help myself think. I can express my feelings to myself and listen to myself as to another, and I can also address myself and stir myself to action. It is difficult to see how Scripture could fulfill these three functions, since as the word of God it is directed to others. Yet, the notion may prove useful in our analysis of two hypotheses.

At some point in a biblical text, there may occur a moment of monologue, caught up, as it were, in the movement of a dialogue. It is as though some strictly private papers were to be published along with the work, now that the author is dead. It might be that the Book of Ecclesiastes contains some passages of monologue, unless, of course, the "I" is merely a stylistic device of the author. It would be difficult to think of Qoheleth writing this book just for himself, but it is not impossible that here and there he has set down sections which are predominantly monologue. Similarly, it is quite possible that St. Paul has included in his letters some moments of soliloquy, some intimate reflections in which he poured out his soul. But in every case, as we have said, the predominant current is dialogue, and whenever monologue is present it is borne along on its movement; and all of the work, as we have it today, is addressed to the reader. In the canticle of Moses, there are certain lines in which by a literary fiction God is portrayed in interior monologue.

143

I said: I will scatter them,
I will blot out their memory among men;
except that I feared the scorn of the enemy,
lest their adversaries judge it amiss. . . .[15]

Even more important is the instance of prayer, more specifically, inspired prayer.[16] We have, for example, in Psalm 73 a monologue which is really a troubled, dissatisfied reflection on the traditional doctrine concerning the retribution made to the good and evil. However, most of the Psalms are predominantly dialogue in form, praising God or making supplication to Him. Some have objected that this human praise of God has, after all, no effect on God, and is in reality but a pouring out of one's soul in monologue. It can have a certain function in society if the Psalms are recited together. Others have maintained that the sole function of the prayer of petition is to provide a personal stimulus on those occasions when we are moved to action, or to be a simple unburdening of our heart when we remain inactive.

Such ideas are untenable: The inspired prayer of the Bible can always initiate dialogue in the mystery of grace, and such prayer actually reaches God. God really hears our song of praise, and this is our greatest dignity; He lets Himself be really touched by our supplications, and this is our greatest hope. The most intimate of our interior reflections is a "pouring out of our heart before God." But this does not mean that prayer does not have its elements of monologue.

Pour out your heart before Him (Ps 62:9).

With a loud voice I cry out to the Lord;
with a loud voice I beseech the Lord.
My complaint I pour out before Him;
before Him I lay bare my distress. . . .
I cry out to You, O Lord:

[15] Dt 32:26–27. On the question of interior monologue in literature, cf. R. Humphrey, *Stream of Consciousness in the Modern Novel*, Berkeley, 1962, esp. ch. 2, "The Techniques: Interior Monologue."

[16] On the question of prayer from the point of view of comparative religion, cf. F. Heiler, *Prayer*, New York, 1958; for a theological view, cf. H. Fries, art. "Gebet," in *Handbuch Theologischer Grundbegriffe*, and Hans Urs von Balthasar, *Prayer*, New York, 1961.

I say, "You are my refuge. . . .
Attend to my cry" (Ps 142:2–4, 6, 7).

. . . the Lord has heard the sound of my weeping;
The Lord has heard my plea;
The Lord has accepted my prayer (Ps 6:9–10).

Our prayer, made up of inspired words, the Our Father or the Psalms, is a real dialogue. Such prayer is a response to God for the goodness He has shown; it is communion with God, a manifestation of ourselves to Him, and a power which enables us to move Him. This may be an anthropomorphic and analogous way of speaking, but it is not false. In inspired prayer, human language in its reality as dialogue reaches a transcendent fulfillment. It is a plenitude conferred on it by the very fact that it is inspired.

Prayer written under the motion of the Holy Spirit is the word of God teaching us to pray. Man utters this prayer. God cannot reveal Himself as a sinner or as in need, but He can reveal Himself as Savior, as accessible and concerned, the companion of our wanderings now and through life and forever.

We will conclude this section with an example from the Gospels. The Word made flesh was walking one day through Galilee and He came to a city gate. Just then a widow came out from the gate weeping and following the corpse of her only son. Jesus Christ "was deeply moved when He saw her." Jesus shared all that is human. This quality, related by St. Luke in his narrative statement, is also a characteristic of the Scriptures in the realm of language. Christ "approached and touched the bier—the bearers halted. Then He said: "Young man, I say to you, rise up!" This efficacious word of Christ, addressed in the imperative and expressing concern, is also a characteristic of the Scriptures. "And the dead man sat up and began to talk." This is the effect of our hearing the word of God: We take life and begin to speak, we establish a dialogue.

OTHER FUNCTIONS OF LANGUAGE

Scholars customarily add to the primary function of language in dialogue or monologue, other functions which they call secondary and which can be classified as the aesthetic and ethical functions of language. Among aesthetic factors, there are such things as the question of plasticity in narrative, the evocative quality of onomatopoeia, etc., while among ethical considerations there are the questions of lying, euphemism, etc.

G. Söhngen, in the book to which we have made reference before,[17] has lately constructed a well-balanced system coördinating language, philosophy, and theology, erected along the lines of the functions of language. His work is divided into three major sections, each of which contains four subdivisions. The sections are devoted to the study of: the logical functions of language, the aesthetic functions, and the dynamic-ethical functions. The four logical functions are considered in their vital orientation toward conceptual precision. They are: denomination, enunciation, syllogism, and finally term. The four aesthetic functions are: the imitation of things, personal expression, metaphor, and world conception, with the third of these functions (metaphor) playing a dominant role in the study as is indicated by the title of the book. The dynamic-ethical functions are also four in number: Efficacious action, witness and declaration, persuasion, formation of opinion through dialogue. The proportion which the author has established between these three groups of four sections, as well as their harmonious interrelation, is well-nigh ideal.[18]

The one hundred twenty pages of Söhngen's book provide suggestive, closely worded reading, and though we have not time here to investigate the book further, we recommend it to anyone who may wish to pursue this line of thought more thoroughly. The aesthetic functions of language will form the subject of study in the next chapter, while the dynamic or "energic" functions will be studied at the end of the book.

Before going on, however, we would like to note here how closely Söhngen's categories resemble the psychological classification of the three functions of language that we have been considering. What Söhngen calls "action and persuasion" can be reduced to the third function, "address," since they are directed to an audience or an interlocutor, while "declaration" or "profession" is actually a total form of "expression" by which a man commits himself in the presence of others to something in the realm of morality or religion, and which can demand an equivalent response from

[17] *Analogie und Metapher* (cf. ch. 2, n. 13).
[18] See the review by H. G. Fritzsche in *TLZ* 89, 1964, pp. 373–375.

others. Thus, in the Scriptures God declares Himself and requires in response our declaration of faith—it is a reciprocal or dialogue movement. Söhngen also contributes a nicely shaded distinction within the third elementary function of language ("address") with his categories of action and persuasion. The dynamism of the spoken word can have either of these as its effect when addressed to another. The last part of his book treats of the dialogical functions of language quite completely; he gives less attention to the monological functions, however.

Krings proposes another line of thought altogether.[19] Rather than distinguish the fundamental functions of language, he speaks of the basic forms of speech. There is first the discursive form, which is the successive and temporal division of the unity by means of logical relations which maintain and manifest the unity in dialectic. The second form of speech is that which "actualizes" reality by rendering it present in the very act of saying it: This is the language of poetry and cult. The third form is called "existential": It is at once the manifestation and full realization of a man in that act by which he engages himself. Krings' terminology is quite different from the preceding studies, and it reveals its close connection with some modern trends in philosophy. Of the forms he discusses, the second is most relevant to our purposes, since most of the inspired text is poetic and is actualized in the cult.

APPLICATION TO INSPIRED LANGUAGE

Let us see some of the consequences of our preceding reflections as they are applied to the inspired word. If God has assumed only the first function of language, the statement of doctrines and ideas on the one hand, and the presentation of facts on the other, then our task is to extract this "inspired" element, separating it from the dross of what is human and not inspired. We will then refine the part that we have extracted by means of formulas that are more and more precise, until the Scriptures will no longer be necessary since they will have been brought to their ultimate goal. (Recall how Söhngen's first function of language tends toward conceptual precision.) We will have in the formulas of dogmatic theology and the conceptualized propositions of speculative theology a purified

[19] The article "Wort" in *Handbuch Theologischer Grundbegriffe*.

form of the "inspired" doctrine, and the Bible will be superfluous. Such has been the practice—though neither openly proclaimed nor defended—of some schools of theology.

In regard to the events which the Bible relates, we could, with a "statement-centered" preoccupation, assume the polemic stance of the controversialist: St. Robert Bellarmine, for instance.[20] Bellarmine set out to prove that sacred Scripture was inferior to tradition and moreover unnecessary. One of the reasons he alleged for this is that Scripture relates many events, which have no connection with doctrine. These facts are not recounted in order that we might believe, rather we believe them because they are recounted. And since the events are only proposed for their informative value, and have no particular doctrinal relevance, it is not necessary to elaborate them conceptually; our only duty is to believe that they happened, and the only problem in their regard is historicity. We adduce this example here to show that such an attitude is not a chimera of our own inventing.

But if the informative or statement function of language is the only one that is inspired, and if this function finds its *raison d'être* in doctrine, why are there so many repetitions in the sacred text? Why so many past events which have no interest for us, why the dialectic of a Qoheleth or Job?

On the other hand, once we admit the plurality of functions in sacred language, we see more clearly why the early Fathers sought and found in Scripture not only Christian doctrine, but also Christian prayer and life. In this integral language of the Bible, there is no such distinction between dogma and life, between theory and practice, which weighs so heavily on us moderns and which we are attempting to correct precisely by a return to the Scriptures and the liturgy.

Liturgy is meant to actualize the language of the Bible in all three of its functions. The reading out of the text is a proclamation which presents the facts of salvation, which highlights God's self-expression, and which is addressed to us in order that we may respond. In liturgy, the Scriptures become once again the medium of dialogue.

[20] Cf. J. R. Geiselmann, *Die Heilige Schrift und die Tradition*, Quaestiones Disputate, no. 18, Freiburg, 1962, section 7.

And in private prayer, too, we do not ordinarily begin with doctrinal propositions and then turn them into a language which is more personal and vital; rather, we spontaneously adopt the language of the Scriptures in the integrity of all its dimensions.

There is yet another way of dissecting the sacred text: It is performed by a new existential interpretation.[21] The inspired (watch the metaphor) function of Scripture is that which calls me to an existential response; it is based on the nature of the existential declaration made by the author. However, in its active function of eliciting my response, this declaration can and indeed ought to be separated from the language in which the author first expressed it. The testimony of the author must be transposed completely into another language if it is to fulfill its function in me. Whatever there is of statement, of doctrine, or of events, can be left aside; and even the function of addressing or impressing me is better described as a meta-function of the biblical text. Thus, the designation "inspired" is a deceptive metaphor which must itself be transposed entirely into another formula in order to be meaningful, in which it means: "Having a power to speak directly to me."

In the theology manuals which treat of inspiration, there is usually a chapter entitled, "The Extent of Inspiration." This chapter has been occasioned by the efforts of some authors to trim down the Scriptures, leaving certain sections of the Bible outside the pale of inspiration. They wanted to omit casual remarks or passing phrases, which are not doctrinal and have no reference to faith or morals. Some have performed a dissection along the latitudinal lines of the text, omitting phrases, sentences, and verses, and combining the rest to obtain a book "purely inspired." Both the solution and this whole manner of posing the question are rejected today. Others made a deeper incision and distinguished, as we have already noted, between matter and form, content and style, ideas and words. This is, of course, the famous discussion on "verbal

---

[21] This whole question is very much in the forefront today. The "Elenchus Bibliographicus" in *Bib* 1963 lists fourteen titles referring to Bultmann. Cf. R. Brown, "After Bultmann, What? An Introduction to the Post-Bultmannians," CBQ 26, 1964, pp. 1–30, with the works referred to there, esp. L. Malevez, *The Christian Message and Myth. The Theology of Rudolf Bultmann*, New York, 1960; and *The Later Heidegger and Theology*, ed. J. M. Robinson and J. B. Cobb, Jr., "New Frontiers in Theology" series, New York, 1963.

inspiration" which Pesch attempts to refute within thirty well-compressed pages. Again, let us say that such limitations on the charism of inspiration find few supporters today.

Benoit divides his chapter on the extent of inspiration in the following way: "To all the faculties, to all those who concurred in the composition of the book and to the whole content." This frame of reference is more inclusive. In line with such a scholastic outlook, we would add that the charism of inspiration extends to all the functions of language. For we cannot limit the action of the Spirit to only this or that dimension of language.

Bibliography for Chapter 5

Language's Three Functions. The basic work is K. Bühler, *Sprachtheorie. Die darstellungsfunktion der Sprache,* Jena, 1934. A study of his work can be found in R. Ceñal, *La teoria del lenguaje de Carlos Bühler,* Madrid, 1941. Kainz accepts for the most part Bühler's position. Söhngen seems to be unaware of Bühler's work.

Language and Monologue. The best study is in Kainz's book, *Psychologie der Sprache,* vol. 1, part 3, A 2, "Die monologischen Sprachfunktionen"; in the same volume, part 3, B, Kainz speaks of the other functions of language. His classification is curious, but the list is interesting and can serve as a basis for further reflection. A more balanced categorization is found in Söhngen's book, *Analogie und Metapher, Kleine Philosophie und Theologie der Sprache,* Munich, 1962, which we discuss in this chapter.

Application to Inspired Language. The use that the liturgy and theology make of inspired language will be given in their bibliographies later on. In regard to the existential view of language, cf. M. Heidegger's essays, "Remembrance of the Poet" and "Hölderlin and the Essence of Poetry," found in *Existence and Being,* Chicago, 1949. Excellent discussions of this aspect can be found in the "New Frontiers in Theology" series, vol. 1, *The Later Heidegger and Theology,* ed. by J. M. Robinson and J. B. Cobb, Jr., New York, 1963, and vol. 2, *The New Hermeneutic,* same editors, New York, 1964.

6. The Three Levels of Language

Language is actualized on three fundamental levels with some intervening strata and many areas of interpenetration. The three fundamental levels are: common language, technical language, and literary language.

COMMON LANGUAGE

Common language is the ground for all the rest. It is the language of familiar intercourse—to which we return with the joy of a child; it is the language in which we share our love and our ideals. The great wealth of this language lies in the area of personal communication; its precision is only moderate. Common language spontaneously actualizes the three fundamental functions of language. Sometimes it answers our zest for knowing; then at other times, though its objective content is minimal, it offers us the joy of personal exchange with a friend; or, finally, it can give us the satisfaction of influencing others with our words.

This is the language of ordinary conversation, familiar and social, so dedicated to the reality which it communicates that the process of transforming experiences, objects, and events into a series of significant sounds, takes place unconsciously—we are annoyed by someone who "listens to himself talking"—and only mistakes or some striking phrase recall us to an awareness of the fact of language.[1]

Words such as these, produced spontaneously, do not result in phrases that are meant to perdure, but to reveal. Valéry says of

[1] For an analysis of this aspect of speech, cf. Kainz, *Psychologie der Sprache*, vol. 3.

such a phrase, *"elle se dissout dans la clarté."* It is meant to pass, and as it passes it communicates, as a moving river which joins both its sides, or even as a zipper which by passing interlocks the two pieces of cloth.

Common language can be reduced to little more than a utilitarian schema: such is the language when buying and selling and travelling (it includes especially numbers and also gestures which emphasize or supply); it is "German in two weeks" or "basic English." This is not the same as a limited knowledge of a foreign tongue; such a barrier can be overcome by great powers of communication (we remember how once in Rome a Spaniard who knew about ten words of Italian yet held an audience of Americans in suspense with the tale of his adventures). Even a language poorly mastered can be a means of communication; utilitarian language, on the other hand, is a means of preserving one's distance as though in an effort to avoid being soiled by contact.

Does such everyday conversational language exist in the Bible? St. Jerome, defending the inspiration of the Epistle to Philemon, says:

There are many things in the Epistle to the Romans and to the other churches, especially to the Corinthians, which are written in a simple and almost everyday style.[2]

We should note that St. Jerome's use of the word "simple" (*remissius*) is a technical term in rhetoric, designating a low and a simple style. Epistolary style is more easily given to using common language. Leo XIII, defending biblical inerrancy in those passages which describe nature, says of the authors of Scripture:

They did not seek to penetrate the secrets of nature, but rather described and dealt with things in more or less figurative language, or in terms which were commonly used at the time. . . .[3]

Pius XII, speaking about historical passages, gives a similar explanation:

[2] *"Inveniri plurima et ad Romanos, et ad ceteras Ecclesias maximeque ad Corinthios remissius et quotidiano pene sermone dictata. . . ."* "Comm. on Phil," PL 26, 637.

[3] ". . . *quare eos, potius quam explorationem naturae recta persequantur, res ipsas aliquando describere et tractare aut quodam translationis modo, aut sicut communis sermo per ea ferebat tempora, hodieque de multis fert rebus in*

When some persons reproachfully charge the sacred writers with some historical error or inaccuracy in the recording of facts, on closer examination it turns out to be nothing else than those customary modes of expression and narration peculiar to the ancients, which used to be employed in the mutual dealings of social life and which, in fact, were sanctioned by common usage.[4]

However, neither St. Jerome nor the recent encyclicals answer our question with an unequivocal affirmative, since it is not the question they explicitly propose to themselves. Common language in its pure state does not exist in the Bible. But insofar as it is the ground of all language, from which proceed the other types and to which they return, common language cannot be totally absent from the sacred text.

In the religious language of a private prayer to God, speech may lose importance or consistency; the language act can become automatic and flow on uniting me to God. But this is not the language of the Bible or the liturgy. We have said that the other levels of language grow out of common language. In the case of inspired language, there was no preëxisting adequate religious language to be subsequently raised by the action of the Spirit. Rather, common language, ordinary and profane, provided the raw material from which inspired language drew its resources, except, of course, in those cases in which the inspired authors used and adapted the religious language of other peoples. However, since all language reverts back one way or another to common language, the inspired word can have an indirect influence on common religious language, and even on ordinary language. A striking witness to this fact is provided by the traces of biblical language to be found in Western literature.[5]

---

quotidiana vita, ipsos inter homines scientissimos." "Providentissimus," EB 121; RSS 22.

[4] "Non raro enim . . . cum Sacros Auctores ab historiae fide aberasse, aut res minus accurate rettulisse obiurgando nonnulli iactant, nulla alia de re agi comperitur, nisi de suetis illis nativis antiquorum dicendi narrandique modis, qui in mutuo hominum inter se commercio passim adhiberi solebant, ac reapse licito communique more adhibebantur." Divino afflante Spiritu, EB 560; RSS 99.

[5] Fritz Melzer follows up some of these traces within the German language in his book, Our Language in the Light of the Ancient Christian Revelation (Unsere Sprache im Lichte der Christus-Offenbarung, 2nd ed., Tübingen, 1962). In chs. 7 and 8, which are especially interesting in this regard, we find

TECHNICAL LANGUAGE

The second level which we must study is that of technical or scientific language.

A mother arrives at the doctor's. She is with her six-year-old boy, and she is very excited. She bursts into a series of explanations interspersed with words of compassion; she heaps up detail on detail amid a stream of tenderness; then she asks the help of the doctor. The doctor tries to calm the woman in order to sort out the facts which interest him from those which confuse him. He proposes a list of questions, in order to reduce the explanation to symptoms. He continues this until he arrives at a precise diagnosis, which he expresses in a language which the mother does not understand, but which she receives confidently; finally, he prescribes a remedy and gives her a prescription. The mother had used all the resources of her maternal language operating at full speed. However, the doctor did not allow himself to be "impressed" by these "expressions"; rather, he subjected them to a sifting process in order to arrive at his objective. The boy's ailments became "symptoms," the vague descriptive phrases became an exact, precise diagnosis. The language of the mother has been reduced to the language of the clinic. A policeman or a lawyer proceeds in the same way in order to transform an agitated, controversial story into a judicial or criminal brief.

When man as worker (*homo faber*) develops a specific technique, or when man as thinker (*homo sapiens*) evolves a science, he immediately elaborates a scientific or technical language. Even primitive people who had mastered certain techniques, fishing, hunting and so forth, likewise possessed in their language certain categories of precise terms. In our Western culture, the Greeks were the outstanding creators of scientific language.[6]

Technical language proceeds from common language by a proc-

---

the following subtitles: "The Death of Pagan Words"; "The New Life of Pagan-German Words"; "Words Derived from Latin"; "Derived translations." By way of proof, he selects a few Christian words which begin with the letter "D," following out their semantic evolution, their relations, and their derivatives. In ch. 10, we read the title, "How Prayer Has Influenced Language."

[6] For a treatment of the language of primitive peoples, cf. Kainz, *Psychologie der Sprache*, vol. 2, pp. 90–169.

ess of detachment, delimitation, and division. It detaches itself from what is personal and subjective, in order to reach a maximum of objectivity, or, to say the same thing in another way, it attempts to inhibit the expressive function of language and its function of address, in order to remove the contingent qualities of concrete language and produce a quasi-universal or at least easily translatable medium of communication. It uses abstract concepts which it continues to subdivide down to the smallest precision. Its sentences are short and simple, easily qualified by circumstantial descriptions.[7]

The ideal of technical language would be an absolute series of terms. As a matter of fact, such a utopian ideal has been pursued by logistics, but the result has been a series of mathematical formulas, not true language. However, this utopian extreme does serve at least as a concrete example of the goal to which technical language aspires. As Heisenberg[8] has shown, the most refined aspects of physics cannot prescind from some elements of common language, and at the same time they retain metaphors which they have more or less standardized.

In technical language, each word is important. Terms must remain fixed in their meanings and precise in their use; formulas must be exact, all their elements sacrosanct (a professor in an examination wants the "precise term"). The conceptual system of a science becomes in its turn an instrument of thought and further discovery, thus joining the two aspects of "the thing accomplished" (*ergon*), and the "power to accomplish", (*energeia*).

. Do we find such language in Scripture? Or, to ask the question in another way, does inspiration ever assume a preëxisting technical language? Or, does a technical religious language ever develop under the action of the Holy Spirit? To these two latter questions the answer is yes.

We find in the legal sections of the Bible laws of a casuistic type, employing language which is quite technical and which has been borrowed from the more general culture of the Near East, mediated to Israel through Canaan. The ceremonial laws are also framed in technical language, which does not seem to have been

---

[7] Cf. H. G. Gadamer, *Wahrheit und Methode*, Tübingen, 1960, pp. 392–395.

[8] Cf. W. Heisenberg *et al.*, *Our Modern Physics*, New York, 1961.

the original creation of the biblical authors.[9] We must be careful, however, not to confuse technical language with the established formulas or the "*topoi*" which may characterize a type of literature or a literary school: Though these latter may be fixed, they are not used as technical terms.[10]

More important than this assumption of technical language is the process of "technicalization" by which common words assume a technical significance. Such a process was implied in the second question we asked above, concerning the development of a technical religious language under the influence of inspiration.

Let us study three examples in which this process is at various stages of development.

(1) The Book of Deuteronomy has a special vocabulary to designate the law and its precepts: *huqqim, mishpatim, miswot, debarim, 'edot, tora, dibre hattora*. This series of seven words, everyone of which has a technical shade of meaning, are consciously confused and combined by the author, in order to convey to us a sense of fullness and interpenetration.[11]

(2) We find in Chapter 7 of the Book of Joshua a very interesting literary procedure which exploits all the semantic possibilities of the Hebrew word "*herem*." The word means fundamentally "dedicate" or "consecrate," but usually in the sense of making a sacrificial offering to God of one's enemy or booty in a holy war. From this sense are derived the ideas of the extermination of a people or of the warriors, and the dedication of precious objects to the cult.

The Israelites broke the law of consecration. . . . they sequestered some things from the consecration (1). . . . they took from the consecration (11). . . . they have become execrated themselves . . . unless you destroy the things that are consecrated (12). . . . there is desecration among you . . . until you remove the consecrated things (13). . . . he who is found desecrated (15).

[9] The basic study is still that of A. Alt, *Die Ursprünge des Israelitischen Rechts* (cf. *Kleine Schriften*, vol. 1, pp. 278–332, Munich, 1959).

[10] Some aspects of this question and a bibliography can be found in our "Hermeneutics in the Light of Language and Literature," *art. cit.*, p. 371; cf. ch. 4, n. 5.

[11] N. Lohfink, *Das Hauptgebot. Eine Untersuchung literarischer Einleitungsfragen zu Dt 5–11*, Rome, 1963, pp. 54–58.

This change of meaning, operating concretely within the same word, conjures up the image of some powerful reality, mysterious yet active. The author can create this impression by his use of a word; there is no need to describe or name this presence exactly.

(3) This is the way that St. Paul uses the Greek word "*amartía*," which is not so much a technical designation of an individual sin, as a deep and terrible reality: the world of sin actively manifesting itself.

It is not legitimate to approach such passages with the outlook of a technician, nor is it exegesis to reduce to a specific and technical meaning a word which an author has left imprecise in its resonances.

A word or a formula can acquire a certain fixity because of its constant use in a definite context; it begins to assume some of the qualities of a technical term. For example, the formula "a land flowing with milk and honey" is redolent of mythopoeic thought, and evokes the image of a land inhabited by the gods, abounding in luxuriant vegetation which requires no work to procure. The Israelites borrowed this phrase from Canaan, and applied it to the land which God had given them. They sang these words in their cultic credo and used them in their doctrine. Thus, the formula became relatively fixed and technical without, however, losing its mythic resonances which were sometimes latent and sometimes actualized. In much the same way, certain institutions or religious practices possessed a fixed vocabulary and phraseology which in time became quasi-technical.[12] We can see a similar process operative in pairs of words which are opposed or complementary. Thus, for example, the word "*mamlaka*," which ordinarily means "kingdom," takes on the sense of "king" in the contrast, "*goymamlakto*," "the people—their king." "*Am*" usually signifies simply "people"; however, when it is opposed to the word "*goyyim*," it takes on the meaning of "chosen people."

A similar phenomenon can be observed in the way in which a certain fact or name undergoes a process of spiritualization and

[12] That K. Baltzer follows this line of investigation is evident from the title of his book, *Das Bundesformular*, Neukirchen, 1960. Lohfink, in the work just cited (n. 11), also adopts this orientation, as does Richter in his *Traditionsgeschichtliche Untersuchungen zum Richterbuch*, Bonn, 1963.

abstraction. Speculation tends to deprive such realities of their concrete existence and they take on the nature of a symbol. Such, for instance, is the explanation of the various biblical descriptions of the "manna" in the desert.[13]

This process received a powerful impulse when the Hebrew Bible was translated into Greek. The Greek language itself, the more reflective mentality of the men of this later age, and the fact that long distant events and institutions had by now become a "book," all combined to produce this process of spiritualization. As it translated, the Septuagint tended to spiritualize many concrete formulas, and to convert simple designations into technical terms, at times eliminating the symbolic quality of the original, and at other times seriously reducing it. In this way, the process of "technicalization" was accelerated. At the same time, however, the tendency toward spiritualization resulted in a new series of symbols, since concrete reality took on a spiritual meaning, and acquired, in the process of receiving a new name, a new and deeper synthesis on a theological level. Thus, the Greek translators prepared a sort of intermediate language which became an invaluable instrument in the hands of the early Christian theologians who were attempting to formulate the mystery of the Christ-fact for their fellow Christians and their prospective converts. The Septuagint is a spiritual bridge, erected by divine Providence between the Old Testament and the New.[14]

Of course, when these words and phrases have once acquired a technical or quasi-technical meaning, they also assume a certain mediating capacity in their new role as formulas; it is important to find just the right word and use it consistently, especially when there is question of making a translation. Then, too, these terms and formulas can serve as the basis for a biblical theology, either by maintaining the terms at the technical level they have reached in the Scriptures, or by continuing the process with the aid of our modern thought categories.

There is a greater proportion of technical elements in the language of the New Testament, especially in the theological specula-

[13] Cf. G. von Rad, *Das formgeschichtliche Problem des Hexateuch*, Gessammelte Studien zum Alten Testament, Munich, 1961, pp. 9–86.

[14] Authoritative information regarding the Septuagint can be had by consulting *Mitteilungen des Septuaginta Unternehmens*, Göttingen. Among the authors, cf. esp. the works of J. Ziegler and I. L. Seeligman.

tion of St. Paul. For, while St. John remains intensely symbolic, St. Paul at times strives for a certain conceptual exactitude, though he, too, respects the frontiers of mystery.

A full analysis of the Bible's technical language is of special relevance in hermeneutics or the science of interpretation. In a study such as ours, it suffices merely to note the fact. Because of the unity of the Spirit and the continuity of His action, inspiring different authors of successive ages, this process of technicalization must be attributed to His activity. It is a progressive revelation, incarnating revelation in a continuity which is advancing. Inspired language is the medium for this dynamic process.

Apart from inspiration, a theology which would aspire to the level of science must develop a technical theological language as an instrument of thought and exposition. We shall have to return to this point later on.

LITERARY LANGUAGE

Literary language springs from the same soil, the same common language, as do the other types of speech. It does not arise from utilitarian language, yet neither is it merely anti-utilitarian. It does not arise from technical language as though it were a parallel specialization moving in the opposite direction. Ortega has defined abstract poetry as "a higher algebra of metaphors," yet this itself is a metaphor.

Literary language does not proceed from common language by means of detachment, purification, and specialization, as though it were some "pure poetry" desiring to exist in a state of complete and absolute purgation, hermetically sealed and containing its own quintessence. Rather, literary language proceeds from common language by raising it to a new power. Rarely does the language of conversation enable us to share all the wealth of an experience, or to communicate the richness of what we live within ourselves: Common language is unable to confer on such realities an adequate objectivity. Many factors can concur to offset this inadequacy: the context, previous acquaintance, a whole series of hyperlogical elements that can accompany dialogue. But often, as we leave a conversation, we feel the distance, the impotency of the words, which have been uttered, and which have only half-accomplished their task. There is a sudden spark, but we are obliged to dissipate it in the extended intricacies of our explanation; a vital intuition becomes too self-conscious or remains inert; the urgency of dialogue robs us of words; the very intensity of our feeling inhibits at times its best expression. These are the moments in which we complain: "I didn't know how to say it. . . . I couldn't find the words. . . ."

Literary language does not have to resign itself to this dilemma, but attempts to actualize experience and make it fully objective, exploiting all the functions of language by causing them to yield their maximum productivity. A literary man takes advantage of every expressive possibility in his language, even those possibilities which have never been actualized before. When he feels that his language is failing him, he does not acknowledge himself conquered, rather he reaches out and intensifies his effort; the very shortcomings and unyielding nature of his medium serve only to incite him, as marble challenges a sculptor.

To empower is not the same as to multiply, and in this instance it is certainly not the increase of multiplication. Literary language often delights in density and concentration. What a world, and how much soul there is in some poems of just a few verses:

> To see a world in a grain of sand
> and Heaven in a wild flower,
> hold Infinity in the palm of your hand,
> and eternity in an hour.
>
> BLAKE

By means of this force, and for the sake of it, literary language stylizes and simplifies, skipping over insignificant spaces.

In literary language, words have an absolute importance, and they are sought with the greatest care. They are not merely a way of saying something completely separable from what they say. Words are important for their sound quality, for their rhythm in a phrase, for their aura of associations, and for their resonances in the periphery of our consciousness. . . .

A certain painter once said to his friend Mallarmé: "I also am a poet; many thoughts come to me, however I cannot find the words." Mallarmé answered him: "Poetry is made with words." According to Valéry:

Meaning is not for the poet the essential nor, ultimately, the sole element of language; it is but one of its constituent factors. . . . Then, too, the simple notion of the meaning of words is not sufficient in poetry; I have already spoken of resonance. . . .[15]

For this reason, poetry always remains but partially translatable, and sometimes it cannot be translated at all.

Poetry delights in multiplicity, it accepts and even seeks ambiguity (Empson); it works with images and symbols, declining logic. Poetry fuses the objective with subjectivity; it creates a presence which is almost magic.

Finally, literary language which seeks to be permanent, ordinarily achieves this stability in the written work.

Do we find literary language in the sacred Scriptures? A greater part of the Old Testament and a good proportion of the New belong to this level of language. In a process much the same as that described above in relation to technical language, the sacred authors availed themselves of a preëxisting literary language, and, under the motion of the Holy Spirit, developed a literary medium of their own.

This fact, which is of some importance in a study of inspiration, has the greatest consequences in hermeneutics, for inspiration takes upon itself and actively exploits all the rich possibilities of literary language.

The Scriptures, then, are a reality of literary language. Their resources are abundant and their content full. They are an integrally human reality, and not simply a doctrinal textbook. They can contain all of revelation, but not in propositional form (Scripture and tradition).

Since the language of Scripture is literary, it demands a literary interpretation, and yet every interpretation still leaves the text unexhausted.

Such to us are the holy writings: they give birth to truth, yet they remain virgins, keeping closed the mysteries of the truth.[16]

---

[15] "Signification n'est donc pour le poète l'élement essentiel, et finalment le seul, du langage; il n'est que l'un des constituants. . . . De même la notion simple de sens des paroles ne suffit pas à la poésie; j'ai parlé de resonance. . . ." L'invention esthétique, Oeuvres ed. by J. Hytier, Paris, 1962, tome 1, pp. 1414ff.

[16] . . . τοιαῦται δ' ἡμῖν αἱ κυριακαὶ γραφαί, τὴν ἀλήθειαν ἀποτίκτουσαι καὶ

Such wealth of meaning can be viewed in different ways, all of which may be substantially correct. Since this language is literary, its content—and not only its meaning—can be manifold. Such multiplicity can be rationalized in successive interpretations, yet these must remain, individually and collectively, unequal to the original expression (R. Petsch).

Since this language is literary, it is not coarse or commonplace, nor can it be made commonplace in order to make it popular. Men must be lifted up and introduced to an understanding of the Scriptures so that they can appreciate its language and its message. The people of God must not be coarse.

Since this language is literary, it cannot be simply transposed to the level of technical language. It must retain its images, its symbols, and its concretization, which reveal and veil the mystery without rationalizing it (theology).

Since this language is literary and not merely intellectual, we are not entitled to go back to some supposed previous conceptual stage of its development which the author has subsequently "clothed" in literary form. This language comes before concepts, notions, and terms, and its meaning cannot be obtained by a systematic purification of its literary qualities (theology).

Since this language is literary, its interpretation cannot consist formally of a conceptual categorization and propositional presentation of its contents. We must proceed from the first, elementary understanding of the literary text to one that is deeper and more explicit, and thence to the content of the message.

Since this language is literary, it confers on words a substantial value; it subsists in them and lives by means of them; it is not a disembodied set of ideas which lives and moves independently of the words which incarnate it.

Since this language is literary, it obliges us to the greatest respect and discretion in applying the principle of "what the author wished to say." A literary man ordinarily says what he wishes to say. The principle is valid insofar as it disqualifies a superficial reading of the text, one that would be boorishly naïve, without feeling for the text, coarse, and "out of focus." But the principle is invalid

---

μένουσαι παρθένοι μετὰ τῆς ἐπικρύψεως τῶν τῆς ἀληθείας μυστηρίων. St. Clement of Alex., "Stromata 7, 16," PG 9, 529; GCS 3, 66.

if by it is meant that the author said what he did not wish to say, and failed to say what he wished, as though literature were some curse which descends on a literary man and clings to his bones. The principle is legitimate insofar as it does not allow us to treat the text simply as a text, but rather sharpens our appreciation of it as a medium in and by which a subjectively experienced reality receives its new objective existence.

In describing the demand placed upon an exegete by the literary nature of the text he studies, we have been forced to sketch an outline of the whole process of exegesis. Before going on, it may be worth while to discuss these ideas a little more completely. The following pages will therefore circle back, as it were, over the area we have just covered; there will be some reptitions and some new points of view.

A Comparison of the Various Levels

The above distinction had, necessarily, to be somewhat schematic. In reality, all three levels of language must be open to one another, even to the point of compenetration, if technical and literary language are to be truly rooted in the common ground of everyday speech. Our next step is to study these three levels in comparison with one another, pointing out where they are opposed and where they lie open to one another.

Common Language and Technical Language

Ordinary language exists before its technical development. It offers to technical language the words which become specialized in terms, and it places various radical forms at the disposition of technical language, so that the latter can evolve and distinguish its concepts (unless, of course, technical language borrows its terminology from an ancient or foreign language, as we often do with Greek). Also, the syntactical structure of common language provides the means by which sentences are constructed and demonstrations established. Syntax provides not only the framework, but also the "mortar" of the construction.

Technical language in its turn gives to everyday speech some of its formula and expressions. As these become popular, they lose their rigid precision and become capable of enriching common lan-

F

guage (much to the annoyance of the scientists; for not only do people plunder their terms, they then go off and confuse them: "chain reaction," "antibiotic," "complex"). This lowering of technical language to the level of common speech is widespread in our modern culture due to the multiplication and effectiveness of the media of communication.

Sometimes science takes up an obvious and simple fact already expressed in common language. When such a simple thing is transposed into technical language, it provokes a reaction, first of surprise, and then of humor: "So that's what they wanted to say! They could have done it without all that fanfare!" At the present time, sociology is the prime example of such procedure. Though the danger of pedantry is obvious, the transposition is legitimate insofar as it renders all the concepts precise, and allows them to be handled exactly.

The Old Testament does not raise human experiences to the level of sociological science, but contents itself with a simply literary expression in proverb, character portrayal, etc.

Common Language and Literary Language

Ordinary language also precedes literary development, and is the raw material for literature. Literary language prefers to keep a certain distance from everyday speech. Usually, it begins in hieratic or stylized formulas, and gradually approaches realism. However, if it insists on maintaining its distance for too long a time and proceeding on a tangent from common speech, it can easily degenerate into isolationism or snobbishness. Then it must reëstablish ties with common language in order that its anemic poetry may be restored to vigor (T. S. Eliot).

Biblical language knows moments of great stylization—the first Book of Genesis, and of great refinement—the Book of Job, but it never becomes isolated or snobbish. And, insofar as we can judge today, it constantly drew its nourishment from the language of the people for whom it was destined. This is one way of understanding the phrase "Sitz im Leben": literature with its roots deeply embedded in the life of the people.

Literary language exerts a great influence on common language by modifying it, rendering it more flexible, and expanding it. Often, metaphors crystallize and become part of the ordinary vocabulary; many literary phrases have become standard expressions, clichés, or commonplaces. Leo Spitzer once said that grammar is style in the frozen state.[17]

Biblical language, through its numerous translations, has exerted an influence on the common language of all Christian lands (Melzer). These traces allow us to find our way back to their common source, and to revitalize expressions which have become profane. Such investigations can provide the language of preaching with valuable means of making its message relevant without becoming vulgar.

Literary Language and Technical Language

Technical language and literary language travel along different roads. Technical vocabulary can be very old, though, of course, no older than the technique which it embodies, while as a system literary language is always older than technical language. A study of their interrelations can be of help to us in understanding the Scriptures.

Earlier in this chapter, we cited two recent encyclicals. It will be useful to recall some of their teaching here:

. . . they did not seek to penetrate the secrets of nature, but rather described and dealt with things in more or less figurative language, or in terms which were commonly used at the time, and which in many instances are daily used at this day, even by the most eminent men of science.[18]

Those customary modes of expression and narration peculiar to the ancients, which used to be employed in the mutual dealings of social life, . . .[19]

Leo XIII speaks of ordinary language, of metaphor (which can be part of literary language), and of scientific language; he denies that the sacred authors were interested in the latter. Pius XII refers to ordinary language in a section which is concerned with literary forms; indirectly, he excludes scientific language. According to the

---

[17] In every nation with a cultural history, the study of one's native language includes the reading of its masterpieces (we usually start with Shakespeare in high school).

[18] *Supra,* n. 3.

[19] *Supra,* n. 4.

teaching of the popes, the Bible does not use the scientific language of astronomy or of the other natural sciences, nor the scientific language of our modern, critical history.

If we continue this line of thought a little further, we will discover that the biblical authors used a literary language in which elements from both common and technical language are still present, but transformed. The language of the first chapter of Genesis is not that of conversation. This solemn categorization of nature is based on the observations of the science of the period which, as we have seen, had already compiled lists of things according to groups. What is interesting to note is the fact that this "science" is completely transposed into a literary language of extraordinary density. There are no metaphors; this language derives from that dawn-age of naming which preceded metaphor. At the same time, there is a conscious distance, maintaining itself above all that is common and ordinary, while using the most common of words.

The story of the plagues in the Book of Exodus is told in a restrained literary language of epic proportions, which has more than a touch of irony, and yet never stoops to vulgarity. Many scenes from the lives of the patriarchs or in the stories of kings and prophets may appear at first glance to be quite ordinary and told in very common language, yet they are in reality extremely stylized compositions. A successful literary transposition of events consists largely in the skillful selection of crucial instants, and the skipping over of insignificant spaces. Dialogues with three or five exchanges, a bargaining process all done on a page—these are not the accomplishments of ordinary language.

When the medieval scholastics talked of the "modes" of the Scriptures, they had posed to themselves this same problem and they had resolved it correctly. Scripture does not employ the "modes" (which means the language) of science, consisting of definition, distinction, and argument; it uses the "modes" of literature.

So far, we have discussed in a general way the type of language found in the Bible, and we have seen that it is literature. At this point, it is possible to push the investigation further, comparing technical language and literary language and studying the relations that exist between them.

Technical language can take as its point of departure the literary descriptions given of a certain reality, which in this first stage depend completely on images and symbols. The beginning of philosophy among the pre-Socratics was intensely symbolic. The "water" of Thales is not our H_2O any more than the "fire" of Heraclitus is our "chemical reaction," or the "atoms" of Democritus our "constellation of protons and neutrons." These objects of early study were "elements," held fast in their quality as symbols, yet made already somewhat remote by the first stirrings of philosophical reflection. Whenever a new stage of philosophical reflection begins, it is not unusual to find once again a system of images and symbols prior to a conceptual development: Such is the case with Bergson and Teilhard de Chardin. But even writers as abstract as the scholastics speculated about the nature of the prophetic charism, invoking such realities as "the light of divine Truth" and the "mirror of eternity." Söhngen delights in filling three whole pages with images taken from the writings of no less a person than Kant! [20]

After this second stage of systematic conceptualization, technical language returns to literary language for the third stage in its own development, that of didactics or exposition. It uses images and symbols to clothe its conceptual functioning and conclusions. Now, we are entitled to pass from the words of the professor to "what he wishes to say" or "what he is trying to get across." The pity is that some professors of hermeneutics know only this third stage, and have attempted to enclose the biblical poets within its limits.[21]

Technical language can present literary language with some formulas or terms to be exploited by the poet's imagination. The transposition into literature of technical terminology is a relatively modern effort: Góngora tried it in poetry, and it is a common device in the modern essay.

Literary language can develop in the direction of technical language, as we have seen, by a process in which symbol is purified or rationalized ("instrument" becomes "instrumental cause"), or by

[20] Söhngen, *Analogie und Metapher*, pp. 65–68.
[21] The classification of the literature of the Old Testament which is current in our manuals can be misleading. They speak of the historical books, the prophetical books, and the didactic books, putting in this latter category the Book of Job, the Psalms, and the Canticle. Then, in addition, they usually reserve a consideration of Hebrew poetry for the introduction to the "didactic" books, in which they consider little more than parallelism and meter.

the constant repetition of a word in exactly the same sense, by the fixity of a certain formula in a given context, or finally by a process of spiritualization.

Literary language can be partially transposed into technical language by extracting the conceptual or propositional content and reformulating it. This results in a certain detached vision of the whole or in a conceptual paraphrase. The process of extraction ordinarily leads to an extract, and this, of course, is not equal to the original. There are some for whom such a procedure is the ideal of exegesis; however, this is not exegesis, but transposition. Some, whose background and outlook is conceptualist, may think that only conceptual formulation of a reality is intelligible, or at least that it is more intelligible. But this leaves aside the whole question of fidelity in interpreting a text which is not conceptual, or of fidelity in laying hold of a content which may be transcendent and pertain to the realm of mystery. Conceptual transposition of a text is not the same as exegesis: It is a distinct function, and one which is of the greatest importance.

On this map which we have traced, indicating the various frontiers, we have located one of the most vital questions of modern theology. There is charted here in outline form the problem of the relation between Scripture and tradition, and we have broadly indicated the problem of the relationship between sacred Scripture and theology, between biblical theology and dogmatic theology.

The effort at transposition is always operative in the preparation of a dogmatic definition. Scholars search for phrases which are more and more precise, in an attempt to frame statements and propositions which will formulate a truth contained in our faith. At one time, there will be the transposition of a biblical passage, at another, the formulation of a subtle link which binds together several passages. Even though a dogmatic formulation can never exhaust the Mystery or any individual mystery, it is nevertheless true that it is definitive and cannot be invalid. In its turn, such a definition does not exclude complementary formulas, nor other definitions which carry on the initial effort without rendering it obsolete.

Since dogmatic formulation continually strives for a precision which can only be achieved by concentrating more and more exclusively on a given area, it is easy to understand how Scripture will always contain more revelation than is formulated in dogmatic definitions. If the Scriptures had used a technical language, they would undoubtedly be more precise, but they would not be so rich.

Then, too, dogmatic formulas cannot prescind completely from symbols and images, since these have an essential function in the presentation of the mystery of salvation.

The biblical expression is superior to the dogmatic expression of a mystery, because it is formally the word of God. The dogmatic expression—after it has been distilled—is formally the word of the Church, and as such has specific functions which are not fulfilled by sacred Scripture. Thus it comes about that though the Scriptures contain all the revelation in a literary form, they are not completely self-sufficient. Often, what is called the "authentic interpretation" is, according to the terminology of these pages, an "authentic transposition" which encloses and defines a part of the total content. As an assertion it is true, but it does not exclude other, complementary, assertions. However, the attempt to ignore dogmatic definitions in the name of fidelity to the Scriptures is a failure to recognize the vitality of the word of God which demands and evokes these diverse forms of expression in order to give free range to its own inner dynamism.

A second transposition of biblical language is effected by scientific theology. Since it is a science, it has need of the instrumentality of technical language with its concepts and propositions. But where will theology get this instrument, and how will it perfect its serviceability in the cause of science? We can distinguish theoretically three sources: Theology either begins with dogmatic definitions, or adopts the conceptual equipment of some philosophy, or assumes the formulations found in the Scriptures.

The first line of approach is not direct, but reciprocal, since theological reflection is precisely the means by which dogmatic formulations are prepared. It is not only unhistorical, but positively ingenuous to imagine that the wording of the definitions was somehow esoterically whispered successively into the ears of the bishops and popes until the moment when they wished to make public the formulation. The experience and the reports of the deliberations during the sessions of Vatican II ought to have cured anyone who suffered from such naïveté, and to have inoculated him for the future. The other half of this reciprocal activity can be seen in those theological treatises which begin with the formulations achieved thus far in her history by the magisterium of the Church. This is a normal and necessary avenue of approach, but it is important not to confuse the road with its destination.

Scientific theology also speculates with the aid of a philosophical system external to revelation. For the scholastics, this instrument was the philosophy of Aristotle. Roger Bacon describes the relation between revelation and philosophy this way:

All wisdom is contained in sacred Scripture, but it must be made explicit by the use of law and philosophy; for just as that which is contained in the fist unfolds out into the palm, so all the wisdom useful for man is contained in the sacred writings, but not explicitly—its unfolding pertains to Canon Law along with philosophy.[22]

No one can deny the validity and effectiveness of the Aristotelian instrument in the hands of the great scholastic theologians. And by the same token, no one can insist that this system be the principal or unique instrument of theology for all ages. A different cultural context can, in principle, both demand and supply a different instrument for speculation.

There is one thing, however, that can never be lacking in the science of theology without incurring the risk of irreparable harm: There must be prolonged and studied contact with the expressions used in Scripture. The language of the Bible must always have a position, a privileged position, in scientific theology.

But this seems to contradict the entire preceding explanation. If the language of the Scriptures is literary, and the language of theology is technical, how can theological language be scriptural?

Obviously, what is intended is not a restriction of all theological language to just those terms found in the Bible. Theological language must begin from the Bible, and must maintain its contact with biblical language, in order to widen its horizons and restore its vitality.[23]

The best illustration of this fact is found in the terminology used

---

[22] ". . . tota sapientia concluditur in Sacra Scriptura, per ius tamen et philosophiam explicanda, ut sicut in pugno colligitur, quod latius in palma explicatur, sic tota sapientia utilis homini continetur in sacris litteris, licet non totaliter explicatur, sed eius explicatio est ius canonicum cum philosophia." Opus Maius, Pars II; cited by Pesch, no. 163.

[23] Cf. L. Alonso Schökel, "Biblische Theologie des Alten Testaments," SZ 172, 1963, pp. 34–51.

by the foremost students of biblical theology themselves. Gerhard von Rad, for instance, who is distinguished for his deep intuitive understanding of the Old Testament world, and for his gifts as a writer, does not restrict himself solely to the language of the Bible, but transposes many notions into a more conceptual frame of reference: "The dissolution of the patriarchal faith in the fertility cult of Canaan," "the intimation of a new salvific activity," "familiarity with the deeds of Yahweh in history." Phrases such as these are certainly not the language of the Bible.

In the New Testament, St. Paul has provided us with a rich theological vocabulary, yet here, too, the need has been felt to continue the process of conceptualization. The great theological dictionary founded by G. Kittel is not being written exclusively in biblical terms, but incorporates a whole tradition of German conceptual formulation. But then, if the professors of biblical theology cannot remain within the terminology of the Scriptures, why demand it of professors of systematic theology?

Analytical, speculative, and systematic theology can never consider themselves perfectly developed. There will always be biblical formulas and phrases awaiting transposition into the more conceptual language of theology. And by this process of returning to the language of Scripture in order to begin its journey anew, scientific theology keeps itself alive. In this sense, it is always legitimate to strive to make theology more biblical. The materials for such an effort are at hand: indirectly in the intermediate sources—biblical dictionaries, studies of biblical themes, monographs on biblical theology, and directly in the quiet, constant reading of the sacred text itself. A great part of the task left for theology is a work of language, in the deepest sense of that term.

CONCLUSION

We have cut a vertical cross-section into language in order to study its various levels. But this cross-section does not reveal an historical succession as do the various archeological strata of a "tell."

In a chronological schema, we would have to distinguish primitive language from cultured language. But such a distinction would be of little help in a study of the inspired word, since the language of the Bible is not a primitive language, but rather one which was

born and grew in an already existing culture. Though biblical Hebrew may be poor in adjectives, have a limited vocabulary, and
possess a very simple syntactical structure, it has in its favor an
extremely subtle conjugation, and when handled by its great poets,
it achieves sonorous force and elemental vigor.

It may be of interest to some to know that the language of the
Old Testament possesses power rather than refinement (though in
its handling of sound it can teach us some lessons), and both its
nouns and verbs have an almost solid quality in their concreteness.
These at least are the characteristics of the language which was
used by the biblical authors and which has come down to us; naturally, they cannot provide a complete description of all Hebrew.
On the other hand, Greek, as we all know, is one of the most
cultivated languages which ever existed. The New Testament is
content to exploit but few of its possibilities.

Bibliography for Chapter 6

Common Language. Most aspects of common language and its realization in the speech act are treated in discussions of the more general
aspects of language. There is a very interesting article by John Wild in
The Philosophical Review repeated in *PT* 2, 1958, pp. 150–161, "Is
there a World of Ordinary Language?" Since there is no other place in
which to mention Wittgenstein, the following articles are mentioned
here: there are three articles in *Philosophical Studies* (Maynooth):
H. A. Nielsen, "Wittgenstein on Language," 8, 1958, pp. 115–121;
C. B. Daly, "New Light on Wittgenstein" (part one), 10, 1960, pp.
5–49; (part 2) 11, 1961–1962, 28–62; cf. also M. J. Fairbanks,
"Language-Games and Sensationalism," *The Modern Schoolman* 40,
1963, pp. 275–280.

Technical Language.   There is an interesting article by A. N. Whitehead, "The Organization of Thought," in *The Limits of Language*, ed.
by W. Gibson, New York, 1962.

Literary Language. A discussion of the way in which language is
actuated in literature can be found in "Language and Literature,"

ch. 11 of E. Sapir's *Language*, New York, 1921. Part four of the book, *Theory of Literature*, by Wellek and Warren is also very helpful. The best treatment of linguistics and literature is found in Leo Spitzer's *Linguistics and Literary History*, New York, 1962. Cf. also D. Alonso, *Poesía española*, Madrid, 1950.

III
THE INSPIRED AUTHORS

ΥΠΟ ΠΝΕΥΜΑΤΟΣ ΑΓΙΟΥ ΦΕΡΟΜΕΝΟΙ
ΕΛΑΛΗΣΑΝ ΑΠΟ ΘΕΟΥ ΑΝΘΡΩΠΟΙ

7. The Psychology of Inspiration

The charism of inspiration, considered formally as an action of the Holy Spirit, cannot be scrutinized by psychological investigations. However, the human literary activity which is moved and directed by the Holy Spirit can be subjected to speculative study and its result called "a proposed psychology of inspiration." A title for this chapter which would be more exact though less manageable would be something like, "The Psychology of the Inspired Human Literary Process."

Someone might ask if an analysis such as we propose is legitimate or even useful; perhaps it would be better to leave inspiration wrapped in its mystery. While, again, someone might object that the study of the human process of literary creation in an effort to understand the charism of inspiration is no more helpful than an analysis of the mathematical reasoning of a professor (who teaches in the state of grace and with a supernatural intention) to an understanding of the workings of grace.

But this objection overlooks an important distinction. Grace has no specific reference to mathematics, but inspiration is directed specifically to the act of language, and it is this which differentiates it from the other charisms. In undertaking a study of this question, we are but following in the footsteps of those who have written treatises on the subject of prophecy and inspiration.[1]

[1] If anyone still feels that such an analysis is not necessary, he is invited to go on to ch. 8.

THE LEONINE DESCRIPTION

Modern manuals usually base their treatment of the question on the following description of inspiration given by Leo XIII in his encyclical, *Providentissimus Deus:*

Hence, the fact that it was men whom the Holy Spirit took up as His instruments for writing does not mean that it was these inspired instruments—but not the primary author—who might have made an error. For by supernatural·power He so moved and impelled them to write—He so assisted them when writing—that the things which He ordered, and those only, they, first, rightly understood, then willed faithfully to write down, and finally expressed in apt words and with infallible truth. Otherwise, it could not be said that He was the Author of the entire Scripture.[2]

We find this passage in that part of the encyclical in which Leo XIII is talking about inerrancy, and rejecting the false opinion of those who maintained that there were errors in the Bible but that these were due to the human authors, not to God. The Pope denies the validity of such a distinction and bases himself on the principle already defined: "God is the author of the entire Scripture," adding to this a speculative elaboration of what is meant by "author." The description of inspiration which is here given is thus not presented for its own sake, but is subordinated to and in the context of the question of inerrancy.

Any discussion of this Leonine description of inspiration should begin·with an affirmation of its fundamental validity. A psychological schematization retains its validity so long as it is taken as such; it loses its validity the moment that it offers itself as the complete and adequate expression of the reality.

If we leave aside cases of completely mechanical writing or other instances of abnormal or pathological phenomena, we can schematically break any literary process down into the following stages: an intellectual stage in which there is knowledge of one kind or an-

---

2 "*Quare nihil admodum refert, Spiritum Sanctum assumpsisse homines tamquam instrumenta ad scribendum, quasi, non quidem primario auctori, sed scriptoribus inspiratis quidpiam falsi elabi potuerit. Nam supernaturali ipse virtute ita eos ad scribendum excitavit et movit, ita scribentibus adstitit, ut ea omnia eaque sola, quae ipse iuberet, et recte mente conciperent, et fideliter conscribere vellent, et apte infallibili veritate exprimerent: secus, non ipse esset auctor Sacrae Scripturae universae.*" EB 125; RSS, p. 24.

other, a volitional stage in which there is a free decision to objectify knowledge in writing, and a stage of execution in which the
intention is realized. In reality, these three stages intermingle, and as
each unfolds it may adopt different forms, yet this does not invalidate the fundamental correctness of the schematization.

In a study of the problems connected with the inspired literary
process, it is quite helpful to adopt this schematization and then
pursue the investigation by differentiating further within each stage
of the schema. This is the method followed by most modern manuals; we wish first merely to reproduce and summarize their presentation.

The Description Given by the Theology Manuals

(1) The Intellectual Stage: The human author can receive his
knowledge directly from God through a previous revelation, and
this can come about in diverse ways: a vision, the ordering of
phantasms in the imagination, or an intellectual perception. It is
also possible that the human author arrive at his knowledge by his
own efforts: his experience, his study, the consultation of sources
etc. In this case, the inspired writer makes an interior judgment
concerning his acquired knowledge and affirms, explicitly or implicitly, that "it is so." This judgment is made with the aid of
divine light, "in the light of divine truth," and this illumination
forms an integral part of the process of inspiration. Because the
light is divine, the judgments made in virtue of this light are
divine. Note that it is not the statement as such which is only the
matter of the judgment that is inspired, but the affirmation of its
truth—the formal element in the judgment. And since this formal
element is of divine truth, it demands the assent of our faith to
the reality revealed. It is not necessary or even usual that the
hagiographer be conscious of the divine influence in his soul.

(2) The Volitional Stage: "No prophecy ever came about by the
will of man." God moves the will of a man to write without destroying his freedom. This usually transpires without any conscious
awareness of the movement on the part of the one inspired, though
the divine action infallibly achieves its purpose. The movement
must be interior and physical; it may at times also be moral, governing the circumstances which prompt the author to write. Under

this motion of God, a man's decision is divine: God is the author of the process by which the book comes about, and thus He is the author of the book.

(3) The Stage of Execution: This is the act of writing which the author accomplishes by himself or through others; it is the act of expressing the message in apt terms, without error. The process by which the work is realized is not under a special supernatural influence, but is carried out with the aid of a certain divine assistance which guarantees that the terms are apt and that there is no error. This assistance does not consist in a physical motion acting directly on the executive faculties.

We are sure that, as the reader studied the above description, he felt a veritable surge of questions and objections welling up within him—more even than he could express to himself: "The outline has become much too schematic. . . . The description is over-simplified. . . . It concentrates on the one example of a writer. . . . Is the creative imagination of a poet an executive faculty? . . . What about all those things in the Bible which are not formal judgments or doctrine? . . . The whole question of literary expression is treated as secondary. . . . There is no appreciation of the psychology of language. . . . The restriction of a prophetic insight to a charism of knowledge seems awkward. . . ."

We can remain calm, however, and proceed with our investigation. Others also have felt the inadequacy of the schematization, and have attempted in their theological speculations to render the description more realistic and more supple.

THE DESCRIPTION GIVEN BY BENOIT

We give Benoit's name to this description since he is responsible for its present and justifiable notoriety. Benoit himself tells us that the first person to propose the distinction was Nicolaus Serarius, an exegete of the sixteenth century. We find the following text in his *Prolegomena Biblica* (Mainz, 1612):

. . . Secondly, God illumines the mind of the writer with a certain light which is either entirely supernatural, or natural but supernaturally conferred or increased. This light is given in order to enable him to perceive what is dictated or to judge, or to do both. Thirdly, this

180

judgment, which is made by the writer concerning what has been dictated, is either theoretical or practical. It is the former when the writer judges that what has been dictated, is true. It is the latter when he judges that he should write these things, in just these words, in this way, and at this time.[3]

The theoretical judgment has as its object, the true; the practical judgment has as its object, the good—an end to be achieved. The theoretical judgment is in the order of knowledge, the practical judgment has to do with activity. Both these two judgments exist and are diversely operative in the inspired authors.

In the case of the prophet, for instance, his announcement of the certainty of coming doom—"You are going into exile"—is the statement of a true proposition made in the name of God. The predominant factor in the oracle was the speculative judgment. However, when the prophet preaches a sermon to the people, his aim is to persuade and convert them, his intention is centered on the good end to be achieved. Here the practical judgment predominated, initiating and directing the literary activity, willing a certain goal and selecting the means toward it.

When the speculative judgment predominates, it elicits a practical judgment concerning the advisability and the means of communicating itself. When the practical judgment predominates, it utilizes various aspects of speculative judgments, ordering them to its own end. An evaluation of any text must first take into account which type of judgment predominates; if it is the theoretical judgment, we seek the truth of the statement and affirm its inerrancy; if, however, the practical judgment is predominant, we seek the practical truth, or the correspondence between what is intended and how and whether it is achieved.

Both procedures are inspired, each realizing the charism analogi-

---

[3] "*Secundo. Intellectum scriptoris illuminat Deus luce quapiam vel omnino* SUPERNATURALI, *vel naturali quidem, sed* SUPERNATURALITER DATA *vel aucta. Et hoc vel ad* PERCIPIENDUM *tantum, quod dictatur; vel ad* IUDICANDUM *tantum, vel ad utrumque. Tertio. Hoc autem iudicium, quod a scriptoribus de dictatis fit, vel* THEORETICUM *est vel* PRACTICUM. *Illud est, quando scriptor iudicat ea quae dictantur, esse vera. Hoc autem practicum est, quando iudicat ea sibi scribenda, et his quidem verbis, isto modo, isto tempore.*" Both Desroches and Grelot cite Serarius. Most probably, the source for all these citations is the ample quotation from Serarius found in *Institutiones Biblicae,* put out by the Pontifical Biblical Institute, 6th ed., Rome, 1951 (the above text was taken from the 5th ed., Rome, 1937, vol. 1, p. 32—tr.).

cally according to its own nature, and each judgment gives rise to a process of execution in which the faculties engaged are operative with the aid of a special divine assistance.

Benoit has lately summed up his thought in three propositions:

1. The writing of the sacred Scriptures calls for speculative judgments as well as practical judgments.

2. These speculative judgments need not precede the practical judgments; they may accompany these latter or come after them.

3. Again, these speculative judgments may be modified under the influence of the practical judgments.[4]

Further on in the same article, enlisting the aid of another distinction proposed by A. Desroches,[5] Benoit enumerates three types of judgments, not merely two:

[1] An absolute speculative judgment, or one "purely speculative," which is made in regard to the truth considered in itself. . . . [2] A speculative judgment with regard to action, which considers the truth in relation to activity . . . the thing to be done is viewed as possible. . . . [3] A practical judgment which has as its proper object practical truth, that is, truth considered in its relation to a right desire . . . which tends unerringly to the goal of art—the work achieved.[6]

The distinction of Benoit is elaborated with an eye to the problem of inerrancy. It enables him to gradate the various degrees of commitment with which the authors make their affirmations down to and including those cases in which, while in the process of

---

[4] "1. *La composition des livres saints exige des jugements spéculatifs surnaturels en plus des jugements pratiques. 2. Ces jugements spéculatifs ne sont pas forcément antérieurs aux jugements pratiques, mais peuvent leur être concomitants ou postérieurs. 3. Ces jugements spéculatifs peuvent être qualifiés par l'influence des jugements pratiques.*" RB 70, 1963, p. 358.

[5] *Op. cit.*, "Jugement pratique et jugement spéculatif . . ." (cf. ch. 2, n. 50).

[6] "1. *Le* JUGEMENT SPÉCULATIF ABSOLU *ou 'purement spéculatif,' qui porte sur la vérité considéré en elle-même, sans aucun rapport, même possible, à l'opération; 2. le* JUGEMENT SPÉCULATIF D'ACTION, *qui a pour objet 'la vérité dans son rapport à l'oeuvre,' mais ne la considère encore 'que comme objet de connaissance, comme mesure et norme appréciative des moyens'; 'l'opérable y est considéré comme possible.' On peut songer à l'appeler 'spéculativo-pratique,' encore que A. Desroches y répugne; 3. le* JUGEMENT PRATIQUE, *qui a proprement pour objet la vérité pratique, c'est-à-dire la vérité 'prise par rapport à l'appétit droit . . . qui tend d'une façon impeccable à la fin de l'art, qui est l'oeuvre.'*" Art. cit., n. 5, pp. 361–362.

achieving a practical goal, they utilize statements without being completely committed to their speculative validity.

This same article includes an historical survey of recent discussion concerning the nature of the two judgments. We find there the opinions of Franzelin, Levesque, Crets, Clames, Pesch, Merkelbach, Lagrange, and Bea.

This line of thought, which we have named Benoit's, has undoubtedly made a great contribution, and has refined and nuanced the Leonine description considerably, bringing it closer to the psychological reality of literary creation. However, we still believe that the needs of the problem have not been entirely met, first, because the whole outlook gravitates too closely around the question of judgment, and secondly, because the operative or executive powers —so eminently creative in a poet—are assigned a negligible function. While recognizing, then, the value of these investigations, it seems that the time is ripe to essay another direction in the study of the problem, one that is more positive and more open to modern acquisitions in contiguous areas of research. That is to say, we would like to relate this problem to the study of literary creativity.

A Description Drawn from Literary Creation

We will proceed in this analysis first by elaborating a description of literary creation in general, basing ourselves on what writers themselves have said. Then we will attempt an application of this description to the biblical authors, again basing ourselves on what these authors have said and also on what their works can tell us.

Both stages in this investigation are liable to objection. In relation to the first stage, it might be pointed out that there is no "common doctrine" in this matter: There are only disparate testimonies whose selection and classification cannot result in a representative description. The second objection is more serious in that it denies that there is any parallel between an author in our culture and the men who wrote the Bible: The whole concept of "author" is so different that if the term is not equivocal, the analogy is too remote to be useful in an intellectual inquiry.

It is certainly true that the biblical authors are not romantic or modern poets. Their approach to literature is quite different.

Their composition often consists more in working with material already formed than in true creativity. The prophet is not concerned with his success as a literateur, but with announcing the message of God. And the biblical authors in general do not attempt to express their own personality or style in their work.

Let these differences be granted. Still, we do not think we have the right to exaggerate them; an analogy is still possible. Sometimes we wonder whether those who so vigorously deny any resemblance between literature in general and the Bible are not really trying to pacify their own consciences in order to leave themselves free to approach the biblical authors with an utterly unique set of criteria and methods; other investigators give the impression of possessing little appreciation of literary values. Whoever would maintain that the Old Testament contains no literature and no poetry has a rather unique concept of these realities.

Think for a moment of the Canticle of Canticles—or the smaller units which compose it; think of the Book of Job—minus its additions; or of the introduction to Ecclesiastes; or of some Psalm or page from the prophets. If, while reading these, our artistic sense is awakened, then the literary world in which they move cannot be so alien to our own. And as we study each work in turn, the spiritual affinity which we discover is quite sufficient justification for the analysis we are about to undertake. Then, too, we need only reflect on the distance between works which we include within the ambit of our own culture: The differences between the *Ars Poetica* of Horace and that of Verlaine are great indeed, yet no one thinks them insuperable.

An Artist with Language

Let us begin with a pen-sketch of an artist in our own culture. Usually, he is a man possessing a capacity to experience many things intensely. These experiences need not be specifically poetic; much of what he lives is shared by the lot of men: disappointment in love, for example. He is capable of deeply personal experiences and at the same time, by reason of some mysterious sympathy with men and things, he can enter into the experiences of others and relive them. Life itself breaks in to make its impact and set up these intense vibrations, but then, so does literature: An artist usu-

ally has a unique grasp of poetry. In art, a man gives himself up to
his experiences, admitting all their vividness and their pain.

> O ancient curse of poets!
> Being sorry for themselves instead of saying,
> forever passing judgment on their feeling
> instead of shaping it; forever thinking
> that what is sad or joyful in themselves
> is what they know and what in poems may fitly
> be mourned or celebrated. Invalids
> using a language full of woefulness
> to tell us where it hurts, instead of sternly
> transmuting into words those selves of theirs,
> as imperturbable cathedral carvers
> transposed themselves into the constant stone.
>
>   That would have been salvation. Had you once
> perceived how fate may pass into a verse
> and not come back, how, once in, it turns image,
> nothing but image, but an ancestor,
> who sometimes, when you watch him in his frame,
> seems to be like you and again not like you:
> you would have persevered.[7]

[7] "O alter Fluch der Dichter,
die sich beklagen, wo sie sagen sollten,
die immer urteiln über ihr Gefühl
statt es zu bilden; die noch immer meinen,
was traurig ist in ihnen oder froh,
das wüssten sie und dürftens im Gedicht
bedauern oder rühmen. Wie die Kranken
gebrauchen sie die Sprache voller Wehleid,
um zu beschreiben, wo es ihnen wehtut,
statt hart sich in die Worte zu verwandeln,
wie sich der Steinmetzeiner Kathedrale
verbissen umsetzt in des Steines Gleichmut.

"Dies war die Rettung. Hättest du nur EIN Mal
gesehn, wie Schicksal in die Verse eingeht
und nicht zurückkommt, wie es drinnen Bild wird
und nichts als Bild, nicht anders als ein Ahnherr,
der dir im Rahmen, wenn du manchmal aufsiehst,
zu gleichen scheint und wieder nicht zu gleichen:
du hättest ausgeharrt."
Rilke, from "Requiem for Wolf Graf von Kalckreuth." German text,
Sämtliche Werke, Insel-Verlag, 1955, vol. 1, p. 663. English translation by
J. B. Leishman, *Rainer Maria Rilke. Selected Works*, vol. 2, New York, 1960,
p. 209.

Recall, for instance, the complexity of Shakespeare, or Lope de Vega, the intensity of Antonio Machado or Donne, the self surrender of which Rilke speaks, or the sublime experience of St. John of the Cross, occasioned by a love poem. Though such people may seem to have something of the romantic about them, they are not all of this school of literature (none of the authors just mentioned is a romantic). Much of what is being written today, and many of the greatest classics, can lay claim to like intensity, complexity, sympathy, and self surrender—Petrarch or Fray Luis of Granada, for example—yet the same cannot be said of those exercises in imitation practiced by many notable writers, such as those responsible for the Petrarchism so prevalent in sixteenth century Europe.

Curiously enough, the artist, even as he abandons himself to the flood tide of his experience, remains somehow aloof from it, as though he had to divide himself in order to contemplate his own experience. To the entirety of the self-surrender there is opposed this distant vantage point from which the surrender is surveyed. The artist gives himself up to the intensity of love or pain as few men can, and yet he preserves a clear reflective consciousness of himself, observing himself in love or pain, and drawing from this quarry the stones for his trade. Rilke has magnificently described these aspects of an artist, and Thomas Mann has taken them as the theme for some of his stories: "Tonio Kröger" or "Tristan," for example. In some writers, this reflective distance is very great; it is a characteristic of the classical writers, but it can also be the sign of a self-scrutiny which is wholly modern. Then, again, as an artist views the experiences of others, he can keep too great a distance, replacing sincere sympathy with cold curiosity, and defensively erecting his vantage point into an unpitying egotistical security. However, a man must be somewhat detached from an experience, be it his own or another's, if he is to write of it.

A great artist begins with an intuition which forms the dominant life center and unifying principle of his work; such, for instance was the experience of a playwright such as Shakespeare or Calderón or the great Russian novelists. Poets, too, of lesser breadth, also begin with a dominating and unifying intuition: Keats, Juan Ramón, Valéry, etc.

Finally, the literary artist has the gift of language. Easily or painstakingly, he makes language serve him, harnessing it, or forging it to his task. The facility of Lope de Vega is in marked contrast with the struggles of Schiller; Tolstoy wrote *War and Peace* six times.

If we wish now to convert these four characteristics of linguistic artistry into a process, we should maintain the same order: experience, reflective vision, intuition, and execution. For the moment, let this schema (one more schema) rest at that, and let us look now at the other extreme in literary creation; not now at the massive geniuses, but rather at the honest craftsman of language with his modest poetic grace and unspectacular insights, and even at the craftsman copier who has not received the gift of poetry at all. There are times when even the greatest artist finds himself alone with his craft as his only resource; and it is at such times that creativity can begin from craftsmanship. Valéry can be our witness:

> The poet is awakened in a man by some unexpected happening, some event outside himself or within him: a tree, a face, a "subject," an emotion, a word. Sometimes it is the desire for expression which sets the thing in motion, a need to translate experience; but sometimes it is just the opposite, there is some fragment of style, some hint of expression which is searching for a cause, which seeks a meaning somewhere in my soul. . . . Note this possible duality: sometimes a thing wishes to be expressed, at other times a means of expression is looking for something to serve.[8]

SOME BIBLICAL EXAMPLES

With this preliminary information, let us undertake to explore the Promised Land of the Old Testament. We do not know if we will return with grape clusters the size of a man, or whether the complex terrain will overwhelm us. At any rate, it is worth the try.

---

[8] "*Le poète s'evéille dans l'homme par un événement inattendu, un incident extérieur ou intérieur: un arbre, un visage, un 'sujet,' une émotion, un mot. Et tantôt, c'est une volonté d'expression qui commence la partie, un besoin de traduire ce que l'on sent; mais tantôt c'est, au contraire, un élément de forme, une esquisse d'expression qui cherche sa cause, qui se cherche un sens dans l'espace de mon âme. . . . Observez bien cette dualité possible d'entrée en jeu: parfois quelque chose veut s'exprimer, parfois quelque moyen d'expression veut quelque chose a servir.*" Paul Valéry, *Oeuvres*, ed. by J. Hytier, Bibl. de la Pleiade, 1962, vol. 1, p. 1338.

A Great Poet

One of the most intense lyric pieces of the Old Testament is, undoubtedly, the poem of Hosea about his unfaithful wife.[9] Aside from some questions of detail, there is general agreement concerning the basic meaning of the poem, its substantial unity, and the power of its language. Everyone can appreciate, either immediately or on reflection, the powerful way in which marriage, the Promised Land, and the divine mystery are fused in the forge of his intuition.

One may question the possibility of reconstructing the creative process by which this poem came into being, but it will be worth the effort to try, availing ourselves of the narrative material in other chapters. Hosea appears to have been someone deeply in love with his wife; his love was strong, exclusive, and irrevocable, but his wife was unfaithful. He feels within him a deep, persistent pain which sinks down and lodges in his heart. Total love has become grief, and grief gives rise to anger, which, in turn, strives to turn into hate in order to dull the pain, but it cannot—this love refuses to be destroyed, it lives on memory and finally conquers. Now, up to this point in our reconstruction, Hosea is not yet a poet; he is only a husband who has been tragically deceived.

At some point, he succeeded in stepping back from himself, and looking at his pain. Perhaps he started to ask himself the reason for his grief, or perhaps he began to complain of a choice which he considers to have been made by God. In this atmosphere of heavy storm clouds, there is a sudden flash of blinding light and his experience is illumined from above; it becomes transparent and reveals in an instant its own deepest meaning. There now appears, not Hosea and his beloved, but God and His people, or, better, this very real experience of Hosea is seen to be a reflection and imitation of God's love for Israel. The prophet's experience had to be deep and painful if it was to convey any notion of the depth of the divine passion.

The insight was poetic: The prophet now feels the urge to transform his intuition into poetry so that in this form it will continue to have existence and reveal to others the love of God which he has discovered. So he sets himself to work, bringing to bear all his mas-

[9] Hos 1:2–3:5.

tery of language and his craftsman's patience: He listens to the sound of his words as he combines them; he measures the rhythm of his phrases; he elaborates his images with consistency; and he intensifies the dramatic movement of his piece, sustaining it up to the conclusion. As he works, he receives new insights which round out and support his original intuition, and as he manipulates words, his meaning becomes clearer, richer, and more delicately blended.

Hosea passes from the scene, but his poem remains. He knows that his poem is an oracle. He passes it on as the word of God, and it is as such that we receive it and read it.[10]

Accepting the above hypothesis as substantially correct, we can go on to ask the question: At what point did the motion of the Spirit begin to be operative? Pesch's remark that "Many times, poets are obliged to endure a cold sweat in their effort to clothe their thought fittingly," [11] does not adequately describe the process. This picture of a poet as a tailor seeking to outfit his ideas is a bit rationalistic. Poetry is not that kind of a sweatshop, or even a designer's salon.

What makes Hosea the author of his poem? The experience of life as such does not pertain to the creative process, except as preparatory for it; it provides the material for the poem. Literary activity has its true beginning in an intuition which provides the force and directive energy to the whole process in which it itself achieves objective existence. Thus, in our case we have to consider that the intuition of Hosea pertains to the realm of the charismatic: At this point, at least, the action of the Spirit must begin. The process which follows, in which intuition is given literary existence and solidity, transforming the preëxisting material into a poem, will then be dominated by this intuition under the influence of the charism.

The process of execution is a creative function: It is here that the powers of the poet in respect to language are acting in creative harmony:

---

[10] Even though it is not introduced by "Thus says the Lord," or something similar.

[11] ". . . ut exemplo sunt non soli poetae, qui saepe sudant et algent ad inveniendum vestitum aptum cogitationum suarum." No. 414.

. . . this state in which we are intimately affected, and in which all the properties of our language are indistinctly but harmoniously evoked.[12]

The error of many authors who treat of inspiration is found in the fact that they envisage the poem or the work to be written as already existing before it is given verbal form. This latter factor is considered quite secondary, and all that is demanded of it is that it be "apt." In poetry, and in literature more generally, the work only exists in its verbal expression; the central intuition becomes objective and communicable only in its literary realization, and the activity by which this existence is conferred characterizes a literary author or poet. (Let us recall here the words of Mallarmé: "Poetry is made with words.")

Obviously, then, we cannot place the specifically literary activity of the author outside the realm of inspiration. Neither can we decompose the process into a series of practical or speculative-practical judgments concerning the aptitude of a given literary formulation. We do not deny the existence of such judgments: Sometimes they are explicit and extend to the very last effort at expression; sometimes they are implicit, contained in the joy of a single, dazzling discovery. But we maintain that literary realization is greater than, and prior to, any such judgments. We cannot equate an intuition which contemplates its object with a speculative judgment which affirms explicitly or implicitly the truth of a proposition. The intuition may be accompanied by some tacit affirmation, "it is so"; but we find it difficult to reduce a poetic intuition to some form of speculative judgment.

The poetry of the Old Testament, at least a large portion of it, cannot be explained by the psychological description and its enumeration of various judgments; consequently, the charism in virtue of which it is inspired does not correspond to the schema proposed.

The example taken from Hosea has its limits as an hypothesis. For some centuries past, commentators, on account of a certain moral scrupulosity, have considered the matrimonial incident related by Hosea to be pure fiction—a species of allegory. Many

---

[12] "*Mais cet état de modification intime, dans lequel toutes les propriétés de notre langage sont indistinctement mais harmoniquement appelées, . . .*" Paul Valéry, *op. cit.*, n. 8, p. 1334.

modern commentators, however, accept the historicity of the fact, since it provides a psychological basis for the oracle. Others insist on what is called "symbolic action," which can be a real historical episode or merely pantomime. Even if we are inclined to see the action as symbolic, we believe that it is a genuine historical occurrence. Those who minimize the psychological factor do not hesitate to recognize the intensity of feeling present in the poem. This means that, though they deny the historical basis of Hosea's experience, they must by that very fact accord to him an extraordinary poetic capacity to enter into the experiences of others, and use them as the raw material for his own poetic creation.

A Simple Craftsman

Let us pass now from the great poet and prophet of love to an anonymous craftsman of a later date who had not a pennyworth of poetic temperament. He is a lover of the law, that law which is beginning to be an intermediary reality while at the same time maintaining its immediate link with God. It has occurred to our author to express his love and the glories of his beloved, the law, in verse. It will be a series of phrases which will convey the sense of totality and perfection. He has decided to use a stylistic artifice, an alphabetical acrostic which consists in beginning each verse with a letter of the alphabet. This technique had been used before in Hebrew literature: in a few Psalms, in the description of an "ideal wife," [13] and in the lamentations attributed to Jeremiah. In the lamentations, there are passages in which each strophe contains three verses, all beginning with the same letter. The author of our Psalm is going to surpass them all: In order to express the idea of plentitude, he will begin eight consecutive verses (seven plus one) with the same letter, which, multiplied by the twenty-two letters of the alphabet, gives to the "poem" a length of one hundred and seventy-six verses, each having six accents. Already the inspiration and proposal are not very poetic.

And so he sets to work: for the first strophe—the letter "aleph." This gives us two "happy's"; a conjunction, "but"; an adverb, "then"; a preposition, "to"; a pronoun, "you"; an interjection, "would that"; and a verb in the first person future, which in He-

13 Prv 31:10ff.

brew begins with aleph. Naturally, the first word sets the tone for the rest of the verse or hemistich, with the result that from verse to verse there is no continuity—only succession.

The first strophe succeeded in avoiding a superabundance of "filler words." The second strophe, beginning with the letter "beth," repeats the preposition *"be"* (with, in) six times, and adds one "blessed": He has not sweated unduly over this. The third strophe—the letter "gimel"—reads nicely: "Ideal," "open," "stranger," "consumed," "rebuke," "take away," and then concludes with two "indeeds." The fourth strophe—the letter "daleth"—has to resort five times to the word "ways."

Our author arrives at the fifth strophe, which has to begin with the letter "he." (In our Hebrew dictionaries, the letter "h" takes up but a few pages.) He counts on using *"hinne"* (behold, lo), which he saves for the last verse. He searches painstakingly, and finally resorts to a colorless artifice. There is in Hebrew a conjugation which in the perfect tense has as preformative *"ha."* This conjugation is called *"hifil,"* and it expresses the notion of causation. We will translate the initial word of each verse, using our English "make" as an auxiliary: "make me understand," "make me appreciate," "make me walk," "make my heart incline," "make my eyes turn away," "make your words firm," "make shame pass from me," and then "behold I desire your precepts." We ought to say in defense of the author that perhaps he did not have our outsider's awareness of verbal roots and conjugations; in any case, his literary activity consisted at this point in a hunt for "h's." Where, then, is the poetic inspiration? There is none. However, the charismatic inspiration must be present.

If someone were to read this last strophe with a theological preoccupation, he would be positively enthusiastic; the author has voiced a profound truth. With all his love for the Law, and with all his expressions of the desire to keep it, he has enunciated here the most important fact about the Law: that its observance is more the work of God than of man. These causative verbs are the proof of it: "make my heart incline," "make my eyes turn away," "make me walk," "make me appreciate that I might keep your law." . . . God not only gives commandments, but also the power, the grace, to keep them. This is the great theological lesson contained in this rather prosaic prayer.

But if we turn our attention back to the literary efforts of the author, we see that his intention was not so much to teach theology as to find "h's." How should we interpret this craftsman's work in terms of inspiration? In general, we would say that the initial idea of the acrostic form multiplied by the number eight occurred under the influence of the Spirit; the patient pedestrian realization of the idea was also directed by the Spirit in such a way that, as the author strove to compose his work, he received new insights with which he could express and develop his love for the law. This love was the remote material for his verses, the point at which it took on the nature of inspiration is found in his craftsman's choice of a literary form.

Someone wishing to use the description of Benoit or Desroches, would say that the Psalm began with a practical judgment or a speculative judgment concerning action, and that this initial judgment gave rise to and modified subsequent speculative judgments. But he should not neglect to complete Benoit's description, acknowledging the decisive importance of verbal realization as a truly formative factor in the process by which the work is composed. This factor must also be accorded a place within the influence of the charismatic motion of the Spirit.

Joining now these examples of the two extremes, Hosea and Psalm 119, we can better appreciate the words of Valéry, which are worth repeating here:

The poet is awakened in a man by some unexpected happening, some event outside himself or within him: a tree, a face, a "subject," an emotion, a word. Sometimes it is the desire for expression which sets the thing in motion, a need to translate experience; but sometimes it is just the opposite, there is some fragment of style, some hint of expression which is searching for a cause, which seeks a meaning somewhere in my soul. . . . Note this possible duality: sometimes a thing wishes to be expressed, at other times a means of expression is looking for something to serve.

This is the place to defend the Leonine description against the inhibiting strictures it has had to endure in some theological manuals. The Pope speaks of the sacred authors as "conceiving correctly in their mind," but this term "concept" is quite broad. It can refer to concepts which are clearly defined, or to a very general idea, or it can even refer to the "conceiving" of a literary work.

193

Why must we interpret this term in the encyclical as referring exclusively to concepts and judgments? In our description of the creative process in Hosea, the first thing "conceived" was an intuition from which grew the general plan of the work. There then followed an intermediary stage characterized by a movement toward its realization, and finally the actual execution by which the intuition was given verbal existence. This same amplitude can be accorded the other Leonine phrase, "aptly express," which can refer to the authentic literary contours given to the initial conception (the phrase which follows, "with infallible truth," need not be identical with "apt"). If the Pontiff's words are thus understood, we can place emphasis on this third stage of composition, leaving for a later moment the question of "writing."

A Tree

Here is a very likely example of the same process of intuition. Valéry, in his list of things which can touch off poetry in a man, puts "a tree" at the head of the enumeration. One morning, just before Spring, a prophet was walking in the countryside and suddenly came upon a tree already in flower. The sight of it suggested its name, and the prophet said it aloud. As he pronounces the word, its obvious etymology comes into his mind: the almond tree has a name in Hebrew which is derived from the word "to watch," because it seems to be so anxiously on the watch for Spring and ready to flower early. As he hears himself say the name, there is a flash of association: "the watching tree"—"God on the watch" (*maqqel shaqed—Yahweh shoqed*). The name of the tree resounds with the echoes of a higher reality: God watching in history to make good His word. The spark of intuition contained a transcendent analogy.

Jeremiah recognized the insight as a message from God, and set to work to transform it into a communicable form. For this purpose, he enlisted the aid of a device already known since the time of Amos,[14] and perhaps even topical in prophetic utterances:

> The word of Yahweh came to me:
> What do you see Jeremiah?
> I said:
> I am looking at a branch of the vigilant tree.

[14] Am 7.

194

And Yahweh said to me:
Well seen!
For I am keeping vigil over my word
bringing it to completion.[15]

As we have constructed it, the inspired process begins with a flash of insight, is followed by a movement or impulse to write, and finally is completed by the exercise of the writer's craft. The last step could hardly be called creative in this instance, since it consisted in "re-filling" a used formula.

We like to compare this example from Jeremiah with a *poema Castellano* by Antonio Machado Ruiz. As the poet walked along, his eyes rested on an elm tree: A ray of light passed through its dormant branches and somehow caught the color of a few tiny leaves just appearing on the tip of one of its shoots. In this tree, just about to regain its verdure, the poet sees the mystery of life itself with its Spring and its hope: the gray melancholy of the branches intimate the secret. He decides to record this discovery before the tree be cut down and disappear.

. . . . .
Elm tree, let me record on this paper,
the favor of your vernal branches.

My heart is looking
also, toward the light and toward reliving,
another miracle of springtime.[16]

And though the medium is more complex, the same intuition resounds in these lines of Hopkins:

Not of áll my eyes see, wandering on the world,
Is anything a milk to the mind so, so sighs deep
Poetry tó it, as a tree whose boughs break in the sky.

[15] Jer 1:11–12.
[16] ". . . . .
olmo, quiero anotar en mi cartera
la gracia de tu rama verdecida.

"Mi corazón espera
también, hacia la luz y hacia la vida,
otro milagro de la primavera."
Antonio Machado, "A Un Olmo Seco," *Poesías Completas*, Madrid, 1955, p. 169.

Say it is ásh-boughs: whether on a December day and furled
Fast ór they in clammyish lashtender combs creep
Apart wide and new-nestle at heaven most high.
They touch heaven, tabour on it; how their talons sweep
The smouldering enormous winter welkin! May
Mells blue and snow white through them, a fringe and fray
Of greenery: it is old earth's groping towards the steep
Heaven whom she childs us by.[17]

The poet of Castile and his English counterpart recognized in elms and ash boughs a human meaning in their cosmic mystery; the prophet from Anatoth, magnetized by his calling, saw divine meaning in an almond tree. The prophet couched his message in an accepted literary formulation of incisive brevity; the Spanish poet used the form of a "confession," revealing the state of his soul as it faced the vision of the elm tree; and the nineteenth-century English Jesuit adopted a sonnet form.

The Area of Probability

Our description of a walk in the countryside is a reconstruction. Perhaps the thought occurred while the poet looked out of the window. Some say that the flowering branch was really a staff made of almond wood (we don't know if the grain is that easily recognizable); even so, the role of the name "watching tree" remains, though its poetic resonances be somewhat diminished. Those who consider that the branch was seen in a vision or was only imagined, must still allow for the poetic role of its name. However, there is no need to have recourse to extraordinary visions when we know, for instance, that Jeremiah received an oracle while watching a potter at work (18:1ff.); and when there is the example of something as homespun as a boiling pot about to tip over (1:13ff.), we need not imagine a preternatural occurrence.

The example taken from Jeremiah provides us with a good illustration of the way in which the actual craft of poetry writing was profoundly influenced by tradition, and this may serve as a sample characteristic of most of the poetry of the Old Testament in which traditional forms and formulas played such a large role.

Jeremiah also tells us in his "confessions" of the interior impulse

[17] "Ash Boughs," *Poems of Gerard Manley Hopkins*, ed. W. H. Gardner, New York, 1959, p. 164.

he felt, which he could not restrain, driving him to give to the words he heard within himself an objective literary existence:

> You led me on, O Yahweh,
> and I let myself be led.
> You forced me, and you won.
> And I? —a laughingstock all day,
> sport for every passer-by.
>
> Whenever I speak, I shout Violence!
> Plunder is my cry.
>
> For Yahweh's word to me—
> scorn and derision all the day long.
> I said:
> I will not remember it,
> no more will I speak in his name.
> Then in my heart it turned to fire
> burning, imprisoned in my bones.
> I am weary holding it in,
> I can no longer.[18]

This reminds us of the "spiritual compulsion" which Stephen Spender avows in his article, "The Making of a Poem." [19]

In the poem of Jeremiah which we quoted above, he refers to his oracle as consisting of the word "Violence!" According to von Rad, this is the cry by which someone who is being oppressed demands protection or justice.[20] The role of the word in context can be variously explained: (1) It could be a summary of Jeremiah's message put here in this form for functional reasons. (2) It might be a germinal word, capable of being articulated in a full oracle, as for example in the oracle of the almond tree; a single cry becomes the seed of a whole poem, setting its tone and providing its theme. (3) It could be the oracle in its entirety; an elemental inspiration suggests but one word and causes it to be pronounced. In such a situation, intuitions and judgments in regard to literary realization count for nothing. The unadorned cry acquires its concrete mean-

---

[18] Jer 20:7–9.
[19] Cf. R. W. Stallman, *Critics and Essays in Criticism. 1920–1948*, New York, 1949.
[20] G. von Rad, *Genesis*, Philadelphia, 1961; cf. pp. 123, 187.

ing within the vital context of the people. We ought to note, of course, that such single-worded oracles were not left in their isolation in the collections of prophetic sayings as we have them, but this does not exclude the possibility of their existence in the prophetic preaching.

A Detail of Style

We are going to take a quick glance at the prophet Isaiah as he gives literary shape to a matrimonial litigation carried on between God and his people or his city. The exclamation *"ay"* could, in the instance we are studying, be said either, as *"ayka"* or *"ayk"* (which became in later pronunciation *"eka"* and *"ek"* respectively); Isaiah chooses the bisyllabic form. There are two words for city, *"ir"* and *"qirya"*: here he chooses the latter. In order to see the reason behind these choices, it will suffice to read out loud the following alternatives:

> 'ayk hayetá lezoná 'ír ne' maná
> 'ayká hayetá lezoná qiryá ne'maná.[21]

The reality of the verse, and consequently of the poem, is changed because of the emphatic fivefold rhyme scheme found in the second of the two lines. Here, if we wish to speak of a judgment, we must place it in the choice between stylistic alternatives (Marouzeau—style consists in choice). The verse is not a simple statement or a judgment of truth; it is a cry and a complaint uttered by God. The intelligible content is dissolved in the expressive utterance. If the poet chooses to give to the divine complaint a form in which there are two more rhymes than need have been, then this choice is inspired, because the total message is more impressive and more revealing in this heightened literary form. Intensity is a dimension of the spirit (Bruno Snell) which plays an important role in interpersonal communication and in literary language. We have to realize that the technique and the style of Isaiah were elaborated under the influence of the Holy Spirit, and that the resulting literary work in all its dimensions is an inspired message. We may note in passing how aptly this verse illustrates the manner in which literary language assumes and exploits the possibilities inherent in common language.

[21] Is 1:21.

Imitation in a Psalm

We are going to prescind for a moment from the origin of Psalm 29. The activating force in the poem is the experience of a storm which, in itself, is but the material for the work. In an overpowering experience of the tempest, a man perceived the awesome yet fascinating presence of God. The storm is to his symbolic intuition a theophany—a manifestation of God in power. This perception of transcendence is the igniting point of the poem. In order to give his intuition an objective existence, the poet chooses the form of a liturgical hymn, and this selection of form dominates the whole tenor of the piece, which appears as a communal song of praise. As he shapes the poem, the author stylizes the storm in a series of seven thunder claps, nouns which can almost be felt, and which are dynamic subjects for his phrases. These factors came to light as he strove to execute his poem in an *élan* of genuine creativity.

So far, this example seems to be exactly the same as that of Hosea. But there is a new factor. This Psalm is in all probability of Canaanite origin, and has been adapted by an inspired biblical author. The probable provenience of the Psalm poses a new question: Who is inspired? At what point in the process did the action of the Spirit begin, and in what terms are we to describe this action? We will attempt an answer.

The Hebrew author experienced a storm in a way very similar to his Canaanite predecessor. There need be nothing unusual in this, considering the fact that a storm is a common enough occurrence, and taking into account the symbolic thought context in which both minds moved. Seeking to objectify his experience, the biblical author recalls or finds this Canaanite Psalm whose aptitude he easily recognizes and on which he works, retouching it and making additions and changes. It is almost the same process which we saw in the case of the question-and-answer formula employed by Jeremiah: more imitative than creative, but no less inspired.

Or there can be another explanation: An Israelite poet reads this Canaanite Psalm and is deeply and sympathetically affected. The power of the poetic word, re-creating the event and manifesting its content, causes in the reader the same experience as that first had by the author, except that this time the intuition vibrates within

199

the context of a faith in Yahweh. There is continuity and communion between the two experiences insofar as the Israelite relived
the previous emotion and intuition; and there is a real transposition insofar as the religious meaning of the poem has been specified in a new significant context. As the Hebrew reader strives to
give form to the experience touched off by the poem, he finds that
the best medium is the poem itself, and in this phase of literary
execution, he adapts it to a new context of faith making use of the
name of God, and God's relation with His people. His adaptation
was a creative process in that it substantially modified the meaning
of the poem. This is not a thing which can be established statisti-
cally by counting the number of words he changed, but must be
appreciated by observing the resonances set up by replacing the
preëxisting word figure in a new context, most probably with a
marked economy of artifices. In this second hypothesis, we can locate the action of the Spirit in that moment when there was a
relived experience in a new key, and then in the fundamental
choice to repeat the previous poem, as well as in the actual technique by which it was adapted to a new religious purpose. Observe,
however, that we admit a religious plane common to both experiences.

This is, as a matter of fact, that which would distinguish our
example from another, whose process of transposition we can control quite closely: We refer to the poem about the shepherd boy by
St. John of the Cross. We now possess the original love poem
which served as his model; it does not really excel other poems of
its type and era. The mystic, whose whole life force was polarized
by the Lord Jesus, read the poem and felt a living flame. Seeking to
confer existence and a communicability to the fire he felt within
him, he took the poem, retouched it here and there, and transposed it to a completely new image-context. The result is astound-
ing:

> A shepherd lad was mourning his distress,
> Far from all comfort, friendless and forlorn.
> He fixed his thought upon his shepherdess
> Because his breast by love was sorely torn.
>
> He did not weep that love had pierced him so,
> Nor with self-pity that the shaft was shot,

Though deep into his heart had sunk the blow,
It grieved him more that he had been forgot.

Only to think that he had been forgotten
By his sweet shepherdess, with travail sore,
He let his foes (in foreign lands begotten)
Gash the poor breast that love had gashed before.

"Alas! Alas! for him," the shepherd cries,
"Who tries from me my dearest love to part
So that she does not gaze into my eyes
Or see that I am wounded to the heart."

Then, after a long time, a tree he scaled,
Opened his strong arms bravely wide apart,
And clung upon that tree till death prevailed,
So sorely was he wounded in his heart.[22]

A critic with a positivist turn of mind, before the original was discovered, suspected a similar process and sought to establish the

[22] "Un pastorcico solo está penado,
Ajeno de placer y de contento,
Y en su pastora puesto el pensamiento,
Y el pecho del amor muy lastimado.

"No llora por haberle amor llagado,
Que no le pena verse así afligido,
Aunque en el corazón está herido;
Mas llora por pensar que está olvidado.

"Que sólo de pensar que está olvidado
De su bella pastora, con gran pena
Se deja, maltratar en tierra ajena,
El pecho del amor muy lastimado,

"Y dice el Pastorcico¡ Ay, desdichado
De aquel que de mi amor ha hecho ausencia,
Y no quiere gozar la mi presencia,
Y el pecho por su amor muy lastimado!

"Y a cabo de un gran rato se ha encumbrado
Sobre un árbol do abrió sus brazos bellos,
Y muerto se ha quedado, asido de ellos,
El pecho del amor muy lastimado."

Text and translation taken from *The Poems of St. John of the Cross. The Spanish Text with a Translation by Roy Campbell*, New York, 1951, pp. 42–43.

lines of dependence for the verses of St. John of the Cross. Another critic, now that the model has been found, might see in it the complete explanation of the mystic's poem. He would go back to the "original," not bothering with the work of St. John since, for him, this is "a pure plagiarism with hardly an original detail." This critic, whom we have invented for the sake of illustration, has not entered into the poem: He has not understood it, and thus, of course, cannot explain it. He is forced to maintain that the work of St. John of the Cross has no interest for him. But genetic analysis and statistics are not the instruments by which poetry is detected. The example of St. John of the Cross illustrates a common literary procedure in Spain during *"el siglo del oro"* known as *"a lo divino,"* by which profane works were taken as the inspiration for other works "with a divine intention." The originals were at times quite pedestrian as literature, though at other times they possessed a certain poetic charm.[23]

St. John of the Cross effected a transposition from a profane level to one intensely religious by the analogy of love. This process sheds light on similar transpositions made by the biblical authors: For example, the chant of field workers—a love song—made expressive of God's love for his people (the song of the vineyard—Is 5:1–7), or a sentinel's song (Is 21:11–12), and most probably the love poem which we call the Canticle of Canticles, are the result of this type of transposition.

We do not doubt that in the case of Psalm 29, it is possible to isolate speculative judgments directed toward activity—concerning the aptitude of a Canaanite Psalm for the Israelite liturgy; and practical judgments—concerned with the adaptation necessary to effect this transposition. If the first judgment is explicit, the others are concomitant with the exercise of the technique required to realize it, and are thus consequent on the effort and the choice. However, we are not sure that this type of analytic dissection is particularly useful here, whereas the moments of conception and execution mentioned in the Leonine description when they are broadly interpreted can provide real insight.

---

23 Cf. Dámaso Alonso, *Poesía española. Ensayo de metodos y límites estilísticos,* Madrid, 1950, pp. 256–258.

A Narration

The story of the ten plagues in the Book of Exodus[24] is not a lyrical composition, nor does it burst forth from an intensely lived experience; it is a narrative of epic proportion, manifesting a calculated process of composition. No one can reasonably doubt that the author of the story as we now have it utilized preëxisting narrative material, some of which was contained in the Yahwistic account, while other elements pertained to the Priestly tradition. Some of the plagues were duplicated in these two compositions, others varied in their telling, and still others were simply diverse. The role of the personages involved, the tenor of the refrains used, as well as some other fixed formulas, were also different in the "J" and "P" traditions. But this does not matter: Our author took the two versions as the basis and source for his own composition. He chooses the number ten, because it is a simple figure on which to structure a story, and because of its capacity to signify seven plus three. The first and second plagues finish ambiguously; the third is decisive— "The finger of God is here." The fourth plague begins a mounting wave of affliction which subsides at the sixth plague, in order to prepare for the solemn entrance of the seventh: a theophany, which is announced in sonorous tones and culminates in the confession, "I have sinned." The eighth plague is preceded by a new prologue, announcing God's intentions and initiating a fresh series of calamities and concessions which culminate in the slaying of the first-born. We will not stop here to point out other ways in which the differences in the two preëxisting accounts are smoothed out or covered over (not always successfully). The final result is an epic narration of dynamic composition which, as such, is the work of the last author. (We presume, of course, that no one will equate "epic" with "pure fiction.")

In this instance, the most creative activity of the author lay in his work of composition, since the material and the formulas were already given. The execution was subordinated to a predetermined structure, and the whole was permeated by an epic tone which was intended to reveal the grandeur of the divine activity. We must, then, situate the impulse of charismatic inspiration within the whole process of composition from the very first choice of a struc-

[24] Ex 7–12.

ture until the whole work was realized. It is not difficult to describe this case in terms of speculative and practical judgments, or, indeed, in terms of conception and execution.

SUCCESSIVE INSPIRATION

The last example which we have just considered is of special importance, because many parts of the Old Testament as it has come down to us were composed in much the same way. The explanation of these passages forces on us a question which could be phrased like this: Are the preëxisting formulas and materials inspired, or is only the last stage of composition, the canonical text, inspired?

This is the question of "successive inspiration." Back in the time when Pesch and others were writing their manuals, it was possible to envisage the process of composition as having taken place in a way similar to our modern experience. Moses wrote his Pentateuch, Isaiah wrote his book, etc. But such thinking is untenable today. Many books of the Bible were composed in successive stages of literary creation: There were the traditions of local cult shrines, the composition of the Yahwist, the Elohistic variant on the same theme, the Priestly account with its cultic and legal interest, the various redactions and combinations of the above and other traditions; there were *"chansons de geste,"* both secular and religious, collected in larger groups, unified on the basis of a religious theme, and rounded out by some passages of theological reflection (the Book of Judges); there were additions made to bring a text "up to date" (the last lines of Psalm 51); the insertion of the name "Judah" in oracles first addressed only to Israel is a commonplace. We find such procedures as the collection in a new dynamic unity of three oracles which were at first separate and of slightly different intent (as in Is 8); and so forth.

Must we imagine the Holy Spirit standing by with arms folded watching the whole process and then, just at the very last minute, stepping in to "inspire" the final stage of composition? Are we obliged to consider only the collector, or editor, or corrector as inspired? Ought we then to think that "inspiration" was only operative in the later period of Jewish history, between the Exile and the time of Esdras?

Such questions, obviously, answer themselves. A theory of inspiration so meager that it shuts out the Holy Spirit during the most creative moments in the composition of a work and then opens the door when there is practically nothing left to do, seems to us quite unacceptable. We are obliged to allow for some form or other of "successive inspiration" in order to explain the facts and apply the principles correctly. Wherever there is a real literary and religious contribution, there the Spirit acted. At the level of profane composition of non-Israelite origin, it is not necessary to invoke the charism of inspiration, and the same is true of a level of simple collection with no literary contribution. The books of the Bible grew along with the life of the people, and the Holy Spirit, far from looking on indifferently, was active in this process of growth and concomitant literary activity, breathing into it mysteriously yet powerfully.

Grelot treats this question by distinguishing three types of charisms which are related: (1) the prophetic charism in the Old Testament and the apostolic charism in the New Testament for the proclamation of the word of God; (2) the functional charism of language, by which the proclaimed word is preserved, elaborated, and developed; (3) the literary charism of language, by which the results of the former are fixed in written form. These three charisms all have relation to the word, that is, to language, but in varying degrees; the last mentioned is the least intense, but nonetheless essential in the constituting of the "Sacred Book." [25]

The Tone of a Work[26]

The example we gave above of the story of the plagues in Egypt suggests some other considerations. We spoke there of an "epic tone," which in the poet was an attitude of soul in the presence of his theme, and in the work was its unifying structure. We can attribute to this "tone," as a subjective attitude of the author, a creative function, because of its influence over the whole of the execution of the work in its structure and unity. If this attitude is not to be identified with the initial intuition, it certainly flows easily from

[25] Cf. the article of P. Grelot referred to above (ch. 2, n. 14).
[26] On the question of literary "tone," cf. W. Kayser, *Das sprachliche Kunstwerk*, Berne, 1948, esp. the last part of the book.

it, and as such must be considered to be under the influence of the Spirit.

The author of the Book of Judith envisaged his protagonist in an "heroic tone," while the tone of gentle irony pervades the characterization of Jonah. Joel (1:17–18) hears the bellows of the starving cattle with a compassion that is almost lyric. The tone of drama is felt in Nahum's contemplation of Nineveh's fall (2), or in the Book of Daniel's description of the scene in Belshazzar's dining hall where an empire changed hands (5).

The attitude or "tone" of soul on the part of the author determines the way in which the work is concretized as it receives its objective existence; in turn, the work determines the "tone" which the sympathetic reader will derive from it. For this reason, the tone of a biblical work assumes an important function as revelation, one which is at times as important as the thing being told. We find it very difficult to reduce this attitude or tone to any kind of "judgment," yet we cannot imagine that such an important factor could lie outside the influence of the charism of inspiration.

The New Testament

The New Testament presents us with less variety. The Gospels began to acquire their consistency in a stage of oral tradition which was nevertheless Gospel. It was at this stage that they received many of their literary forms: There were larger units of composition such as the Passion narrative, and smaller unities which can be discerned because of the similarity of their structure: miracle stories, conflict stories, parables, etc. All of this provided the preëxisting material for the evangelists in their original work of literary composition.[27]

The literary efforts of the evangelists were profoundly personal contributions, and that is why each of them offers us a picture of Christ which is different yet complementary. They retain many of the forms and phrases which were found in the material that lay

[27] In regard to the formation of the Gospels, cf. X. Léon-Dufour, *Les Évangiles et l'Histoire de Jésus*, Paris, 1963; V. Taylor, *The Formation of the Gospel Tradition*, New York, 1957; C. Dodd, *The Apostolic Preaching and its Development*, 1st ed., London, 1936; J. R. Scheifler, *Así nacieron los Evangelios*, Bilbao, 1964. The bibliography and notes in this latter work are especially valuable.

before them, imposing on it a higher unity deriving from an overall narrative schema and theological interpretation. Without a doubt, the literary work of the evangelists was inspired from the moment of the original intuition or intention which grew out of a personal understanding of Christ, until the last patient touches of redaction. It is not as certain that the previous stages of composition were inspired, but considering the extent of the influence that this stage had on the later literary Gospels, it seems reasonable to suppose that the successive elaborations of the material which later became the Gospels was inspired also.

The letters are in large measure doctrinal with parenetic material interspersed. Often, they give literary stability to formulas which were part of the apostolic preaching, thus posing for us the problem of where to place the emphasis in an analysis of their compositions: Is it in their writing or in their speaking? (we will treat of this problem in Chapter 9). The first Epistle of St. Peter is presented as a collaborative undertaking: "I write you this brief appeal through Silvanus, our trusty brother" (5:12). It appears as though the work of Silvanus was more than secretarial, and that he played a real role in the framing of the inspired message, which means, of course, that he was also inspired. The Epistle to the Hebrews seems to be a homily approved and recommended by St. Paul; but we cannot imagine that inspiration began with his "subsequent approval." The letters, especially of St. Peter and St. Paul, incorporate material found in the ancient liturgy. They refer to "spiritual canticles" (Eph 5:19; Col 3:16), and even quote from early hymns (Phil 2:5–11), or professions of faith (1 Cor 15:3ff.).

The New Testament has effected an immense work of transposition in which the Old Testament is placed within the new context of the Christ-fact. There is more here than the simple application of a few explicit prophecies, or the attempt to elucidate others that are more obscure; nor is it merely a question of the homiletical, theological, or pastoral use of a few passages from the ancient writings. The whole of the Old Testament is seen in the light of the glory shining on the face of Christ Jesus that transforms and elevates it by conferring on it a fullness of meaning which crowns its insights and tendential aspirations with a perfect but unsuspected plentitude. The new context is charged with transforming power. The original sense of the text is not denied but is rather transposed by its new context, being caught up in a dynamic movement and sharing a higher life. Thus, the Old Testament, to use Origen's favorite theme, becomes Gospel.

Once the Logos had touched them, they raised their eyes and saw only Jesus, no one else. Moses, the law, and Elijah, prophecy, had become one thing; they had become one with Jesus who is the Gospel. And so things are not as they were before; there are no longer three, for these three have become one Being.[28]

This transposition was effected by Christ, first of all by the very fact of His Incarnation, and then by His words which conveyed His own mystery and explained it. We see Him at Nazareth proclaiming: "Today in your hearing, this text has come true" (Lk 4:21); we hear Him explain, "but let the Scriptures be fulfilled" (Mk 14:49), and in a special way after the Resurrection, when "He began with Moses and all the prophets and explained to them the passages which referred to Himself in every part of the Scriptures" (Lk 24:27). It is not quite exact to say that the Church received the Bible directly from the Synagogue. The Bible was given to the Church by Christ, and all the apostles, fathers, doctors, and saints of the Church have understood and followed this example.

This transposition of meaning, this filling with meaning, is a true literary activity, one which Lohfink calls the "hagiographical act." [29] It is an activity by which literary form is given to a new and mysterious reality that completes the meaning of the older texts by joining them in a transcedent unity toward which they tended, but which they could never attain or demand. If this view is cor-

---

28 Ἀγγὰ μετὰ ἀφὴν τοῦ λογοῦ, τοὺς ὀφθαλμοὺς ἐπαράντες εἶδον Ἰησοῦν μόνον, καὶ οὐδένα ἄλλον. Ἕν μόνον γέγονε Μωϋσῆς ὁ νόμος καὶ Ἡλίας ἡ προφητεία Ἰησοῦ τῷ Εὐαγγελίῳ. καὶ οὐχ ὥσπερ ἦσαν πρότερον τρεῖς οὕτω μεμενήκασιν, ἀλλὰ γεγόνασιν οἱ τρεῖς εἰς τὸ ἕν. "On Matthew, t. 12, 43," PG 13, 1084.

The same thought is expressed in a slightly different way in his sixth homily on Leviticus:

"Doceat te Evangelium, quia cum transformatus esset in gloriam Jesus, etiam Moyses et Elias simul cum ipso apparuerunt in gloria, ut scias quia lex et prophetae, et Evangelium in unum semper conveniunt, et in una gloria permanent. Denique et Petrus cum vellet eis tria facere tabernacula, imperitiae notatur, tanquam qui nesciret quid diceret. Legi enim, et prophetis, et Evangelio non tria, sed unum est tabernaculum, quae est Ecclesia Dei." "Hom 6 in Lev," PG 12, 468.

29 In art. cit. (cf. ch. 6, n. 11).

rect, then the activity by which the fullness of meaning is conveyed was performed under the action of the Holy Spirit, and the necessity for a "spiritual understanding" of the Old Testament follows ineluctably.

SYNTHESIS

Now that we have seen the variety existing in the ways and results of literary activity, we would like to propose another schema, intended as complementary to those which we have already seen. It has three levels: the material, the intuition, and the execution.

(1) *The Material of a Literary Work.*

The stuff of which literature is made is living experience—one's own or another's—which has been appropriated. It may be a single vivid occurrence, or a series of events which accumulate in the consciousness with the rhythm: experience—reflection. The material that a novelist uses can be the experience of his own life, or it can be the life around him which he considers or discovers; it can come directly from life, or through the medium of something which is read. This material can be theoretical knowledge, or a series of facts, or some preëxisting literary elaboration.

Strictly speaking, the material does not pertain to the creative process, and has interest only because of its relation to the future literary work, insofar as it is transformed by the productive activity of the writer. It is in this light that we should view the biblical events, the court records, the preëxisting profane literature, etc. These things may exist as the result of a special action of God; they may be instances of a divine intervention in history, but they are not yet the object of the charism of inspiration.

(2) *The Intuition.*

At times, the light of understanding comes only after a long and painful period of gestation, and then in a flash, the formless mass of our experiences takes shape, and we see the results of our searching. At other times, the intuition comes suddenly, without any awareness of a period of preparation, and our soul is held, as it were, in suspense. We experience the insight as something unsuspected, imperative, or serene, which fills us with a sense of light and the joy of discovery. It may be that we have caught the message of a symbol, or perhaps some analogy reveals a new dimension of reality.

This intuition becomes the life center, activating and illuminating the whole process to follow. It is what Stephen Spender calls the initial idea, it is masculine or germinal. Proust has pointed out how intuition precedes the work of the intellect, and Virginia Woolf has stressed its unifying power; it is itself simple. Pirandello, in a memorable passage, describes how, as he was at grips with some personalities which had presented themselves to his imagination, there came to him an intuition which shed light on the whole complex and was the seed of his *Six Characters in Search of an Author*. Writers are all in accord in assigning intuition as the true starting point for a work, and as the catalytic energy which fuses preëxisting material.

If the biblical authors have this in common with their literary counterparts, then we must maintain that this intuition in them takes place under the influence of inspiration, and that it manifests a reality, though not in propositional form. There must, of course, be some latitude allowed for variation in the intensity and extent of these germinal intuitions. The Bible is not a collection of nothing but masterpieces.

(3) Execution.

Consequent on the intuition, there may occur an impulse, felt as an inner necessity, to write or to compose. Goethe speaks of some poems which occurred to him all of a sudden, and demanded to be composed without delay with such insistence that he felt an instinctive or hypnotic force impelling him to write immediately.

This interior urge sets the whole process of execution in motion. It is directed toward an activity which the writer performs in regard to language; that is to say, the whole process by which the "poetic idea," or seed, or intuition is made objective, is ordered from the very moment of its inception toward language.

We ought not to consider language as some lifeless stone; it is a medium possessing a certain capacity to work along with the artist. By language we mean, as we said before, not merely the dictionary and the grammatical dimension of words, but the whole complex of possibilities and resonances assembled in a given linguistic entity.

But language can also present to the writer an aspect of resistance. Anyone can appreciate this quality of language who has tried to translate poetry, while maintaining the force and shades of the original. But even when we compose in our own language, we can encounter this resistance which will give rise either to a sense of challenge or to a "lapidary style," in which language is treated like a stone. When certain poets complain that their poem does not correspond to their interior vision, it is possible that, apart from the exaggerations of the romantics, they are referring to this resistance of language which has not been overcome by their intuition and technique. This is true not only of poetry or literature, but even didactic treatises can experience the intractability of words, thwarting the attempt of a teacher to hit upon the right formulation. Pesch speaks of this common experience in his discussion on the psychology of inspiration:

Someone can have the intention to write, and know what he wants to write, and still hesitate and labor in order to find the right expression of what he wants to say. This is true not only of poets who sweat and shiver in order to find apt clothing for their thought, but also of other writers who, after having removed all doubt as to what they want to say, still often cannot find the right way to say it, except after a long series of attempts, and then not infrequently in later editions they say the same thing in different words.[30]

Pesch does not sufficiently consider the act of expression as a creative element in composition. But to a large extent, the talent of a writer is found precisely in the art of expression. We do not readily accept the excuses of a bad writer who makes appeal to his profound and genial intuitions.

Actually what a writer does, is to transform his material, the world and his experience, into an organic significant system com-

[30] "*Potest aliquis velle scribere et scire, quid scribere velit, et interim anxius haerere et laborare de elocutione rerum scribendarum, ut exemplo sunt non soli poetae, qui saepe sudant et algent ad inveniendum vestitum aptum cogitationum suarum, sed etiam alii scriptores, qui saepe omni dubitatione iam remota de rebus, quae dicendae sint, modum dicendi convenientem non inveniunt nisi post multa tentamina, et in posterioribus editionibus easdem res non raro aliis verbis exprimunt.*" No. 414.

posed of words. This takes place by an act of language in which all the possibilities and resonances of language collaborate.

In the process of giving expression, new intuitions occur and are subordinated, and other, lesser insights are gained; but sometimes a greater intuition arises, dethroning and enlisting the former, and the work takes a new direction.

This collaboration of language in the act of realizing a work stands out clearly in writers who have a great sensitivity for language. Such men—trained perhaps in philology—have a feeling for the roots of words, and are often able to pass from a verbal analogy to one that is ontological.

At the end of the process, which may have been easy or painful, direct or intricate, the finished work emerges. It contains the preëxisting material in a different mode of being. It confers on the intuition an objective existence, though not enunciating it by way of proposition, and the work of execution, either manifest or hidden, receives stability.

An attentive analysis of the biblical writings sometimes reveals to us the work of execution. We do not know if it came easily to the writers, or if it cost them something, but the fact is there. These men labored over a language they had received and allowed it to come to their aid. Sometimes they capitalized on the sound of its words; sometimes they employed the alternating rhythm of parallelism to convey a sense of balance; sometimes they quickened the rhythm in order to concentrate their message.[31] All of this labor must be seen as having taken place under the motion of the Holy Spirit, for it is mainly here that we find the charism. The role of the sacred writers consisted in transforming into a significant word-system the history of the people, their own personal experiences, the insights they received from God, the meaning of history, the works of salvation, the response of the people of God. . . . Inspiration is a charism of language, and language is forged at this stage of literary production. There is no problem in imagining two expressions of the same thing, both inspired, and one better than the other; they can even be from the same author, and indeed often are.

Before this stage of activity, the word does not exist, there is no word of God. It is in this process of expression that the word is

[31] We have treated this aspect, with many illustrative analyses, in *Estudios de Poética Hebrea*, Barcelona, 1963.

realized, and if the Bible is the word of God, it is because He has directed this process. The being of the words is their signification or meaning, and the being of the work is in the system of significant words. In the word of the Bible, revelation is present and available—it is the meaning of the words. We have avoided here using the expression "revelation is contained" in the words. Such terminology tends to make one think that there is some real distinction between the word as receptacle and the meaning as its content. But this is false; the meaning is realized in the word, and the being of the word is its meaning. Otherwise, it is nothing but fruitless sound.

The motion of the Spirit hovers over the language act of the sacred writer, and makes of it an act of revelation. The context of the Spirit and the context of the Logos—these two, which are united ontologically, meet here again at the term of our analysis.

Postscript

There are some who would not wish to see this chapter conclude without a more detailed discussion of the operation of the faculties which collaborate in the process of execution. But such a discussion would be interminable. There would have to be some treament of the sense of rhythm which plays such a large part in some passages, and which can register the most delicate shade of emotions; then there is the question of phonetics—the role of sound and tone in literary expression; we would have to enter into the question of imagination as creative and imitative, for this is essential in poetry. There should also be some consideration for the discernment of various shades and resonances of meaning, as well as an attempt to assess the various semi-conscious factors which find expression in a literary work.

It will be sufficient and briefer to invoke the principle of Benoit with regard to the analogous nature of inspiration: The charismatic influence extends to all the faculties according to their specific function in literary activity. To complete this statement, we will only add that this functioning is not parallel, but organically interrelated, and thus the charismatic influence should be conceived as central and all-pervasive.

Bibliography for Chapter 7

The Psychology of Inspiration

The Description Given by Benoit. It is probably best to begin with Benoit's most recent article, "Révélation et Inspiration," *RB* 70, 1963, pp. 321–370. (See *Aspects of Biblical Inspiration* translated by J. Murphy-O'Connor and S. K. Ashe, Chicago, 1965.) His other works are referred to there and the positions they set forth modified and clarified. The first part of the article, "Revelation and Inspiration According to St. Thomas" is dedicated to giving a more ample and flexible view of the Angelic Doctor's thought. The second part, "Revelation and Inspiration in the Bible," is also marked by a suppleness of treatment in regard to the sacred text. The third part, "Criticism and Suggestions in regard to the Modern Discussions," terminates the work and attempts to interpret the data in the light of the categories of speculative and practical judgment. The work of A. Desroches, *Jugement pratique et jugement spéculatif chez l'Ecrivain inspiré*, Ottawa, 1958, is a thesis of one hundred and forty pages. Its orientation is descriptive, its documentation meager. There is also the very competent thesis of Denis Farkasfalvy, *L'inspiration de l'Ecriture Sainte dans la théologie de Saint Bernard*, Studia Anselmiana, no. 53, Rome, 1964.

An Artist with Language. Since this aspect of the psychology of inspiration is seldom treated at length in manuals, the bibliography will be somewhat ample in order to familiarize readers with the names and opinions most current in this field. Monographs on inspiration have sometimes attempted to describe the psychology of inspiration: H. Lusseau in his *Essai sur l'inspiration scripturaire*, Paris, 1930 (a thesis defended in 1928), dedicates a chapter to this topic before discussing the description of *Providentissimus Deus*; it consists of thirteen pages. Among the authors cited, one finds Pesch, Billot, Schiffini, and St. Thomas; there is a citation from Boileau, and Pascal is also represented, along with some nineteenth-century French orators. A. Desroches in his work also dedicates a chapter to the psychology of the literary author (pp. 107–123). His authorities are Cajetan, St. Thomas, John of St. Thomas, and Aristotle. There is one quote from Chateaubriand, one from Maritain, and two from Longhaye. Such a method is simply insufficient. In order to discuss this question properly, we must begin from a wider experience of literature and techniques of composition. It would be impossible to cite all the authors who have exercised some influence on the ideas which we propose in the "Description Drawn from Literary Creation." The purpose of the enumeration which follows is, as we have said, to provide a point of departure for those who wish to study this aspect of the problem more fully.

From a philosophical point of view, the question of creativity has been studied only recently. The essays of Heidegger, mentioned in the bibliography of Chapter 5, are an interesting beginning. There is a good article by Carl Hausman, "Spontaneity: Its Rationality and Its Reality," in *IPQ* 4, 1964, pp. 20–47, in which there is a review of the opinions of Whitehead, Husserl, Hartmann, etc.; the bibliographical material in the footnotes is also valuable. J. Maritain in *Creative Intuition in Art and Poetry*, New York, 1953, treats of this theme in Thomistic categories (on Thomism's effort to account for the fact of poetry, cf. Curtius, *European Literature and the Latin Middle Ages*, p. 227). Maritain writes from his own experience as an author, and with a real sympathy and familiarity with poetry. The most important chapter for the topic which interests us here is ch. 4, "Creative Intuition and Poetic Knowledge." In the same tradition, but harder to follow, is the little study by T. Gilby, *Poetic Experience* (Essays in Order, no. 13), New York, 1934; ch. 9, "Presence," is especially good.

It is very important in a study of artistic creation to consult the statements of artists themselves, and in this regard we are fortunate to have good material in English. Brewster Ghiselin in *The Creative Process*, New York, 1955, collects the testimony of mathematicians (Poincaré, Einstein), musicians (Mozart), painters (van Gogh, Picasso), sculptors (Moore), and various literary authors. Charles Norman in *Poets on Poetry*, New York, 1962, presents the views of sixteen different English-speaking poets on their art; not all of these speak of the creative process, but all make interesting reading; the same can be said of the collection of essays in *The Limits of Language*, compiled by W. Gibson, New York, 1962, which includes in part 2, "Consequences of the Problem, Testimony from Artists and Writers"—articles written by Sartre, Virginia Woolf, Wallace Stevens, etc. There are four other excellent studies of the same type: H. Block and H. Salinger, *The Creative Vision. Modern European Writers on their Art*, New York, 1960; W. Allen, *Writers on Writing*, New York, 1948 (the essays here are all good and they are organized with great perception. We have used this book a great deal). M. Cowley, *Writers at Work*, New York, 1959 (a series of interviews, treats of the techniques of composition); and John W. Aldridge, *Critiques and Essays on Modern*

Fiction. 1920–1951, New York, 1952, which contains a wealth of valuable material, and a good bibliography: under part 2, ch. 2, "Writers on their Craft," there are fifty-six titles listed, and under part 3, ch. 3, "The Artist and the Creative Process," there are eighty-nine books and articles listed.

There are some good works that treat of creativity by an analysis of the works and the artists who produce them: A. Maurois, *The Art of Writing*, New York, 1960; Wallace Fowlie, *Jacob's Night*, New York, 1947. P. Valéry discusses both aspects in the series of essays which make up *The Art of Poetry*, New York, 1961; cf. especially "Problems of Poetry."

8. The Author and the Community:
The Sociology of Inspiration

We have often spoken of "the inspired author," presupposing that the inspired writers were individual authors. But is this not a modern idea of literary production, one that is inapplicable to the period and mentality of the biblical authors? According to some, we ought to speak of an inspired people rather than inspired authors. Inspiration would be a charism commonly held, a great wind which sweeps and whirls through the land of Palestine. To speak of inspired authors is to dole out the Spirit with a medicine dropper; the Spirit animates the whole of the Chosen People, all of the body of the Church. This is how we must view the Bible; it is the work of a whole people.

This idea, though still quite imprecise, is current in some circles today, and this invites us to treat of it explicitly under the somewhat simplified heading, "The Sociology of Inspiration."

SCHLEIERMACHER

The precursor of this theory seems to have been Friedrich Schleiermacher. The father of semi-rationalism also has some things to say about the Holy Spirit. According to him, the Holy Spirit is the spirit of the community: this is a thoroughly romantic concept, one enshrined in the magic word "*Geist*." It suffices to recall with what enthusiasm the romantics listened to the "spirit" of a people; Herder (a pre-romantic) studied the "spirit" of Hebrew poetry; Humboldt sought out the "spirit" of various languages. The Holy Spirit of the Church is the religious spirit which it has received from Christ, which is an arational impulse. Christ has "in-spirited" into the Church the true religious spirit, and in this sense has inspired all its activity, including the writings of its holy books. The historical writings are inspired in that the community recognizes itself and its deeds in them, and directs the conservation of its records. This is said of the New Testament: as for the Old Testament, only some fragments are inspired, because the Spirit is somehow there, even though it had not yet become fully defined as the common spirit of the Church.

We should note these two points: the spirit of the community activates, inspires literary activity; and the spirit of the community recognizes and expresses itself in narratives. So far, we have seen only the social dimension of the problem.

Schleiermacher goes on to coördinate the social factor with the personal factor: the Spirit of Christ was received by the apostles, and they are the ones who form the spirit of the community. All the activity of the apostles as individuals was inspired, and this includes their literary activity. Thus, the two factors, social and personal, are coördinated.[1]

In criticizing Schleiermacher, we should note first of all that we cannot conclude that an idea is automatically ridiculous or false, because derived from a romantic origin or context. Schleiermacher tried to find a compromise between the rationalism prevalent in his time and the Christian world outlook; thus, some of his ideas can be purified from error and transposed to a Catholic key, as has already been recognized by the theologians of the school of Tübingen.[2] For we, too, believe that the Holy Spirit animates the Church as a body; however, we do not go on to identify the Person of the Holy Spirit with communal feeling.

FORM CRITICISM

At the beginning of the century, the sociological outlook began to penetrate into the exegesis of the Old Testament. Pedersen wrote a

---

[1] But, of course, his refusal to admit that the Holy Spirit is a Person of the Trinity is unacceptable. We can not admit his explanation of the Spirit as something merely human and social, which is participated in by the individual. It is this humanism of Schleiermacher which irritates Karl Barth so much.

[2] Cf. P. Dausch, *Die Schriftinspiration. Eine biblisch-geschichtliche Studie,* Freiburg, 1891, esp. [tr.] "The Catholic School at Tübingen," pp. 186–192.

book on the social life of Israel, *Israel. Its Life and Culture*,[3] which rescued the Old Testament from intellectual rarefaction and placed it within the life of the people. Hermann Gunkel with his famous formula, "*Sitz im Leben*," sought and found the social situations which acted as origin and medium of transmission for many literary types, the cultic context of many of the psalms, for example. Neither Pedersen nor Gunkel gave any formal consideration to the problem of inspiration. In fact, Gunkel rejected the idea explicitly: "The pretty myth of inspiration has already vanished." Nevertheless, the social dimension of the Bible had been firmly established.

From Gunkel, the burden of the labor passed to the New Testament, due to the work of four pioneers: Dibelius, Bultmann, K. L. Schmidt, and Bertram. According to them, the synoptic Gospels are not the work of the evangelists—secondary redactors of minor importance, but of the whole Christian community, stimulated by the challenge of its various activities and needs.[4]

The words and deeds of Jesus, or those attributed to Him, are collected in stereotyped formulas which originated in and were transmitted by various specific "life-situations" (*Sitz im Leben*), which determined the form or pattern which the pericope or saying would take (form criticism). The community is creative and literarily active, and thus it is pointless to seek out the author of each literary unit: many have collaborated, and there are many authors. The most that can be done is to distinguish the Palestinian community from the Hellenistic community. The community in its cult effected the apotheosis of Christ, and thus from the cult, later on, there was derived the dogma of the divinity of Jesus (Bertram); the community in its missionary activity recounted or invented miracles in order to strike back at the propaganda used by the Hellenistic cults; the community placed on the lips of Jesus the solutions to problems it was experiencing.

This is not the place for an extensive criticism of such a theory, which has its origins in the writings of Durkheim, except to men-

[3] Foto reprint with additions, New York, 1959.
[4] A particularly clear exposition of this question can be found in Ed. Schick, *Formgeschichte und Synoptikerexegese. Eine kritische Untersuchung über die Möglichkeit und die Grenzen der formgeschichtlichen Methode*, Neutestamentliche Abhandlungen, no. 18, Münster, 1940. Other works are listed below in the bibliography.

tion that the theories of the French philosopher entered late into the study of the New Testament, long after they had been discredited in other areas of thought.

There is, however, in the theory an element of truth which is accepted and adopted in Catholic study of the New Testament, namely, the fact that the material worked on by the synoptic authors has its roots within the life, thought, and worship of the early community, and that it came to them, at least in some instances, already possessing a literary form. But the community here envisaged was organized and not a formless mass; it was governed by responsible leaders, and still possessed some early witnesses to the things which were being recorded. Lately, there has been a tendency to reëvaluate the intense and conscious work of the evangelists; this line of thought is being developed by a method known as "redaction criticism" (*Redaktionsgeschichte*).

The authors cited above do not consider the problem of inspiration, but the Catholic version of this theory must ask the question: Who is inspired? It seems logical to consider that the literary material, before reaching the hands of the gospel authors, had already experienced the influence of the charism of inspiration. This material had already been formulated and fashioned to some degree, and thus it is not a question of preëxisting material, but of material which is specifically literary.

KARL RAHNER

Karl Rahner takes another approach to the problem.[5] His effort is directed to penetrating and concretizing the meaning of a formula already venerable in the study of this question. What does it mean to say that God is the author of sacred Scripture?

The Church knew an initial stage of formation or "crystallization" at the time of her foundation which was not merely a moment of time, but extended throughout the apostolic age, that is, roughly, the first generation of eyewitnesses. Now, one of the constituent factors in this process of self-formation was the activity by which the Church declared and expressed herself in formulas which are permanent, definitive, and binding on future generations. This activity, which is an essential component in the

[5] *Inspiration in the Bible*. Cf. bibliography.

Church's structure, is that by which the Church's self-awareness achieves literary objectivity. God in His historic and salvific action founded a Church as an historical and eschatological reality, and caused it to crystallize in a structure which included all its essential components. This means, then, that God caused that activity by which the Church achieved literary self-expression, since this is one of her essential component factors; He determined this by an infallible and formal pre-definition. In this way, God is the author of Scripture. Thus, for example, God and St. Paul are both authors of the note to Philemon: Paul is the author of the note as such, and God is the author of the action by which the Church, through this note, gives expression to her charity—a constituent factor of her being. There is one common effect of the two activities, but there are two diverse formalities. In a similar way, the Old Testament is the expression of the community of the covenant people which prepared for the definitive fact of the Church.

We should note here that, according to Rahner, this activity of self-expression is accomplished in the Church by individual persons responding to specific occasions within her life, and under the impulse of the unifying direction of the Spirit. Those who accuse Rahner of denying the fact of personal inspiration either have not read or have not understood him. It is simply that he does not enter into the question as to how God actuated this formal pre-definition in each human author.

Rahner perfectly coördinated the personal and social aspects of inspiration, aptly stressing the ecclesial context of both the inspired authors and the works they produce. This is his greatest contribution to the discussion of the problem (and we seem to hear in it a distant echo of Schleiermacher).

Pierre Benoit touches on the question rather hastily. He speaks in his article on the analogies of inspiration[6] of a "dramatic inspiration": It is the motion of the Spirit directing the people in their historical activity, and providing the theme and the material for the inspired books. Considered from the point of view of its origin —the Spirit, and of its ultimate place in the sacred writings, this common activity partakes of the context of scriptural inspiration. As we mentioned before, we find this terminology unsatisfactory, and we would prefer to use the word "charism" to indicate the

---

[6] "Les analogies de l'inspiration," in *Sacra Pagina, op. cit.*

common denominator of these gifts, and then go on to distinguish various differences and relations.

D. J. McCarthy has undertaken a study of this question in a recent article, "Personality, Society, and Inspiration." [7] His opening remark that "the Bible was formed in, by, and for a society" is nicely balanced by some judicious reflections on the personal factor within tradition which sustains the society. The sacred author, writing for the community, knew that his work would be actively received and used by the community; the community took up his work, used it, and elaborated on it. We may not speak of some "impersonal" source of these works, but at most of anonymous authors.

John L. McKenzie

The theme of the social character of inspiration has been proposed with particular emphasis by J. L. McKenzie in a brief article which acknowledges its dependence on the works of Rahner and Benoit.[8]

The article treats of a series of problems, formulated quite forcibly, which derive from the critical study of biblical literature. It is dated April, 1962, and we note that, independently, it coincides with some of our own preoccupations in this area, such as the question of successive authors[9] and that of the relation between speech and writing. In regard to many basic points, we agree with McKenzie, for example, on the fact that the biblical authors functioned as members of a community. All that we wish to note here are a few positions which we think are exaggerated.

It seems to us that he exaggerates the picture somewhat when he attempts to break it down into its individual components:

We know, or we think we know, that in the ancient world the manuscript was treated with great freedom; it was subject to the revision and expansion of each successive owner, and it is this constant process which has created our critical problems. In oral tradition, the material is flexible to the extreme, and it can be said without exaggeration that each successive bard or balladist was the creator of the story anew.[10]

[7] Cf. bibliography.
[8] Cf. bibliography.
[9] Cf. "XVII Semana Biblica Española," 1956, published in 1958.
[10] Art. cit. (bibliography), p. 117.

To say that the last statement is not an exaggeration seems to us to be equally an exaggeration. It is a fact that in the Bible we have vestiges of ancient written tradition. In any oral literary culture, there is a body of trained "reciters" who claim fidelity to an accepted version of what they relate; in Israel as among other peoples, there was the preservative and conservative factor of the cult, in which such texts were handed on.

It seems to us that there is another exaggeration, due to a lack of shading, in the neat opposition established between a modern author who wishes to express his individuality and the biblical author desirous of concealing his individuality in order to be the voice of the community. Many authors of our culture have been the authentic voices of their society and wished to be so, while some biblical authors express themselves in the first person—the prophets and wise men, for example. It is, however, certainly true that the degree of reflective self-consciousness has increased in man because of the self-awareness of the Renaissance, the cultivated self-reflection of the romantics, and liberal individualism. It is also true that a modern author wants to be known and recognized, whereas the fact that the name of an ancient writer was preserved was often due to the devotion of his disciples; but ancient times knew pseudonymous as well as anonymous authors.[11] In this regard, McCarthy's article, referred to above, is more to the point.

There is a third consideration: here and there, McKenzie refers to the biblical authors as the spokesmen of their society. In a general sense, this is quite true, but this generic meaning can be further specified, as we will see later on.

When McKenzie speaks of the experience which the prophets received from God, and of their efforts to articulate it,[12] he introduces once again the personal element which complements the social aspect of inspiration.

Once the exaggerations have been reduced, McKenzie's theory

---

[11] The fundamental study on this point is by J. A. Sint, *Pseudonymität im Altertum. Ihre Formen und Gründe*, Innsbruck, 1960. He was criticized by M. Forderer (*Gnom* 33, 1961, pp. 440–445) and answered in ZKT 83, 1961, pp. 493ff. For a later period, cf. K. Aland, "The Problem of Anonymity and Pseudonymity in Christian Literature of the First Two Centuries," *JTS* 12, 1961, pp. 39–49.

[12] *Art. cit.*, p. 121.

does not force the personalities of the authors into an amorphous mass, but rather gives them their roots in a society. In this sense, inspiration can be considered a communal charism which does not dispense with, but rather demands, the voice of its spokesman.

Israel expressed her faith and recited her traditions through her priests, prophets, kings, poets, sages, and even through her bards and balladists who created and transmitted oral traditions.[13]

There is another interesting point touched on in this article, namely, the fact that biblical criticism has given us a new awareness of man's social dimension, which fits in nicely with our renewed sense of the Church. This aspect, not explicitly formulated by the author, gives a special importance to the article.

EVALUATION

What should we think of such theories? We should first of all reject any notion of an amorphous community which is somehow creative; there is no such thing as a literary work produced by "everybody," and there is no need to revive the romantic theory which dissolved a work of art back into the masses. We reject this latter idea, not because it is romantic, but because it is wrong; there were many intuitions in that school of thought which will have to be rethought one day. But this aspect of the *"Volksgeist"* view of literature is certainly not one of them.

At first sight, it may seem as though the process which we have referred to as "successive inspiration" differs little from the romantic view. However, it is one thing to place a work indiscriminately within the masses, and quite another to discern in a text the combination of various sources, traditions, and redactors as in the Pentateuch, or to distinguish between an author and an editor as in the Book of Isaiah.

We would like now to adopt another point of view in order to appreciate the social dimension of the inspired books and their authors: let us look at this mystery from the angle of language and literature.

[13] *Art. cit.*, p. 120.

LANGUAGE

We should recall here what was said about language as a social reality, and the limits of this dimension which we sketched in that discussion. Someone learns a language with its stock of words already formed, its power to develop new words by analogy, its outlook and expressions, its delicately shaded areas of meaning, and all the treasures of appreciation and description which have been deposited within it over the centuries. He consciously develops the power and the manner of communicating himself to another, of thinking and of being influenced; and in this sense, a person remains forever modified by the social dimension of the language he has learned.

Such modification is, however, only the remote preparation for the charism of inspiration: When Jeremiah complained that he did not know how to speak, he was alluding to his lack of literary competence; and Isaiah received the consecration of the power of speech which he already possessed. We are considering here a certain *energeia* or power of language which collaborates in the execution of a literary work, and which thus provides a means by which the society of the inspired author influences his work. And since language is not a purely inert factor in the literary process, we can envisage society present and active by means of language, during the whole of the author's effort. But we should not exaggerate this influence; many others, equally indebted to society for their language, use it without thereby becoming inspired.

When someone uses a language, it is possible for him to surrender himself to it simply and accept it as it is, adopting its formulas, idioms, and clichés; or he can submit to the inherent power of the language with a certain ingenuous realism, perhaps employing its sound patterns without fully grasping their meaning. And even if he does not go to this extreme, he can still accept language without any discussion, when he should have maintained a certain considered distance.

In many ways and in varying degrees, however, each individual usually adapts a language to his own needs and temperament, thus asserting his liberty in relation to the possibilities of the language: in this lies the greatness of language as a medium by which human liberty receives expression and realization. This liberty with language is in direct proportion to one's mastery of it; thus we see the balance between the personal and social factors in language: The personal is expressed in a social medium, manifesting and realizing itself in relation with other persons by means of a common possession. In this instance, the social dimension of language enters into the question of inspiration, which is a personal charism of communication, actuated and expressed in a social context and through a social medium.

The possibilities of a language are in some degree limited. We do not refer here to all the remote possibilities which, if accumulated, would actually change the language. There are some who maintain that everything can be said with language, everything can be translated. This is true, but only partially.

Let us consider a language in the concrete:[14] It has a limited number of words which express reality in a certain way, and whose contiguous areas of meaning or *"Sprachfeld"* serve to limit the meanings possible to each (Good morning—Good day; yellow— orange—red, etc.). There are words in other languages which express shades of thought intermediate to those which we possess. When we wish to translate these intermediate shades, we must have recourse to circumlocution or paraphrase. Perhaps the original and the translation will say the same thing at least in regard to the informative content, but the total content of one will not equal the other. And even if we are able to give full expression to the original so that its overtones are understood, we do it by a multiplicity of words, and we still lack conformity to the literary tone of the original. An incisive expression is never adequated by a paraphrase. We may perhaps seek to overcome the gaps in the language we are using, by having recourse to technical terms, but this means that we have left the domain and level of language.

The possibilities and limitations of translation are well expressed by Ezra Pound in his essay on "How to Read":[15]

If we chuck out the classifications which apply to the outer shape of the work, or to its occasion, and if we look at what actually happens,

---

[14] An excellent work on these aspects of language is that by J. Trier, *Der deutsche Wortschatz im Sinnbezirk des Verstandes; die Geschichte eines sprachlichen Feldes*, Heidelberg, 1931.
[15] *Literary Essays of Ezra Pound*, ed. by T. S. Eliot, New York, 1960, p. 25.

in, let us say, poetry, we will find that the language is charged or energized in various manners.

That is to say, there are three "kinds of poetry":

Melopoeia, wherein the words are charged, over and above their plain meaning, with some musical property, which directs the bearing or trend of that meaning.

Phanopoeia, which is a casting of images upon the visual imagination.

Logopoeia, "the dance of the intellect among words," that is to say, it employs words not only for their direct meaning, but it takes count in a special way of habits of usage, of the context we expect to find with the word, its usual concomitants, of its known acceptances, and of ironical play. It holds the aesthetic content which is peculiarly the domain of verbal manifestation, and cannot possibly be contained in plastic or in music. It is the latest come, and perhaps most tricky and undependable mode.

The melopoeia can be appreciated by a foreigner with a sensitive ear, even though he be ignorant of the language in which the poem is written. It is practically impossible to transfer or translate it from one language to another, save perhaps by divine accident, and for half a line at a time.

Phanopoeia can, on the other hand, be translated almost, or wholly, intact. When it is good enough, it is practically impossible for the translator to destroy it save by very crass bungling, and the neglect of perfectly well-known and formulative rules.

Logopoeia does not translate; though the attitude of mind it expresses may pass through a paraphrase. Or one might say, you can not translate it "locally," but having determined the original author's state of mind, you may or may not be able to find a derivative or an equivalent.

It is often in these areas of limitation that a great artist scores his triumphs, finding new solutions which then enlarge the area of possibilities in a language. This may occur in the ordering of words or in their combination; think of Góngora, Péguy, or cummings. A writer, by the way he uses language, has an indirect influence on the community which shares his medium.

We can envisage an activity of this type within the context of inspiration: Not only does society influence the writer by means of language, but, reciprocally, the writer can exercise an influence on those who read him. This type of activity on the part of the sacred writers has conferred on us many new possibilities of thought and expression in the sphere of religion.

There is also another factor to be considered: Just as a society develops its language in virtue of a common sentiment and outlook, so, after the language has been established, it acts as a cohesive force within the group. In a certain sense, language is a constitutive factor in a society. And this is true of the society of man in general, or of the smaller divisions within the human family. If we Christians are a people "called together," it is because we have all responded in faith to a call, to a word. And one of the cohesive forces of our community is the religious language which we share. This common language is inspired, not precisely as Hebrew or Greek or English, but as biblical. There is another important social dimension to the charism of inspiration. Few Christians are called to play a creative role in the development of religious language; this was the vocation of the inspired writers, and, as is the case with all charisms, it was conferred "for the good of the Church." We should not fear the liturgical reforms which have been and are now being introduced. We will be joined together as the people of God far more effectively by a shared understanding of biblical language as it reaches us through translations, than by a common incapacity to understand its Latin expression. The language of the Bible will continue through the centuries to sink deeper roots in the Church, to expand its own social dimension while acting as a factor of unity.

To sum up, then: (1) Man receives from language a certain general modifying influence; (2) he receives through language the influence of others, as they use speech concretely; (3) he works with language, expressing his liberty by his exercise and mastery over its possibilities; (4) by means of his speech, he influences others. The first two factors are prior to inspiration; the last two may enter into the inspired language process. Thus, through language in itself, inspiration acquires a social dimension.

LITERATURE

Usually, a future writer or author begins by learning, that is, by reading, listening to, and assimilating the literary works which have preceded him. He enters into a tradition—a prerequisite for any life—adopting its outlook and literary forms, and thus allows himself to be prepared traditionally and socially for his future activity. In the Bible, this preparation precedes the inspired process.[16]

The next step is taken when a literary man, without abandoning his capacity to learn, begins to create, utilizing that which he has received from the community. In his literary activity, he can have any one of a number of varying degrees of social integration, which we will classify under three general headings:

(1) The first possibility is that he will speak or write in the name of the people: *vox populi*. When the people hear him, they will recognize themselves and take him to themselves as *their* poet. He gives expression to the mind of the community in such a way that the community considers itself the author of his sentiments and thoughts, while yet recognizing and honoring the privilege and prestige of *its* spokesman. It may happen that because of distance in space or time, the community does not know the author, even though it accepts his works.

This is popular poetry in the best sense of the term, which is far from being the degeneration of true poetry to the level of vulgarization. It may easily come about that people will begin to sing the poetry, making it its own, and forgetting the author completely. This is an instance when "popular" would be equivalent to "anonymous." The song is not the product of an amorphous community; it is, rather, that the name of the author has disappeared because he has so identified himself with his people. No one has expressed this truth better than Manuel Machado, who himself composed so many "*soléas*" which are popular in this best sense of the word:

> Until the people sing them
> verses are really not verses;
> and when the people sing them
> no one remembers their author.

> Such is the glory, my friend,
> of those who write songs of the people;
> to hear it said quite simply
> that they were written by no one.

[16] For counsels on the formation of a writer, cf. A. Maurois, *The Art of Writing*, New York, 1962, esp. ch. 1, "The Writer's Craft."

Strive, then, to have your verses
go out to the people and finish
by ceasing to be your own,
that they may belong to others.

He who can fuse his heart
with the life-soul of his people,
will find that he loses his name
and gains eternity.[17]

In this sense, many of the liturgical pieces in the Old Testament are popular and social; and this is true also of some of the narrative material, as well as of the Proverbs—these latter were once well defined as "the wisdom of many and the wit of one" (Lord John Russell).

(2) The second way in which a man can be related to his society is by exercising his activity on it: directing it, reacting against it, leading the way for it as a precursor. In the case of opposition, the poet is social in the sense that he is stimulated and sustained in his purpose by the resistance of the community. The whole reason why he speaks or writes is his people, his community; he does not go off from them in desperation, or retreat in fear; he confronts them.

[17] "Hasta que el pueblo las canta,
las coplas, coplas no son;
y cuando las canta el pueblo,
ya nadie sabe el autor.

"Tal es la gloria, Guillén
de los que escriben cantares:
oir decir a la gente
que no los ha escrito nadie.

"Procura tú que tus coplas
vayan al pueblo a parar,
aunque dejen de ser tuyas
para ser de los demás.

"Que al fundir el corazón
con el alma popular,
lo que se pierde de nombre,
se gana de eternidad."
"Cualquiera Canta un Cantar," Manuel y Antonio Machado, *Obras Completas*, Madrid, 1947.

The greater part of prophetic literature pertains to this type in its social dimension. Jeremiah is a good example. God made him "a fortified city, a pillar of iron, a wall of brass" against his own people. And when his words produced, not conversion, but mockery, the prophet tried to escape, but God sent him back to the battle.

Unamuno is not a popular writer, but his works have a great power of communication. Let us listen to some of his principles: "The first thing necessary for one who wishes to write with effect is that he have no consideration for the reader and show him no mercy." ". . . to be able to accomplish this, he will stick you with a hot needle, in order to hear you yell." ". . . to irritate the public may become an obligation in conscience." Unamuno is a social author, he is aggressively so: "To be fought against is one way of being sustained and stimulated"; yet we would not say that Unamuno is the "voice" of his people.

The public can influence and modify a literary work, even to the point of endangering its quality; a writer receives this influence as a demand, a provocation, and a threat. If he knows how to apply concession and self-defense in the proper doses, then society plays a positive role of collaboration. In the activity of the prophets, the community is a conditioning factor in the literary work, at least in the way it reacts to the prophet. This social dimension may be prior to the process of inspiration, or it may permeate the whole process itself.

(3) We have in our culture the literary man of the ivory tower or the garret, the accursed poet, sealed off, fit only for initiates, a stranger to society and contemptuous of average people. This species of hot-house poet, removed or indifferent, is not found in the biblical garden. Not even the author of Ecclesiastes—an extreme case—can be classified in this category; he is thinking out loud and challenging the secure routine of the reader.

This is all we can find of a social dimension to inspiration. We cannot offer any more. Yet what we have seen is a true complementary factor in the realm, always open and attainable, of the individual. The explanations of Schleiermacher and Rahner fall principally in the first of our divisions, the author who gives expression to the sentiments of the community and in whose writings the community recognizes itself. Benoit's description does not extend beyond a consideration of the materials which are to enter into the work. McCarthy insists primarily on the living reception and use of the work on the part of the community.

We will treat of other social aspects of inspiration in Chapter 10, in the discussion of a literary work as such. We may say in this connection, however, that the greatest influence that society exercises on a writer is found in its character of audience or public. In a reality such as literature, whose very nature implies reference to another, the term of that reference is a constitutive factor in its production and finds concrete expression in the work itself. However, it is not exact to say that the charism of inspiration moves and directs the activity of the people in its capacity as audience. We should rather say that the sacred author was inspired to write his work with reference to the community. There is a parallel and complementary charism possessed by the society which receives the work; they are the people of God, the Church.

Bibliography for Chapter 8

The Opinions. The best account of the opinions is found in the authors themselves: Schleiermacher's *Der Christliche Glaube* is now translated into English: *The Christian Faith*, 2 vols., New York, 1963. Rahner's work on inspiration is in the English "Quaestiones Disputatae" series of Herder and Herder, *Inspiration in the Bible*, New York, 1961 (the German original is reviewed by M. Zerwick in VD 36, 1958, pp. 357–365 and by A. M. Dubarle in *RevScPhTh* 24, 1959, p. 106). The articles discussed in this chapter are J. L. McKenzie, "The Social Character of Inspiration," *CBQ* 24, 1962, pp. 115–124; D. J. McCarthy, "Personality, Society, and Inspiration" *TS* 24, 1963, pp. 553–576.

Form Criticism. Most of the discussions about form criticism are concerned with its historical and literary conclusions rather than with its sociological presuppositions. There is a good evaluation by P. Benoit, "Reflexions sur la '*Formgeschichtliche Methode,*'" *RB* 53, 1946, pp. 481–512 (*Exégèse et Théologie*, Paris, 1961, pp. 25ff.), and a chapter in Wikenhauser's *New Testament Introduction*, New York, 1958, pp. 253–276; R. Schnackenburg wrote an article on form criticism in

ZKT 85, 1963, pp. 16-32, which is summarized in *TD* 12, 1964, pp. 147–152. The Instruction of the Pontifical Biblical Commission, *On the Historical Truth of the Gospels* (April 21, 1964), contains some positive statements in regard to form criticism. The article by J. Fitzmyer is very helpful as a commentary: "The Biblical Commission's Instruction on the Historical Truth of the Gospels," *TS* 25, 1964, pp. 386–408. A slightly different orientation can be found in C. Kearns, "The Instruction on the Historical Truth of the Gospels," *Ang* 41, 1964, pp. 218–234.

Sociology and Language. The book of Weisgerber, *Das Gesetz der Sprache*, mentioned previously, though it exaggerates certain positions, can be used here, especially section 1, which deals with the sociology of language. Weisgerber cites A. Sommerfelt, *La Langue et la Société*, Paris, 1938.

Sociology and Literature. A good treatment and an ample bibliography can be found in Wellek and Warren, *Theory of Literature*, ch. 9, "Literature and Society."

9. Speech and Writing

So far, we have usually avoided using the term "writer" when speaking of the biblical authors. But why this hesitation in using a formula already universally accepted?

There is no doubt that the formula is current in theology, and widely accepted by tradition. If, for example, we read the description of Leo XIII,[1] we find that in eight lines of text, words deriving from the root *"scribere"* occur five times: The Holy Spirit "took up men as His instruments for writing"; the sacred writers are contrasted with God, the author; God moved them to write; He assisted them while writing; the author willed faithfully to write down. . . . Someone might want to capitalize on the distinction made by the Pope between God as author and man as writer, resurrecting once again the view that human activity should be restricted to that of a secretary. But such a position would be opposed to the whole tenor of the encyclical. Nevertheless, it is true that in this description, the hagiographers are looked on simply as being writers. (Hagiographer means sacred writer.)

Pesch's description of the four stages in the hagiographer's activity is a good example of the classical view of the matter:

[1] "*Quare nihil admodum refert, Spiritum Sanctum assumpsisse homines tamquam instrumenta ad* scribendum, *quasi, non quidem primario auctori, sed* scriptoribus *inspiratis quidpiam falsi elabi potuerit. Nam supernaturali ipse virtute ita eos ad* scribendum *excitavit et movit, ita* scribentibus *adstitit, ut ea omnia eaque sola, quae ipse iuberet, et recte mente conciperent, et fideliter* conscribere *vellent, et apte infalibili veritate exprimerent.*" EB 125; cf. RSS, p. 24. Emphasis added.

234

. . . *first,* he must conceive the idea of writing a book, that is, he must make a judgment as to what is to be written; *second,* he must consider how those things which he thinks should be written, ought to be expressed in words; *third,* he must decide to commit to writing those things which he has mentally conceived; *fourth,* he must carry out his decision either himself or through another. That these are the necessary steps is obvious without more consideration.[2]

The word "write" is absent from step four of the above description, in order to allow for the presence of a secretary, at least in those cases where inspiration does not require that the inspired writer be himself an amanuensis. In the rest of his study, Pesch never considers the sacred authors anything but writers. For him, the matter is so clear as to need no discussion.

Among recent studies, Rahner uses this terminology when he refers to the situations in the life of the Church which occasioned the writing of the text; he admits without difficulty that there is a distinction when he elaborates his theory of the Church speaking and expressing herself, and then concretizing this expression in the fact of writing.

Actually, this manner of speaking is very ancient and has its roots in the Bible itself: The New Testament authors cite or comment on the Old Testament, calling it "the writings," "what is written," etc., and we can read in the New Testament the statement that Moses wrote (Mk 10:5; Lk 20:28; Jn 1:45; 5:46). The Fathers, as we have already noted, were familiar with the term "hagiographer."

THE PROBLEM

The outlook and the terminology of the manuals generally reflect a view of the Scriptures which considers them as the result of a writing process: for each book there was an act of writing. Moses wrote the Pentateuch, Isaiah the work which bears his name, David wrote the Book of Psalms, and so forth. Though the act may have extended over a long period of time, it can be considered a psycho-

2 ". . . debet IMPRIMIS *mente concipere ideam libri scribendi seu debet iudicare, quid scribendum sit; debet* SECUNDO *considerare, quomodo res illas, quas scribendas iudicat, verbis exprimere velit; debet* TERTIO *habere voluntatem ea, quae mente concepit, scripto mandandi: debet* QUARTO *hoc consilium exsecutioni mandare aut per se aut per alium. Haec esse necessaria est per se evidens."* No. 414.

logical unity, and it pertains culturally to that type of activity familiar to us, the very activity by which the author of the manual produced his own book.

However, modern historical and critical studies have done away with such a simple view of the matter: we can no longer envisage one act, there were many acts on the part of different and successive authors, and not all of these acts consisted in writing strictly so called —a large place was occupied by oral activity both in composing and in transmitting the material now found in the Scriptures. The New Testament itself often uses the word "speak," avoiding, in regard to the prophets, the use of the word "write."

> Heb 1:1: God spoke to our forefathers . . .
>
> 2 Pt 1:21: Men, moved by the Holy Spirit, spoke in behalf of God.
>
> Lk 1:70: . . . He proclaimed by the lips of His prophets. . . .
>
> Acts 3:21: . . . of which God spoke by His holy prophets (cf. Acts 4:29, 31).
>
> Acts 8:25: . . . giving their testimony and speaking the word of the Lord.
>
> Acts 28:25: How well the Holy Spirit spoke to your fathers through the prophet Isaiah. . . .
>
> Rom 3:19: All that the law says, it addresses to those who are under its authority.
>
> Heb 7:14: Moses said nothing in regard to priests of this tribe. . . .
>
> Jas 5:10: Take the prophets who spoke in the name of the Lord.

In all of these texts, we find a preference for words relating to speech when they describe the prophets, as well as some references to Moses' activity as being one of speech, and there is a description of the apostles "speaking the word of the Lord."

Oral composition and oral transmission are among the facts commonly accepted today in biblical studies. However, it is much easier to admit a change in the factual situation which a theory is considering, than to change the formulas in which the theory expresses itself. In our case, the formula is found in the phrase "the inspiration of the Scriptures." Formerly, the word "write" covered the whole process and was considered as one act; now we see that the writing of the text is only one step in the process by which it was produced, and this raises a new question: Is the oral activity inspired or is the written activity inspired, or are both inspired?

One either extends the charism of inspiration to cover all the phases of the process—and they are analogous—or restricts it to the moment of writing.

The second alternative has the appearance of fidelity to the commonly held view, yet it must be admitted that once the meaning of a term has been changed, the continued use of a formula is a change in its sense, and is a departure from what is considered common doctrine. Moreover, this second alternative runs the risk sometimes of considering inspiration as an act which enters in only after the word of God has been constituted and fixed in expression, and thus could seem to be a reversion to the view, already rejected, which holds that inspiration consists in a "subsequent approval."

On the other hand, the moment in which the act of writing takes place is indispensable and cannot be left outside the role of charismatic influence. If we are to possess sacred writings, then they must be written; and if they are to be written, there must be someone to write them; if the Holy Spirit wished to give to us the Scriptures, He had to move, in some way, the men who wrote them. All of this is so obvious as to be almost tautology; so obvious, in fact, that we dispense ourselves from thinking about it. We should reflect, however, that from this fact alone we cannot conclude that the technique and process of composition were also accomplished by writing.

It is nearly a century and a half since a theologian of Tübingen, John Baptist Drey, posed the problem quite precisely:

A curious thing: Was that not the work of God which the apostles, daily, and in many places and for many years, preached by word of mouth before it occurred to them to write any of it down? That first community of Jerusalem, and the others, and the early Christians in general, did they only hear the word of the apostles and not the word of God; did it only become the word of God when they read it? [3]

Drey's articles were published in 1820 and 1821. The problem that he posed went by unnoticed and disappeared. Today, now

[3] "Sonderbar! War denn das kein Wort Gottes, das die Apostel täglich und aller Orten und viele Jahre lang mündlich predigten, ehe es ihnen einfield, auch darüber zu schreiben? Jene erste Gemeinde von Jerusalem und die andern alle, überhaupt die ersten Christen hörten also nur das Wort der Apostel, kein Wort Gottes; dies ward erst, als sie es geschrieben lasen." P. Dausch, Die Schriftinspiration . . . , p. 188; cf. ch. 8, no. 2.

that our knowledge of the process by which the Old and New Testaments were composed is much more developed, the problem returns and demands a solution.

It is an incontestable fact that a good proportion of the Old Testament existed and was transmitted largely through oral tradition before being fixed in a written form (though there are some who go to extremes in this regard). In the New Testament, an oral tradition preceded the redaction of the synoptics: The Gospel came before the Gospels. Where, then, should we locate the charism of inspiration?

SOLUTIONS

Benoit has devoted a great deal of consideration to this question. In his first study, composed as notes and commentary on St. Thomas's tract on prophecy, he distinguishes between a prophetic inspiration, moving a man to pronounce an oracle, and a literary inspiration, by which a man is moved to compose a book.

In this regard, we might distinguish two distinct vocations, as it were: the first one impels one to *repeat an oracle* which has come down from heaven; the other compels one to *compose a book*. We shall designate them by the two standard terms, "prophet" and "sacred writer." . . . For the *prophet*, who receives from God a message to deliver, the speculative judgment occupies the foreground. . . . The case of the *sacred writer* is quite different. He receives from God an impulse to compose a book. . . . This time the action of inspiration will first affect his practical reason and will have for its primary object the practical judgment. . . .[4]

Benoit wrote this in 1947. Twelve years later, he modified this distinction, and this modification also is apparent in the English

[4] "On peut à ce sujet distinguer comme deux vocations distinctes: celle qui fait RÉCITER UN ORACLE descendu du ciel et celle qui pousse à COMPOSER UN LIVRE. Nous les désignerons par les deux noms typiques du "PROPHÈTE" et de l' "ÉCRIVAIN SACRÉ." . . . . Dans le cas du PROPHÈTE qui reçoit de Dieu un message à délivrer, c'est le jugement qui occupe le premier plan. . . . Il en va autrement de l' ÉCRIVAIN SACRÉ qui reçoit de Dieu l'impulsion de composer un livre. . . . Cette fois la motion inspiratrice atteindra d'abord la raison pratique de l'écrivain et aura pour objet premier le jugement pratique. . . ." La Prophétie, by P. Benoit and P. Synave, New York, 1947, pp. 317-318. The English translation above is Prophecy and Inspiration, New York, 1960, pp. 106-107.

translation of *La Prophétie*.[5] On the psychological level, we find: inspiration in the order of knowledge—cognitive; inspiration in the order of speech—prophetic, apostolic, oratorical; and inspiration in the order of writing—hagiographical, scriptural. On the social level, we may distinguish between inspiration in the order of speech or action (dramatic, prophetic, apostolic) and scriptural inspiration, which is an attempt to overcome the limitations of time. These distinctions need to be developed more fully, but Benoit has the merit of at least discerning their necessity and situating them correctly.

Grelot's treatment is much clearer and better developed:

We should, then, first examine fully the question of the charisms which are related to the word of God before going on to the study of scriptural inspiration.[6]

In the Old Testament, prophecy (in the strict sense of the term) founded the community, as it were, by bringing to it the word of God. Then, other charisms followed which structured the community, in order to allow the word to maintain its existence there and to develop its potentialities. Throughout the whole of this process of development, scriptural inspiration gave to the word, from time to time, a written form, so that the community could refer to this writing as to the norm of its faith. At the end of this period, Christ, the Word of God made flesh, brought to men the fullness of revelation, by His words and by His acts; by that very fact, He showed forth the ultimate meaning of the ancient writings. But this revelation is made explicit in the message of the Gospel; and thus we see the role accorded to the apostolic charism in founding the Church . . . to which it brings the word. After this charism, there come other charisms to structure the living tradition of the Church, so that the word will maintain itself there and bear fruit throughout the course of time. This is the meaning of the hierarchical magisterium which, with the aid of the Holy Spirit, continues to watch over the apostolic deposit of faith. At the same time, this deposit has received a written and fixed expression which is due to the scriptural inspiration conferred on certain of its early recipients

[5] The modification appears in the 1959 article in *Sacra Pagina* cited above (ch. 8 no. 6); the modifications in the English of *La Prophétie* can be seen on pp. 125–127, esp. of *Prophecy and Inspiration*.

[6] "*Il sera donc utile d'examiner dans toute son ampleur la question des charismes relatifs à la Parole de Dieu avant de passer à l'étude de l'inspiration scripturaire.*" RSR 51, 1963, p. 349.

endowed with charismatic functions, who were sufficiently close to the apostles to be able to witness directly to their legacy.[7]

The term "inspiration" is qualified by the adjective "scriptural": It is a subsequent charism whose function it is to fix the message in writing, and as such it is subordinate to other charisms which have to do with the preservation and development of the word, and these in turn are completely dependent on the prophetic and apostolic word. In this way, we have a unified context: the word, a differentiation of charismatic gifts, and inspiration in the strict sense for the written expression of the word. It is obvious that this type of scriptural inspiration cannot be treated by utilizing the categories of the manuals without any recognition of the change in their content.

It is not so easy to see in Grelot's description how the charismatic activity of some of the authors in the sapiential tradition is at the service of the prophetic word, nor is there any well-developed consideration of what is involved in the literary stability given to the word by writing.

We see in Benoit and Grelot an effort to distinguish the activity of speaking from that of writing in their analysis of the charism of inspiration. But is it legitimate to make a problem out of something which is so simple and clear? Everyone talks of the Bible as the sacred books, the sacred writings, the *sacra pagina*; the term "Bible" itself signifies book or books, its authors are called hagiog-

[7] "*Dans l'ancien Testament, la prophétie (au sens fort du terme) fondait en quelque sorte la communauté de salut en lui apportant la Parole de Dieu. Ensuite d'autres charismes venaient structurer cette communauté, pour permettre à la Parole de s'y conserver et de développer ses virtualités. Tout au cours du développement, l'inspiration scripturaire donnait occasionellement à la Parole une forme écrite, pour que la communauté puisse se référer à cette Ecriture comme à sa règle de foi. Au term des temps, le Christ, Parole de Dieu faite chair, a apporté aux hommes la révélation totale par ses paroles et par ses actes; du même coup il a dévoilé le sens définitif des anciennes Ecritures. Mais c'est par le message évangélique que cette révélation s'est explicitée; de là le rôle du charisme apostolique, comme fondement de l'Eglise . . . . , à qu'il apporte la Parole. Après lui, d'autres charismes viennent structurer la tradition vivante de l'Eglise, pour que la Parole s'y conserve et y fructifie au cours de temps. Tel est le sens du magistère hiérarchisé qui, avec l'assistance de l'Esprit Saint, continue encore de veiller sur le dépôt apostolique. Celui-ci cependant a fait l'objet d'une fixation écrite, grâce à l'inspiration scripturaire dont on bénéficié certains dépositaires des fonctions charismatiques, encore assez rapprochés des apôtres pour pouvoir témoigner directement du dépôt légué par eux.*" Ibid., pp. 364–365.

raphers (sacred writers), and the Old Testament itself is often cited in the New Testament simply as "the writings." This tradition had existed for millenniums; what basis can there be for trying to qualify it?

Before approaching the biblical problem directly, we will first consider the fact of language in general, without trying to make any immediate applications.

SPEECH AND WRITING

Language is primarily spoken; word is primarily sound. A lack of the ability to read or write is a perfectly human thing; it existed for thousands of years, though now it is only the inheritance of small children.

Writing is a secondary and simplified means of recording. Even speech is a stylized and simplified "mimesis" of reality, both interior and exterior, but at least it has the dimensions of tone, inflection, and rhythm which our system of notation does not register. Compare, for instance, the system we use for registering speech with that which we use for the notation of music: in this latter, we indicate movement—allegro, andante, presto; intensity—piano, forte; changes in speed—rallentando, accelerando, crescendo, diminuendo; the nature of the rhythm—staccato, legato, etc. Actually, our system of speech notation is quite primitive, and the reason, at least partially, is that we have neglected the primary word.

Writing is a system of symbols, three times removed from the reality it expresses—it is the graphic notation of sound which itself represents an interior word. The primary function of writing is the conservation of the spoken word.

Once a culture has developed the art of writing, the written notation begins to develop a series of functions of its own, and can exercise a reciprocal influence on the spoken language. Some writers speak in a style characteristic of written literature;[8] and one of the psalmists compares his tongue to the quick pen of a scribe (Ps 45).

[8] A. Maurois recalls his conversation with Rudyard Kipling: his mannerisms, his subtle capacity to insinuate, and the general impression he gave of a man possessed of ancient wisdom, or like some prophet of the Old Testament. *The Writer's Craft*, p. 18; cf. ch. 8, n. 16.

Writing can give to the spoken word a juridical value: there have been contracts since the culture of Sumeria. A text can assume a magical function, as in the Egyptian execration texts. Writing stabilizes the fluid process of oral tradition; it inhibits the process by which phonetic and semantic changes are introduced into a language, and it tends to become the norm for speech: Good writers set the pace for good speakers. Writing even has an influence on the pronunciation of a language, for the reading or writing of a language can be mastered by those who cannot pronounce it correctly ("I read French, but I cannot speak it"). The literary existence of a thing facilitates repetition and diffusion, while maintaining a normative standard.

In our day, we have reached the stage where we think in terms of a series of books: Huge machines devour paper and ink and turn out mountains of literature, new "series" or "collections" are begun every day, and editors pursue authors—at least some authors. But then, at the other extreme, we have, happily, a rebirth of interest in the spoken word, captured on phonograph records and tapes, which are able to be repeated without the intermediary of a written medium and the impoverishment of being contained within some thirty or so graphic characters and ten signs of punctuation.

In a culture in which writing is already prevalent and predominant, there is a danger that some authors will lose awareness and feeling for the primary reality of the spoken word. They think in terms of letters, rather than in terms of sound, and they imagine that others near them or far from them in time or distance think, or thought, as they do.

O. Jespersen makes the very penetrating observation that the majority of linguists are helpless in the face of a living language because, unknowingly, they take writing for speech, and they are incapable of thinking in a context of sound rather than in one of written characters.[9]

Edward Sievers opposed this tendency toward "literalism" with his analyses of the sound quality of literature (in the Bible as well), and the new structural analyses take the sound patterns of a piece

[9] "Noch eindringlicher legt O. Jespersen dar, dass ein grosser Teil der Linguisten der lebendigen Sprache hilflos gegenüberstehen, weil sie unbedenklich die Schrieft für die Sprache nehmen und unfähig sind, in Lauten statt in Buchstaben zu denken." F. Kainz, Psychologie der Sprache, vol. 6, pp. 30–31.

as their point of departure. Jespersen's indictment of literary critics is also valid in regard to much of the thought on biblical inspiration. We ought, then, to rethink the problem, bearing in mind this central fact which has been all too often disregarded: the spoken word is primary.

THE TECHNIQUES OF COMPOSITION

In our culture, the art of writing has been well developed and printing has correspondingly been made easier by the reduction in the cost of paper (compare the ancients' esteem for writing materials—palimpsests, papyrus, etc.—with our modern phenomenon, the waste basket). As a result, there is a clearer distinction made between the two methods of composition—oral and written—which corresponds more or less to the temporal distinction between ancient and modern techniques.

In ancient times, oral composition was the normal procedure. This technique employs a great number of stereotyped formulas and artificial mnemonic devices. Because of these, the composition possesses a certain rigidity, which oral tradition undertakes to soften: In our own times, the relation is much the same as that which exists between folk songs and recorded music. Concomitant with this type of composition there arises a body of professional bards, storytellers, or ballad singers, who have their own techniques of memory and recitation while maintaining a basic respect for and fidelity to a normative version of their material.

To the stage of primitive oral composition and its oral transmission, which usually lasts for some time, there succeeds the written stage in which the work is stabilized. This implies that that which is known orally is appreciated enough to be conserved; we have the example of the enthusiasm of the romantics for folklore which has become an organized movement in our own day.[10] This literary stabilization is a service to society: Tradition is given a wider diffusion thereby, while maintaining a fixed form; variants are reduced and the text becomes normative.

Written composition is both more rigid than oral and more free: There is a fixed text which is regarded as unchangeable, but

[10] There is a society dedicated to the study of folklore, called "The Folklore Fellows," with its own periodical, *Folklore Fellows' Communications.*

there is a greater freedom from stereotyped formulas and other devices to aid the memory. It is easy in this mode of composition to utilize the written works of others; our modern scholarly works derive in large part from contact with other books (sometimes involving the cult of footnotes to the point of fetishism).

Even the very method of writing itself can have an influence in turn on the process of composition: When one composes at a typewriter, he usually settles more quickly for the formulation of his expression, especially in regard to word order. One scholar will compose the outlines of his conferences or class lecture by hand, but he will use a typewriter when he writes an article, while another will first work out the formulation of everything by hand before typing it out. Others, gifted with a facility for expression, have, with the aid of modern dictating machines, returned to the methods of an earlier age. Since the written word lacks many possibilities of expression, there have been attempts to give this medium another dimension: We find extreme examples of this in the efforts of some to convey effects with the printed lines of their poetry—in some of the work of George Herbert, e. e. cummings, Apollinaire, etc.

There are some authors, mostly poets, who compose mentally; this is a form of oral composition, or at least non-written composition. When the poem is complete, they commit it to paper. However, the ordinary method of composition, which has been in use for centuries, is to use paper as a testing ground, writing and rewriting until the final form is achieved.

LITERARY COMPOSITION OF THE BIBLE

The art of writing was already well known (cf. Jg 8:14); there was a functionary known as a scribe, and court records were kept. Papyrus was imported, and parchment and vellum were produced; often texts were partially scraped off a hide, so that it could be used again (the original of a palimpsest found at Qumran dates from the eighth century B.C.). Wood or metal tablets inscribed with a stylus were also employed, and in some cases potsherds were used, the characters being painted on rapidly with a small brush (Lachish letters). Yet the excavations in Palestine reveal hardly any written documents: This may be due to the fact that the climate is hard on any papyrus (only a dry climate, such as that in Egypt or the caves of Qumran or Murabbaat, is able to preserve papyrus), or it may be that written material tended to be concentrated in official quarters, such as the palace or temple.

Other data point to the fact that certain biblical poems were written down as early as the eleventh or tenth centuries B.C. This is indicated by the traces of an ancient system of writings still found, though not always understood, in the Massoretic text. (This has been established by the work of Albright, Cross, and Freedman.)

The Bible itself has many things to say about the way it views writing. The Covenant, laws, the Decalogue, the blessings and curses, must be written (Nm 5:23; Ex 24; Dt 4–5). According to ancient custom, the writing of a contract conferred on it a juridical status, and we may suppose that this custom prevailed in Israel. Also, writing made possible a fixed and authoritative text, to be used at the annual renewal of the Covenant. Thus the writing of a text is not merely the graphic notation of what is spoken: it is a new act constitutive and meaningful, which makes a word into a juridical instrument, an immutable norm, or a witness for the future.

A census is the same type of thing. The Book of Joshua (ch. 18) describes the distribution by lot of the Promised Land, and adds that this distribution was registered in a sort of property list. As the story stands, the act by which ownership was conferred consisted in a divine allotment by which God gave portions of his land to his people. Yet this divine act had to be juridically recorded. In this case, the act of writing did not constitute the act of allotment, but was the subsequent juridical instrument, ensuring the right to property already possessed. However, in Psalm 86 it seems that the act of writing was constitutive of the juridical effects which followed from the fact that someone "was born here." From the moment that his name was inscribed, a person was formally incorporated into the people with equal rights of citizenship, and by this act the city of Sion was constituted the mother of the nations.

Writing is often employed simply to overcome the barriers of distance and time. Letters are the means men use to extend their words a great distance: There are examples of these in the Old Testament, and a good proportion of the New Testament is made up of letters. When men attempt to overcome the dimension of time, they are looking to the continuity of their community: This motive is operative in the People of God, and in such a situation the act of writing easily confers upon the word the role of witness. Psalm 102 expressly recognizes this function of writing, which preserves the message against time and serves as a sort of testimony:

> For Yahweh rebuilds Sion,
> and is seen amidst his glory.
> He regards the prayer of the needy,
> and does not contemn their prayer.
>
> Let this be written for a generation to follow,
> a people then created will sing Yahweh's praise.
> (Ps 102:17–19)

The future generation, which was yet to be created, had not been witness of these salvific acts of Yahweh. In times gone by it was the function of the cult to actualize the past events of salvation history, and we can hear the echo of the ancient preaching style in such phrases as: "Yahweh our God made with us a Covenant at Horeb. Not with our Fathers did he make this Covenant, but with us, we ourselves, who are here today, all of us the living" (Dt 5:2–3). This function is attributed to the written word in the Psalm we have just seen: The written fact will incite the people to praise. In verse 9 of Psalm 149 we seem to have an allusion to a written judicial sentence: "To execute on them the written sentence, this is the glory of all his faithful." Perhaps in this case the written text was looked upon as the juridical act necessary for the validity of the sentence.

The testimonial quality of a written document stands out clearly in Chapter 8 of Isaiah: "The record is to be folded and the sealed instruction kept among my disciples" (8:16; cf. v. 20). Jeremiah, Chapter 36, is an interesting example of the prevalent attitude in regard to the preservative function of writing. There we see the king attempting to obliterate the prophetic word, by cutting up the scroll Jeremiah had dictated, and throwing it into the fire. But the word was greater than the king's scheming, and because it was alive in the memory of Jeremiah, it was written again and preserved for future generations.

The sapiential literature contains references to the art of writing. In the case of the Proverbs, we see a very academic activity by which the sayings of the sages were collected, compared with variants, and included in collections which, at times, were composed outside Israel. The activity by which these collections were formed reminds us of our present-day specialists in folklore, though the efforts of these ancients seem to have been motivated by more religious considerations. And, as we will see in the following chapter, this activity had about it the literary qualities characteristic of any anthology. At the end of the Book of Ecclesiastes, we read this statement made by a disciple in regard to the master's technique of composition:

Besides being wise, Qoheleth taught the people knowledge, and weighed, scrutinized and arranged many proverbs. Qoheleth sought to find pleasing sayings, and to write down true sayings with precision.

We may sum up our survey of the biblical information in regard to writing by saying that writing is not always a mere graphic notation of the spoken word for the sake of preservation. It may also serve to add a juridical value to a word, either by constituting the juridical fact, or as a subsequent instrument, and it may also be a testimony or a norm.

Another series of facts indicate that part of the biblical literature had a prehistory in which it existed in oral form. The basic task of the prophets was that of proclaiming the word, and we see this in the accounts they leave of their vocation and in descriptions such as that of the "evangelist" or herald of good news in Is 40:9, who is bidden to "cry out at the top of your voice." However, I do not think that we can conclude from the command given to Jeremiah in Chapter 36 to write his oracles, that he had not written anything before. It is possible, but such a conclusion seems a bit oversimplified. In regard to the New Testament, we have the witness of the text itself to the intense oral activity which was carried on prior to and contemporaneous with the activity of writing.[11]

An analysis of the sound factors in some prophetic oracles and in other poetic passages demonstrates clearly that they were com-

---

[11] This is, as we have seen, the principal argument of J. B. Drey. Cf. A. H. J. Gunnweg, "Mündliche und Schriftliche Tradition der vorexilischen Propheten als Problem der neueren Prophetenforschung," *FRLANT* 73, 1958. B. Gerhardsohn, *Memory and Manuscript. Oral and Written Transmission in Rabbinic Judaism and Early Christianity*, Uppsala, 1961. For another aspect of the question, cf. B. S. Childs, *Memory and Tradition in Israel*, "Studies in Biblical Theology," no. 37, London, 1962.

posed to be recited aloud: They were poems made expressly to sound and resound.[12] At the same time the exquisite care in regard to the sound dimension of language and to rhythm which is often manifest in these poems indicates that they had already attained a literary stability before they were written down. In such cases, the process by which they finally achieved written form was often little more than a simple recording, or consisted merely in adding some verses or glosses. Sometimes this literary activity lay in constructing larger harmonic unities, utilizing and respecting the individuality of "bells" which had already been cast (the image is Gunkel's). Analysis also shows that there were often successive stages of written composition in which a similar process was operative in regard to preëxisting written material. We sometimes get the impression that this material was handled with greater freedom than were some of the oral sources.

Thus, we cannot automatically identify the fact of being written with the ultimate stage of literary fixity. Some pieces were already fixed in an oral stage of composition, while there were written documents which were reworked many times before achieving literary stability. The type of literature in question is often as important as the technique of composition, be it oral or written, in determining the point at which a piece receives a final and fixed form. There are some genres which by their nature are fixed once and for all, they are untouchable. "Do not touch it any more, the rose is like that" (Juan Ramón). Then there are other types of literature which demand that the climax be in a fixed form, a play on words or something similar, but which leave a good deal of liberty to the creative capacity of the narrator. And there is the literary form of improvisation which finds a place at times in the dramatic arts (*"recitare a soggeto"*).[13] There are times when we have in the Bible two versions of the same text: There are instances of this in the Psalms, and the Proverbs provide many examples. At other times, it seems as though the cult fixed the final form of a text, while it was still in

---

12 See our *Estudios de Poética Hebrea*, ch. 5, "Estilística del material sonoro."
13 Modern study in folk songs has served to illustrate both the fixity of certain formulas, referred to as "floating verses" or "floating lyric material," and the extreme variability and adaptability of verbal expression. Cf. A. Lomax, *The Folk Songs of North America*, New York, 1960; *The Folk Songs of Peggy Seeger*, New York, 1964.

the oral stage. Thus we see that the fixity of a work of literature can result from many causes and can have many results.

THE WORD

These facts, which indicate a very complex possibility of relations between speaking and writing, have caused modern authors to differ widely in their theories about inspiration, or at least in their terminology, when speaking about it. Benoit uses as his generic term the word "inspiration," which he subdistinguishes as being "oratorical" (prophetic or apostolic), "scriptural," and that which is commonly called the inspiration of the Bible, which is, "cognitive plus scriptural" or "oratorical plus scriptural." Grelot takes the concept "word" as his central consideration, and uses the word "charism" as his generic term, reserving "inspiration" to designate the last stage in which the text is given written form, though he affirms the existence of other charisms which produce, preserve, and develop the word.

I also have preferred (independently) to take "word" as the central consideration, and this is the principal reason why I have chosen to write about "The Inspired word," rather than "Inspiration."

His Excellency Neophytus Edelby, Titular Archbishop of Edessa, expressed the Eastern view of scriptural inspiration in his intervention of October 5, 1964, at the third session of Vatican II:

Scripture is a prophetic and liturgical reality; it is a proclamation more than a book, it is the testimony of the Spirit in regard to the Christ-Event whose privileged moment is the Eucharistic Liturgy. By this testimony of the Spirit, all of the plan in regard to the Son reveals the Father. The post-Tridentine controversy has tended to view Scripture almost exclusively as a written norm, whereas the Oriental Churches see in Scripture a consecration of Salvation History under the species of the human word, and they consider this consecration as inseparable from the consecration of the Eucharist in which all history is summed up in the Body of Christ.

We are going to concentrate on this theme of "consecration," transposing it back into the past. History is revelation which prepared the coming of Christ, made it actual, and prolongs it. In a wide sense, history is anything that has happened: events, words, religious experiences . . . All of this first existed as event until, as the result of a choice, certain of these events became language in an oracle or a psalm, a story or a prayer. The activity by which event becomes word, is an activity of language in an inclusive sense. This activity transpires under the charismatic influence of the Holy Spirit, whose overshadowing makes it fruitful. The "holy" offspring which is thus born "is called" the word of God, just as that which is born of Mary as a result of the Spirit's overshadowing is called the Son of God. That transcendent moment in which event becomes word is the same moment at which the word becomes the word of God.

However, since in the generation of a word the process is more varied than in the generation of a man, the fundamental reality comes about differently in different situations. In the abstract, our main interest in concentrated on that moment in which event becomes word, and it is to this moment that the charism principally has reference. In the concrete, this moment is found or is developed within differing activities.

Sometimes[14] oral composition results in a finished work, and the written notation merely gives to it a literary stability. In this case, the oral process of composition must be considered inspired.

Sometimes the oral composition results in a work which is substantially fixed, but which undergoes a series of adaptations and changes within a controlled oral tradition, until it reaches a stage of literary fixity. In this case, inspiration would have been present in all those who made a real literary contribution to the work, including, of course, the original author. It may be that all of the previous process was but preëxisting material for a true literary creator who then brings it to its final stage; then we would have the following case.

Sometimes the composition is a written process which utilizes preëxisting materials either oral or written. This true process of composition, not merely a work of edition or collection, is inspired. It is difficult to decide in each individual case how much of the preëxisting material is inspired. Sometimes the entire process of

[14] The examples that we give here indicate the minimum. We cannot exclude the action of the Holy Spirit at other stages in the composition, yet neither can we demand it.

composition is effected through writing. This composition is inspired, and it is the type of inspired activity usually envisaged by the manuals.

In these cases, and we could add others, we must posit an action of the Holy Spirit which governs the activity by which the text is written, since in the concrete order of salvation, God has willed that His word be preserved and transmitted to us by writing: "All these things happened to them by way of symbol, and they were written for our instruction" (1 Cor 10:11). The fact of writing is at least an integral part of the total process of inspiration, since without this final activity we should not have the Scriptures in the Church. And this activity makes present the "testimony," as it were, of the Spirit.

The fact of writing adds, or can add, to the meaning of words, by making them a definitive norm or by incorporating them into a larger, sacred, and all-embracing context. This substantial addition of meaning really affects the concrete being of a word, and as such it is brought about by the charismatic activity of the Spirit.

Let us recall here once again the words of Tertullian:

The words [of the prophets] and the miracles they performed in order to lead men to faith in the divinity, are now kept in the treasury of literature.[15]

And those of St. Augustine:

God has spoken first by the prophets, and then by Himself, and then by the apostles what he judged sufficient; and he has provided those writings which are called canonical, and which are of the highest authority.[16]

Those things which are actually written bring to us the guarantee of their inspiration: "As such, they have been confided to the Church" (Vatican I). The Church receives them as written and hands them on. With all tradition, we can reverently use the formula "sacred writings" in connection with this other venerable phrase: "He has spoken through the prophets."

When the process of literary stabilization is finished, there then begins or continues the process of recitation, application, and in-

15 PL 1, 435; cf. ch. 4, n. 7.
16 PL 41, 318; cf. ch. 3, n. 24.

terpretation; this process may itself be oral or written, it is always living and free. Since the object of this process is the work already completed, we will reserve to the next chapter a closer study of its nature.

When the question of speech and writing is posed in this way and applied to the notion of inspiration, there arises a whole series of questions: What is the relation between Scripture and tradition? Is it possible that there are fragments or formulas truly inspired, which never achieved the final stage of written expression? If there are, is it possible to find and recover them? For the moment, we will restrict ourself to the simple enunciation of the questions.

Bibliography for Chapter 9

Speech and Writing. The fundamentals of the problem can be found in Kainz's *Psychologie der Sprache*, vol. 4, ch. 1; cf. also L. Lavelle, *La parole et l'écriture*, Paris, 1947.

The Techniques. The works referred to in the bibliography of Chapter 7 under "An Artist with Language" are relevant also here, especially the discussions of technique in A. Maurois, *The Art of Writing*, ch. 1, "The Writer's Craft," and M. Cowley, *Writers at Work, op. cit.*

IV
THE INSPIRED WORK

10. The Inspired Work

THE WORK OR THE AUTHOR?

Of the two biblical texts which are classical in the tract on inspiration, one (2 Pt 1:21) refers to the authors—"borne along by the Holy Spirit, men spoke in behalf of God," while the other text (2 Tim 3:16) refers to the written works themselves—"All of Scripture is inspired." Which of these two affirmations is the more basic?

The Fathers seem to have preferred the second formula, though, of course, not exclusively:

The Scriptures are perfect because they were pronounced by the Word of God and by His Spirit.[1]

How could all the Scripture bear witness to Him, unless it proceed from the one and the same Father? . . . The Son of God is sown throughout all the Scriptures.[2]

It is impossible that those letters be not sacred, which not only sanctify but divinize. And so the sacred writings, or the volumes which are made up of these sacred letters and syllables, the Apostle designates as inspired.[3]

The New Testament itself, when it cites the Old Testament, usually refers to it as "the Scripture" rather than naming individual authors, though again this is not an invariable practice.

---

[1] Cf. ch. 2, n. 56.

[2] "Quomodo igitur testabantur de eo Scripturae, nisi ab uno et eodem essent Patre. . . . Scilicet quod inseminatus est ubique in Scripturis ejus Filius Dei." St. Irenaeus, "Adv. Haer.," PG 7, 1000.

[3] ἱερὰ γάρ ὡς ἀληθῶς τὰ ἱεροποιοῦντα καὶ θεοποιοῦντα γράμματα ἐξ ὧν γραμμάτων καὶ συλλαβῶν τῶν ἱερῶν τὰς συγκειμένας γραφὰς τὰ συντάγματα ὁ αὐτὸς ἀκολούθως ἀπόστολος θεοπνεύστους καλεῖ. St. Clement of Alex., "Exhortation to the Greeks," ch. 9, PG 8, 197, 200.

The medieval commentators also preferred the second formula. The whole theory of the four senses was not applied by the Middle Ages to the authors of Scripture, but to the books, to the works themselves: the allegorical sense, and the tropological and anagogic senses, were there in the text, visible to the Christian who read with faith. They never asked whether or not the author of this or that book of the Old Testament perceived these senses with the same precision that they did.

When scholastic speculation began on the prophetic charism, the problem was discussed from the point of view of the mind of the prophet, more especially his knowledge. The tract was usually referred to as "Concerning the Prophetic Knowledge." The neo-scholastic movement of the last century concentrated on the psychological aspect of the problem, situating the discussion within the head of the author; this exclusive concentration has not been without its dangers.

The object of the definition of Vatican I is the books themselves, which are "holy and canonical . . . because, being written under the inspiration of the Spirit, they have God for their author, and as such they have been confided to the Church."[4] Note the last phrase: It is not the authors which have been confided to the Church, but their books; and this is the reality which continues to live in the Church.

The manuals which treat of inspiration, preoccupied as they are with the question of the "motion of the Holy Spirit," hardly ever considered this question. If we wish to gain an integral view of the mystery, we must combine the psychological view with one that is more literary.[5]

> Be not like your fathers whom the former prophets warned:
> "Thus says the Lord of Hosts:
> Turn away from your evil ways and from your wicked deeds."
> But they would not listen or pay attention to me, says the Lord.
> Your Fathers, where are they?
> And the prophets, can they live forever?

[4] D-S 3006; cf. ch. 2, n. 48.
[5] "*Olim dicebant sic: hic est liber a Deo conscriptus. Atqui liber constat non solis rebus seu veritatibus expressis, sed etiam expressione verbali. Ergo Deus ut sit auctor libri censendus est non res tantum scribendas sed etiam verba quibus exprimerentur, in individuo determinasse. Nunc vero solent ab inspiratione personali procedere.*" Pesch, no. 468.

But my words and my decrees, which I have entrusted to my
  servants, the prophets,
Did not these overtake your fathers?
Then they repented and admitted:
"The Lord of Hosts has treated us according to our ways and
  deeds,
Just as He determined he would." [6]

*We may make an accommodation of these words and apply
them to our question: Where are the sacred authors now? Are
they alive now, here in the Church of God on earth? No, but their
words still reach us, their books still live on in the Church.*

*When the theologians say that inspiration refers primarily to the
authors and secondarily to their books, they are speaking of temporal priority, and are taking care to reject anything that might appear to favor the theory of subsequent approval.*

Theopnuestos is said primarily of the man, secondarily it is said also of
the book composed by such a man.[7]

*In the order of intention, and therefore of importance, the
works are primary, and all the effort of the authors and their vocation is orientated toward the work to be produced. We might say,
though with some exaggeration, that Jeremiah means nothing to
us; what interests us is his work, because his work is the word of
God.*

*In this preoccupation, we find ourselves in agreement with the
modern tendency in literary criticism.[8] There was a time when the
science of literary investigation consisted in studying the life and
times of the author; the work was reduced to a symptom, included
for its value in the depth analysis of the writer, and at times as
proof of his pathological state. Some rationalists even applied these*

---

[6] Za 1:4–6.
[7] "Theopneustos est igitur primario HOMO; secundario autem ita vocatur
scriptum a tali homine compositum." Bea, op. cit., p. 6 (cf. ch. 1, n. 26).
[8] This is the orientation of the work mentioned before of Wellek and
Warren, Theory of Literature (ch. 4, n. 18). The two principal parts of the
book are concerned with "The Extrinsic Approach to the Study of Literature"
and "The Intrinsic Study of Literature." This is also the approach of Leo
Spitzer, and in general of the Stylistic Analysis School of literary criticism.
For a study of the various tendencies, cf. M. Wehrli, *Allgemeine Literaturwissenschaft*, Zurich, 1951. For a treatment of the methods of analysis, cf.
S. E. Hyman, *The Armed Vision*, New York, 1947.

methods to a study of "The Strange Experiences of the Prophets." Today, however, scholars are agreed that the proper object of literary science is the work itself, and that a study of the author and his epoch in the light of sociology, psychology, the history of ideas, etc., has a place only insofar as it aids in understanding the work.

In some circles, it used to be considered a great achievement if one could show that a work usually attributed to Smith was really the work of Jones, and with this triumph the investigation rested. But we are yet entitled to insist: Very well, the work was written by Jones and not Smith, nevertheless it still deserves to be studied in its own right.

These considerations, both of the biblical text itself and of the modern tendency of literary criticism, have prompted us to devote a separate chapter to a study of the inspired works.

What Is a Literary Work?

Usually, literary language is actualized in a literary work. Outside of a literary work, such language may do service in some other capacity—a conversation, a technical work, etc. Thus, it may happen that a conversation is a work of art—as was said of the conversations of Cocteau, though it may also come about that literary forms become common and thereby lose their elevation. There are works of a pedagogical nature whose main purpose is to impart technical knowledge, which still deserve a place among the works of literature—*L'Histoire naturelle* of Buffon, for example.

The intuition of the poet, or novelist, or dramatist, along with his subjective participation in reality, and the experiences he chooses to relate, acquire objective consistency in his work. This consistency is made up of words, of language forms whose own existence is in their signification, and which are communicable.

Is this true also of the Bible? We have already said that a large proportion of the Bible employs literary language. Is this language used to produce a series of individual works? Before proceeding to a comparison of the literature of the Bible and that of other literary works, it will be helpful to delineate the area of our analogy.

A work in the Old Testament may differ greatly from a modern work in the manner of its production; a work which has undergone successive elaborations at the hands of successive authors, and which achieves its final form by being incorporated into the work of yet another author, has not known the same process of composition as a novel by Mauriac. However, the process ought not to be identified with the work, and it is possible for the biblical processes to result in a true literary unity. We might recall, for instance that some sections of Macbeth seem to derive from the work of Thomas Middleton, and recall also the literary process we saw in St. John of the Cross's poem, "The Shepherd Boy," or that which produced the epic narrative of the ten plagues.

It might also be objected that there is a real divergence in the intention of a biblical author. It is usually said that a literary work is disinterested; it attempts to present reality for our contemplation and not primarily to stir us to action. Moreover, that which it would have us contemplate is found within the work itself, which is a self-contained, self-justified world.[9] The biblical authors, on the

[9] We must, however, maintain some presence of the intention of the author in his work. When Valéry protests that he desires not to "say" but to "make" (*poiema*, *poiesis*), he is reacting against an excessive expressionism which can degenerate into an absence of form. But in his reaction, Valéry goes too far. Could anyone seriously think that "The Graveyard by the Sea" says nothing? Rilke expresses himself more subtly when he asks of poets that they "say instead of feeling sorry for themselves," and that they "transmute into words those selves of theirs, as imperturbable cathedral carvers transposed themselves into the constant stone." In general, we might say that the poet or the artist gives himself up to his work and to its fashioning in such a way that the work is foremost in his mind and perhaps occupies all his conscious attention. But this immediate intention does not exclude the presence, albeit temporarily hidden, of a greater and more far reaching intention which reasserts its claim to conscious ratification at the proper time. It is this general intention to be of service to mankind, to the truth, or to God which in actual fact exercises its influence in the consummation of the work.

St. John of the Cross wrote poetry very well; whether it cost him much labor or little is not important. It is quite possible that in his case the presence of God dominated him even during the composition of the poem. What is important is that this presence did not destroy, but rather elevated and intensified the poetic and technical capacities of the author. Great poets, in their dedication to the work which they create, realize a great ambition to know, to say, and to reveal.

"Art for art's sake," as an explicit program of activity, can be a reaction against romanticism, but it is a perversion of something human. It effects its own retribution in the artistic destitution, insincerity, and lack of fidelity to art itself which follow in its train.

What we mean to say is that the supposed opposition between literary and biblical writings on the basis of their "intention" is groundless. In some cases, it is the product of a mentality which seeks to preserve Scripture from

I

other hand, are preoccupied with the necessity of proclaiming their message; they desire above all to influence and stir to action; thus, their intention is not truly literary. What this objection is really saying, is that the works of the Bible should be compared with another type of literature which is also capable of producing real literary entities: It is the literature of commitment, of message, of action; the literature of a "movement," but it is still literature. Again, we can take the example of St. John of the Cross: "Art for the sake of art, or even art pared to the bone, had no interest for him." [10] He had no intention of producing "works of art," yet what other Christian poetry can approach his?

It is possible to discuss this question on another plane. In a work of language, the human spirit reveals itself as it creates, and it manifests the world as re-created. Every work of art is the creation of a world achieved by imposing a form; every human creation effects something new and is a revelation. In this sense, art is essentially expression (though not precisely expressive); it is language. A work of literature as it transposes the practical or cosmic world to the world of representation, strips it of its bounded quality and makes it deeply significant; it shows forth clearly the truth of the being of this world, not by a series of statements (though these are not excluded), but by a process of re-presentation. When we say that a work is false, we do not refer to its propositions. Thus, to classify Scripture as a work of art is not to deny that it conveys meaning; it is rather to penetrate into the manner in which it intends to signify. The Emperor of Assyria, the proud, self-satisfied conqueror, is presented to us, and his reality, unforgettably experienced in the light of God, when we enter into the "mimesis" effected by Isaiah.

> Are not my commanders all kings?
> Is not Chalane like Charchamis,
> Or Hamath like Arphad,
> or Samaria like Damascus?

---

the slightest taint of "art for art's sake"; but this puritanism is itself occasioned by the contrary exaggeration. What mattered to the prophet was the proclamation of the message of God, and so he wished to compose a poem. His logic is admirable. It was precisely because the divine oracle meant so much to him that he was intent on its literary perfection.

[10] ". . . *le tenía sin cuidado el arte por el arte y aun el arte a secas.*" D. Alonso, *Poesía Española* (cf. ch. 7, n. 23), p. 280.

Just as my hand reached out to idolatrous kingdoms
that had more images than Jerusalem and Samaria,
Just as I treated Samaria and her idols,
shall I not do to Jerusalem and her graven images?

By my own power I have done it,
and by my wisdom, for I am shrewd.
I have moved the boundaries of peoples,
their treasures I have pillaged,
and, like a giant, I have put down the enthroned.
My hand has seized like a nest
the riches of nations;
As one takes eggs left alone,
so I took in all the earth;
No one fluttered a wing,
or opened a mouth, or chirped! [11]

There are some who imagine that to speak of biblical poetry or of literary works in the Bible is to render the Scriptures worthless. It means, they think, that the Bible thereby loses its importance as revelation, and therefore any importance whatsoever. It is true that methodologically one may institute a stylistic analysis of the text, prescinding for the moment from its total meaning, but to speak of the Bible as literature is not to restrict it to this specialized field. To say that the Bible is literature is not to say that it is unimportant.

But is not such an opinion a distortion of the facts? It is difficult to read the Epistle of St. James as a work of literature, and the same can be said of many of St. Paul's exhortations. We can still speak of such examples as "works," though we may doubt their aesthetic qualities. The liturgy continues to use such texts, not simply in order to discharge a duty toward them, but to reveal to us the Church in and through a moment of her existence. These passages or books were not taken up by the Church merely to satisfy some obligation.

All of this implies that we must accord to the term "work" an ample connotation, one that will extend from a sermon to a covenant. Having thus qualified the limits of our investigation, we are entitled to begin a description of a literary work, concentrating on

[11] Is 10:8–14. Cf. "Tres imagines de Isaías," EstBíb 15, 1956, pp. 74–79.

its most characteristic factors. We will then pass on to apply the analogy to the Bible, respecting the reservations necessarily implied.

THE LITERARY WORK

What is the nature of a literary work? There is an excellent treatment of this question in Chapter 12 of *Theory of Literature* by Wellek and Warren;[12] we will content ourself here, therefore, with giving a summation of their analysis. A literary work does not exist in the material dimension of writing—the paper, the type, the ink, etc.; nor in the written text, which is only a graphic notation, nor in the sequence of sounds uttered by the speaker or reciter, since this would result in making the work non-existent when it was not actually being recited. We cannot place the work of literature in the experience of the reader, which is manifold and changeable; nor in the experience of the author, which may be only partially objectified; nor in his intention, which may remain little more than that; and it is to no avail to seek the existence of a work in a certain amalgam of experiences on the part of society.

A literary work is a precise system of words, ordered one to another and having meaning; it is a structure or a system of structures. As a structure already accomplished, it is a realized act, and at the same time it is a potentiality which can be actualized. It is to this system that the graphic notation, as well as its readers and reciters, must have reference.

This description is applicable not only to a unified work which was born of a single dominant intuition, but also to a work of composition which utilized preëxisting materials, and even to a collaborative work in which one mind is principally directive and others coöperate. It applies in varying degrees to a proverb, a poem of two verses (Juan Ramón, Montale), a novel such as *War and Peace*, or an intricate drama, such as some of Calderón's mystery plays.

MULTIPLE STRUCTURE

A literary work possesses a multiple structure. That is, it has various levels of existence. In an ideal instance, these various levels are

[12] Cf. ch. 4, no. 18.

interrelated in harmony or counterpoint, in coördination or in designed dissonance.

There is first of all the level of sound with its various possibilities of expression, linked to the meaning of the words and giving pleasure to the ear; then there is the level of rhythm with its power to form and express; this is an ordering factor, providing a scheme for order, but it is also flexible, registering and conveying the tempo of the emotions. Built on these, and permeating them, there is the stratum of meaning with its concentric circles of connotation and resonance evoked by juxtaposition and association; this gives rise to the image level, embodying and reflecting the analogies of being, and producing fruitful and unsuspected insights. The image level gravitates toward small dynamic constellations whose structure is more or less actively determined by the inherited culture of the author. Moreover, these partial literary forms even exist in certain more generic structures, known as literary genres or types. Then there is the level of concept or idea or thought, virtually activating the whole structure, though actually existing in varying degrees of explicitness and conscious ratification.

These various strata realize and manifest the intellectual, imaginative, and emotional levels of man's existence, and thus actualize the three functions of language which we have seen before.[13] Dámaso Alonso has described this interweaving verbal structure with great sensitivity and literary experience; he finds outstanding examples of it in poetry. If we wish to extend and apply his description, we will be obliged to restrict the field of investigation and concentrate on certain aspects according to the nature of the work we are studying: poetry, prose, hymn, doctrinal treatise, narration, etc. We ought to allow room for the introduction of factors which can affect, either positively or negatively, the total meaning of a work, and we must allow for those cases in which the composition, especially of preëxisting material, has not resulted in a perfect interrelation of the various levels. The advantage of studying an ideal case lies in the fact that it allows us to

---

[13] " 'Sit quidvis simplex dumtaxat et unum,' said Horace. It seems almost the reverse of the truth. 'Complex dumtaxat et unum' would be better. Every real poem is a complex poem, and only in virtue of its complexity does it have artistic unity." W. K. Wimsatt, The Verbal Icon. Studies in the Meaning of Poetry, Lexington, 1954, p. 81.

describe the reality more fully, and alerts our receptivity and critical sense to the whole gamut of possibilities. If we begin with instances in which the possibilities are only minimally realized, we may develop a certain deafness or color-blindness with regard to some dimensions of literary reality. If someone were to study music only from the aspect of melody, he would undoubtedly be able to appreciate, say, monodic compositions, but he could not very well raise them to the position of a general norm for all music. He must also study harmony, counterpoint, tone, etc.

From what we have said about plurality, certain conclusions present themselves spontaneously. It is impossible to exhaust the appreciation and the analysis of a work by taking only one aspect of it, be this its conceptual level, the emotional or imaginative strata, the literary personality created, the action or plot, the desire to influence, etc. The necessities of method or the requirements of training may require that we concentrate on one aspect or another, but we must remember that it is but one aspect and nothing more, and that by isolating this aspect we have changed it somewhat, divorcing it from the total system in which it exists. I may extract from the rich complexity of an existing work an aspect that appeals to my temperament or state of soul, or present scholarly preoccupation; but I can never legitimately identify the aspect of my choice with the totality of the literary work.

When speaking about inspiration, we said that the inspired process was ordered to and reached fulfillment in the work. Now, if we take the case of a biblical work which actually and fully possesses all the levels of existence we have been describing, we are forced to ask ourselves whether or not inspiration extends to all of them. Should we consider that inspiration affects only certain strata of a biblical work? May we exclude, for instance, the expressive function of language as this is actualized by rhythm? Must we eliminate the resonances of a turn of phrase, and restrict its allusions in order to arrive at its purely conceptual significance as being the only one inspired? Or should we not rather consider as inspired the work as a whole in its total concretization with every level of its existence according to its own nature and the role it plays in the over-all language system?

We should note, however, that to affirm that all the levels of an inspired work are influenced by the motion of the Holy Spirit is not the same thing as to make all of them of equal importance: We cannot raise a rhythmic pattern to the status of an infallible proposition. When we say that the human nature of Christ was assumed by the Person of the Word, we do not exclude from the Incarnation any corporal member or organ or tissue, yet neither do we reduce the complete human organism of the man Christ to a uniform mass of "humanity." Each member, and organ, and tissue is assumed according to its particular function: the tongue for speaking, the hand for curing, the feet for walking, the nerves for receptivity and suffering, the blood for life and death. The same applies also to Our Lord's emotional life: weariness and fear, tenderness and compassion, anger and pity. We ought to regard the works of literature in the Bible in a similar way, for they are an image of man. The work in its totality is inspired, and this affects each element and stratum according to its nature and function; thus, the revelation of God gains entrance to us by every facet of our being which can be influenced by reality. If it seems to us that the simple, spiritual, and most pure knowledge of God is thereby humiliated, we should accept this mystery of self-abasement as a revelation of love. The Fathers liked to join together the mysteries of the "self-emptying" realized in the Incarnation with that of the divine condescension embodied in the Scriptures.

These same Fathers also delighted in the manifold wealth of the sacred text, and in this, too, their views were echoed by a unanimous choir of medieval commentators: Scripture is a forest, an ocean, a banquet, a heaven with ever-widening frontiers:

"An infinite forest of meanings." —"The deep forest of Scripture." —"With such depth as the deepest ocean." —"Sacred Scripture is the table of a rich man . . . the extent of whose riches cannot be measured." —"It is as impossible to enumerate all the delights which this table contains, as it is to dry up the whole ocean." —"Sacred Scripture is like a swift-flowing river; it fills the depths of the human mind, and still flows on, it satisfies him who draws from it, yet it remains inexhaustible." —"It is measured by the immensity of its mysteries." —"O the marvellous depths of your utterances!" [14]

---

[14] "*Infinita sensuum silva —latissimam scripturae silvam —in tanta profunditate, velut altissimo pelago —Mensa divitis sacra Scriptura est . . . cuius divitiarum altitudinis non est finis. —Huius mensae deliciae tam impossibile est explicare, quam universi abyssi pelagum absorbere—Scriptura sacra, morem rapidissimi fluminis tenes, sic humanarum mentium profunda replet,*

The Fathers and the medieval theologians attributed this plenitude of the Bible to the fact of its inspiration, its divine origin. But
we should not take this to mean that the wealth of the sacred text
is found there despite human activity; it is not some treasure hidden there by God, while the human author was asleep or dis-
tracted; it is, rather, incarnated in the text in the process by which
the text was written. We could say, in keeping with the thought of
the Fathers, that the plurality of the work was assumed by the
charism of inspiration in order to reveal the plurality of the divine
revelation. It is in this context that the medieval authors elaborated their theory of the four senses of Scripture. The following
text of St. Bonaventure is representative of their thought:

The breadth of the Scriptures refers to the number of their parts; the
length, to their account of the times and periods; the height, to their
description of the orderly levels of hierarchies; and the depth, to their
abundant allegorical senses and interpretations. . . . It is entirely
logical for Scripture to have a threefold sense in addition to the literal:
such amplitude consorts with its content, its hearer or disciple, its
origin, and its end. It consorts with its content, for scriptural teaching
is concerned with God, with Christ, with the works of salvation, and
with the things of faith. God is the Being covered by the Scriptures;
Christ is the power; the works of salvation are the action: and the
things of faith are the sum of all three aspects. Scripture's manifold
meaning consorts with its hearer. None but the humble, pure, faithful,
and attentive can hear it properly. As a deterrent to pride, a mysterious and profound signification is hidden under the shell of its obvious meaning. The very depth that lies beneath the humble word re-
proves the proud, chases out the unclean, drives away the insincere,
and awakens the slothful to search the mysteries. . . . Scripture's
manifold sense is proper to the source whence it comes: God, through
Christ and the Holy Spirit speaking by the mouth of the prophets and
of the others who committed its doctrine to writing. Now, God speaks
not with words alone, but also with deeds, for with Him saying is
doing and doing is saying; moreover, all creatures are the effects of
God's action, and, as such, point to their Cause. Therefore, in Scripture, which is received from God, both words and deeds are meaningful. Again, Christ the Teacher, lowly as He was in the flesh, remained

---

*ut semper exundet; sic hauriente satiat ut inexhausta permaneat —myster-
iorum immensitate extenditur. —Mira profunditas eloquiorum tuorum!"* H.
de Lubac, *Exégèse Médiévale*, Paris, 1959–1961, vol. 1, pp. 119ff.

lofty in His divinity. It was fitting, therefore, that He and His teachings should be humble in word and profound in meaning: Even as the Infant Christ was wrapped in swaddling clothes, so God's wisdom is wrapped in humble images. Finally, there was variety in the manner whereby the Holy Spirit brought enlightenment and revelation to the hearts of the prophets. As no mind is able to hide from Him, and as He was sent to teach all truth, it was fitting that His doctrine should harbor several meanings within a single utterance. Scripture's manifold sense also accords with its End. It was given to guide man's thoughts and actions so that he might arrive at his true goal; and since all the rest of creation was designed to serve him in his ascent toward his heavenly home, Scripture takes on the very diversity of created things, to teach us through them that wisdom which leads to eternal life.[15]

The text of St. Bonaventure with its orientation toward the "four senses" is the usual expression of what was the accepted method for drawing out the riches of the sacred text. As he moves from the realm of practice to a consideration of the fittingness of these four dimensions, he presents a theological view of Scripture.[16]

[15] "*Consistit autem ipsius latitudo in multitudine suarum partium, longitudo vero in descriptione temporum et aetatum, altitudo in descriptione hierarchiarum gradatim ordinatarum, profunditas in multitudine mysticorum sensuum et intelligentiarum.*" . . . *Subiecto inquam competit, quia ipsa est doctrina quae est de Deo, de Christo, de operibus reparationis et de credibile. Subiectum enim illius quoad substantiam est Deus; quoad virtutem, Christus; quoad operationem, reparationis opus; quoad omnia haec est ipsum credibile.* . . . *Competit etiam hoc auditori . . . ut ipsius profunditate in humilitate litterae latente, et superbi comprimantur, et immundi repellantur, et fraudulenti declinentur, et negligentes excitentur ad intelligentiam mysteriorum.* . . . *Competit etiam principio a quo est: quia est a Deo, per Christum et Spiritum Sanctum loquentem per ora prophetarum et aliorum qui hanc doctrinam scripserunt. Quoniam autem Deus non tantum loquitur per verba, verum etiam per facta, quia ipsius dicere facere est, et ipsius facere dicere; et omnia creata tamquam Dei effectus innunt suam causam; ideo in Scriptura divinitus tradita non tantum debent significare verba, verum etiam facta. —Christus etiam doctor, licet humilis esset in carne, altus tamen erat in deitate: ideo decebat ipsum et eius doctrinam habere humilitatem in sermone cum profunditate sententiae.* . . . *Spiritus etiam sanctus diversimodo illustrabat et revelationes faciebat in cordibus prophetarum: ipsum etiam nullus latere potest intellectus, et missu erat omnem docere veritatem; ideo competebat eius doctrinae, ut in uno sermone multiplices laterent intelligentiae. Competit nihilominus ipsi fini: quia Scriptura data est ut per ipsam dirigatur homo in cognoscendis et agendis, ut tandem perveniat ad optanda.*" Breviloquium, pp. 202–206 (cf. ch. 3, n. 13).

[16] This wealth or fruitfulness is not exclusively due to the literary nature of a work. A simple formula or statement of the truth can contain a world:

We should also note, however, that this notion of the abundant riches of the sacred text is applied to the Bible as a whole. It cannot be predicated indiscriminately of every single part. There are sections which have a very modest role in the over-all context; there are others which, if divorced from their context, would seem poor indeed. A book of ceremonies makes no pretensions at being a complete literary work, fully activating all the levels of its existence; nor does it present itself as the most apt means of inspiring sublime sentiments. But a book of ceremonies, seen in relation to the cult, which is its frame of reference, assumes new dimensions of meaning, and can reveal unsuspected depths of theological insight. This is the case with the Book of Leviticus. An experience and a good piece of advice can soon be depleted; yet, when integrated in a whole series, such sayings can shed light on the meaning of human existence. This is exemplified by a work such as the Book of Proverbs.

Either extreme in this regard is dangerous. There is an enthusiasm which sees profundity everywhere, and a skepticism that hesitates to see it anywhere. Neither is correct, but it is foolish to imagine that skepticism is a better guide to the meaning of a text than enthusiasm.

Much can be said in a few words. This is especially true when the statement embraces a wide horizon of human experience. In such a case, the depth of the original formula is made explicit in successive articulations. This is exemplified in the simple formulation of some great intuitive insight which then becomes the principle of multiple and repeated reflection.

On the other hand, that quality of a literary work in virtue of which it embodies such wealth, can be shared by works which are not, in the strict sense, literary compositions. We see this verified in those great intellectual constructions which are embued with an immense spiritual fecundity— despite some errors—that cannot be simply equated with the sum total of their propositions. The *Summa Theologica* of St. Thomas, St. Augustine's *City of God*, Hegel's *The Philosophy of History*, a play by Calderón or Shakespeare, all of these must certainly be classified as "rich," and all of them possess a similar intellectual beauty.

There is no doubt that such compositions as the Epistle to the Romans, or to the Hebrews, fall within the category of literary work in the wide sense. The modern analytical technique known as *Redaktionsgeschichte* tends to accord the same judgment in regard to the Gospels. There are some books, such as Ben Sira, whose quality as a literary work still escapes us; but perhaps future study in this direction may yield some agreeable surprises.

Structured Plurality

The second thing we ought to note about this plurality is that it is structured. A literary work is a dynamically interrelated unity whose parts can be determined by analysis, but which cannot be truly understood without that which Dámaso Alonso calls "a total intuition." [17] Alonso applies this term especially to poetry, which, as he notes, proceeds from just such an intuition. We can, however, extend its application by analogy to any kind of literary work, including those which have resulted from a carefully designed plan or composition, or even those which are conscious imitations. If there exists such a thing as a merely juxtaposed series of phrases, then, of course, we would have to read it that way, allowing each statement to be autonomous and separate.

This raises the delicate question of context. An anthology which a good poet makes of his own verses is, theoretically, the juxtaposition of autonomous poems, written and conceived separately. Nevertheless, the selection of these poems and their organization creates an over-all context which is capable of shedding light on each individual poem by highlighting resemblances, antinomies, key words, similarity of structure, etc. If I pick up the collected poems of T. S. Eliot, read them through, and then return to the first poem, I see it in a new light. I experience the two factors which unify the collection: the fact that one man wrote all these poems, and the secondary fact of their being chosen and organized in an anthology.

Then there is the example of an anthology created from the works of a school of poetry, or of a period or theme. The context thus created becomes a secondary unifying factor whose worth depends primarily on the capacities of the compiler. If done well, this context allows the individual works mutually to shed light on one another. If, however, the compiler be an irresponsible dunce, he will produce not a context, but confusion: if, for all practical purposes, he takes lines, stanzas, titles, and notes, and tosses them in a hat, shakes it, and then sets them down in the order in which he draws them out, we hardly think it worthwhile to read or study his work. The Bible did not come about in this manner, though there

[17] *Op. cit.* (n. 10, and ch. 7). Cf. also Leo Spitzer, *Linguistics and Literary History*, New York, 1962, esp. ch. 1.

269

was undoubtedly a series of successive anthologies, giving rise to the final unity.

Would we be entitled to call this anthology a "work" of literature? Yes, analogically; it possesses structure and plurality and can be read and analyzed as such. This is what exegesis does when it compares passages, formulas, schemata, and themes. And this is what the liturgy does when it selects and reorganizes a series of smaller units.

The total view of a work is obtained by reading it through completely, since a literary work is essentially temporal, as is its medium, language. This temporality is not the sum of its moments, nor a series of partial and autonomous readings. However much we analyze a text, separating unities and studying them, we must return to a total vision of the work in order to make a synthesis. Thus, in New Testament study there is first the discipline of form criticism, by which individual units are isolated and explained in virtue of their genesis within the early community; this is followed by "redaction criticism," in which the units are seen within the structure of one of the Gospels, and their mutual relations are studied in this dimension, as well as in comparison with the other Gospels; then there is the further synthesis which presents the theology of the synoptics or of all the Gospels on one theme or aspect of New Testament teaching. This can be further integrated into an over-all "theology of the New Testament." In the liturgy, on the other hand, the predominant emphasis is on the over-all unity which is presented in the liturgical cycle: the history of salvation and the mystery of Christ. As we will see further on, this sense of unity is achieved in large part by the power of the liturgy to repeat and re-present.

Thus, it appears that the unity achieved in the Bible is variable and does not always coincide with our norms and procedures. Because of its character as public revelation, its over-all unity by which it transcends the individual work of each author is its most important aspect. This unified structure is derived from the plan of God to which it bears witness and of which it is itself a part; there is also the unity of tradition extending over millenniums, which it sums up and which finds expression in the process by which one inspired theologian accepts and builds on the work of his predecessors, as well as in the process by which individual units and strands were united and transposed, as they were incorporated in ever larger anthologies. Finally, there is the unity achieved by the Scriptures within that process by which the Church took the Scriptures to herself, added to them, and used them to effect and express her own crystallization. This whole objective process is one more reason why we cannot be content with a psychological exegesis which restricts itself entirely to the mind of the author as the only norm for determining the meaning of the text. The transcendent unity of the Bible does not suppress its lesser structural unities; rather, it enshrines them. Thus, the various types and levels of unity which are to be found therein become themselves a vehicle of revelation and facilitate understanding.

The structural unity of a work gives rise to another interesting consequence: It is possible to arrive at the life center of a piece of literature by many different roads, and having once arrived there, it is possible to view the whole from within this center. The center we are referring to is the center of the work, not that of the author. Tolstoy describes this phenomenon by using the image of converging lines: "In a work of art, the important thing is to achieve a focal point wherein all the lines converge and from which they emanate." Maritain speaks in this connection of the "immanent action" of a poem.

Sometimes the work itself indicates avenues of access to its life center; at other times it seems closed, and some minor level of its existence provides the key. Then there are times when the particular temperament or sensibilities of the reader dictate the means of entrance. A scholar may work for long periods of time and finally announce that he has found the key; this is not pride, but only the enthusiasm of the specialist. The Bible in its totality leaves many doors open so that the people of God may enter into its Holy of Holies. It is a pastoral duty to keep these doors open and to point them out to God's people.

What we have said about avenues of approach must be applied variously according to the nature of the work in question: There are some works which seem to have only one door, and this is not only hard to find, but also does not allow everyone to pass through without distinction. In the Bible, there are sections and even whole works which are difficult to understand; not everything is equally accessible and uniformly easy to expose. This is why the liturgy of the cathedrals (as distinct from that of monasteries) has always favored a selective reading.

CONSISTENCY

Another characteristic of a literary work is its inner consistency, its capacity as a self-enclosed entity to maintain its individuality (an individual according to the philosophers is something which is "one in itself and distinct from other things"). But this distinction does not mean that it is "closed to the public," or that it cannot be received and used by society. What gives this consistency to a work is its form. As Henry James puts it: "Form alone takes, and holds and preserves substance." [18]

Let us recall what we said about the language of conversation. When it is true dialogue and not technical discussion, conversation is completely realized in its passage. Its influence may be profound, even decisive in someone's life, still conversation exists by and for its passing (even if it is indiscreetly taped on a recorder). An interview for a periodical or for a television program is not a simple conversation, but a conventional form of "literature," and in this sense approaches the nature of a "work"; the same can be said, for example, of the conversations between Eckermann and Goethe.

A conversation exists in passing, but a literary work seeks to subsist, and it achieves this in an organized language system. The medium here becomes constitutive as well as revealing, and this is the meaning of Lützeler's phrase, "In science, language is at the service of meaning [sinndienend], in poetry language makes meaning [sinnbildend]." [19] While a dialogue unites two people by its flow, a literary work stays there like solidified concrete. Such things as light literature or writings entirely committed to the moment, may be exceptions to this, but these do not nullify the standard norms, nor are such things found in the Bible.

In the plan of revelation, God has willed to make Himself known in artifacts of language which are not completely grasped in a day, but are meant to last "from generation to generation." This fact was appreciated by the Fathers when they instinctively preferred to

[18] In a letter to Hugh Walpole, May 19th, 1912. *The Letters of Henry James*, selected and edited by P. Lubbock, New York, 1929, vol. 2, p. 237.
[19] *Einführung in die Philosophie der Kunst*, Bonn, 1934, p. 10.

speak of the work rather than of the author, when they discussed the Scriptures.

But was it always so? Have all the inspired works lasted down to our times? Theoretically, of course, we cannot put limits on the Holy Spirit; He could very well have inspired works which were only destined for their time. How many prophets spoke the word of God, and never wrote it? When St. Paul says that "All these things happened to them by way of symbol, and they were written for our instruction, on whom the terminal point of the ages has come," he said that of all the things which are in the Scriptures, but he did not necessarily mean that everything that happened to the people of old was written down, or that once having been written it was preserved for us. Admitting this possibility, we can go on to ask whether or not it is probable that the Holy Spirit acted in this way. In Geiselmann's theory of the canon, such a procedure is presumed:[20] The Church has chosen from among inspired works those which she found necessary or fitting—nature is prodigal in the abundant production of life, and the Holy Spirit is prodigal in His gift of inspiration. On the other hand, there are authors who deduce from the nature of inspiration the fact that it must be rare.

From what we know today about the formation of the Bible, it is reasonable to suppose that there were other inspired works which did not endure; the evidence does not allow us to go further than this probability. The whole question is, as a matter of fact, a bit academic, since, when we speak of sacred Scripture, we are referring to those books which have been "confided to the Church."

WRITING

A literary work possesses consistency because of its realization in a structured system of words, but not precisely because it is written. I might preserve a conversation by means of a tape recorder, but this adds nothing to its nature as a passing reality; a great work of drama might be lost, and then instinctively we feel that violence has been done to something which by its nature ought to endure (recall the efforts of the literary school of ancient Alexandria to form a canon).

The way in which a literary work is preserved is secondary. The

[20] *Die Heilige Schrift und die Tradition* (cf. ch. 5, n. 20).

bards relied on their memory, our culture has developed the written word with its various ideograms, sign systems, etc. God has chosen writing as the means of preserving and transmitting the words He has inspired, and this is why we call them the Scriptures.

It is interesting to reflect, however, that what we actually conserve is not the work, but its notation. If I look at a score of Beethoven, I cannot say that it is his *Pastoral*. A symphony is a system of orchestrated sounds, whereas what I hold in my hand is nothing but sheets of lined paper with little black dots on them. I cannot put my ear to the paper in order to hear the symphony. In the same way, writing only preserves the "score" of a literary work; it is, however, the means of access to the work itself.[21]

Since we live in a culture which abounds in written texts, and since the technique of writing and printing has a reciprocal influence on the techniques of composing, we have reached the point where we have identified the work with its written expression. We read poems in a subdued voice (that is, we don't read them), and we conceive of language in terms of letters and not sounds. Imagination can supply; orchestra directors read a new score, and hear the music without sound, but the majority of men must hear the music if they are to know the work; and there are some who read the score, even as they listen to the piece.

In the field of literature, however, the majority of readers feel no need to hear what they are looking at, even going so far as to read a play silently.

The sacred books are merely the notation of the word of the inspired message; they are nothing more, and nothing less.

This consideration of the consistency of a literary work and of the relation it bears to written expression, brings us to another of its qualities which we would like to describe.

REPETITION

A literary work can and indeed must be repeated. In a conversation, we only repeat something or ask to have something repeated when it was not understood; we repeat a poem, either reading or

[21] Cf. L. Lavelle, *La parole et l'écriture*, Paris, 1947, and Gadamer's *Wahrheit und Methode* (cf. ch. 6, n.7), II, 1, b, "Die Verwandlung ins Gebilde und die totale Vermittlung."

reciting it, precisely because we have understood it, and as our understanding grows so does our joy in repeating the experience.

In literature, a work only conveys its message when it is actualized in the process by which a reader or listener creates it once again. Many readers repeat a work, but it remains inexhaustible. The reader or reciter actively re-creates the work, yet it remains intact. The work is changed slightly under the active influence of the one who recites it, yet it always maintains its identity; it is repeated indefinitely, but it is not multiplied.

This is the paradox of a poem which subsists in its written expression. It does not actully exist when it is not being repeated; it is not truly repeated, unless the reader creates once again its unifying life principle, but it is never repeated identically in the same way.

A literary work is a presentation which is only actualized in its re-presentation: this re-presentation (in the broad sense of that word) makes the work present again, and thus allows the work to actualize its own re-presentation. Repetition presents the work in the act of expressing something and of thus realizing its meaning. Actualization implies presence, the real repetition of a work, and not the simple act by which its existence is remembered; it is a vision being lived in the present.

This is the way that the Church receives and keeps the sacred writings. It is not a question of a mere material conservation, but of a handing on, a tradition, of the works of the Bible, so that the faithful may repeat and relive them, actualizing and ratifying the intuition which gave them birth. This is the meaning of the ancient adage that meditation on the sacred text reaches perfection *quando lector fit auctor* (when the reader becomes the author), and it is the source of that privileged position which the Scriptures hold in the liturgy, the whole purpose of which is to "recall" and "re-present" the salvific acts of God in history.

Let us imagine these two possibilities: A community of monks knows all the Psalms by heart and recites them every day; then, during a persecution, they are deprived of any written exemplar of the Psalter. A Christian has a lovely bound copy of the Psalms in a deluxe edition, but he never reads it. In the first instance, the inspired words are not lost; in the second, they never existed.

FIDELITY

The necessity that a literary work has of being repeated, poses the question of fidelity. Because of the fact that a work only actually exists as repetition, which necessarily implies multiplicity and variability, there is a permanent norm and certain limits of tolerance in which the variations must move. For the sake of clarity, we will illustrate this with examples taken from the world of music and the theatre.

Ought there to be a stable tradition governing the manner in which the Baroque theatre of Calderón should be presented? Is the stage setting now used by Wagner's grandsons faithful to the work of the master? How quickly should we perform the works of da Vittoria or di Lasso? In order to provide practically for these types of questions, our culture has formed two groups of men to whom, in a certain sense, the works have been confided. First, there is the corps of interpreters: the pianists, the directors, the actors, the poetry readers, etc. Then there is the corps of critics, historians, theorists, etc. These groups sustain a force and are, in turn, sustained by it; it is the force of living tradition. In this force, as it is kept alive, there resides the control exercised by society in receiving and appreciating the re-creation of the works of art. Every pianist gives a personal interpretation to a work by Beethoven, while remaining within the limits of substantial fidelity. By means of these repetitions, we possess a living and uninterrupted tradition. An orchestra director is expected to have passed through a very demanding technical formation—counterpoint, composition, the theory of music, etc. However, in the last analysis it is up to him to re-create the work in each concrete performance. He himself finds it very helpful to listen to recordings of a symphony directed by the composer.

This interpretative tradition is transmitted in our Western culture with a great measure of fidelity; still, the differences in sensibility and outlook necessarily bring with them changes in the manner of interpreting each work. It pertains to the corps of critics and scholars to see that the modifications do not exceed the limits of a substantial fidelity to the original.

We have concentrated on the example of music, because there our experience of successive interpretation is undeniable. It is another matter in literature, so long as we think that every silent reading of the text is valid. It is fashionable today to consider as ideal that type of reading which moves as fast as possible, and there are even courses advertised to teach people to read three pages a minute. This is all right for periodicals and for the mountains of paper passing over the desk of an administrator, supplying him with background and committee reports. But I cannot speed up an adagio of Bach; no one will admit the theory that if I play the tape recorder twice as fast as I ought to, I can hear twice as many symphonies in the same time—in fact, I will have heard nothing. But this is the kind of thing that is often said about the repetition of literature in general, and even of poetry. If we are so pressed for time that we have only half an hour, at least let us not waste it completely by trying to "read" thirty pages of poetry or sixty of narrative.

One of the functions of a liturgical recitation of the Scriptures will be to maintain a moderate tempo. It is certainly to be hoped that the new techniques of recording poetry readings, plays, etc., will create once again a sense of the sound dimension of these works, and impart a feeling for their tone and rhythm.

In the Church

Since the sacred text only actually exists when it is repeated, and since this text has been confided to the Church, it follows that it is the Church's responsibility to have certain groups who devote themselves to maintaining the living tradition and assuring fidelity to the works received. In this case, however, the normal, human reality of a group of critics and scholars is raised to a higher sphere, that of the Spirit. What is a simple fact of human culture is also in this context a charismatic reality.

First, there must be a body of men who can authoritatively interpret the sense of the sacred text and set the limits of tolerance within which personal variations will remain authentic throughout the generations of readers and reciters. This corps, invested with authority, will be able to perform its task with much greater security and deep fidelity than any purely human institution, since it possesses within it, still active and dynamic, the same Spirit who first inspired the works. We call this body the magisterium.

This first group usually works in collaboration with another subordinate body: that of the technical experts who apply the methods of analysis and criticism, as well as other techniques of human science, to the text, in order to remove the obstacles and prepare the way for a deeper and more vital appreciation of the sacred books. They correct interpretations that have wandered from the right path, though not, of course, with the authority proper to the magisterium. Since they apply the methods of the human sciences to a book which is also human, it is possible and even normal that they will discover new aspects, even though they may not be charismatically enlightened by the Holy Spirit. In this case, the human contribution of technique leads to a greater understanding of the message of God, since all the levels of the literary work, each according to its own nature and function, have been permeated by the Holy Spirit. Then, too, these experts, as good Christians, enter into the life center of the sacred text, and participate in their own way in the activity of the Spirit within the Church. Thus, the scholars prolong and refine the interpretations of the magisterium, and prepare for those of the future.

A wide field is still left open to the private student, in which his hermeneutical skill may display itself with signal effect and to the advantage of the Church. On the one hand, in those passages of Holy Scripture which have not as yet received a certain and definite interpretation, such labors may, in the benignant providence of God, prepare for and bring to maturity the judgment of the Church; on the other, in passages already defined, the private student may do work equally valuable, either by setting them forth more clearly to the flock and more skillfully to scholars, or by defending them more powerfully from hostile attack.[22]

A third group in the Church who actively receive and transmit the living tradition in regard to the text are those who recite it. Their usual place is within the liturgical action. The scope of their

[22] "Nam privato cuique doctori magnus patet campus, in quo, tutis vestigiis, sua interpretandi industria praeclare certet Ecclesiaeque utiliter. In locis quidem Divinae Scripturae, qui expositionem certam et definitam adhuc desiderant, effici ita potest, ex suavi Dei providentis consilio, ut, quasi praeparato studio iudicium Ecclesiae maturetur; in locis vero iam definitis potest privatus doctor aeque prodesse, si eos vel enucleatius apud fidelium plebem et ingeniosius apud doctos edisserat, vel insignius evincat ab adversariis." Providentissimus Deus, EB 109; RSS, p. 15.

activity has been greatly reduced over the centuries, but in our day, due to the great liturgical renewal and the restored prominence of the word of God, this office in the Church will become correspondingly important.

We call his third group the "Order of Readers" (*Lectores*). In the light of what we have said about the interpretative and actualizing functions of repetition, it is easy to see what an important role this is, and how necessary it is to form good readers. They must be men whose character and training will enable them worthily to "re-present" the sacred text, not only in its intellectual content, but at every level of its plurality and structure. But this is a question of something more than dignity in the sense of splendor; the very being of the inspired work is, or ought to be, made actual in its repetition. The authentic existence of the word of God depends for its reality not only on the magisterium and the scholars, but also on the readers at the liturgy. This is not the place to excuse negligence by an appeal to the omnipotence of God; we are here in the realm of the mystery of word of God, a mystery which is made present in and through men, and which reaches its culmination in the Incarnation. The word of God addressed to men becomes human once again in the intelligible and expressive voice of the reader, as the people of God assemble to listen to the voice of God. In this message, addressed at this moment to this community, the whole chain of authors, editors, and scribes is brought to fruition.

The authority of the magisterium, the *sensus fidelium*, and the labor of the exegetes, are not divergent forces variously applied to the text; they make up that one hierarchic unity in which tradition is alive and active, one force, sustained by the Spirit, which flows out from the Word and returns to the Word.

Bibliography for Chapter 10

What Is a Literary Work?   The best treatment in English is found in Wellek and Warren, *Theory of Literature*, ch. 12, "The Mode of Existence of a Literary Work of Art." In this chapter, the authors cite the fundamental work of R. Ingarden, *Das literarische Kunstwerk*, Halle, 1931, in which a phenomenological approach is applied to the problem of the existence of a literary work, and various levels or "strata" are distinguished. Cf. also H. G. Gadner, *Wahrheit und Methode*, Tübingen, 1960, and Dámaso Alonso, *Poesía Española. Ensayo de metodos y limites estilisticos*, Madrid, 1950. A phenomenological view of a literary work seems presupposed to the method outlined by L. Spitzer in ch. 1, "Linguistics and Literary History," in the book of the same name.

11. The Work and Its Translation

All that we have said about a literary work forces us to raise the question of translation. If the work only exists in its repetition as being its actualization and re-presentation, are we entitled to say that it receives an authentic repetition when it is translated?

God has spoken to us in very definite human languages, and He has respected the fact that language is not a medium through which we receive disembodied ideas, but a real medium of communication. If, then, I do not understand those languages, what good is it to me that God has spoken?—He has not spoken to me.

We have accepted the two terms "interpret" and "re-present" as synonymous in some areas of meaning, especially as applied to drama. To re-present is to interpret; to interpret something is to render it present once again. Can we say of that particular kind of interpretation which is called translation that it truly re-presents the work? We might note in passing that in many languages there is a semantic interpenetration between "interpret" and "translate." Greek has the word "ermeneuein," and in medieval Latin there was "interpretari," which was contrasted with "exponere" or "comment on the text." Translation is such an established art in our culture that we take it for granted; the average reader of Dostoevski or Mauriac never gives it a thought.

When we come to the problem of holy Scripture, the best procedure seems to be to accept the fact as it is, and then begin our reflection on it with the help of some background considerations.

The primary and immediate fact of our religious life ought to be the fact of the liturgy; now, the liturgy proclaims the word of God, and I either do not understand this word, or I understand it in a *translation. Beginning from this fundamental experience, we will cast a look backwards over the history of biblical translations.*

AN HISTORICAL REVIEW

The apostles were not totally unfamiliar with Hebrew, though the language they spoke was Aramaic. When they went to preach to the Gentiles—whose language and culture were Greek—and when they began to write, they cited the Old Testament according to the ancient Greek translation, known as the Septuagint. The one Gospel which, according to tradition, was written in Aramaic, was very soon translated and adapted for a Greek audience, and this translation is our canonical text. Following this example, the majority of the Fathers used the Septuagint, and, of course, read the New Testament in Greek, as they did the later books of the Old Testament (when they were considered canonical), which were composed in Greek. Some of the Fathers studied Hebrew, in order to penetrate the Scriptures more deeply; Origen, in his famous Hexapla, arranged the Hebrew text, its transliteration, and the then known Greek translations, in parallel columns for easy reference and comparison.

In the second century, culture began to center on Rome, becoming more explicitly Latin, so that Greek was no longer the language of the Western part of the Empire. A product of this Romanization was a series of Latin translations, and Pope Damasus, desirous of having a normative version, entrusted this work to St. Jerome. A scholar, thoroughly versed in the literary and rhetorical traditions of Greek and Latin, St. Jerome had undertaken the study of Hebrew and Aramaic in order to read the Scriptures for himself in his beloved *"hebraica veritas."* By correcting previous translations (with varying degrees of thoroughness), and by producing new translations, he finally achieved a vernacular translation for the people—in Latin, of course. (Every language is vernacular, during the time that it is actually in use; after that, it becomes either a foreign language or a dead one.)

Throughout the centuries in which the Latin culture predominated in the West, St. Jerome's translation became more and more widespread, until it eventually came to be considered the popular (*vulgaris*) Bible, the Vulgate. When non-Latin European cultures began to emerge, however, translations were soon made into their languages. Sometimes the whole Bible was translated, and sometimes only passages: liturgical pericopes, the Gospels, the Psalter, were all put into these new cultural media.

The Reformation gave a new impulse to the movement toward vernacular translations; some were made from the original languages, some were translations of the Vulgate, and Luther's translation was put into other European languages. This movement had a profound influence on the literary development of the various national languages. In some countries, Catholics reacted by producing their own vernacular translations of the Vulgate, though at times utilizing the translations of their enemies, the Protestants.

The Renaissance introduced a new emphasis on classical Latin and fostered the study of languages. This resulted in new translations in Latin which were more elegant or more literal (including interlinear translations); these new versions were made both from the original and from other ancient versions. In order to reduce the danger of confusion, however, the Council of Trent chose from among all the Latin translations the one called the Vulgate, and imposed this as normative for the Western Church; at the same time, certain limits were set for translation into the vernacular. These two Tridentine decisions received a rigorist interpretation in some countries.

Toward the end of the eighteenth century, as the Enlightenment was flourishing, Benedict XIV urged that translations be made of the Vulgate, and various writers in different countries responded by producing works of genuine literary merit (Petisco, Martini, et al.).

In our times, the directives of Pius XII have given an extraordinary impetus to modern translations from the original languages, so much so that publishing of the Scriptures has taken on some of the aspects of a business with the inevitable danger to quality.

These few facts can help to provide a background for the experience of any modern reader of the Bible who finds himself confronted with a wealth of translations to choose from. I read the Confraternity of Christian Doctrine translation; my friend reads Knox; the new curate likes the "RSV," the pastor still reads the Vulgate. But who is reading the word of God? Wouldn't it be better to make one English translation for everybody? Or perhaps we ought to insist on Latin for the whole Western Church, or teach everyone Greek and Hebrew. Isn't there any translation which is considered more reliable than another for those who cannot read the original languages? Well, there are two ancient translations which have always been regarded by tradition as specially privileged.

THE GREEK TRANSLATION KNOWN AS THE SEPTUAGINT

Recently, scholars have been airing the problem of the Septuagint: Is the Septuagint, they ask, part of the inspired corpus of the Scriptures, or is it merely a translation of the inspired books?

Some authors argue in this manner: The writers of the New Testament cite the Septuagint version as "the Scripture," that is, as the word of God; but in some instances, the Greek text differs from the Hebrew original. Therefore, it should either not be cited as Scripture, or it should be considered inspired.

So long as the translation is faithful, there is no difficulty, but when the Greek text does not correspond with the original, I cannot cite it as Scripture or as a translation of Scripture, unless, of course, this Greek text is itself inspired. But there are such citations, as a matter of fact, made by the authors of the New Testament; what right, then, do we have to say that just these verses are inspired?

The Septuagint translates the original quite well in some places; in other places, however, it does not render the Hebrew text at all, simply because the translator did not understand it. Then again, there are passages which transform the original, continuing or initiating a semantic evolution and transposing the whole to a new mentality and culture.

In the case of a simple misunderstanding, it seems somewhat hardy to maintain that the Holy Spirit has effected the deformation of a text He once inspired in order now to present it to the Church. It would be more in keeping with the general nature of the divine salvific providence to say that he permitted human imperfections, which do not substantially alter the message, as the text was transmitted or interpreted. Such things are already found in the Hebrew text.

There are instances when the text is transformed or transposed, and here we have an example of a new interpretation or representation. It is certainly wrong to think that all the recitations and readings of the original were perfectly equal and faithful to the point of identity. This would be to deny the nature of the work as something which needs to be repeated and finds it existence in repetition. A translation which transforms (as opposed to one which deforms) is but one more step in this direction. It involves the selection of one aspect of the original with a subsequent emphasis on it. Thus, there may occur a concentration on the conceptual aspect of a work, a minimizing of its symbolic quality, a spiritualization of the image, etc. This is the same sort of thing that we find in the various recitations of a work; there are those which are reserved and intellectual, others which are impassioned, still others which are contemplative, or dedicated to action, etc. Such variations in recitation and transpositions in translation are not opposed or foreign to the original which is present under that aspect of its total potentiality which has been actualized. In all these cases, however, we must maintain that the ultimate norm is not the translation, but the original. If the sacred writers cite a translation in this way, they are citing a possible interpretation of sacred Scripture.

But there are times when the New Testament authors invoke a text which departs from the meaning of the original. In these instances, a new element enters in: It is that activity which we call "making use of a text." This process is subsequent to and distinct from the purely interpretative function of repetition.[1] We can use a text to illustrate something, to support an argument, to stimulate reflection, or by way of allusion and ornamentation. We do not enter into the work, but rather subject it to another intention which is foreign to its own, but which is not necessarily opposed to it. A literary man knows how to use the words, phrases, and images of another in a way which is neither a simple citation nor an interpretation.

The authors of the New Testament can use the Old Testament in much the same way: developing an argument according to the rabbinic standards of the day, introducing an allusion or reflection which sheds light on the mystery of Christ, etc. This use of another

[1] Cf. C. H. Giblin, "As It Is Written. A Basic Problem in Noematics and Its Relevance to Biblical Theology," CBQ 20, 1958, pp. 327–353, 477–498.

text, since it is a literary activity which achieves objective existence in the work, is an inspired process. However, inspiration does not convert the free use of a text into a citation or interpretation. It is a literary procedure in its own right, one that is inspired, and one that allows more liberty to the author who uses the text.

Such are the possibilities. We are, after all, confronted with the inspired text, not with its authors. That which transpired in the mind of the author as he wrote with attention and conscious reflection, does not exactly adequate the reality of his work, especially if the work enters into the stream of a living tradition. In a certain sense, the work exceeds the author. As Kainz has remarked of this problem:

The statement of a theorem can develop a fecundity never foreseen by the scholar who first chose or found the words to express his new insight, and this fecundity may well go far beyond the initial intention of its author. A capacity for being exploited may attach itself to the original formula in such a way that it takes a direction quite other than that which was intended and for the sake of which it was conceived. Or, later on, there can occur some play on words or gloss which brings to light a real fecundity never even imagined at the beginning. . . . The formula has proved once again to be more intelligent than its creator.[2]

What Kainz says of scientific thought is all the more applicable to literary work wherein repetition, interpretation, and use have a much greater legitimate ambiance.

Returning now to the Septuagint, we may distinguish three different levels: the meaning of the Hebrew original, the meaning of the Greek translation, and the literary use made of this latter in the New Testament. Benoit and Auvray defend the inspiration of the first two levels as being the only way that we can understand

2 "Ein Lehrsatz kann eine Fruchtbarkeit entfalten, an die der betreffende Forscher gar nicht gedacht hatte, als er eben diese Worte für seine neue Erkenntnis wählte oder fand, eine Fruchbarkeit also, die über die Ausgangs-intention ihres Schöpfers weit hinausreicht. An die vorhandene Formulierung kann sich eine Auswertbarkeit schliessen, die in ganz anderer Richtung liegt als der, auf die der Satz ursprünglich zielte, um derentwillen er konzipiert war. Ja es kann ein wortspielhaft erlebter, ein glossomorpher Einfall im weitern Verlauf eine sachliche Fruchtbarkeit erweisen, die anfänglich nicht zu vermuten stand. . . . Die Formel war wieder einmal gescheiter als ihr Schöpfer." Kainz, Psychologie der Sprache, vol. 1, pp. 259–260.

the citation in the New Testament.[3] But we believe that there is another alternative—to place the inspiration in the first and the third levels. The Hebrew original is inspired, and the New Testament use made of its Greek version is also inspired. It then follows that St. John had no intention of defining for us, with the help of faultless philology, what Isaiah meant in a given text.

We do not pretend to close the discussion once and for all with the solution we have proposed; there is no definition of the magisterium which settles the issue. The majority of scholars do not consider that the Septuagint is inspired, and the articles of Benoit and Auvray have not met with wide acceptance.

However, the ancient Greek version of the Old Testament will always retain the privilege of having been for all practical purposes the Bible of the writers of the New Testament and of the Church during her period of formation. This privileged position is still actively accorded to the Septuagint by the Oriental Church.

THE VULGATE

The other translation which commands our special reverence is the Vulgate. It was the text of the Western liturgy for more than a thousand years; centuries of theologians have studied it, and generations of Christians received from it their faith and devotion, and in turn gave these expression through its phrases.

No one ever thought of calling the Vulgate inspired, but there have been those who considered it the only reliable text from which to receive the word of God. It will suffice in this regard to cite the post-Tridentine theologian Melchior Cano, who has exercised a vast influence on later ages through his *De locis theologicis*.

CHAPTER 12 In which are set forth the arguments of those who wish to maintain that for the understanding of sacred Scripture recourse must be had to the Hebrew and Greek sources.

CHAPTER 13 In which there is proved the authority of the ancient Vulgate edition, and that recourse is not to be had now to the Hebrew and Greek Text.

CHAPTER 14 In which the arguments in Chapter 12 are refuted.

Among Cano's own arguments, one finds this polemical position:

[3] Cf. the works referred to in the bibliography.

The scholars among the Hebrews, that is, our enemies, strive with great effort to corrupt the Hebrew text, in order to render it contrary to our exemplars, as Eusebius relates in his *Ecclesiastical History*, Book 4, Chapter 18. And the Greeks do the same thing in many places; in order to twist the Scriptures to fit their theories, they violate the New Testament.[4]

When responding to the arguments of those who wish to have recourse to the original languages, Cano supposes that the translator who produced the Vulgate was endowed with a charism similar to the prophetic charism, but he does not go on to make this declaration of his more precise:

> . . . either the ancient translator rendered the sacred writings through a special grace of the Holy Spirit, or the Latin Church has not possessed for all these centuries the Gospel of God, but of man. You may object that the translator was not a prophet. Certainly, he was not a true prophet, but he possessed a charism very closely approximating that of prophecy (as Titelmann has rightly asserted) which I have shown to be necessary for the translating of the sacred text. Especially was this necessary, so that the Latin Church would have an edition of the sacred books which it could safely follow in matters of faith and morals.[5]

Finally, in Chapter 15, Cano recognizes the utility of knowing Hebrew and Greek: in order the better to converse with infidels, when the Latin text is not as strong; in order to get various mean-

---

[4] Liber ii Cap 12 "*Ubi eorum argumenta ponuntur, qui suadere volunt, in sacrarum intelligentia Scripturarum, ad fontes Hebraicum et Graecum recurrendum.*"

Cap 13 "*In quo veteris vulgatae editiones autoritas demonstratur, et quod non est nunc ad Hebraeos Graecosve recurrendum.*"

Cap 14 "*In quo argumenta capitis duodecimi refutantur.*"

"*Item Hebraeorum doctores, nostri videlicet inimici, multo studio contenderunt textum Hebraicum corrumpere, ut vetus testamentum nostris exemplaribus facerent esse contrarium, ut Euseb. lib. 4. eccl. hist. 18. refert. Graeci quoque eadem contentione multis locis, ut scripturam ad suum sensum traherent, novum testam. violarunt.*" Liber II, Cap 13.

[5] "*. . . aut veterem interpretem Spiritus sancti peculiari dono sacras literas convertisse, aut ecclesiam Latinam multis retro seculis non Dei habuisse Evangelium, sed hominis. Cum igitur objicit, interpretem non fuisse Prophetam. Sane vero propheta non fuit, habuit tamen (ut Titelmannus recte asseverat) spiritum quendam prophetico vicinum & proximum: qualem necessarium esse ostendimus sacris literis interpretandis. Imo qualis erat necessarius, ut ecclesia Latina editionem sacrorum librorum haberet, quam tuto in fide & moribus sequeretur.*" Liber II, Cap 14.

288

ings from the same passage, so that one may understand idioms, turns of phrase, and proverbs; and in order to understand the Hebrew and Greek words incorporated in the Latin text.

This position was common doctrine, at least in practice, for many centuries. When the acts of the Council of Trent were published, it was evident that zealous theologians of subsequent periods, in their polemic preoccupation, had exaggerated and solidified an extreme position. In his encyclical, *Divino afflante Spiritu*, Pius XII authoritatively interpreted the Tridentine decree:

Nor should anyone think that this use of the original texts, in accordance with the methods of criticism, in any way derogates from those decrees so wisely enacted by the Council of Trent concerning the Latin Vulgate. It is historically certain that the Presidents of the Council received a commission, which they duly carried out, to beg, that is, the Sovereign Pontiff in the name of the Council that he should have corrected, as far as possible, first a Latin, and then a Greek, and Hebrew edition, which eventually would be published for the benefit of the Holy Church of God. If this desire could not then be fully realized, owing to the difficulties of the times and other obstacles, at present it can, we earnestly hope, be more perfectly and entirely fulfilled by the united efforts of Catholic scholars.

And if the Tridentine Synod wished "that all should use as authentic" the Vulgate Latin version, this, as all know, applies only to the Latin Church and to the public use of the same Scriptures; nor does it, doubtless, in any way diminish the authority and value of the original texts. For there was no question then of these texts, but of the Latin versions, which were in circulation at that time, and of these the same Council rightly declared to be preferable that which "had been approved by its long-continued use for so many centuries in the Church." Hence, this special authority, or, as they say, *authenticity* of the Vulgate was not affirmed by the Council particularly for critical reasons, but rather because of its legitimate use in the Churches throughout so many centuries; by which use, indeed, the same is shown, in the sense in which the Church has understood and understands it, to be free from any error whatsoever in matters of faith and morals; so that, as the Church herself testifies and affirms, it may be quoted safely and without fear of error in disputations, in lectures, and in preaching; and so its authenticity is not specified primarily as *critical*, but rather as *juridical*.[6]

---

[6] "*Neque arbitretur quisquam hunc primorum textuum usum, ad critices rationem habitum, praescriptis illis quae de Vulgata Latina Concilium Triden-*

Among all the diverse Latin translations in the Latin Church, for public use, the Vulgate is to be preferred. This is the moderate scope of the Tridentine decree.

As a matter of fact, anyone who wants to become directly acquainted with our rich theological tradition has to know the Vulgate, since it was the dogmatic basis for centuries of theological thought in the West. But that does not mean that the Vulgate must always retain this position, nor can it continue to be a sincere expression of faith and devotion for those who cannot understand its language, except in the sense that these people make a global act of faith in the contents of the sacred writings. It has even less right to be considered the ultimate norm of interpretation and re-presentation.

Just as a director of an orchestra or theatrical production, as he strives to produce his own interpretation, must take into account interpretations of the masters and other recognized authorities, so, too, future interpreters of the Bible must always accord to the Vulgate the respect and authority due to a magisterial performance.

---

tinum sapienter statuit, ullo modo officere. Constat enim e litterarum monumentis Concilii Praesidibus fuisse creditum, ut ipsius Sacrae Synodi nomine Summum Pontificem rogarent—quod illi quidem fecerunt—ut Latina primum editio, dein vero et Graeca et Hebraica, quoad fieri posset, corrigerentur, in Ecclesiae Sanctae Dei utilitatem tandem aliquando vulgandae. Cui voto, si tunc propter temporum difficultates aliaque impedimenta non plene responderi potuit, in praesens, ut fore confidimus, doctorum catholicorum collatis viribus perfectius ampliusque satisfieri potest. Quod autem Vulgatam Tridentina Synodus esse voluit latinam conversionem, 'qua omnes pro authentica uterentur', id quidem, ut omnes norunt, latinam solummodo respicit Ecclesiam, eiusdemque publicum Scripturae usum, ac nequaquam, procul dubio, primigeniorum textuum auctoritatem et vim minuit. Neque enim de primigeniis textibus tunc agebatur, sed de latinis, quae illa aetate circumferebantur conversionibus, inter quas idem Concilium illam jure praeferendam edixit, quae 'longo tot saeculorum usu in ipsa Ecclesia probata est.' Haec igitur praecellens Vulgatae auctoritas seu, ut aiunt, AUTHENTIA non ob criticas praesertim rationes a Concilio statuta est, sed ob illius potius legitimum in Ecclesiis usum, per tot saeculorum decursum habitum; quo quidem usu demonstratur eamdem, prout intellexit et intelligit Ecclesia, in rebus fidei ac morum ab omni prorsus esse errore immunem; ita ut, ipsa Ecclesia testante et confirmante, in disputationibus, lectionibus concionibusque tuto ac sine errandi periculo, proferri possit; atque adeo eiusmodi AUTHENTIA non primario nomine CRITICA, sed IURIDICA potius vocatur." EB 549; RSS, pp. 91–92.

MODERN TRANSLATIONS

Having considered the qualities of the two privileged translations, we may now go on to discuss modern translations.

Every translation must answer the needs of its age. The Vulgate itself was a vernacular translation, made into the language which was currently spoken and written in the Western world of that time. Just as the Septuagint and the Vulgate exercised a great influence on the formation of the language of Christians, so the new translations will influence the religious language, both cultic and theological, of their epoch.

The principal object of this task is to achieve an "interpretation" or "repetition" of the original work in such a way that when the translation is recited, the whole structured language system exists again here and now.

But is this possible? If the work is a structured system, how is it possible that in a new language the same interrelations and structure will exist again? It is impossible to be equally faithful to all the levels of the original. The better one knows the original language, the more difficult translation appears; the more deeply one has penetrated the original, by intuition or by analysis, the more does one despair of translating its riches. Croce declares that a literary work of art can never be translated; Edward Sapir, however, himself a master in the study of language, recognizes the fact that, "nevertheless, literature does get itself translated, sometimes with astonishing adequacy." [7] His explanation of this fact is, however, disputable.

Because of the plurality of the work itself, and because of its need to be repeated, it is possible and even necessary to have many translations in order that all the aspects of the original may be the better appreciated. Just as the Septuagint effected a spiritualization of certain symbols and images, so we may continue this process of conceptualization as long as we keep in mind the grave danger of transposing a literary work into the realm of technical language. This would only serve to obstruct the authentic actualization of the inspired work. Along this road there lies in wait the "logical fal-

[7] *Language*, p. 222.

lacy" which we have already treated of in an article dealing with the techniques of translating Hebrew poetry.[8]

Though we admit the possibility of various translations existing at the same time, due to the mutual inadequacy of the languages, still there is an ideal toward which all must strive: The text must approach as far as possible a real capacity to repeat and actualize the original with immediacy and unity.

A theatrical work should be translated primarily for the stage, a piece of lyric poetry for recitation, and the translation of the Bible should look towards its liturgical proclamation. We would like to point out here two principles of rather ample scope which must be operative in order to achieve this ideal.[9]

(1) The principle of stylistic level means that we must pay attention to the plane on which the original moves; we must note its "tone": It may be that of conversation, lyric, oratory, or of elevated prose. We may allow poetry to lose its rhythm in translation, but we cannot permit poetry to become prose. A prosaic translation of poetry is not a translation, but a betrayal (unless, of course, one is only preparing a "trot" for those who are going to consult the original). In order to render the tone of the original, logic will not suffice; there must be a feeling for the work, born of familiarity.

(2) The principle of stylistic system means that the original work must show forth its own system, in order to become the life center of the translation. The translator discovers this system and its "soul" by intuition, trial, and analysis. If in a particular poem the factor of sound is predominant, then the translation must also make this its central consideration, even to the point of subordinating an imagined terminological exactitude. Thus, if the name of a tree mentioned in a poem were selected, not for botanical reasons but for alliteration, then it would be unfaithful to the original to abide by the botany and neglect the alliteration. The same can be said for factors of rhythm, image, plasticity, idea, etc.

A frequent temptation of Western minds, especially of professors, is to make the translation more precise than the original; as

---

[8] "Traducción de textos poéticos biblicos," *EstBíb* 19, 1960, pp. 311–328.
[9] We have treated of the technique of translation, giving examples in a series of articles: (1) "Traducción de textos poéticos hebreos," *CB* 17, 1960, pp. 170–176. (2) "Traducción de textos poéticos," *CB* 17, 1960, pp. 257–265. (3) "Traducción de textos poéticos," *CB* 18, 1961, pp. 336–346. (4) "Textos poéticos: análisis y traducción," *CB* 19, 1962, pp. 282–294.

though the original were a system of genera which must be reduced to species. The symbol becomes a concept; a suggestion becomes an affirmation, and so forth. Another temptation is that of trying to have the translation explicitly convey all the resonances which the original owes to its general context. An integral translation will strive to realize the total context, so that the resonances will be heard and felt as contextual, rather than as completely explicit in the one passage.

There is always the temptation to regard literal translation as the best, and though this can be useful, it is not faithful. It is a temptation to demand that the translation be always harmonious and smooth; many times it is in the dissonance or erratic rhythm of the original that the expression consists. Paraphrase always offers a great temptation. There are many more temptations that beset the translator, but this is not the place to enumerate or develop them, since this is not a practical treatise on the art of translation.

It was the fact itself of biblical translation that interested us. It is the unavoidable consequence of the fact that the divine word has become incarnate in human speech. Since its original concretization in one language, one author, one work, the word of God seeks wider scopes for its energy—it seeks to reach every man. "St. Paul wrote to one city; through St. Paul and through that city the Holy Spirit has written to all" (Chrysostom).

The inspired word demands translation by its very nature, and translation is an exalted and arduous service of the Word.

Bibliography for Chapter 11

The fact of translation in regard to the Bible is vividly brought home to anyone who consults the "Elenchus Bibliographicus" in *Biblica*. In part 3, "Textus et Versiones," which prolongs as it were the corresponding treatment in any standard introduction, there are often as many as one hundred and twenty titles. Among the ancient versions, we find: the Targums, the Septuagint and other Greek versions, the Vetus Latina, the Vulgate, Ethiopian, Armenian, Coptic, Georgian, Gothic, Old

Slavic, and Syriac. The ancient translations are valuable in attempts to restore a faulty passage in the original, but their interest here lies in the witness they give to the diffusion of the word of God by means of translation. In regard to the art of translation in general, there is the work edited by W. Arrowsmith and R. Shattuck, *The Craft and Context of Translation*, Austin, 1961; most of the articles are concerned with translations of the classics, but the Introduction and the chapter "Impossibilities of Translation" by W. Winter are of a more general orientation. There is an appendix of twenty-two pages in which the observations of various Latin and English authors (including St. Jerome and the translators of the King James version) are presented. A more technical treatment of the same problem can be found in G. Mounin, *Les problèmes théoriques de la traduction*, Paris, 1963.

A discussion of the modern translations made by the translators themselves can be found in their introductions or in separate articles and books, as in the case of R. Knox, *Trials of a Translator*, New York, 1949; Theophile Meek, who did so much of the work in the *Chicago Bible*, propounds some of his principles in "Old Testament Translation Principles," *JBL* 81, 1962, pp. 143–154.

The Septuagint. P. Benoit has two articles on the inspiration of the Septuagint: "La Septante est elle inspirée?" in *Vom Wort des Lebens* (Festschr. für M. Meinertz), Münster, 1951, pp. 41ff.; (*Exégèse et Théologie*, vol. 1, pp. 1ff.), and "L'inspiration des Septante d'après les Pères," in *L'Homme devant Dieu. Mélanges offerts au Père Henri de Lubac, Exégèse et Patristique*, Paris, 1963, pp. 169–187. And P. Auvray has an article in *RB* 59, 1953, pp. 321ff, "Comment se poser le problème des Septante." A. Vaccari treats of the citations of the Septuagint in "Las citas del Antiquo Testamento en la epístola ad Hebraeos," *CB* 13, 1956, pp. 239ff. Recently, P. Grelot has expressed his approval of the position of Benoit and Auvray: "Sur l'inspiration et la canonicite de la Septante," *Sciences Ecclésiastiques*, 17, 1964, pp. 387–418.

The Vulgate. In addition to the standard treatment in the introductions, there is the work of Dom Chapman, *Notes on the Early History of the Vulgate Gospels*, New York, 1908. The study most relevant to our purpose is A. Allgeier "Haec vetus et vulgata editio. Neue worte und begriffesgeschichtliche Beiträge zur Bibel auf dem Tridentinum," *Historisches Jahrbuch* 60, 1940, pp. 142–158; *Bib* 29, 1948, pp. 253–290.

Modern Translations. The fundamental article is the collaborative work edited by J. Schmid, "Moderne Bibelübersetzungen. Eine Übersicht," *ZKT* 82, 1960, pp. 290–332. There is a discussion of various modern translations by way of review in the biblical periodicals (cf., for example, the reviews of *The New English Bible* in the "Elenchus Bibl.," *Bib*, 1962, nos. 703–705; 1963, nos. 763–764). R. Nida's long interest in this field is summed up in his *Toward a Science of Translating*, Leiden, 1964.

12. The Reception of the Work

When, by means of translation, we have achieved an actualization of the inspired work, it still remains only potentially actualized until the moment when it is recited publicly or read privately.

When the people of God are united in the liturgy to hear the word of God being proclaimed out loud in a language they can understand, there above all the word of God finds full existence. To the profession of faith which declares that "He spoke through the prophets," we can add this other profession: "Who now comes to speak to me in the reader at the liturgy."

. . . Christ is always present in His Church, especially in her liturgical celebrations. . . . He is present in His word, since it is He Himself Who speaks when the holy Scriptures are read in the Church.[1]

In the liturgy, God speaks to His people and Christ is still proclaiming His Gospel.[2]

The act of understanding consummates and completes the process of language. That which has been given objective existence is once again made subjective. Language actualizes and manifests what is interior, a work actualizes an experience by means of language, and repetition actualizes the word-system of a work; but all these still remain somehow in potency, and the potency receives its definitive actualization when the reader or listener receive it.

A re-presentation is for others, otherwise it remains an abortive

[1] ". . . Christus Ecclesiae suae semper adest, praesertim in actionibus liturgicis. . . . Praesens adest in verbo suo, siquidem ipse loquitur dum sacrae Scripturae in Ecclesia legentur." Const., no. 7.

[2] "In Liturgia enim Deus ad populum suum loquitur; Christus adhuc Evangelium annuntiat." Const., no. 33.

effort or play. In private reading, the reader is the audience, and if he reads out loud, he becomes both spectator and actor.

The reception of an act of language is not a passive operation, as though the spectator or listener can give themselves up to a blissful inertia. It is, rather, in every phase of the process, an intense spiritual activity. This complete activity transpires without our being fully aware of it, in the simple act by which we understand something expressed in language. It is more intense in dialogue, still more so perhaps in the reception of a complete literary work. This activity, like so many other human operations, can become a real pleasure, whether it be the pure activity of reception or the reciprocal activity of communication with another person. Dialogue demands response, and this is what consummates the act of listening. If the words of the one speaking to us are meant to influence us, then our response must be in acting. These are the two fundamental forms of response—in word and in act.

A literary work also requires these two types of response. A work which poses problems and communicates the author's reflections, demands of me that I also reflect and take a stand; a work which challenges, demands that I act.

In the liturgical action, the whole community, except for the onlookers, takes part in the act of re-presentation. But are there really spectators? In a certain sense, no. Someone who comes only to watch, to look on, does not enter into the reality, and therefore does not receive the liturgical action, since this can be appreciated only from within. Would we say, then, that the liturgy is a play? Insofar as it is a re-presentation which wishes no one to be really an onlooker, it can be called play. Guardini, in his classic book on the spirit of the liturgy, has a whole chapter on the liturgy as play. He saw the total meaning of this notion: The liturgy is a sacred reënactment presented before God. God is, in a certain way, the onlooker of the play which men enact in order to praise and glorify Him.

Such is the wonderful fact which the liturgy demonstrates; it unites art and reality in a supernatural childhood before God. That which formerly existed in the world of unreality only, and was rendered in art as the expression of mature human life, has here become reality. These forms are the vital expression of real and frankly supernatural life. But this has one thing in common with the play of the child and the life of art—it has no purpose, but it is full of profound meaning. It is not work, but play. To be at play, or to fashion a work of art in God's sight—not to create, but to exist—such is the essence of liturgy. From this is derived its sublime mingling of profound earnestness and divine joyfulness.[3]

The whole assembly sings a Psalm and the word, the inspired word, comes into play, achieving through the community its full actualization. The whole assembly hears the word of God proclaimed, and they must respond with word and action: Not only with the liturgical action, but with the action of the whole of their lives, which then becomes energized and enlightened by the power of the Word.

In a secondary sense, the liturgical action can be of interest to a non-believer or a Christian of another community, and it thus acquires another value added to its primary meaning. But when this aspect of being a play becomes commercialized and looks for tourists, God leaves, and the play is no longer sacred. The work does not now receive its consummating actualization, and becomes instead a falsehood.

The liturgical actuation gives the work a new dimension of actuality: The re-presentation is a presence of the Word. Not the contents of the work, insofar as they are different from and anterior to it, but the meaning of the work itself which is revealed in the re-presentation—this is the vehicle for the word. We are referring here to the word as it is present in the liturgy.

Since the actualization of the inspired work is effected by the active participation of the community entering thus into the reality, it is easy to understand why the *Constitution on the Sacred Liturgy* makes such great efforts to restore this aspect of the liturgical action: not only in the Eucharistic action itself, but also in the liturgy of the Word:

Pastors of souls must realize that, when the liturgy is celebrated, something more is required than the mere observation of the laws governing valid and licit celebration; it is their duty also to insure that the faithful take part fully aware of what they are doing, actively engaged in the rite, and enriched by its effects.[4]

---

[3] R. Guardini, *The Church and the Catholic, and the Spirit of the Liturgy*, New York, 1935, p. 181.

[4] "*Ideo sacris pastoribus advigilandum est ut in actione liturgica non solum*

Mother Church earnestly desires that all the faithful should be led to that full, conscious, and active participation in liturgical celebrations which is demanded by the very nature of the liturgy. Such participation by the Christian people as "a chosen race, a royal priesthood, a holy nation, a redeemed people (1 Pt 2:9; cf. 2:4–5) is their right and duty by reason of their Baptism." [5]

THE WORK AS MEDIATOR

When we insist on the importance of the work, on its structured consistency and inner dynamic unity, we do not mean that it is living in the formal sense of that term. A literary work is the manifestation of a meaningful reality, it subsists in itself, yet its subsistence lies in its meaning.

Artists themselves often witness to this enduring, independent existence of a literary work. From among the many possible testimonies, we adduce these lines of W. K. Wimsatt:

The poem is not the critic's own and not the author's (it is detached from the author at birth and goes about the world beyond his power to intend it or control it).[6]

A poem should not mean but be. It is an epigram worth quoting in every essay on poetry.[7]

Rilke's "Requiem for Wolf Graf von Kalckreuth" contains the same thought in a more nuanced form:

We only watch the poems that still climb,
still cross, the inclination of your feeling,
carrying the words that you had chosen. No,
you did not choose all; often a beginning
was given you in full, and you'd repeat it
like some commission. And you thought it sad.
Ah, would you had never heard it from yourself!

---

observentur leges ad validam et licitam celebrationem, sed ut fideles scienter, actuose et fructuose eandem participent." Const., no. 11.

[5] "Valde cupit Mater Ecclesia ut fideles universi ad plenam illam, consciam atque actuosam liturgicarum celebrationum participationem ducantur, quae ab ipsius Liturgiae natura postulatur et ad quam populus christianus, 'genus electum, regale sacerdotium, gens sancta, populus adquisitionis' (1 Pt 2:9; cf. 2:4–5), vi Baptismatis ius habet et officium." Const., no. 14.

[6] The Verbal Icon, p. 5 (cf. ch. 10, n. 13).

[7] Ibid., p. 81.

Your angel sounds on, uttering the same
text with a different accent, and rejoicing
breaks out in me to hear his recitation,
rejoicing over you: for this was yours.[8]

In a work, I live somehow with other persons, I come to know events and things, and often I feel myself in the company of the author as he speaks. We might say that in the work and through the work we come into contact with things and events and with the author. Some prefer the formula "in the work," others prefer to describe this contact as taking place "through the work." Without any pretensions at settling the question, we would tend to choose the first formula.

Contacting Events in the Work

Events, which are by their nature passing, limited, and irreversible, achieve stability in a system of words which we call a literary work. This is the principle underlying all narration, which, in its turn, is the subsisting memory of a community. When event becomes word, it is not merely repeated, but receives in the process a human and personal interpretation. To interpret is not to falsify; as a matter of fact, it is just the opposite. It means to penetrate into the meaning of an event and transpose superficial appearances to the level of intelligibility (there can, of course, be false interpretations).

There is a school of painting which attempts to interpret and manifest the interior meaning of things by distorting their external appearances, simplifying lines, changing colors and shapes, etc. This is a form of expressionism, and it has more truth in it than the naïve preoccupation with what "things really look like." Thus,

---

8 *Nur den Gedichten sehn wir zu, die noch*
über die Neigung deines Fühlens abwärts
die Worte tragen, die du wähltest. Nein,
nicht alle wähltest du; oft ward ein Anfang
dir auferlegt als Ganzes, den du nachsprachst
wie einen Auftrag. Und er schein dir traurig.
Ach hättest du ihn nie von dir gehört.
Dein Engel lautet jetzt noch und betont
denselben Wortlaut anders, und mir bricht
der Jubel aus bei seiner Art zu sagen,
der Jubel über dich: denn dies war dein.
Sämtliche Werke, p. 662; Translation by Leishman (cf. ch. 7, n. 7).

van Gogh pictures the sun as a great gyrating power which imparts its movement to all the beings on the earth. Is the monochromatic sun of a "realist" painter actually more true? (We once saw in *The Illustrated London News*, pictures of the sun taken from high altitude balloons, and they bore a striking resemblance to the sun envisaged by van Gogh.)

In order to interpret an event, a narration may highlight one aspect and neglect others, liberating the event from its bounded temporal existence, making it capable of being remembered and recited, and raising it to the level of a universal reality without being false to the deepest concrete meaning of the event.

In sacred Scripture, we meet many events which are interpreted and transmitted in a structured system of words. Inspiration guarantees for us that this interpretation is profoundly correct. A scholar could go to the Bible and abstract from it the facts and events he needs to reconstruct a critical history; his reorganized series of extracts is not inspired, neither is his interpretation. What he has gained in his recapturing of "things as they really were," he has lost in the inspired "expressionism" which revealed the deepest meaning of the events. For while these happenings were, undoubtedly, human actions, they were also the actions of God, and by that fact revelations of God in history. As they took place on this globe, they looked like any other events, but the sacred author saw their inner significance, and this was the living intuition which dominated the whole process by which his work was realized.

In the work, we come into contact with events as interpreted; in order to repeat or re-present the work, this transcendent dimension which constitutes the revelation of God must be preserved. It is not the simple empirical fact, which is unrepeatable by its nature, not is it a pure poetical repetition, even though this might possess validity and depth; it is, rather, that which in the event made it salvation history and thus is deeply relevant to our lives. These sacred events reach us in the biblical "work" as re-presented in the liturgy. As events, their deepest meaning is in the fact that God acted in them. As present in the work, and actualized in the liturgy, they are the events in which God acts now.

For Yahweh rebuilds Sion,
and is seen amidst his glory.

He regards the prayer of the needy,
and does not contemn their prayer.

Let this be written for a generation to follow,
a people then created will sing Yahweh's praise.[9]

Contacting the Author in the Work

We do not wish to consider the work of an author as a symptom by which we can classify him as "introverted," "psychotic," or "neurotic." This would be to look on the author as an object of scientific investigation (if such procedures can be called scientific), but it is not knowing him as a person. We wish instead to have a dialogue which is truly human and not merely utilitarian. But is it possible to have such access to an author by means of his work? Does he desire it? Or is the work a total presence, meant once for all to relegate the author to a dignified aloofness?

It is sometimes said that present literary investigation concentrates on the work and nothing but the work, and that the author is not of any interest. This reaction against the psychologism of an earlier generation has led, in turn, to some exaggeration. It is perfectly true that our literary analyses are not primarily concerned with the private life of the author: how he dressed, what kind of whiskey he drank, the name of the woman who presently caught his fancy and to whom he dedicated a sonnet, etc. To know the family name, the social class, and the dates of birth and death of Laura is not exactly the overriding preoccupation of a literary study of Petrarch. Personal information about the author only interests us insofar as it has influenced his work and left its mark there.

But it is no less certain that a reader can relive the intuition of the author, and can thus approach him as a person, stand by his side, and share his vision for a few moments. Both men may now repeat the same words and in them find themselves united in joy or pain, or it may be that the reader follows the author, dimly aware that he is approaching something, but not quite reaching it. A literary work can be a real manifestation of an author; and this is true not only of lyric, but also of epic poetry and drama.

This capacity to manifest the author is obvious in the case of lyric poetry, but there are two things that we must bear in mind: At times, a poet is moved to create by way of reaction against his

[9] Ps 102:17-19.

experience, as a form of compensation or liberation, and in this case it is important to be able to sense the nature of the revelation being made through the work. At other times, the author puts himself in the place of someone else, and then his self-revelation is "once removed," so to speak; it is conveyed through the person he has assumed.[10]

An epic can also manifest its author. We must look to the selection, disposition, and interpretation he has given to the events he narrates. The selective process is most significant in what it leaves out, for often an omission is more motivated than the decision to include something. There may be some philosophical or theological principle at the center of a narrative composition, even though it never be formulated. An author may manifest a tendency toward apologetics, a penchant for storytelling, an enthusiasm for ideals, a preoccupation with exactitude, etc. The mentality of the author is there concretely in the work; it is not necessary nor even possible to contact it by a series of inferences or syllogisms.

An author may speak through the characters he creates (here, though we will be repeating concepts which we saw in Chapter 2, we are not repeating the analogy we used there to help us understand inspiration). In some rare cases, an author can make his characters speak with Sophoclean ambiguity—Oedipus Rex, Caiaphas in St. John's Gospel, etc. There is also the other extreme in which an author enters into his own work by means of one of his characters, and addresses his audience directly; he may do this boldly, and make it apparent to all, or he may choose to disguise it, leaving only a clue. Between these two extremes, there is the whole gamut of possibilities: An author may keep his distance from characters, and he may by the force of the context in which he puts them convey to us his personal feelings about them. This is clearly seen, for instance, in the novel with a thesis: as when an author condemns a "bad" person to defeat and frustration, and when he crowns the efforts of the "good" character with success and happiness. Other authors surround their characters with affection and intuitive understanding—think of the relation between Cervantes and Don Quixote—and this show of paternal affection is itself a way the author has of speaking to us. The average reader enters right into the world of the novel and never gives the **author**

[10] Cf. W. Kayser, *Das sprachliche Kunstwerk*, Berne, 1954, pp. 191ff.

a thought. Then at the end there may come a flash of insight or a moment of deep reflection, and he realizes that the author was there all the time, there in the novel, living along with the reader in his contemplation of reality as it presented itself to him in the re-creation effected by the author.

We do not wish to discuss here whether or not this experience of the living presence of the author is of a purely aesthetic or literary nature. We personally think that it really belongs to language. Nor do we wish to maintain that this experience is absolutely universal: that it happens to all readers, whenever they read any book. We wish only to appeal to the experience of many readers. We know some who have a real love for Antonio Machado, Dostoevski, the author of Ecclesiastes—a lyricist, a novelist, and an essayist. And this experience is sufficient to warrant our going on to ask the cardinal question.

Contacting God

In the work, we contact the author. Is it possible, then, in the Bible to contact God? We do not, of course, refer here to the modes of syllogistic and inferential thought. It is true that God has willed that this human author tell me this or that event, this or that way, and that what is written here is a manifestation of the will of God. But is that all that I can find there? Is it only a witness to a decree of God?

The Fathers understood this aspect in a deeper and more immediate way (though, of course, they respected the analogy they were dealing with). God has initiated a dialogue, and He allows me to enter into His heart.

Let each one consider that through the tongue of the prophets we hear God speaking to us.[11]

What is Scripture, but a letter from Almighty God to His creature? . . . Strive then each day to meditate on the words of your Creator. Come to know the heart of God in the words of God.[12]

[11] St. John Chrys. Cf. ch. 5, n. 7.
[12] "Quid est autem Scriptura sacra, nisi quaedam epistola omnipotentis Dei ad creaturam suam? . . . Stude ergo, quaeso, et quotidie Creatoris tui verba meditare. Disce cor Dei in verbis Dei, ut ardentius ad aeterna suspires, ut mens vestra ad coelestia gaudia majoribus desideriis accendatur." St. Gregory, "Letter 31, Ad Theodorum," PL 77, 706.

Through the sacred writers who composed the text, and by means of the world of narrative, God really speaks to me. In the work, I contact God because the work itself is a sort of incarnation in which God has concretized his self-revelation. It is a new creation through a medium, "through the prophets," and yet it is direct: "He spoke."

We have already seen these words of Pesch:

> . . . and, therefore, God speaks to us immediately in Scripture, because Scripture is the word of God in the formal and proper sense. The sacred writers are intermediaries between us and God; they are intermediaries, not in the sense that they are objects by whom we know God, but in a subjective sense, as being the mouth of God, by which He speaks to us.[13]

---

[13] "*Eatenus igitur* DEUS NOBIS IN SCRIPTURA IMMEDIATE LOQUITUR, *quia Scriptura est verbum Dei formale et proprie dictum. Sunt quidem intermedii inter nos et Deum scriptores sacri; at sunt intermedii non ut objecta, ex quibus Deum cognoscimus, sed sensu subiectivo ut os Dei, per quod Deus ad nos loquitur.*" No. 411.

V
THE CONSEQUENCES
OF INSPIRATION

ἀκούσαντες τὸν λόγον τῆς
ἀληθείας

ζῶν ὁ λόγος τοῦ Θεοῦ
καὶ ἐνεργὴς

13. The Context of the Word: Truth

*There are some who prefer to speak of the "effects of inspiration,"
but actually the effect of inspiration is to make of the human word
the word of God, just as the effect of the action of the Spirit in the
Incarnation is the God-Man Christ: "The Holy Spirit will come
upon you and the power of the Most High will overshadow you;
and for that reason the holy child to be born will be called 'Son of
God.' " Because of the action of the Spirit on Mary, because of the
power and the overshadowing, the Child which will be born of her
is really God. Because of the action of the Spirit on the sacred
writer, that structured reality of human words which will emerge is
really the word of God.*

*From this effect there follow many consequences. But once the
terminology has been agreed on, there is no difficulty in adopting
the more usual designation, "the effects of inspiration."*

*It is much more difficult to reach an agreement in another sense
about a final "s" which, though it may appear to be insignificant,
reveals a whole difference of concept. The manuals speak not of the
effects of inspiration, but of its effect, in the singular. From the
action of the Spirit and from the nature of the Word of God, there
is only one "effect"—inerrancy. This one aspect is considered so
important that it occupies half the tract; so fundamental that it
dominates the whole treatment of hermeneutics to such a degree
that hermeneutics becomes the art of saving the Bible from error.*[1]

[1] Pesch does not speak of inerrancy as an effect of inspiration, but he
devotes a great deal of attention to it. Van Laak (1911), after having
proved the existence of inspiration, derives one consequence: inerrancy.
Billot (4th ed., 1929) proposes various consequences: the spiritual sense,
inerrancy, the rules for interpretation. Tromp treats of the question affirming the infallible truth of the Scriptures which he considers under two head-

Imagine, for example, a tract "De Verbo Incarnato," divided into two equal parts: part one—"The Incarnation"; the fact and the mode of its existence—one Person in two natures. Part two— "The Effect of the Incarnation"; the impeccability of Christ. The impeccability of Christ could be proved from Scripture—"which of you can convict me of sin," and by a metaphysical deduction—it is contrary to the nature of the divine sanctity. Then the theory would be applied to answering objections: As a boy, Christ stayed behind in the temple (disobedience); later, He cast out the buyers and sellers from the temple (anger); He exposed the Pharisees (revenge); He slipped away from a threatening crowd (cowardice); He went to banquets and dinners, let Himself be touched by a prostitute, etc., etc. None of these is a new accusation, but they could easily occupy half our tract on the Incarnation.

Would we accept such a treatise? We can already hear the objections: What has happened to the solidarity of all men in Christ, the consideration of our adoptive sonship, the example of His life, His revelation of the Father? Though most of our modern manuals have done away with the classical tract on "The Mysteries of the Life of Christ," still they have not reduced themselves to the narrow limits of the tract we have just made up.

Why, then, has there been such a narrowing of the tract on inspiration, which should follow a structure parallel to that on the Incarnation? The reason is to be found in the history of the last half century or so.

What purpose do the medieval castles and walls serve? Why are there such great walls around Avila or Avignon? Now, because the tourists visit them, and because they are historical and artistic monuments. But castles and walls are built in order to provide habitation and defense during times when there is open hostility or uneasy peace. The building of a castle is an assurance of power; to make a breach in the wall is the first decisive step in conquering a city.

Until the end of the last century, Scripture found itself in a state of war, confronted with open hostility. In an age now remote from us, persecutors demanded that the sacred books be handed over so

---

ings: inerrancy, and the truth within the meaning of the text (literary types). Höpfl-Gut speak of one effect of inspiration: inerrancy.

that they could destroy them, and Christians died heroically in order to save the inspired text. In an age when culture was nearly extinct, the enemy was decadence and negligence, and the monks labored to preserve and multiply copies of the Bible. Toward the end of the last century, the arms of the enemy were directed against the supposed errors of the Bible in an effort to force a breach and enter the sanctuary of inspiration in order to destroy it. The Bible had to be defended; and this is the time when our manuals on inspiration were conceived and constructed. It is not strange, then, that they were surrounded by such great walls of arguments and replies in those sections which dealt with inerrancy.

It would be disrespectful and unfitting to dismantle these walls which still have a function, but we must stop to consider whether or not the wall is the essence of the city, or whether peaceful habitation of the city is not something more important. Certainly, the centuries' long tradition of the Church has regarded the Scriptures with much greater breadth of view, and it seems to me that it is healthier and more balanced to follow this ancient tradition, especially in these times of such wonderful renewal in the appreciation of the Bible.

This is why we return to the division made in Chapter 1—the context of the Word and the context of the Spirit. In the context of the Word, "Truth"; in the context of the Spirit, "Power." Not that these are the unique consequences of inspiration; they are, rather, headings under which we may group the other consequences, while clearly asserting that Truth and Power are found intimately united in the multiple unity of the divine action.

The Fathers of the Church often spoke of the action of the Trinity in the Scriptures, either naming all three Persons explicitly, or uniting the Word with the Father or with the Holy Spirit.

The holy books were written under the inspiration of the Holy Spirit, by the will of the Father of all, through Jesus Christ.[2]

One God, the Father, the Lord of the Old Testament and the New; One Lord, Jesus Christ, Who was foretold in the Old Testament and

---

[2] Διόπερ τοῖς πειθομένοις μὴ ἀνθρώπων εἶναι συγγράμματα τὰς ἱερὰς βίβλους ἀλλ' ἐξ ἐπινοίας τοῦ ἁγίου Πνεύματος βουλήματι τοῦ Πατρὸς τῶν ὅλων διὰ Ἰησοῦ Χριστοῦ ταύτας ἀναγέγραφθαι καὶ εἰς ἡμᾶς ἐληλυθέναι. Origen, "De Princ., bk. 4," PG 11, 359. Cf. R. Gögler, *Zur Theologie des Biblischen Wortes bei Origenes*, Düsseldorf, 1963, "Logos und Pneuma," pp. 282–298.

came in the New; and one Holy Spirit, Who through the prophets preached concerning Christ, and when Christ had come, descended on Him and made Him known. Thus, no one should separate the Old Testament from the New, nor should anyone say that there is one Spirit in the first and another in the second, otherwise he will offend against that Holy Spirit Who is honored along with the Father and the Son.[3]

The Scriptures are perfect, because they were pronounced by the Word of God and by His Spirit.[4]

All these [prophets] were endowed with the Spirit of prophecy and honored by the Word . . .[5]

REVELATION OF A MYSTERY

In the context of the word "Truth," Christ, Who has revealed God, is the Truth. Not only does He speak the truth, He causes it to be and is Himself the Truth. In an analogous and participated way, sacred Scripture, insofar as it is the revelation of God, is the truth.

We can think of this in terms of ontological truth: the manifestation of being and of its meaning; and we can think of it as reflective logical truth, enunciated in propositional form. In the Scriptures, we find a manifestation of being, and its meaning within salvation; we also find many statements made about salvation. In regard to the manifestation of being, we can say that the Scriptures are true; in regard to its statements, we can say that the Scriptures contain truth.

Truth can be considered in its total unity or in its relative unity, as it relates to a point of view (not relative truth, but relative unity); revelation, too, may be considered either in its total unity or in terms of the units of revelation. When we know a person, we possess the truth of that person in a unified way: We express this

---

[3] Εἷς Θεὸς, ὁ Πατὴρ, Παλαιᾶς καὶ Καινῆς διαθήκης Δεσπότης. καὶ εἷς Κύριος, Ἰησοῦς Χριστὸς, ὁ ἐν Παλαιᾷ προφητευθεὶς καὶ ἐν Καινῇ παραγενόμενος. καὶ ἕν Πνεῦμα ἅγιον, διὰ προφητῶν μὲν περὶ Χριστοῦ κηρύξαν. ἐλθόντος δὲ τοῦ Χριστοῦ καταβὰν, καὶ ἐπιδείξαν αὐτόν. Μηδεὶς οὖν χωριζέτω τὴν Παλαιὰν ἀπὸ τῆς Καινῆς Διαθήκης. μηδεὶς λεγέτω, ὅτι ἄλλο τὸ Πνεῦμα ἐκεῖ, καὶ ἄλλο ὧδε. ἐπεὶ προσκρούει αὐτῷ τῷ ἁγίῳ Πνεύματι, τῷ μετὰ Πατρὸς καὶ Υἱοῦ τετιμημένῳ. St. Cyril of Jer., "Catech. 16, On the Holy Spirit," PG 33, 920–21.

[4] St. Irenaeus; cf. ch. 2, n. 56.

[5] St. Hippolytus; cf. ch. 2, n. 19.

unity by dividing and differentiating it in a series of things we know about him—his opinions, his plans, his character, his reactions, his attitudes, tastes, and ideals. Since a person does not manifest himself to us in one total act by which we enter into the simplicity of his life center, we get to know him through a series of truths, or, better, units of truth about him. These we can repeat in statement form, when someone asks us about him. Behind all these manifestations and in them, we catch a glimpse of the radical unity of a person. This is his highest truth.[6]

In the same way, God wishes to reveal Himself to us as a Person, inviting us to friendship. He divides His self-manifestation into a long series of salvific acts which give understanding of diverse aspects of His unity. These we call His decisions, His actions, His precepts, or His counsels. We are able to reduce this multiple series to a synthesis, to a higher unity; we can also perceive in these manifestations the presence of the Person Who is revealing Himself.

The unity of revelation is the mystery of salvation in Christ. This is our highest truth,[7] and in itself it is a totality. This one truth can be articulated and divided into a whole series of truths or units of truth. Usually, when we speak of aspects of truths, we think immediately of a series of theoretical propositions: the tract on soteriology—Christ, His activity, His unity, His operations, the sacraments, and these are broken down into a series of theses. Actually, the mystery of Christ is articulated in a series of ordered events, which sum up salvation history. Since we are in the context of truth, we must consider these events in their ultimate meaning. They are significant events; their relation to salvation is their ultimate meaning; their unfolding of the mystery of truth is their ultimate truth. We should here take the term "events" in a wide sense, as including happenings, experiences, and even words, but the predominant medium of revelation for God is in event as a happening. To set forth the meaning of these events is to manifest their transcendent truth. This is fundamentally the truth of Scripture: It is one in the mystery of Christ revealed; it is manifold in that series of events which manifest its meaning as they reveal their own.

[6] The process of getting to know a person resembles the "hermeneutic circle." From the parts to the whole, from the whole to the parts.

[7] *"Jesu corona celsior et veritas sublimior."* From the hymn for Confessors.

Since the sacred writers reveal this truth, they teach us and convey understanding. In this general sense, we may speak of the Bible as a teaching, an instruction or doctrine. Some describe Scripture as the doctrine of salvation; others say that it contains this doctrine. The question is largely one of terminology. However, in neither view are we allowed to take the term in the sense of "ideology" or "theory." We use the word in its wider meaning when we say that life teaches us, or history, or failure.

In some books of the Bible, especially in the New Testament, teaching takes on an obviously didactic aspect, which includes doctrine. But this is not so in the Old Testament, not even in the sapiental books, which are not really very "doctrinal." These were the reasons which led the scholastics to discuss the question of the "modes" of Scripture, which, while they are not those of the scientist, still are more certain. Thus, Scripture is the source and norm for theological truth, even though it does not present itself exclusively as doctrine. Its literary "modes" convey the highest truth.

"God is Love"; "God loved the world so much that He gave His only Son that everyone who has faith in Him may not die, but have eternal life." The first statement is quite simple; the second is complex. Both enunciate and affirm something. They teach with sufficient clarity though their terminology is not conceptual, but symbolic and mysterious. Still, they both retain their character as propositional teaching, as teaching by statement.

In such cases, which are frequent in the Bible, this question of truth is not difficult. The truth is proposed as a manifestation of the mystery which reveals and veils, and thus stimulates the search for greater understanding. This kind of biblical truth is simple, and it suffices to note and affirm its existence. On the other hand, the truth of the literary "modes" of the Bible is more difficult. Following the example of the medieval theologians, we will treat of this aspect separately, and for this purpose will use the categories of our Western culture, since they are more easily understood.

LITERARY TRUTH

Just as life is a teacher, so is literature. Literature, in the full sense, is not a doctrinal treatise. How, then, does literature teach? What is the truth of literature? In this section, we are going to follow

Hans Meyerhoff, whose treatment in Chapter 4 of his *Time in Literature* is especially clear and well-balanced.[8]

Information Is Accidental

A literary work contains a good deal of information: elements of description which touch on life or history, the arts, work, etc. This data, which is integrated accidentally into the work, can be controlled by like information from other sources. It is the object which an historian, sociologist, or archeologist has in mind when he consults the literature of the past. We can learn from the *Iliad* a good deal about the customs of the Mycenaean age and of the epoch in which the poem itself was fixed (eighth century B.C.). In the *Odyssey*, we can learn a good deal about the sailing techniques of that age. All this information does not constitute the specific truth of the literary work, and the specialist who goes to the text only for the sake of its data, never comes in contact with the work as literature.

The Scriptures can also supply us with a good deal of information about the customs and concepts of the ancient Near East. There were two-story houses with pillars supporting the upper story; there were hand mills, operated by two women; the heavens were looked upon as a solid dome; shepherds used slings; people thought that there was a great supply of hail up in the heavens, etc. None of this information constitutes the specific truth of the Scriptures. St. Augustine had already pointed out this fact, and Cardinal Baronius (according to the testimony of Galileo) formulated it this way: "The Holy Spirit wishes to teach us not how the heavens go, but how to go to heaven." (Yet about sixty years ago, L. Murillo tried to find scientific information revealed in Genesis.)

This type of data is not the truth of the Scriptures, and the sacred author may utilize such information with a certain liberty, subordinating it to the truth of his work. He can simplify the facts, he can accept the information without troubling to find out if it is completely exact, he can make up some of the information and use it in his work, he can distort things in the interest of narrative or expression, or he can exaggerate them. This is neither trickery nor whim, but a functional judgment made in virtue of the

[8] H. Meyerhoff, *Time in Literature*, ch. 4, "Literature, Science, and Philosophy."

overriding truth of the work. If the scholar uses the work as a reliable source of information, he must assume responsibility for his own errors and not attribute them to the literary author. We cannot exclude beforehand the possibility that the sacred author made such functional judgments and exercised liberty with the information available to him; he was not writing an encyclopedia.[9]

Theories and Doctrines

Another truth of a literary work is found in the theories or doctrines propounded by the author within the work, either through the mouth of a fictional character or in the form of reflections which interrupt the flow of the narrative. This is not the ideal of literature, but it exists. In the Bible, which is not pure literature, this form of teaching is often found: A reflection on the meaning of a life or an event can be expressed through one of the people in the narrative. Thus, the "Deuteronomist" author puts speeches in the mouths of Joshua, Samuel, and Solomon at turning points in his account of the history of Israel. This obvious literary device proved very helpful to the author as a means of inculcating his thesis, his truth. When he relates the fall of Samaria, and can find no one prominent enough to deliver his message, the author himself takes the stage to explain the meaning of the tragedy.[10]

Truth Properly Literary

Meyerhoff distinguishes between a primary truth and a secondary truth of literature. He calls this latter truth one of "inference." *The primary truth* is the internal coherence of the work which reveals truth to us as a property of being, and as such makes an

[9] This is, we think, what Benoit develops under title of "practical judgment." It would be risky for instance to use the Book of Judith as a source for historical information: Nebuchadnezzar, King of the Assyrians in Nineveh. On the other hand, in a work which sets out to be historical, its truth is the facts themselves along with their interpretation. Tho way that this interpretation is given can determine the literary type of the work: epic, religious, "causal," etc. But even here the facts are not presented in a list, but are incorporated and used according to the purpose of the author.

[10] In the Book of Judith, the author places the discourse in the mouth of Achior, the Ammonite. There is a certain irony in this procedure, as well as a dialectical purpose and a desire to highlight the nature of the religious confession. Though often these speeches are intruded into the narrative with a certain lack of literary finesse, they are valuable since they are frequently a key to the meaning of the whole composition.

appeal to the person. Some critics speak of such a work as "convincing," not in the oratorical sense of persuasion, but in the sense that the work has consistency and reality.

There are many passages in Scripture which are convincing in this sense. Take the description of the drunkard in Proverbs 23:

> Who scream? Who shriek?
> Who have strife? Who have anxiety?
> Who have wounds for nothing?
> Who have black eyes?
> Those who linger long over wine,
> those who engage in trials of blended wine,
> Look not on the wine when it is red,
> when it sparkles in the glass.
> It goes down smoothly;
> But in the end it bites like a serpent,
> or like a poisonous adder.
> Your eyes behold strange sights,
> and your heart utters disordered thoughts;
> You are like one now lying in the depths of the sea,
> now sprawled at the top of the mast.
> They struck me, but it pained me not;
> They beat me, but I felt it not;
> When shall I awake
> to seek wine once again?

Readers instinctively apply such adjectives as "real," "authentic," "convincing" to a passage such as this. In Meyerhoff's terminology, we have here a true artistic presentation, one that is authentic; and there is a true communication with the reader, one that elicits a true response. The text incorporates an experience, personal or otherwise, presents it authentically or truly, and is able to evoke an authentic decision.[11]

But not all of Scripture has this power to convince, especially when the author simplifies events to the point of schematization. Many of the kings appear unconvincing literarily, even though the teaching of the writer be true.

The secondary truth of inference involves a certain generaliza-

11 Ordinarily, this kind of truth involves a moment of recognition in which there is a new perception or a deeper insight. In this act of "re-cognition," there is an increase of knowledge in one way or another. As the reality is presented, it reveals itself manifesting its own truth.

tion. A literary work presents to us new aspects of reality and experience, broadening our knowledge by acquaintance. When discussing the first kind of literary truth, we spoke of the knowledge which can be gained from it by accident, as it were: all the information which the work may contain, but which does not constitute its specific truth. Knowledge which is gained by familiarity is a different thing altogether, and one which is much more integrally human. This type of knowledge is transmitted by literature. The high point of such knowledge is found in the knowledge conveyed of another person, but we can also acquire knowledge of this type with regard to the objects which form part of our life.

The Scriptures often provide us with a knowledge born of familiarity; this is the way we come to know God as Someone Who comes and associates with men. Many other beings then enter the context of our lives as a result of this condescension, and they become familiar to us. This most important aspect of the truth of the Scriptures can never be adequately conveyed in propositional form.

Knowledge by familiarity is the basis of that contemplative activity by which Christians reflect on a passage of the sacred text: As the text is read slowly and its actualization often repeated, it begins to yield its deep truth, until finally he who gazes into it is penetrated by it. The life of Christ reveals the mystery of Christ to those who know it by familiar contact. This is the principle which St. Ignatius proposes to him who would "exercise himself" in the knowledge of Christ, and it is a method far superior to that in which cerebral meditation gives rise to voluntarist decisions. In meditation, the understanding operates according to the laws of deduction and analogy, the truth with which it is concerned is contained in a proposition; in contemplation, the predominant factor is presence, somehow perceived—the mind is free and receptive and thus dynamically active.

A work of literature reveals our own inner meaning and depth, and makes us conscious of ourselves. As we read, we see ourselves in the light of the author or of his work, and in virtue of this knowledge we can respond by acting to change ourselves. This is the meaning of the last line of Rilke's sonnet, ". . . you must change your life." [12]

[12] "*Du musst dein Leben ändern.*" Last line of "Archaïscher Torso Appolos"; cf. *Sämtliche Werke*, vol. 1, p. 557 (*op. cit.*, ch. 7, n. 7).

The Epistle to the Hebrews says that the word of God "pierces as far as the place where life and spirit, joints and marrow, divide. It sifts the purposes and thoughts of the heart." The Scriptures are true in the sense that they reveal to us what we are in the sight of God. In Psalm 50, God comes to confront the sinner in a vivid litigation:

> When you do these things, shall I be silent?
> Or do you think that I am like yourself?
> I will correct you by drawing them up before your eyes.

And man responds to God:

> I acknowledge my offense,
> and my sin is before me always (Ps 51).

What God effects in the Psalm by direct accusation, He can also do indirectly by showing us someone else, David for instance, in his sin and repentance. Without having formulated any proposition, I have been shown the truth about myself, that is, I see what I am before God, and this impels me to repentance and a deeper conversion. The truth of Scripture is "con-vincing" in this sense also; it is the deep and active truth of the inspired word.

A literary work can reveal the structure of a being, of our own being, as we have just seen. An event presented in this way unlocks the mystery of its meaning, and transcends its own limitations.

In the Scriptures an historical event, unique and irreversible, is presented in its inner meaning in such a way that this meaning sheds light on other events. By recounting happenings which can never be repeated, the sacred writer reveals the structure of the history dominated by God; he writes a theology of history, or, at least, one chapter of it. Book two, or part two, of St. Luke's work recounts the life of the early Church. The Church's structure is revealed as an historical institution with an existence in time. Though the Acts of the Apostles is not a treatise on ecclesiology, it gives us the light by which we understand the dynamic reality of the Church.

Meyerhoff concludes by showing the similarity in theme and method between existential philosophy and literature. The principal existentialist authors study and freely quote literary works as a source of knowledge which can shed light on the meaning of existence.[13]

Though the Scriptures do not fit in this category exactly, Meyerhoff's observations can help in understanding what kind of truth, what kind of authenticity and power, we are to find in the Scriptures. In doing so, we will not be far from those medieval thinkers who saw in the "modes" of Scripture a knowledge which exceeds all others in certainty and sublimity.

THE TRUTH OF WITNESS

We can add to Meyerhoff's categories another type of truth—that of the witness. It is a truth which has a juridical quality, but also an existential quality, capable of engaging the whole man. We are not speaking here of the account of an eyewitness which he relates for the pleasure of telling it; this is not testimony in the strict sense of the term. The testimony demanded by the law is an instrument of justice; this is the source of the gravity of false testimony. The testimony demanded and inspired by faith, therefore, must be carried even as far as martyrdom (*martys* in Greek means witness, and in Christian antiquity the Latin designation for a martyr was "*confessor fidei*"). This quality of truth with its juridical element and existential commitment constitutes the prophetic and apostolic vocation.

Sacred Scripture in its more important sections presents the truth in all its power as ineluctably present, forcing its way in. In a wide sense, since all Scripture is salvation history, and a presentation of the mystery of Christ, it can be considered a witness to this mysterious reality. This brings us back once again to the substantial truth of the Scriptures, which we discussed above.

Christ is the Truth (Jn 14:6), and He is a witness to the truth (Jn 18:37). His words bear witness to Himself and to His mission. Christ staked His life on bearing this witness when He was judged. In thus committing Himself to death, He gave His testimony an unshakable authenticity. The whole validity of biblical truth as a testimony rests on this fact, and draws its strength from it. The

---

[13] This is especially true of Heidegger and Jaspers. Sartre not only quotes literature, he writes it.

law and the prophets bore witness in the past (Rom 3:21), and the apostles are to continue it (1 Jn 4:14).

TRUTH IN DIALOGUE

Finite, human truth often resides in a quest. This is so because none of our truths is the whole truth, even though each of them may be complete in itself. The search for truth may take the form of a solitary meditation or of a friendly dialogue. A deduction is truth in the process of becoming; a syllogism is part of a dialectic. The truth is also sought in the clash of opinions, and this itself is a form of dialectic, a "disputed question." A dialectical dispute may mobilize the energies of two individuals or groups or schools of thought, and thus acquire a true historical dimension.

In a didactic or literary treatment, one can adopt either of two methods: He can present the results of his investigation, the conclusion of a syllogism, the accepted text, the correct formula, etc., or he can present the process of investigation as a sort of intellectual lyric or perhaps a drama. This second method was exploited by the unrivaled genius of Plato. His dialogues are "dramatic," and this dynamic quality was not without its effect on the thought of the philosopher. (We can hardly imagine that it made no difference to Plato whether he exposed his thought dynamically or in a series of static, objective propositions.)

Does Scripture ever employ the same method? If it is revelation, it would seem that it should present me with the truth as already realized, proposed by God or in the name of God; revelation is not the product of human searching, and searching is not possible to God. Thus, it seems that there is no room for personal investigation or an inquiry in dialogue.

But the facts contradict this theory. Because revelation is progressive, challenging man and stimulating him to ask questions, it cannot be a block of truth which descends abruptly from heaven. A revelation awakens man, forcing him to search more deeply, and so prepares him for future revelations.

If one of the functions of language—that of monologue—is to sustain the process of thought, and if another function—that of dialogue—is the contrast of opinions as a means of finding and possessing truth in common, then there does not seem to be any reason why this dimension of language must be a stranger to inspiration. Dialogue is too human a thing and too noble to be excluded *a priori* from the Bible.

One Easter day two disciples of Jesus were making their way to Emmaus. As they walked, they discussed the events of Friday. And so they talked over these things and inquired together. St. Luke's term here is provocative: they went along inquiring between themselves— this is the dialogue of Easter morning. And in the midst of their joint inquiry, the Truth joined them; it was Jesus, but they did not recognize Him yet.

The scene here from the Gospel is charged with emotion and with potential. We should not forget this Greek word *"suzetein"*—"to inquire together." The best definition of dialogue would be just that: two persons searching out between themselves the truth and the Truth.[14]

The author of Ecclesiastes includes in his book the process itself of his meditation, that is, he sets about presenting his truth dynamically. It is impossible to understand this book, or the Book of Job, unless we grant that they are dialectical pieces, concerned with the great problem of retribution—they are "disputed questions," and the problem discussed by these two was only satisfactorily answered by Christ. The dialectic preoccupation of the Epistle of St. James is manifest, and the Book of Wisdom seems to be a reply to Ecclesiastes. The Deuteronomist sought out the meaning of events and tried to establish their inner consistency; his was a *"fides quaerens intellectum."*

We see, then, that the Scriptures, especially the Old Testament, also contain the truth by way of inquiry, and that is part of their drama. It shows man faced with the obscure light of mystery, endowed and challenged by the word. Since the sacred text does not present us with all truth in the form of a definitive answer, it remains open to the inquiry and ever deeper penetration of the faithful. It is the Word, imposing on us the obligation to ask questions, directing our inquiry, and, by means of the Spirit, bringing us into the fullness of the truth.

One might, in virtue of some epistemological theory, condemn

[14] L. Alonso Schökel, *Pedagogía de la comprensión*, 2nd ed., Barcelona, 1961, pp. 117–118.

the above exposition as being too complicated, and wish to substitute another series of categories which would be much simpler. Frankly, our intention was rather to point out various aspects of biblical truth which seem to fit badly into the usual compartments. Sacred Scripture possesses a transcendental truth manifesting the Mystery as being, and it contains many logical truths of judgment and statement, in and through which transcendental truth finds articulation.

LOGICAL TRUTH

This one aspect of truth has assumed a great importance in the history of our tract. This truth, which we call logical, is that of a formal statement or proposition. Its contrary, logical error, is the error of a formal statement. Logical truth and logical error are thus found in the well-defined and limited area of proposition, whose structure will allow of only contradictory judgments, affirming or denying the relation between subject and predicate. When confronted by a proposition, we are fully justified in examining its validity with the presupposition that it must be either true or false. In some cases, a distinction may be employed which divides the proposition in two, delimiting the extension of the subject or the predicate. Before such a distinction is made, in strict logic the proposition is not true and false at the same time, but is rather an imperfect proposition, since it does not clearly affirm or deny one thing. The technique of distinguishing, both in the art of dialectic and in everyday life, shows us that not everything which is a proposition linguistically is a strict logical proposition.

So, then, if I go to the Bible preoccupied with questions of logical truth and error, I have prejudiced the issue and have no right indiscriminately to confront every verse of the Bible with my dilemma. To pose the queston in such a way is to limit, at least methodologically, the extent and type of truth to be found in the Scriptures, and to exclude in principle all truth which is not propositional. This narrow view of the question was aggressively put forward by the rationalists, and meekly accepted by a good number of Catholic theologians.

Is it possible, then, to make universal statements in regard to logical truth? We can do so if we put our statements in a negative

form, since a negation has universal dimensions. Some verses of the
Bible contain truth; no verse of the Bible contains error. Just as,
for instance, a positive precept does not bind always and everywhere: "Give alms" does not mean that I must give to every poor
man at every moment. A negative precept is universally binding:
"Do not blaspheme."

I cannot affirm universally that all the Bible contains logical
truth: interjections, questions, commands, suggestions, allusions,
images are not propositions and cannot, by definition, be the expression of logical truth. But I can frame this universal negative:
No part of the Bible contains error, since the above figures of
speech are equally incapable of expressing logical error. This is the
significance of the negative formula, "inerrancy." And though it is
universally applicable to the Bible, it presupposes a very restricted
view of biblical truth. It has the advantage of all such specific formulas of being precise, but the danger begins when it is allowed to
dominate the whole consideration of truth in the Bible, thus reducing the Scriptures to a catalogue of formal propositions. Such an
attitude in its zeal to defend the inerrancy of the Bible finds that it
has dumped into the text truckloads of "logical errors." In order to
avoid this, we must put the question of inerrancy in the larger
context of the truth of the Bible. Then the negative universality
and precision of the term "inerrancy" will work to best advantage.

The principle of inerrancy is easy to understand: God cannot be
deceived, nor can he deceive us. If God proposes something in the
Scriptures, it is true and cannot be false.

. . . and so far is it from being possible that any error can coexist with
inspiration, that inspiration not only is essentially incompatible with
error, but excludes and rejects it as absolutely and necessarily as it is
impossible that God Himself, the supreme Truth, can utter that which
is not true.[15]

The deduction is simple. God has spoken, and God cannot utter
falsehood. It does no good to take refuge in the distinction between the divine and the human in the Scriptures; the truth is

---

15 ". . . *tantum vero abest ut divinae inspirationi error ullus subesse
possit, ut ea per se ipsa, non modo errorem excludat omnem, sed tam necessario excludat et respuat, quam necessarium est, Deum, summam Veritatem,
nullius omnino erroris auctorem esse.*" Providentissimus Deus, EB 124; RSS,
p. 24.

divine, the error human—such a distinction has no basis in the nature of the inspired text:

Hence, the fact that it was men whom the Holy Spirit took up as His instruments for writing does not mean that it was these inspired instruments—but not the primary author—who might have made an error.[16]

But the following deduction is false: God has spoken; therefore He has pronounced a series of propositions. God has rather assumed all the dimensions of human language.

The general principle which follows quite simply from the veracity of God, can get quite complicated when we start to apply it. The situation has been aggravated by the half-century of discussion which was carried on in Catholic circles on the subject of inerrancy. This is not the place to give an historical synthesis of those battles (the maneuvers of which can be studied in the older manuals); we wish simply to note a few of the opinions. There was Salvatore di Bartolo, who restricted inerrancy to matters of faith and morals; Cardinal Newman, who proposed that along with the inspired message there were other things *"obiter dicta"*; Lenormant distinguished between inspiration and revelation: All of Scripture is inspired, not all of it is revelation; only revelation demands our assent to its infallibility.

Leo XIII refused to admit any limitation to inerrancy, and proposed some principles which could be used in resolving diffiulties. His counsels, which extended to the realm of interpretation, can be summed up in this "golden rule" of St. Augustine, quoted by the Pontiff himself:

And if in these books I meet anything which seems contrary to truth, I shall not hesitate to conclude either that the text is faulty, or that the translator has not expressed the meaning of the passage, or that I myself do not understand.[17]

---

[16] *"Quare nihil admodum refert, Spiritum Sanctum assumpsisse homines tamquam instrumenta ad scribendum, quasi, non quidem primario auctori, sed scriptoribus inspiratis quidpiam falsi elabi potuerit."* Ibid., EB 125; RSS, p. 25.

[17] *"Ego fateor caritati tuae, solis eis Scripturarum libris, qui iam canonici appellantur, didici hunc timorem honoremque deferre, ut nullum eorum auctorum scribendo aliquid errasse firmissime credam. Ac si aliquid in eis offendero litteris, quod videatur contrarium veritati, nihil aliud quam vel mendosum esse codicem, vel interpretem non assecutum esse quod dictum est, vel*

The Pope then explains how we should understand what the Scriptures have to say on matters dealing with the physical sciences, and he goes on to suggest that a similar solution be applied to historical questions.

Other attempts to understand the Bible in the context of inerrancy proved unfortunate: There were the notions of "history according to appearances," implicit citations, an immature version of "literary genres," etc. All of these attempts were well-intentioned and contained an element of truth, namely, that once the Scriptures are understood, the question of their being in error disappears. However, good intentions cannot save a defective theory.

Pius XII, in his encyclical, *Divino afflante Spiritu*, repeated the same principle, which we may paraphrase roughly: If we can understand the Scriptures correctly, the errors they supposedly contain will disappear; however, let us have humility to admit that we cannot resolve all the difficulties.

By this knowledge and exact appreciation of the modes of speaking and writing in use among the ancients can be solved many difficulties, which are raised against the veracity and historical value of the divine Scriptures, and no less efficaciously does this study contribute to a fuller and more luminous understanding of the mind of the sacred writer. . . . Nevertheless, no one will be surprised if all difficulties are not yet solved and overcome, but that even today serious problems greatly exercise the minds of Catholic exegetes.[18]

In this way, the principle of inerrancy becomes a negative canon of hermeneutics: There can be no interpretation which implicates the Bible in error. This norm is particularly relevant when dealing with the synoptic question and the frequent discrepancies found in their narratives.

Pesch dedicated sixty-three pages to inerrancy in the second part of his book, which he followed with a supplement in 1926. For

---

me minime intellexisse, non ambigam." "Letter 82, to St. Jerome," cf. EB 127; RSS, p. 25.

[18] "Cognitis igitur accurateque aestimatis antiquorum loquendi scribendique modis et artibus, multa dissolvi poterunt, quae contra Divinarum Litterarum veritatem fidemque historicam opponuntur; neque minus apte eiusmodi studium ad Sacri Auctoris mentem plenius illustriusque perspiciendam conducet. . . . Nemo tamen miretur non omnes adhuc esse difficultates expeditas atque evictas, sed graves etiam hodie quaestiones catholicorum exegetarum mentes non parum agitare." EB 560, 563; RSS, pp. 99, 101.

thirty years, there were no new efforts in this direction; the encyclical of Pius XII was more a change of outlook and approach than a speculative contribution to the problem. In regard to modern opinions, we will merely list some of the recent work which has been done in the field.

Benoit made a real contribution with his notions on speculative and practical judgment.[19] The speculative judgment has the truth for its object and thus, as a human operation, it is open to error. In inspiration, God guarantees the truth of such a judgment. The object of the practical judgment is the good, and as such is not subject to error or truth, but is judged by whether or not it corresponds to what was intended. When a practical judgment enlists speculative judgments for its own purpose, these latter are conditioned by their context. In other words, Benoit insists that before one can inquire as to whether or not a judgment is true or false—in order either to defend or attack it—we must first inquire whether or not that judgment moves exclusively in the realm of logic.

A. Moretti[20] proposes a theory based on the notion of opinion. Opinion, by its nature, pertains to the intermediate zone of probability; it is only an error when, being erroneous itself, it is proposed as true. When we say: "I think . . . ," "I believe . . . ," "It seems to me . . . ," "I would say . . . ," we have explicitly declared that what we are saying pertains to the area of opinion, and we cannot be guilty of error, since we have formally stated that our adherence to what we say is conditioned. In the Book of Ecclesiastes, opinions are put forth explicitly as such, even though the Hebrew terminology is not as neatly categorized. In normal speech, and in much of what we write or give in conferences, there are many implicit statements of opinion which may take the verbal form of a proposition, though they are not really such at all. Usually, the general or specific context suffices to indicate this implicit quality of our statement as an opinion. We cannot exclude beforehand the possibility that the Bible also contains this way of proposing an opinion. The Bible is a human book, and it is not human always to express oneself in a pondered true or false proposition. Our theology manuals are accustomed to gradate carefully the de-

---

[19] Cf. ch. 9.
[20] "De Scripturarum inerrantia et de hagiographis opinantibus." *DivTh* 62, 1959, pp. 32–68.

gree of certitude of each thesis: "Of defined faith," "of faith," "ecclesiastical doctrine," "theologically certain," "common doctrine," "more probable opinion". . . . The language of conversation and that of literature could not do the same without pedantry.

N. Lohfink[21] has lately studied the problem from another angle, and has taken a significant step forward. His primary concern is to provide a formula that will be faithful to tradition, and at the same time be pastoral. In keeping with tradition, we must widen the psychologically preoccupied horizons of the last century, which situated problems and sought their solutions totally within the mind of the author. We must consider the work as a literary reality. This reality is not to be found in a single granulated verse, obtained by artificially pulverizing the context. One may ask whether or not the Bible really contains "books" in our modern sense of the term. Modern study has shown us the organic growth and successive transpositions and integrations which finally culminated in the transposition effected by Christ, Who then confided the Scriptures to the Church. From this it appears that the formula "inspired books" is too vague and problematic. Inerrancy should be predicated of the Scriptures as they have been entrusted to the Church, "and which as such have been confided to the Church." This is the integral and primary meaning of the Scriptures, within which we must find the meaning of its lesser units, books, oracles, verses.

Conclusion

If we have treated the question of inerrancy somewhat briefly, it is not because we think it secondary, but because of other positive considerations. First, every manual provides an ample treatment of the question, from both an historical and a theoretical point of view. Secondly, we have preferred to adopt the orientation of *Divino afflante Spiritu,* which has changed the center of gravity in this problem, and put the stress on hermeneutics. The lesson of the recent past has taught us that an excessive preoccupation with inerrancy can stultify exegesis, while a serene and solid exegesis eliminates most of the problems met with in the defense of inerrancy. Though, as is the case with most slogans, this one oversimplifies

[21] In the article, "Über die Irrtumslosigkeit und Einheit der Schrift," SZ 84, 1964, pp. 161–181, mentioned before (cf. ch. 2, n. 11).

the reality, still it is true to say that for the last sixty years we have been struggling to defend the Scriptures, now we are working to understand them.

One last point: It is neither legitimate nor prudent to consider hermeneutics as an appendix to the consideration of inerrancy. Thus, for example, the method which seeks and describes the literary types in the Bible is not a last desperate measure to save the Bible from error now that all other attempts have failed. It is a fruitful method in its own right, whose purpose is the appreciation and interpretation of the text. Pius XII in *Divino afflante Spiritu* deduces the need for a hermeneutical method from the divine-human nature of the Bible itself: This is the outlook which predominates in Catholic exegesis today, and it is the outlook which should prevail in a treatise on inspiration.

Bibliography for Chapter 13

Literary Truth. In addition to the work by Hans Meyerhoff, *Time in Literature*, there is the work of W. Kayser, *Die Wahrheit der Dichter. Wandlung eines Begriffes in der deutschen Literature*, Hamburg, 1959, which develops its theme by selecting authors representative of each century. Thus, for example, we have: the truth of facts and fiction, to declare the truth while smiling (Grimmelshausen), to declare the truth in images (Gottsched), the truth of form and symbol (Goethe), etc. There is a good treatment and ample bibliographical material in Wellek and Warren, *Theory of Literature*, ch. 10, "Literature and Ideas," and ch. 3, "The Function of Literature."

The Truth of Witness. Söhngen dedicates four pages to this theme in his *Analogie und Metaphern*, vol. 4, ch. 2 ("Die Zeugnis und Bekenntnisfunktion," pp. 107–110). Cf. also R. Asting, *Die Verkündigung des Wortes Gottes im Urchristentum dargestellt an den Begriffen Wort Gottes, Evangelium und Zeugnis*, Stuttgart, 1939.

Logical Truth (Inerrancy). A. Moretti, "De Scripturarum inerrantia et de hagiographis opinantibus," *DivTh* 62, 1959, pp. 32–68; cf. also M. de Tuya, "La inerrancia bíblica y el hagiógrafo opinante," *EstEc* 34, 1960, pp. 339–347, and the article of N. Lohfink mentioned before, "Über die Irrtumslosigkeit und die Einheit der Schrift," SZ 89, 1964, pp. 161–181. There is an article of J. Coppens in which he contests the position of Benoit: "L'Inspiration et l'inerrance bibliques," ETL 33, 1957, pp. 36–57, and an interesting study by J. Forestell, "The Limitation of Inerrancy," CBQ 20, 1958, pp. 9–18. Recently, P. Zerafa discussed the topic in Ang 39, 1962, pp. 92–119, "The Limits of Biblical Inerrancy." J. Coppens has expressed some disagreement with the position of Lohfink: cf. "Comment mieux concevoir et énoncer l'inspiration et l'inerrance des Saintes Ecritures?" NRT 96, 1964, pp. 933–947. Another orientation can be found in O. Loretz, *Die Wahrheit der Bibel*, Freiburg, 1964.

14. Revealed Doctrine and the People of God

THE WHOLE OF REVELATION?

In *Providentissimus Deus*, Leo XIII recommended the Scriptures as an "arsenal" of doctrine:

For those whose duty it is to handle Catholic doctrine before the learned or unlearned will nowhere find more ample matter or more abundant exhortation, whether on the subject of God, the supreme Good and the All-Perfect Being, or of the works which display His glory and His Love. Nowhere is there anything more full or more express on the subject of the Savior of the world than is to be found in the whole range of the Bible.

As St. Jerome says, "to be ignorant of the Scripture is not to know Christ." In its pages His Image stands out, living and breathing; diffusing everywhere around consolation in trouble, encouragement to virtue, and attraction to the love of God. And as to the Church, her institutions, her nature, her office, and her gifts, we find in Holy Scripture so many references and so many ready and convincing arguments, that as St. Jerome again most truly says: "A man who is well-grounded in the testimonies of the Scripture is the bulwark of the Church." And if we come to morality and discipline, an apostolic man finds in the sacred writings abundant and excellent assistance: most holy precepts, gentle and strong exhortation, splendid examples of every virtue, and finally the promise of eternal reward and the threat of eternal punishment, uttered in terms of solemn import, in God's name and in God's own words.[1]

[1] "*Nam catholicae veritatis doctrinam qui habeant apud doctos vel indoctos tractandam, nulla uspiam de Deo, summo et perfectissimo bono, deque operibus gloriam caritatemque ipsius prodentibus, suppetet eis vel cumulatior copia vel amplior praedicatio. De Servatore autem humani generis nihil uberius expressiusve quam ea, quae in universo habentur Bibliorum contextu; recteque affirmavit Hieronymus, 'ignorationem Scripturarum esse*

This paragraph of Leo XIII is a summary of Christian doctrine under the four headings, *"De Deo," "De Christo Salvatore," "De Ecclesia," "De Moribus et De Novissimis."* According to the Pontiff, Scripture contains this doctrine in a way that is unequalled.

Does Scripture contain all the doctrine of salvation? Or to rephrase the question, is the whole of revelation contained in Scripture? Or, as it is frequently posed today, are there two parallel sources of revelation?

Formulated this way, the question has resounded throughout the whole world, and has been echoed in the discussions of Vatican II. In this question, two currents of thought confront one another.

Since we cannot list here all of the many opinions on the matter, or even summarize so lengthy a discussion, we must content ourself with giving an outline of the state of the question. All Catholics agree that there are these two—Scripture and tradition. The Protestants, as a result of the studies in form criticism, agree that there was an oral tradition in the Church before it was subsequently given literary stability; and many Protestants are seeking to discern an interpretative tradition.

Protestants understand the sufficiency of Scripture to mean that the Bible is its own norm (in regard to the canon), and that it provides its own interpretation.

The canonical Scripture, the word of God, bestowed by the Holy Spirit and proposed to the world by the prophets and apostles, is the most ancient and most perfect philosophy of all; it alone perfectly contains all piety and every norm for life. Its interpretation is to be sought from it alone, as it is its own interpreter under the guidance of charity and faith.[2]

---

ignorationem Christi': *ab illis nimirum exstat, veluti viva et spirans imago eius, ex qua levatio malorum, cohortation virtutum, amoris divini invitatio mirifice prorsus diffunditur. Ad Ecclesiam vero quod attinet, institutio, natura, munera, charismata eius tam crebra ibidem mentione occurrunt, tam multa pro ea tamque firma prompta sunt argumenta, idem ut Hieronymus verissime edixerit: 'Que Sacrarum Scripturarum testimoniis roboratus est, is est propugnaculum Ecclesiae.' Quod si de vitae morumque conformatione et disciplina quaeratur, larga indidem et optima subsidia habituri sunt viri apostolici: plena sanctitatis praescripta, suavitate et vi condita hortamenta, exempla in omni virtutum genere insignia; gravissima accedit, ipsius Dei nomine et verbis, praemiorum in aeternitatem promissio, denunciatio poenarum."* EB 86; RSS, p. 4.

[2] "Scriptura canonica, verbum Dei, Spiritu Sancto tradita et per prophetas

When a Catholic speaks of the sufficiency of Scripture, he means that the scriptures "*catholice tracta*," as they are understood in the Church and by the Church, are enough. Geiselmann[3] gives many ancient texts which clearly affirm the sufficiency of the Scriptures. We will cite here only two:

. . . perfect in itself, and for everything sufficient (St. Vincent of Lérins).

. . . the source and summation of all our faith (Hugo of St. Victor).

The Two Theories

So far, Catholics are in unanimous agreement among themselves. Differences begin when the discussion moves to the question of the relation between Scripture and oral tradition. There are two opposing explanations, which we will characterize as establishing a quantitative or a qualitative relation.

The first position maintains that the Scripture contains a series of truths, and that tradition contains some of these same truths and others; tradition adds to Scripture quantitatively. Thus, for example, if in revelation there are 1300 truths, Scripture might contain one thousand of them, tradition another three hundred. Or it might be that revelation is contained partly in Scripture and partly in tradition (the formula "*partim-partim*" was not accepted at Trent).

The second view holds that the whole of revelation is in Scripture, but that it is there in a special way. It is fixed in literature, but it is not purely propositional; it contains some things explicitly and others implicitly; some realities it sets forth in concepts, others in symbol; some truths are given as propositions, others as possible inferences; some fully developed, others in germ. There are neat formulas and also presences existing within and sustaining aspects of the total organic structure. This fullness of revelation in the Scriptures demands by its very nature a process of reading, inter-

---

apostolosque mundo proposita, omnium perfectissima et antiquissima philosophia, pietatem omnem, omnem vitae rationem sola perfecte continet. Huius interpretatio ex ipsa sola petenda est, ut ipsa interpres sit sui, caritatis fideique regula moderante." Confessio Helvetica (1536), cited by Pesch, no. 218.

[3] *Die Heilige Schrift und die Tradition*; cf. ch. 5, n. 20.

pretation, explanation, and development which will never end; and this is tradition. Congar thus arrives at the conclusion that there is no truth revealed only in Scripture, none revealed only in tradition, with the one exception of the truth that must be outside Scripture: "These books are inspired."

These two theories represent two mentalities. The first looks on revelation primarily as proposition; it is not so much the revelation of a Person as the revelation of truths, and truths are propositions. Correspondingly, faith, rather than a total personal commitment, is more an intellectual activity whose object is framed in propositions. But it is clear that there are some dogmas of faith which are not "proposed" in Scripture. That is why the great champion of this opinion in recent times, Lennerz,[4] has requested professors of theology to refrain from their heroic efforts to find "proof texts" for certain theses. But then, a number of these dogmas are not found in propositional form in the early Fathers or in the ancient documents of the magisterium. At this point, the adherents of the propositional theory ought to have recourse to a *"disciplina arcanae"* which has been transmitted from mouth to mouth without ever leaving any traces until that moment when it is publicly proposed. If there be no such recourse, then these men must admit that they are exercising in regard to the ancient documents of tradition an interpretative activity which they refuse to concede as valid in regard to sacred Scripture. Those who maintain this position consider tradition especially in its ultimate stage, of the ordinary and and extraordinary magisterium, and attend much less to the living tradition of the *sensus fidelium* of the entire Church.

The second mentality is more integral and organic: Revelation is not only propositional, it is rather a presentation of the Person of Christ in His acts and teaching. The evangelists had already begun the task of explaining the meaning of the Christ-fact; they gave tradition a literary fixity, but they did not interrupt it. Revelation can assume many literary forms and can exist in life before being formulated. Thus the *"sensus fidelium"* is extremely important when it is joined and subordinated to the magisterium. This outlook seeks first of all to grasp the unity of the two realities in the Church, which we call Scripture and tradition.

Which of these theories is the true one? As of this moment, the

---

[4] Cf. bibliography.

question has not been settled, and still remains a "disputed question."[5] We should rather ask: Which theory is more probable? To answer that question, we cannot rest content with discussion and speculation; we must consult tradition. Here again, the two theories part company in the way they set about studying the problem.

The first theory bases itself to a great extent on the manuals produced during the last hundred years, and the catechisms which, in their capacity of exponents of the "common opinion," serenely propose the quantitative theory. The adherents of this view also cite the way in which certain recent encyclicals have spoken:

It was chiefly out of the sacred writings that they [the Fathers] endeavored to proclaim and establish the articles of faith and the truth connected with it, and it was *in them, together with divine tradition,* that they found the refutation of heretical error, and the reasonableness, the true meaning, and the mutual relation of the truths of Catholicism.[6]

It is also true that theologians must always return to the sources of divine revelation: for it belongs to them to point out how the doctrine of the living teaching authority is to be found either explicitly or implicitly in the Scriptures and in tradition.[7]

Finally, they cite the Tridentine decree, giving it the sense attributed to it by St. Robert Bellarmine:

. . . and seeing that this truth and discipline is contained in written books and in traditions not written . . .[8]

[5] In the volume *De Scriptura et Traditione,* one of the contributors confidently asserts that it is *de Fide* that not all of the revealed truths are contained in Scripture (Augustín Trapé, p. 326). Since he does not say whether or not he understands this of other truths besides the canon of the Scriptures, no one need disagree with the statement.

[6] "*Nam quae obiectum sunt fidei vel ab eo consequuntur, ex Divinis potissime Litteris studuerunt asserere et stabilere; atque ex ipsis,* SICUT PARITER EX DIVINA TRADITIONE, *nova haereticorum commenta refutare, catholicorum dogmatum rationem, intelligentiam, vincula exquirere.*" *Providentissimus Deus,* EB 114; RSS, p. 18; emphasis added.

[7] "*Verum [quoque] est, theologis semper redeundum esse ad divinae revelationis fontes: eorum enim est indicare qua ratione ea quae a vivo Magisterio docentur, in Sacris Litteris et in divina 'traditione,' 'sive explicite, sive implicite inveniantur.'* " *Humani generis,* EB 611; NCWC trans., p. 10.

[8] ". . . *perspiciensque hanc veritatem et disciplinam contineri in libris scriptis et sine scripto traditionibus. . . .*" Decree of the Council of Trent, sess. 4, EB 57.

The second theory[9] has extended its study of tradition to include the most ancient documents, and joined to this a consideration of the practice of the Church, as well as a study of her formulas. Three authors in particular have carried on this historical study of tradition. J. R. Geiselmann has reworked and synthesized the studies of two Tübingen theologians—Kuhn and Möller; he has studied the meaning of the Tridentine definition and its later interpretation, giving attention to the work of the theologians of the later Middle Ages. In his books and articles, which are a mine of information, he has succeeded in creating an awareness of the problem, and has orientated investigation toward a solution that is more integral and traditional. H. de Lubac does not study our problem directly, but in his great work on medieval exegesis whose roots he traces to the work of Origen, thus covering a thousand years of Catholic thought on revelation and the Bible, we are brought to the same conclusions. Y. Congar has dedicated a two-volume work to the problem, the first historical and the second systematic. The plebiscite of tradition consulted by these three men, though it is complex and nuanced, favors the theory of an organic integrated unity. Rahner, for his part, approaches the problem from a speculative point of view, and fully accords with this theory. In the same line of thought, though with variations in interpretation, we can list Beumer in his numerous articles, which are extremely well-informed and enriched with personal insight. We can also list the works of Holstein and Tavard, as well as many diverse monographs whose conclusions are in the same vein. And then, of course, the question has run the whole gamut of the popular press, because of the discussions during the first and third sessions of Vatican II.

Taking the present state of the question into account, we would propose this evaluation of the opinions: The theory and the practice of the Church, which has extended for nearly two thousand years, is not explained by the view which holds for a quantitative relation between Scripture and tradition. Such a view is not adequate to the fullness of the witness of the magisterium in its decrees and teaching, of the Fathers in their preaching and theological reflection, or of the medieval authors who looked to the Scriptures to find revelation. The quantitative theory is new: It is not what

The works referred to in this paragraph are all found in the bibliography.

the Council of Trent intended to define (Geiselmann); it was born of anti-Protestant polemic (Bellarmine); it has been repeated in the manuals without any serious attempt to study the problem. It involves a devaluation of the Scriptures, which is certainly not a tradition in the Church. Now that the Scriptures are being restored to their place in the life of the Church, the problem must be met and solved.

The theory of qualitative relation or organic unity existing between Scripture and tradition explains the traditional thought and practice of the Church much more adequately; it is more consistent with a personalist view of revelation and of faith, and it is more in keeping with the unity of charismatic activity.

Some light can be shed on this question by recalling some of the things we have said in the preceding chapters: the medieval doctrine of the "literary modes" of the Bible, the structured plurality of a literary work, the various types of truth (including the truth of search), the relative autonomy of a work of literature, the work and its context, the repetition of a work as its re-presentation, symbolic thought and expression, inspiration in the context of the other charisms. These and perhaps other realities which we have discussed throughout this book easily find their place within the theory which holds for the organic and integral unity of Scripture and tradition.[10]

THE USES OF DOCTRINE

This question depends in some degree on the former. At this point in the Church's history, in the second half of the twentieth century, a Christian has many means at his disposal by which he can come to a knowledge of revealed doctrine. He can find all of the principal ecclesiastical documents arranged and catalogued in the one volume of Denzinger-Schönmetzer; and if he wishes to study a doctrine or settle a question, he need only consult the index, and then read the history of Christian thought on his point, as it is manifested in the documents of the Church; while the third index will give him an over-all view of this same teaching according to the traditional schema of the manuals. However, while it is true that all

[10] The contrary opinions expressed at the council have served to highlight the problem and have given it added interest, as well as providing a stimulus.

these documents proceed in one way or another from the Scriptures (at least according to the second theory), the reader is liable to consider himself dispensed from consulting the sacred text personally, especially since his manual (*enchiridion*) speaks a language which is more precise and better organized.

But this is not the way to hand on the Christian reality in its fullness. Bellarmine said that the Scriptures were not necessary, but this is polemic, not tradition. If God has confided His revelation in the Scriptures to the Church, the Church must make them available to her children. The Church fulfills this obligation on various levels of her existence. We will, therefore, schematize these levels somewhat, and consider them as three: liturgy, catechesis, and theology.

The Liturgy

In the context of the liturgy, Scripture becomes a teaching when it is read and understood. It is not understood, and thus cannot teach, when the language instead of being a medium of communication is a means of separation: Millions of Christians do not understand Latin. The remedy for this is either to teach everyone Latin, or translate the text:

"But since the use of the mother tongue, whether in the Mass, the administration of the sacraments, or other parts of the liturgy, frequently may be of greater advantage to the people, the limits of its employment may be extended. This will apply in the first place to the readings and directives, and to some of the prayers and chants . . .[11]

The *Constitution on the Sacred Liturgy* has opted for translation, and some think that the question is now completely resolved.

But in reality this is not so. Biblical language, even if translated well, or perhaps because it is well-translated, can seem strange and unintelligible to the people, and lose thereby its capacity to teach. Someone completely unacquainted with St. Paul will not understand him just because he is read out in English. How many peo-

---

[11] "Cum tamen, sive in Missa, sive in Sacramentorum administratione, sive in aliis Liturgiae partibus, haud raro linguae vernaculae usurpatio valde utilis apud populum exsistere possit, amplior locus ipsi tribui valeat, imprimis autem in lectionibus et admonitionibus, in nonnullis orationibus et cantibus. . . ." Const., no. 36:2.

ple, for instance, know the theological wealth contained in the word "Lord" (*Kyrios*) as St. Paul uses it? It has become so familiar that we unconsciously assume that St. Paul meant no more by it than we usually do. Ought we then to translate the Bible into another language that is non-biblical, or should we teach the Christian people the meaning of the biblical language? A bit of both: One of the principal tasks of the liturgical homily is precisely that of making the language of the Scriptures intelligible to the people.[12] Considering the present stage of biblical renewal, we would go so far as to say that this will be the most crucial task for a generation or so. It may be that we should have a sort of homily to precede the reading by way of preparation; or perhaps after the homily which follows the reading, the text could be read again.

Little by little the language of the Scriptures will become familiar to the people of God, and then they will understand the language of God. In this way, with time and patience, the effort at putting the biblical language into a more available medium will have the result of teaching the people the language itself. Then the simple reading of the text will become a real teaching. This teaching achieves new depths because of the liturgical contexts which establish and highlight relations between the texts as they mutually shed light on one another and orientate themselves toward the liturgical action. This is the traditional practice of the Church, somewhat obscured these last few decades.

Although the sacred liturgy is above all things the worship of the divine Majesty, it likewise contains much instruction for the faithful. For in the liturgy, God speaks to his people and Christ is still proclaiming his Gospel. And the people reply to God both by song and prayer.[13]

The sermon, moreover, should draw its content mainly from scriptural and liturgical sources. . . .[14]

[12] We intend here only to outline the problem and schematically to propose a few possible solutions insofar as they touch on the theme of the word.

[13] "*Etsi sacra Liturgia est praecipue cultus divinae maiestatis, magnam etiam continet populi fidelis eruditionem. In Liturgia enim Deus ad populum suum loquitur; Christus adhuc Evangelium annuntiat. Populus vero Deo respondet tum cantibus tum oratione.*" *Const.*, no. 33.

[14] "*Haec vero imprimis ex fonte sacrae Scripturae et Liturgiae hauriatur . . .*" *Const.*, no. 35:2.

By means of the homily, the mysteries of the faith and the guiding principles of the Christian life are expounded from the sacred text, during the course of the liturgical year; the homily, therefore, is to be highly esteemed as part of the liturgy itself; . . .[15]

Catechesis

The other means of imparting sacred doctrine are related to this principal means as preparation or prolongation. Catechesis is a preparation. The Counter-Reformation conceived of this activity as a process by which the child was taught a series of rigid and precise formulas which he did not understand, but which were meant to protect him in the future. Later, under the influence of the Enlightenment, this type of catechism seemed to answer perfectly to the ideal of intellectual precision. The biblical and liturgical renewal of our times has imposed a different orientation: Catechetical instruction as a pedagogical activity adapts itself to the intellectual development of the child; that is, it begins with the history of salvation, moving from events to expressions of a more doctrinal nature. This initiation into the language of the Scriptures brings one into a world in which God becomes familiar; it brings the child into contact with Life. The new catechetical methods spontaneously turn to the Scriptures.

Theology

The doctrine proposed by the liturgy which is prepared for by catechesis is extended and developed by the science of theology:

Most desirable is it, and most essential, that the whole teaching of theology should be pervaded and animated by the use of the divine Word of God. This is what the Fathers and the greatest theologians of all ages have desired and reduced to practice. It was chiefly out of the sacred writings that they endeavored to proclaim and establish the articles of faith and the truth connected with it, and it was in them, together with divine tradition, that they found the refutation of heretical error, and the reasonableness, the true meaning, and the mutual relation of the truths of Catholicism. Nor will anyone wonder at this who considers that the sacred books hold such an eminent position among the sources of revelation that, without their assiduous study

[15] "Homilia, qua per anni liturgici cursum ex textu sacro fidei mysteria et normae vitae christianae exponuntur, ut pars ipsius liturgiae valde commendatur; . . ." Const., no. 52.

and use, theology cannot be placed on its true footing, or treated as its dignity demands.

For although it is right and proper that students in academies and schools should be chiefly exercised in acquiring a scientific knowledge of dogma, by means of reasoning from the articles of faith to their consequences, according to the rules of approved and sound philosophy —nevertheless, the judicious and instructed theologian will by no means pass by that method of doctrinal demonstration which draws its proof from the authority of the Bible.[16]

The principle which the Pope proposes, and which is recommended by the teaching and practice of Christian antiquity, touches on the profound nature of theology, and it is beginning to be realized again in our teaching of sacred doctrine. Sacred Scripture must animate the study of dogma (the "articles of faith"), the exercise of theological reasoning ("their consequences"), controversy ("refutation of heretical error"), speculative theology ("the reasonableness"), and systematic theology ("the mutual relation").

The same Pontiff made restricted application of his principle in a way suited to the theological climate of his time: The student in a university course should begin from the articles of faith (creeds and dogmatic definitions), and proceed by a strict process of reasoning; the professor who does research (as opposed to his classroom work which corresponds to the duties of students just seen) cannot neglect the Scriptures in his investigation into dogma. The student who wishes to prepare himself for the study of the Bible which will be profitable and without peril, begins by studying philosophy and theology according to St. Thomas.

[16] "*Illud autem maxime optabile est et necessarium, ut eiusdem Divinae Scripturae usus in universam theologiae influat disciplinam eiusque prope sit anima: ita nimirum omni aetate Patres atque praeclarissimi quique theologi professi sunt et re praestiterunt. Nam quae obiectum sunt fidei vel ab eo consequuntur, ex Divinis potissime Litteris studuerunt asserere et stabilire; atque ex ipsis, sicut pariter ex divina traditione, nova haereticorum commenta refutare, catholicorum dogmatum rationem, intelligentiam, vincula exquirere. Neque id cuiquam fuerit mirum, qui reputet, tam insignem locum inter revelationis fontes Divinis Libris deberi, ut, nisi eorum studio usuque assiduo, nequeat theologia rite et pro dignitate tractari. Tametsi enim rectum est iuvenes in academiis et scholis ita praecipue exerceri, ut intellectum et scientiam dogmatum assequantur, ab articulis fidei argumentatione instituta ad alia ex illis, secundum normas probatae solidaeque philosophiae, concludenda; gravi tamen eruditoque theologo minime negligenda est ipsa demonstratio dogmatum ex Bibliorum auctoritatibus ducta; . . .*" Providentissimus Deus, EB 114; RSS, pp. 17–18.

At the end of the last century, St. Thomas was considered simply in his role as the author of the *Summas*, and his exegetical labors, as well as the ancient meaning of *"magister theologiae,"* were ignored.[17] At the time of Leo XIII, biblical studies were handicapped by the influence of rationalism: The statement of the Pontiff was far-reaching and courageous, but it was not the last word. Pius XII took a step forward:

> . . . they should set forth in particular the theological doctrine in faith and morals of the individual books or texts so that their exposition may not only aid the professors of theology in their explanations and proofs of the dogmas of faith, but may also be of assistance to priests in their presentation of Christian doctrine to the people, and, in fine, may help all the faithful to lead a life that is holy and worthy of a Christian.[18]

The theological doctrine of Scriptures is placed at the service of the professor of theology, so that he may explain and prove dogma; it is at the service of priests, so that they may present Christian doctrine to the people. We should note here the consequences of our modern specialization: The Middle Ages (including, naturally, St. Thomas) considered the professor of theology (*magister theologiae*) as entrusted with the task of expounding the sacred text: *"legit sacram paginam"*; whereas now his task is to expound and prove dogmas. According to the ancient idea, a homily was meant to explain passages of the Bible; now it has become a process of presenting Christian doctrine, though this is not further defined. Theological doctrine expounded by an exegete (who has become a

---

[17] "St. Thomas's written work in *sacra pagina* must certainly have extended over the whole of his teaching career, since commenting on the Bible was the prime task of the master in theology." M. D. Chenu, *Toward Understanding St. Thomas*, Chicago, 1964, p. 243. Pius XII, in his allocution to the Angelicum, January 14th, 1958, first praised the commentaries of St. Thomas on Scripture, and then concluded. "Quare si quis ea [commentaria] neglegat, minime dicendus est S. Angelici Doctoris plane et plene familiaritate et notitia uti." *AAS* 50, 1958, p. 152.

[18] ". . . *ostendant potissimum quae sit singulorum librorum vel textuum theologica doctrina de rebus fidei et morum, ita ut haec eorum explanatio non modo theologos doctores adiuvet ad fidei dogmata proponenda confirmandaque, sed sacerdotibus etiam adiumento sit ad doctrinam christianam coram populo enucleandam, ac fidelibus denique omnibus ad vitam sanctam homineque christiano dignam agendam adserviat." Divino afflante Spiritu*, EB 551; *RSS*, p. 93.

specialist himself) is considered auxiliary. When the encyclical speaks of "the individual books or texts," it does not take account of biblical theology as a separate discipline.

The directives of Pius XII are an advance over those of Leo XIII, and they point out a road which the concluding paragraphs of the encyclical invite us to follow.

The predominant method of using scriptural doctrine in our theology manuals is that of the "proof from Scripture." If this were only a pedagogical device, leading the student back from the dogmatic formulation to its germinal presentation in the sacred text, it would be acceptable. But the method has created an outlook which puts the reality entirely out of focus: The Bible has become a supply depot for "proofs"; its function is seen as secondary and subordinate to dogmatic theology.

In an article on this theme,[19] we attempted to point out the origin of the "intellectual mechanism" which is called the "proof": It derives from the dialectic of Aristotle, and was imposed by the treatise of Melchior Cano, *De locis theologicis.*[20] Its place is found only when there is question of proving a proposition which is debatable or debated (thesis); or in controversy where, as a methodological procedure, that which is denied by the adverasry (historically, the Protestants) is treated as open to discussion. This same method was used as a means for training students. The aspect of controversy or dispute ended by becoming the exclusive orientation of theology, though, as Lonergan has observed, rhetoric also served to influence the process.

It is useless now to try to improve the proofs from Scripture. What we must do, is reduce the emphasis on proof to its proper and legitimate role, and expand theology more in the direction of its expository functions, as expounding and interpreting the revealed doctrine: this is, to return to the method of the Middle Ages.[21] Such a renewal is already in progress, caused partly by the

[19] "Argument d'Ecriture et théologie biblique dans l'enseignement théologique," *NRT* 91, 1959, pp. 337–354.
[20] Cf. A. Lang, *Die loci theologici des Melchior Cano und die Methode des theologischen Beweises,* Munich, 1925.
[21] Cf. Chenu, *op. cit.* (n. 17). In this connection, paragraph 16 of the *Constitution on the Sacred Liturgy* takes on a special importance: "*Curent insuper aliarum disciplinarum magistri, imprimis theologiae dogmaticae, sacrae Scripturae, theologiae spiritualis et pastoralis ita, ex intrinsecis exi-*

conviction of many professors, and partly by the present dissatis-
faction of most of the students. In both groups, there is a renewed
awareness of the place of Scripture in the Church.

This renewal will draw in its train a whole world of theological
riches; men will discover wealth only dimly suspected before. In
teaching, the factor of time will, obviously, require a selection of
certain themes or aspects for fuller treatment, while others, more
vital in another age, will receive less attention.

These three channels of doctrine, liturgy (and preaching),
catechesis, and theology are not the only means by which biblical
revelation can be actualized, as though the Church in general or its
magisterium were excluded from this need of the Bible. The
Church of God as a whole, and the teaching magisterium must also
listen to the Scriptures, accept them and expound them. These
words of Pesch are still relevant:

The Scripture is a rule of faith from which the Church may not de-
part; she is obliged by its authority as by the authority of God Himself speaking.[22]

The Scripture has been given by God to the ecclesiastical magisterium, so that it learn from it what it should teach to both wise and
ignorant.[23]

In this activity of the magisterium, the exegete can have a subordinate function, since his labors may, in the "Providence of God,
prepare for and bring to maturity the judgment of the Church."

The exegete actualizes the doctrine of Scripture by a theological
exposition of particular passages, and by establishing a biblical theology around some theme or in a more general context. These
studies are extended by dogmatic theology, and echoed by the min-
isters of the word; however, this action is not unilateral and the
roles are not exclusive.

---

gentiis proprii uniuscuiusque obiecti, mysterium Christi et historiam salutis
excolere, ut exinde earum connexio cum Liturgia et unitas sacerdotalis
institutionis aperte clarescant." The "mysterium Christi" and the "historia
salutis" are the central theme of the Scriptures.

[22] "Scriptura fit regula fidei, a qua ecclesia recedere non potest . . ." No.
578.

[23] ". . . ipsi magisterio ecclesiastico etiam Scriptura a Deo data est, ut
ex ea discat, quae doctos et indoctos doceat." No. 579.

All human words need proof and witnesses, but the word of God is a witness to itself, because it must be that whatsoever enunciates incorruptible truth is an incorruptible witness to the truth. But since our God has willed that through the Scriptures we come to know something of His most intimate thoughts and desires, and since the very message of the sacred Scripture is, in a certain way, the mind of God, I will not be silent about anything which God has willed to be known or preached.[24]

Bibliography for Chapter 14

Scripture and Tradition. The fundamental work in this area has been done by J. R. Geiselmann whose work, *Die Heilige Schrift und die Tradition,* we have already cited. In addition, Geiselmann had dedicated other books and articles to this theme, especially "Die mündliche Überlieferung" in *Beitrag zum Begriff der Tradition,* ed. by M. Schmaus, Munich, 1962. One of Geiselmann's studies can be found in English in *Christianity Divided,* ed. by D. Callahan *et al.,* New York 1961 (cf. "Scripture, Tradition, and the Church: An Ecumenical Problem"). The work of Congar is embodied in his two volumes: *La Tradition et les Traditions. Essai historique,* Paris, 1960; *La Tradition et les Traditions. Essai Théologique,* Paris, 1963. In English, we have the excellent work of G. H. Tavard, *Holy Writ or Holy Church,* London, 1959. Lennerz has published most of his work in various articles in *Gregorianum,* and Beumer has most of his articles in *Scholastik.* The majority of authors who treat of the question put the stress on the aspect of tradition. The large volume of seven hundred pages, *De Scriptura et Traditione,* Rome, 1963, contains, in addition to articles treating of the state of the question since Trent (and therefore somewhat polemic in tone), studies from a biblical point of view (Feuillet, Rigaux), patristic doctrine (Ortiz de Urbina on the Oriental Fathers, and Holstein on the Western Fathers after St. Augus-

---

[24] "*Alia enim omnia, id est, humana dicta, argumentis ac testibus egent. Dei autem sermo ipse sibi testis, quia necesse est quidquid incorrupta veritas loquitur, incorruptum sit testimonium veritatis. Sed tamen cum per Scripturas sacras scire nos quasi de arcano animi ac mentis suae quaedam voluerit Deus noster, quia ipsum quidquid vel agnosci per suos vel praedicari Deus voluit, non tacebo.*" St. Salvian, "De Gubernatione Dei, bk. 3," PL 53, 57.

tine), the doctrine of the early reformers, the Orthodox, and the Anglicans. The bibliography by Beumer on p. 85 is especially valuable. The state of the question before the Council is excellently presented by G. Moran, *Scripture and Tradition. A Survey of the Question*, New York, 1963 cf. also in *Herder Korrespondenz* 13, 1958–1959, pp. 349–353 14, 1959–1960, pp. 567–573, Über das Traditionsprinzip." For the period immediately after the Council, see the "Elenchus Bibl." in *Biblica* for 1964, especially nos. 82 and 247. There is also a good résumé of the discussion in *Herder Correspondence* 2, 1965, pp. 16–21, "The Debate on Revelation."

The Uses of Doctrine. A. Grillmeier, "Vom Symbolum zur Summa. Zum theologiegeschichtlichen Verhältnis von Patristik und Scholastik," in *Kirche und Überlieferung*, Freiburg, 1960. The recent discussions about biblical theology must necessarily consider this question. A. Lang's study on Melchior Cano is still valuable, *Die loci theologici des Melchior Cano und die Methode des theologischen Beweises*, Munich, 1925; Karl Rahner has two articles in vol. 5 of *Schriften zur Theologie*, Cologne, 1962: "Exegese und Dogmatik," pp. 82–111; and "Was ist eine dogmatische Aussage?", pp. 54–81. This volume will probably be published in English. The first of these articles can be found in *Dogmatic vs. Biblical Theology*, ed. by H. Vorgrimler, Baltimore, 1964. As mentioned earlier, Lang's study is utilized in L. Alonso Schökel, "Argument d'Ecriture et théologie biblique dans l'enseignement théologique," NRT 81, 1959, pp. 337–354. There is a good but brief discussion of biblical theology in D. Stanley's *Christ's Resurrection in Pauline Soteriology*, Rome, 1961, "Introduction." James Robinson has recently given an excellent evaluation of the problem of biblical theology, seeing the Catholic *Problematik* from a Protestant viewpoint: cf. "Scripture and Theological Method," CBQ 27, 1965, pp. 6–27.

Catechesis and Preaching. These subjects are treated in both Chapters 14 and 15; the bibliography given here will apply to both of them. The fundamental work is that by J. Jungmann, *Die Frohbotschaft und unsere Glaubensverkündigung*, Regensburg, 1936, which has been translated, abridged, and edited by W. Huesman as *The Good News Yesterday and Today*, New York, 1962. In regard to the liturgy and preaching, there is the work of Daniélou, *The Bible and the Liturgy*, Notre Dame, 1956, and an interesting study by A. Wilder, *The Language of the Gospel. Early Christian Rhetoric*, New York, 1964. The volume *La Parole de Dieu en Jésus Christ*, Paris, 1961, has, among others, an article by H. Holstein, "Prédication apostolique et magistère." And the papers of the Strasbourg Congress, *The Liturgy and the Word of God*, already cited, contains an article by F. Coudreau, "The Bible and the Liturgy in Catechesis," Again, the "Elenchus Bibliographicus" of *Biblica* can provide bibliographical information, as also the "Elenchus Suppletorius" in *Verbum Domini*, and the periodical *Worship* devotes many of its articles to this subject.

15. The Context of the Spirit: Saving Power

Sacred Scripture, because it is the inspired word, contains the doctrine of salvation and it possesses the power of salvation. In the context of the Logos—Truth; in the context of the Spirit—Power. Holy Scripture not only teaches us, it acts on us; it not only teaches us to act, it makes us act. This traditional doctrine has been somewhat neglected recently and stands in need of being re-affirmed.

HUMAN LANGUAGE

There is within human language a certain force and power. We have already seen something of this aspect in our discussion of the "impressive" function of language. It is this notion which we wish to develop more fully here.

Fundamentally, the energy of language derives from will and terminates in will through the medium of language expressed and understood. We will discuss now the ways in which this general pattern is realized specifically.

The power of the will is made objective in forceful, significant word forms, which can reach the area of the intellect and create conviction, or the weaker adherence of opinion, or the wider scope of a mentality. From a social point of view, a will radiating out in ever-widening circles can create a public opinion, an enormous force, a collective mentality, or a common conviction.

We call this energy residing in the one speaking authority, and it is a genuine power. But we can also consider this power as it is in language divorced from the speaker, as something significant and literarily structured. Since in human speech the two factors of speaker and thing spoken can be disassociated, we can find instances of men without authority becoming the bearers of a powerful message; and we see cases in which the message, lacking authentic power because it is wrong or evil, still acquires power because of the force of the language or the authority of him who speaks it: this is the charge that Plato laid to the Sophists. This example of evil and error being spread by the energy of agitators, at least shows the power of the word. But there can be no such distinction when God speaks. His authority is invested in his words, and through these it passes to the listener without the aid of artifice.

Secondly, the power made objective can reach the area of the will, calling forth a decision, either in the realm of action or of attitude. This second effect of language we call persuasion, just as we called the first conviction. Conviction prefers arguments, persuasion relies on values and motives. This latter may also assume a social dimension: Oratory is a large part of political activity.

Thirdly, the energy of words may extend into the realm of the emotions, effecting some change or even producing total transformation. Words console, animate, rejoice, impart sympathy, confidence, or peace. In these cases, the word does not so much proceed from authority of will as transmit a deep affective participation which is imparted to the other. The social radiation of this power of the word is more limited except where there is question of elemental feelings. In all these aspects which we have described, we are speaking of language as a medium of communication, as a signifying reality, that is, as identical with its meaning.

In dialogue, these dimensions of language may act in an "alternating current" of influence, increasing in intensity in a number of ways. In order to convince another, I redouble my own conviction; or having begun to convince another, he ends by convincing me, or perhaps we exchange convictions. We may stir one another to action which may be common, complementary or divergent. The affective power of dialogue is obvious.

Since our soul is one, the activities we have described seldom exist as separate realities; usually, one predominates and enlists the other two.

The word of God must have this energy or power in the highest degree. Because it proceeds from an infinite authority and cannot be different from what is good and true, it reaches man wholly. Since it is the word of God, it occurs in the realm of the supernatural; it is for salvation and its power is saving. The word of God is a bearer of grace; it works salvation: "In his word, God not only reveals what grace is, He also imparts grace in that word." [1]

THE DYNAMIC FORMS OF LANGUAGE

There are certain forms in a language which manifest and actualize the "energic" or dynamic quality of speech. We will treat of the principal forms briefly.

Address. The mere fact of calling someone by his name makes him attentive and disposed to listen. There is the call to arms, and the summons to witness. I can invoke the name of another and make him present to myself; I can invoke his name to another in order to obtain a favor. Invocation, when it takes on a social dimension, becomes convocation and refers to a parliament or assembly, including a cultic assembly.

Another form of address is found in the act of *naming,* which establishes someone juridically in an office. In an election, it usually suffices either to name the person in a recognized context, or to write his name on a ballot. The power of the "address" in this case resides in the accumulated naming on the part of a majority of the community.

Address can also take other forms, such as personal invitation, a slogan held in common, etc. When the address is mutual, then one call is echoed by another.

The *imperative* form is a pure expression of will intended to result in action. If it proceeds from one invested with authority in the juridical sense, then it has the force of a precept or a law. If it is based on a right, then it imposes an obligation. In other cases, it may be simply a petition. There are linguistic variations of the imperative, such as the gerundive "No Smoking," the future indicative, etc. The imperative can be mutual, social, etc.

The *question* requires a verbal response, and in this sense it is

---

[1] "*In seinem Wort offenbart Gott nicht nur, was Gnade ist, Gott erweist uns auch in seinem Wort Gnade.*" Volk, in Fries, *Handbuch Theologischer Grundbegriffe,* vol. 2, p. 868.

active or activating. It may be a tacit request or command, as in the case of a judge or a professor. There is a form of question which does not require that one respond to the questioner: this is what is called a "rhetorical question," and it can possess great power. A question of this kind can pursue a man, echoing in his soul for years in order to confront him and demand a radical decision.

The grammatical form of *statement* can also be the bearer of a particular force. There is the sentence which is not only so grammatically, but also juridically, and there are declarations which have extensive juridical effect. There are also statements of principle or policy endowed with all the force of that which they represent; and there are personal declarations which possess the power of example. A man's last will and testament is made in the form of a statement. A declaration can be mutual and can commit both parties for life ("I love you"), and mutual declarations can bind whole societies within their own structure or in relation to one another.

There are other forms of speech which can be reduced roughly to one or more of the above: counsel, exhortation, suggestion, insinuation, recommendation, intercession. Every language has many words to express this dynamic function of language.

Magic formulas pertain to another sphere altogether: These are considered powerful not for what they say, but by the fact that they are said.

Finally, there are blessings and curses, considered by many people to have an efficacy; which indeed they do, within certain religious contexts.

The Scriptures contain nearly all these forms of speech, and, obviously, they lose none of their force by being the word of God. They are, rather, brought to their maximum of intensity, and since they pertain to the plan of salvation, their energy and their action are saving.

The soul by its nature can be corrupted and saved by words. A word can drive it to anger, and again, a word can make it meek; a sordid remark can incite it to lust, and honest words can instill moderation. If, then, a mere word has such force, tell me why do you disregard the Scriptures? If an exhortation can accomplish so much, what will be the effect when the exhortations are from the Spirit? More powerful than fire to melt the heart is the good word which resounds from the divine Scriptures and prepares a man for any good work.[2]

Before studying specific dynamic forms of biblical language, we are going to listen to what the Bible has to say of itself as word, and see how the Bible represents the word in action. We are going to offer a very generous selection of texts in this section, since the doctrine of the power of the biblical word is extremely important and has been somewhat neglected lately.

THE OLD TESTAMENT

The *creative* word. The first chapter of Genesis, that glorious portico of the Bible, is really a liturgy of creation. God calls things to assemble in existence: God's initiative is a word which makes things exist, and creatures respond by their existing. God imposes names on His creatures and by this act establishes order and variety; creatures respond by taking their place within the cosmos. God's word is charged with power, it bears His will, "Let there be light, and there was light. . . . God called the light Day." Neither formless nothingness (*tohu-wa-bohu*) nor the darkness can resist the word of God. But the word of God does not confer existence as some mute and static presence; it creates activity and bestows an irrepressible dynamism:

Be fruitful, multiply, and fill the waters of the seas.

Let the earth bring forth living things; tame beasts, creeping things, creatures of the field, each according to its kind.

Be fruitful, multiply, fill the earth and master it. . . .

Covenant. God "called His son" from Egypt. The existence of the people of God is due to this "vocation," this active word of God. The mob of disparate clans and peoples who left Egypt are

---

2 Ἀπὸ γὰρ λόγων καὶ φθείρεσθαι καὶ σώζεσθαι πέφυκε. καὶ γὰρ εἰς ὀργήν τοῦτο αὐτὴν ἐξάγει, καὶ πραΰνει τὸ αὐτὸ πάλιν. καὶ πρὸς ἐπιθυμίαν ἐξῆψε ῥῆμα αἰσχρόν, καὶ εἰς σωφροσύνην ἤγαγε λόγος σεμνότητος γέμων. Εἰ δὲ λόγος ἁπλῶς τοσαύτην ἔχει τὴν ἰσχὺν, πῶς τῶν Γραφῶν καταφρονεῖς; εἰπέ μοι. Εἰ γὰρ παραίνεσις τοσαῦτα δύναται, πολλῷ μᾶλλον ὅταν μετὰ πνεύματος ὦσιν αἱ παραινέσεις; καὶ γὰρ πυρὸς μᾶλλον τὴν πεπωρωμένην μαλάττει ψυχὺν, καὶ πρὸς ἅπαντα ἐπιτηδείαν κατασκευάζει τά καλά, λόγος ἀπὸ τῶν θείων ἐνηχούμενος Γραφῶν. St. John Chrys., "Homily 2, 10 on Mt," PG 57, 31.

united in their hearing of God's call, and they become a people—God's people—by continual response to the call which saved them: This is what we mean by covenant. In this case, the response to God's initiative is not the simple fact of existence and activity. Here the people must consciously accept and freely ratify the call, expressing their response by active obedience.

Commandments. The word of God which was expressed in the jussive form at creation takes the form of a categorical future in the Decalogue: "You shall not have strange gods," "you shall not kill." Language in the form of an imperative assumes the qualities of a will-act; it is possessed of a certain power which addresses itself to another person precisely as a person. That is, an imperative conveys will to another precisely in his capacity to accept or reject what is conveyed. A command is not magic; the force that it bears is a human force, it is personal and dynamic, but it is not irresistible. When a command is expressed in the future rather than as a simple imperative, it seems to acquire a new capacity and power while retaining its characteristic of being expressly directed to a second person: "Do not kill—you shall not kill . . . do not steal—you shall not steal." When a command is accepted, it achieves fulfillment and becomes capable of forming a society, sustaining a covenant by which men are joined to one another and to God. To hear this word is to obey. A man may close himself off, freely and culpably, so that "hearing he does not hear." In the final age of a new covenant, God will increase the force of His command by engraving his law on the hearts of the people, thus making it an immanent source of man's response while respecting his responsibility.

Within the vocation of the people, and deriving from it, we find the vocation of the individual: the prophets, the servant, the apostles, and this call may also include the imposition of a new name (Abram—Abraham; Simon—Peter).

The context of the covenant includes other aspects of word as dynamic: There is, for instance, the fact of *blessings* and *curses.* The law contains and expresses a whole series of benedictions and maledictions charged with a power which man unleashes not by magic but by obedience or disobedience. The prophet Zechariah has described the power of this word in "surrealist" poetry which catches the terrible and destructive force of this word set loose on the land by the people's infidelity:

Then I raised my eyes again and saw a scroll flying.
"What do you see?" he asked me.
I answered,
"I see a scroll flying; it is twenty cubits long and ten cubits wide."
Then he said to me:
"This is the curse which is to go forth over the whole earth;
in accordance with it shall every perjurer be expelled from here.
I will send it forth, says the Lord of hosts,
and it shall come into the house of the thief,
or into the house of him who perjures himself with my name;
it shall lodge within his house
consuming it, timber and stones." [3]

The Prophetic Word. Sometimes when the prophet pronounces a divine oracle, he acts as a preacher moving the wills of his audience; at other times he predicts the future. Often, this prediction of the future is a force in the present which brings it about, not by way of magic but in virtue of the dynamic power of the word of God. The oracle enters human history as an active element, not merely as a simple statement of what will happen in the future. The fact that many oracles make themselves dependent on the interplay of human wills does not derogate from their authority or reduce the respect due to an inspired prediction. These so-called "conditional prophecies," by the very fact of their being pronounced, enter into and confront human decisions, the future is different because of them, and they have fulfilled their role. The "fulfillment" of what they predict is to be judged by their power, since they are the message of a prophet, not the estimate of a news commentator.

The *declaration* of God is always valid, not because it discovers what already exists, but because it creates the situation in which it is verified; in this, God's declaration resembles a juridical decision. When David repented of his crimes of adultery and murder, he heard the oracle. "Yahweh has forgiven your sin." At other times, the same type of oracle is condemnatory: "For the three crimes of Damascus and for the fourth, I will not hold it back" (Amos 1:3).

The *name* of God (Yahweh) is also dynamic: It is the guarantee of the authority of a command: [4]

[3] Za 5:1–4.
[4] Cf. R. Criado, *El valor dinamico del nombre divino en el Antiguo Testamento*, Granada, 1950.

Keep, then, my statutes and decrees, for the man who carries them out will find life through them, I am Yahweh (Lv 18:5).

You shall not swear falsely by my name, thus profaning the name of your God. I am Yahweh (Lv 19:12).

You shall love your neighbor as yourself. I am Yahweh (Lev 19:18).

The name of Yahweh is a blessing:

You shall set my name upon the sons of Israel, and I will bless them (Nm 6:27).

And the imposition upon a child of a name which includes the name of Yahweh is the means of assuring for this new life God's constant protection.

Not only the juridical decision, but the whole process of litigation (*rîb*), when it is directed by God, is composed of living words: questions, proofs, objections, denunciation, threat, testimony. The word of God pursues man aggressively until it evokes a confession:

> Hear, my people, and I will speak;
> Israel, I will testify against you; . . .
> But to the wicked man God says:
> "Why do you recite my statutes,
> and profess my covenant with your mouth,
> Though you hate discipline
> and cast my words behind you?
> When you see a thief, you keep pace with him,
> and with adulterers you throw in your lot. . . .
> When you do these things, shall I be deaf to it?
> Or think you that I am like yourself?
> I will correct you by drawing them up before your eyes." [5]

At the other extreme, there is the word of the people at *prayer*. This word, possessing a power given it by God, is able to remain immanent while still having an effect in the realm of the divine, reaching to God Himself. A remarkable instance of this power is found in the intercession of Moses which finally prevails against God: "And Yahweh refrained from the evil which he had threatened to do against his people" (Ex 32:14).

[5] Ps 50.

Finally, there is the case where God swears by His own life, thus endowing His word with the very intensity of the divine existence.

In a remarkable work, known as the "Book of Consolation" and which now comprises chapters 40–55 of Isaiah, we find a meditative synthesis of all these aspects of the word of God.

There is the word of *vocation* or calling which governs events:

Who has performed these deeds? He who has called forth the generations since the beginning (41:4).

We find the process of naming by which possession is assured:

But now, thus says the Lord,
who created you, O Jacob, and formed you, O Israel:
Fear not, for I have redeemed you;
I have called you by name: you are mine (43:1).

The prophetic word announcing and effecting the future:

It is I who confirm the words of my servants,
I carry out the plan announced by my messengers;
I say to Jerusalem: Be rebuilt;
I will raise up their ruins.
It is I who said to the deep: Be dry;
I will dry up your well springs.

I say of Cyrus: My shepherd,
who fulfills my every wish (44:26–27).

The word once uttered is unchangeable:

By myself I swear,
uttering my just decree
and my unalterable word (45:23).

The word is heard by the heavens and by kings:

Yes, my hand laid the foundations of the earth;
my right hand spread out the heavens.
When I call them they stand forth at once. . . .
I myself have spoken, I have called him,
I have brought him and his way succeeds! (48:13, 15).

The word which calls confers power on the word of the prophet:

The Lord called me from birth,
from my mother's womb he gave me my name.
He has made my mouth a sharp-edged sword (49:1–2).

These texts, selected from among the more significant, are marked off by a literary device known as "inclusion"; that is, the theme with which the work begins is taken up and echoed, sometimes with the aid of the same words, at the conclusion of the work. The words contained in this Book of Consolation, which is itself a series of poems loosely joined, are active and true because they are the word of God:

> The grass withers, the flower wilts,
> when the breath of the Lord blows upon it.
> Though the grass withers and the flower wilts,
> the word of our God stands forever (40:7–8).

> For just as from the heavens
> the rain and snow come down
> and do not return there
> till they have watered the earth,
> making it fertile and fruitful,
> giving seed to him who sows
> and bread to him who eats,
> so shall my word be
> that goes forth from my mouth;
> it shall not return to me void,
> but shall do my will,
> achieving the end for which I sent it (55:10–11).

This is how the Old Testament looked on the word of God: Not only as a means of knowing, but as a force which is acting. Its sphere of activity is creation in history, especially the redemptive creation of salvation history. We tend to look on such a view as being a bit primitive, ingenuous, allegorical, or imaginative. But we should be careful. The fault lies with us and with our narrow concept and impoverished experience of word in a culture which regards it as nothing more than a conventional and ephemeral "sign." We recognize in theory the power of ideas; actually, in practice we are subject to the power of words more than we realize; to words, not as empty sounds, but as significant realities. Sincere reflection on this fact leads us to a recognition of the "energic" power of human language, and by means of this insight we are prepared to study the saving power with which God endows His word.

THE GOSPELS

The Gospels present Christ to us as speaking and acting, going through the land of Palestine preaching the Kingdom of God and working miracles. Without realizing it, or formulating it explicitly, we tend to make a division in the activity of Christ: By His words He taught us and by His deeds He saved us. [6]

But let us consider an outstanding example in the life of Christ: The raising of Lazarus as told in the Gospel of St. John. We find there the statement: "I am the resurrection and the Life"; not merely "I bring" or "I announce," but "I am." Christ reveals life and gives life because He Himself is the Life, and from Him there radiates the power of life even to the dead, because of His own resurrection from the dead. As the narrative proceeds, we catch a glimpse of the heart of Christ: "When Jesus saw them weeping, He sighed heavily and was deeply moved." In this sincere and heartfelt participation in their sorrow, Jesus manifests and ratifies His deep solidarity with humankind. In His sympathy He established a union with those who are weeping, and with His friend who has been overcome by death. The sisters, in good faith, and some of the Jews, murmuring, seemed to suppose that if Christ had been present, this death would not have taken place: "If you had only been here my brother would not have died . . ." "Could not this man, who opened the blind man's eyes, have done something to keep Lazarus from dying?" No one specifies exactly what they think Christ could have done: The sisters mention only His presence, the Jews recall a past action. Then there is another series of words uttered by Jesus in which He thanks His Father for having heard Him; He does this in a loud voice so that those present will believe in His mission. Finally, He calls out: "Lazarus come forth," and Lazarus comes forth.

What took place in this miracle? We can view it from many aspects: the personal power of Christ, His compassion, His prayer, His word. No doubt, all of these facets of the event were truly part of it: The power of Christ derives from His mission, it is actualized

[6] Cf. K. Wennemer, "Theologie des Wortes im Johannesevangelium. Das innere Verhältnis des verkündigten logos theou zum persönlichen Logos," *Schol* 38, 1963, pp. 1–17. Also O. Cullmann, *The Christology of the New Testament*, Philadelphia, 1959, ch. 9, "Jesus the Word."

in His prayer, expressed in His compassion, and realized its effect through His word. The great danger here is that we will divorce these aspects from the miracle itself, making them the mere trappings or occasion for the exercise of divine omnipotence, as though God acted immediately here, and everything else that happened had no real influence on the event, but was only occasioned by and for the people who were present.

Such a view is really not Christian. Pushed to its ultimate conclusion, it gives rise to the opinion that the omnipotence of God has saved us and that the Incarnation was not really necessary. In a mitigated form, we find such thinking behind the idea that Christ has died and God gives us life, but there is no intrinsic connection between these realities; on the occasion of a word of Christ, God worked a miracle, the word itself effected nothing. Anyone who really believes in the Incarnation cannot accept a view that makes of it and of all the activity of Christ the mere occasion for divine action which is independent of it.

We are not trying here to imagine what God could do, but what He has done. God's love does not seek us while remaining distant; Christ has wept with us. The blind man was not cured by some remote activity on the part of the divine omnipotence; he was cured by a little mud smeared on his eyes by Jesus and by the command to go and wash. We are not saved by some abstract thing we name "the will of God," but by the passion and resurrection of Christ. The Word of Life is not a beautiful Platonic theory, but something we have seen and heard and felt with our hands.

Once this principle is established, it is clear that we cannot restrict the saving power of Christ to actions alone, excluding His words. Just as all the actions of Christ are words because they speak of the Father, so too all the words of Christ are actions and are endowed with power. In the case of Lazarus, the power of Life was in the words, "Lazarus, come forth!"; the words wrought the miracle and at the same time manifested its meaning. It was a power of salvation because, through the word of Christ, His resurrection was present by anticipation. This power of Christ's words is not restricted to miracles, but is found in all His words. It will suffice here to mention instances already known.

Christ's *teaching* was characterized by authority and power: "When Jesus finished this discourse, the people were astounded at

His teaching; unlike their own teachers, He taught with a note of authority" (Mt 7:28; cf. Mk 1:27 and Lk 4:32). The people were struck, not only by the depth and beauty of this new teaching, but even more by the power it held, and which they had experienced. We might give a free translation of the Greek word *"exousia"* by saying that Christ's teaching was "convincing."

Christ's *call* was efficacious: It was a vocation. He repeated this call, and vocation became convocation. He chose twelve of His disciples, and, according to St. Luke (6:13), "named" them apostles; Simon, their leader, He named Peter.

The *command* of Christ held sway over wind and water, over fever and demons; when He willed it, His words were irresistible. The miracles that He worked without words are very few in number; such as the power that "went out from Him" to cure the woman who touched the hem of His robe. A leper made a simple appeal to His will: "If You will it, you can make me clean"; Christ gave expression to His will in an imperative: "I will it, be clean," and "immediately the leprosy left him."

Christ *promulgated* His law with His own authority: "You have learned that they were told . . . But what I tell you is this . . ." And this law can even become beatitude.

Christ's word expresses and effects *forgiveness*: "The Son of Man has the power to forgive sins." And this power is realized in a declaration which saves: "Your sins are forgiven. Go in peace."

Christ pronounced His *prophetic* word over bread and wine and the imminent sacrifice becomes present; bread and wine become body and blood establishing a covenant which is at the same time a testament. By our repeating these words of Christ, His memory and His sacrifice are once again made present.

Christ *prays* to His Father, and the Father hears Him.

The words of Christ are not merely the medium of knowledge; they are themselves spirit and life.

This power of Christ's word is rooted in His person and His mission, and cannot be conceived as something apart from the work of redemption. His words acquire a new force after the resurrection, since they somehow endured along with Him a kind of death, accepting fully the human dimension of limitation and destruction. The words of Christ, even during His life, were powerful, but since the resurrection they have shared in the glory of His risen state, free of the limitations and corruptions of this life and endowed with the fullness of power by the Spirit: "The Word of God is not bound." This is the word which reaches us as Christians. Though it sounds paradoxical, it is still true that as we read the Gospels we perceive the word of Christ more perfectly than did the Apostles who heard them during the earthly life of Jesus. Just as the Eucharist is the body of the Lord, the Kyrios, the Glorified, the Christ, so too the Gospel is the message of Christ in glory. Jesus has traversed the valley of death and emerged to abide now forever glorious and free; His words, too, "will not pass away." Not only are Christ's words more intelligible now that He is risen, they are also more powerful, more capable of imparting life.

In the light of these principles, and in view of the fact that all the power of the inspired word is rooted in Christ, we are going now to consider the rest of the New Testament writings in which the word bears witness to itself.

The New Testament Writings

The New Testament refers to the word of God as Scripture, first applying this to the Old Testament and then by implication to the New Testament.

The Epistle to the Hebrews contains a fundamental passage in regard to the inspired word which, interestingly enough, stresses the effectiveness of this word:

The word of God is alive and active. It cuts more keenly than any two-edged sword, piercing as far as the place where life and spirit, joints and marrow divide. It sifts the purposes and thoughts of the heart (4:12).

In the original Greek of this passage, the word "alive" or "living" is in the emphatic position as the first word of the sentence: We could translate the first line somewhat rhetorically as: "Living is the word of God and active." It is living, as God is the living God, and its activity is the actualization of the power of God: it penetrates into the most intimate depths of a being, reaching that mysterious point of our vital and psychic principle which is touched and permeated by the Spirit. From within, it can judge and condemn because it forces man to take up a position, to make a decision. Faced with this word, it is useless to try to dissimulate or compromise.

Let us look again at the four descriptive words used in this passage to characterize the word of God: alive, active, cutting, piercing. Whoever, in the name of inerrancy, refuses to accept all these terms as valid is accusing the Bible of error. Whoever, in the name of inerrancy, forgets these adjectives is insulating himself from the piercing power of God's word. Let us hope that the living word will not let itself be overcome.

One of the two texts which we have already called "classical" in the tract on inspiration is, when cited in its entire context, a testimony also to the power of the inspired word. The general context is that of a pastoral letter: a series of counsels and doctrines given to a man charged with the care of souls. The "man of God" referred to in the text applies to this type of office, and for such a person the Scriptures are an instrument by which he carries out his task. However, though the text is concentrating on the pastoral duties of a bishop, the realities that it describes are applicable to the life of every Christian.

But for your part, stand by the truths you have learned and are assured of. Remember from whom you have learned them; remember that from early childhood you have been familiar with the sacred writings which have power to make you wise and lead you to salvation through faith in Christ Jesus. Every inspired scripture has its use for teaching the truth and refuting error, or for reformation of manners and discipline in right living, so that the man who belongs to God may be efficient and equipped for good work of every kind (2 Tim 3:14–17).

In the work of salvation which comes about through faith in Christ, that is, by accepting Him and committing oneself to Him, sacred Scripture has a very special role to play: It has the power to make a man wise with a wisdom that is not a theoretical mastery of a science or practical competence in a craft, but rather personal knowledge of God. Timothy has known the Scriptures familiarly since childhood; there is no need to convince him of their power: The sacred writings possess a "spirit" which makes them uniquely apt and efficacious in the apostolic ministry.

There is in St. Paul's description a certain sense of integrity and fullness conveyed by the descriptive words he has chosen and by the broadening rhythm in the last phrase. He mentions the inspiration of the Scriptures because he wants to stress their power. Obviously, they would not possess such a power if they were false or mistaken. Immediately before the passage we quoted, St. Paul had said: "Wicked men and charlatans will make progress from bad to worse, deceiving and deceived." Thus, the first consequence, the very reason for inspiration at all, is that the word of God may act effectively in the Christian life and in apostolic activity.

St. Thomas, commenting on this passage, has this to say about the power of the word:

Thus, the effects of Scripture are fourfold: in the speculative order, to teach the truth and to refute error; in the practical order, to take from evil and to incite to good. Its ultimate effect is to bring men to perfection.[7]

There is another very interesting passage in this same letter. St. Paul is speaking of his "Gospel," of the message he proclaims whose substance is Christ, risen and glorified. But this message is not something in the order of a mere fact that can allow itself to be silenced or suppressed, or even opposed by contrary propaganda. What St. Paul preaches is the message concerning the risen Lord, and as such it cannot be imprisoned:

Remember Jesus Christ, risen from the dead, born of David's line. This is the theme of my gospel, in whose service I am exposed to hardship, even to the point of being shut up (2 Tim 2:8-9).

The earliest letter of St. Paul which we possess is his First Epistle to the Thessalonians. St. Paul had preached at Thessalonica and his word had been the word of God; God had spoken through him. The Thessalonians had accepted this preaching, knowing that it was the word of God. They did not receive it as some merely human word, but, aided by the Spirit, they accepted it in all its reality. This word which the believers received was not a simple statement of fact or theory, but an active and living power:

[7] "Sic ergo quadruplex est effectus sacrae scripturae, scilicet docere veritatem, arguere falsitatem, quantum ad speculativam: eripere a malo, et inducere ad bonum, quantum ad practicam. Ultimus effectus eius est, ut perducat homines ad perfectum." "Comm. on 2 Tim 3:16, 17" (in Marietti ed., nos. 127–128).

This is why we thank God continually, because when we handed on God's message, you received it, not as the word of men, but as what it truly is, the very word of God at work in you who hold the faith (1 Th 2:13).

The Epistle to the Romans contains two passages which are very instructive in regard to this theme of the power of God's word. The first is found at the beginning of the letter and provides an outline of all that is to follow:

I am not ashamed of the Gospel. It is the saving power of God for everyone who has faith. . . . (1:16).

The Gospel here is the preaching of St. Paul, the message which he brings of the mystery of Christ: This Gospel is not merely concerned with the saving power of God, it is that power in action. And, as is the case with the whole of salvation, the sphere of this power is faith. There is nothing mechanical or magical about this: Man can freely refuse it. But he who receives this Gospel, receives salvation.

The other passage is found at the end of the letter, and is a synthesis of the Christian life. The mystery of Christ has its center in His death and resurrection. Christ suffered and died, and the Father raised Him up and glorified Him. We must die and rise with Christ, sharing the sufferings of His life, and His glory. We share His death when we suffer as Christians, we share His resurrection when we are strengthened and consoled. The marvelous thing about this mystery is that it is precisely in suffering that we come to know this consolation and encouragement. It is through fellowship in His sufferings that we experience the power of His resurrection, and this experience strengthens our hope of final glory, which will itself be a full participation in the glory of the risen Jesus. To suffer with endurance is a grace; to experience Christ's consolation is part of the same grace, and this encouragement is given to us by the Scriptures:

All that was written of old, was written for our instruction; so that by the endurance and encouragement of the Scriptures, we might have hope (Rom 15:4).

The word translated as "encouragement" is, in Greek, "*paraklesis*," which contains an inevitable allusion to the Paraclete, the

Spirit who consoles, instructs, and encourages, the Spirit sent by the glorified Christ, the Spirit Who inspired the Scriptures.

There is a similar thought in the first book of Maccabees:

. . . So, though we have no need of these, since we find our encouragement in the sacred books that are in our keeping . . . (1 Mac 12:9).

In the First Epistle of St. Peter, we find an exhortation to fraternal charity: This mutual love must be based on the fact that we share a common birth. We are related spiritually, and should maintain and express the family ties that bind us together. This spiritual birth was not brought about by corrruptible seed, but by a seed that is incorruptible, the word of God, living and abiding. God lives and imparts His life to others; His life is eternal, and thus He can impart eternal life. He does this through the medium of His Word, Who likewise is eternal. The word of God referred to in the passage below is the Old Testament, which, since it is from God, must abide; it does not pass away, but is consummated and realized in the word of the Gospel.

Having purified your souls by obedience to the truth so that you love your brothers sincerely, love one another deeply and purely. You have been reborn, not from a corruptible seed, but from one that is incorruptible; by the living and enduring word of God. For

> "All flesh is grass
> and all its glory like the flowers of grass.
> The grass withers,
> the flower fails.
> But the word of the Lord endures forever."

And this word is the Gospel announced to you (1 Pt 1:22-25).

The progress of this word of God is told in the Acts of the Apostles, which traces the growth and consolidation of the Church. We should note this ecclesial function of the word: When the Church was being formed, it entered into her very structure, and now it remains there vital and active.

The word of God now spread more and more widely; the number of disciples in Jerusalem went on increasing rapidly . . . (6:7).

Meanwhile, the word of God continued to grow and spread (12:24).

365

In such ways the word of the Lord showed its power, spreading more and more widely and effectively (19:20).

Not only the man who believes, but even inanimate creation can be sanctified by the word of God. It was created by the word of God and is good and beautiful; eating and drinking, matrimony, and all the goods of the earth should be received with gratitude:

For everything that God created is good, and nothing is to be rejected when it is taken with thanksgiving, since it is hallowed by God's own word and prayer (1 Tm 4:4).

God takes the initiative in the work of salvation; just as at creation His powerful word called all things into existence, so now His word calls to the true life the chosen part of His creation, the Christians. Our response must be the humble acceptance of the word which God sows within us, in order that it may produce our salvation.

On his own initiative He has brought us to birth by the word of truth, so that we might be a sort of first fruits of His creatures. . . . Away, then, with all that is sordid and the malice that hurries to excess, and quietly accept the message [Logos] planted in your hearts, which can bring you salvation (Jas 1:18, 21).

By way of conclusion to this section, let us hear the moving words of St. Paul's farewell address to the elders of Ephesus. They could well form the basis for a meditation on this mysterious aspect of the word of God:

You know how, from the day that I first set foot in the province of Asia, for the whole time that I was with you, I served the Lord in all humility amid the sorrows and trials that came upon me through the machinations of the Jews. . . . And now, as you see, I am on my way to Jerusalem, under the constraint of the Spirit. Of what will befall me there I know nothing, except that in city after city the Holy Spirit assures me that imprisonment and hardships await me. For myself, I set no store by my life; I only want to finish the race, and complete the task which the Lord Jesus assigned to me, of bearing my testimony to the gospel of God's grace. . . . I know that none of you will see my face again. . . . And now I commend you to God and to his gracious word, which has power to build you up and give you your heritage among all who are dedicated to him. . . . (Acts 20:17–32).

All of St. Paul's apostolic activity had for its purpose the building up of the Church of Christ in order to impart a share in the inheritance of heaven by his proclamation of the good news. This activity was coming to an end in one area of the Church, and the Apostle could not leave until he had provided for the continuance of his work. He commends the Church at Ephesus to its pastors, and he commends the pastors to God and to the word of God: This word will continue to build up the Church, and confer on it the heritage of the Kingdom of God.

We never knew St. Paul personally, we did not follow him in sadness as he boarded the ship; yet he has left us his word, and we have received it for what it really is—the word of God. This word continues to build up within us, and through us, the Church of God.

THE FATHERS

The Fathers of the Church well understood this farewell message of St. Paul: They continued to build up the Church with the word and to profess their faith in its saving power.[8]

Therefore, brothers and sisters, following the God of truth, I am reading you an exhortation to pay attention to that which is written, that you may both save yourselves and him who is the reader among you.[9]

The holy Scriptures, and wise rules for conduct, are the high roads of salvation.[10]

Truly, these letters are holy and divinizing.[11]

We say that the sources of salvation are the holy prophets, evangelists, and apostles; for these, with the assistance of the Holy Spirit,

[8] Cf. the work of Gögler which we have cited frequently (e.g., ch. 13, n. 2), esp. the section, "Die Macht des Wortes," pp. 270–274.

[9] "Ὥστε, ἀδελφοὶ καὶ ἀδελφαί, μετὰ τὸν Θεὸν τῆς ἀληθείας ἀναγινώσκω ὑμῖν ἔντευξιν εἰς τὸ προσέχειν τοῖς γεγραμμένοις, ἵνα καὶ ἑαυτοὺς σώσητε καὶ τὸν ἀναγινώσκοντα ἐν ὑμῖν. 2 Clem 19:1. Greek and English both taken from Loeb Classical Library, The Apostolic Fathers, vol. 1.

[10] Γραφαὶ δὲ αἱ θεῖαι, καὶ πολιτεῖαι σώφρονες, σύντομοι σωτηρίας ὁδοί. St. Clement of Alex., "Exhortation to the Greeks, 8," PG 8, 188.

[11] Ibid., ch. 9 (cf. ch. 10, n. 3).

have communicated to the world the sublime and heavenly saving word.[12]

From the field we derive the comfort of wheat, from the vine the fruit which sustains us, from the Scriptures the doctrine which gives life.[13]

Drink of Christ that you may drink His words. His word is the Old Testament, His word is the New Testament. The divine Scriptures are taken as drink and consumed as food when the sweetness of the Eternal Word sinks into the very marrow and powers of the soul.[14]

The ancients used the Scriptures to drive out demons, to bless infants, and to cure the sick; and these practices are not totally unknown in the Church of our own day.

THE MAGISTERIUM

And it is this peculiar and singular power of Holy Scripture, arising from the inspiration of the Holy Spirit, which gives authority to the sacred orator, fills him with apostolic liberty of speech, and communicates force and power to his eloquence. For those who infuse into their efforts the spirit and strength of the Word of God speak "not in word only, but in power also, and in the Holy Spirit, and in much fullness" (1 Th 1:15).[15]

Nor does "the word of God, living and effectual and more piercing than any two-edged sword and reaching unto the division of the soul and the spirit, of the joints also and the marrow, and a discerner of the thoughts and intents of the heart" (Heb 4:12), need artificial devices and human adaptation to move and impress souls; for the Sa-

---

[12] Σωτηρίου δὲ πηγὰς εἶναί φαμεν τοὺς ἁγίους προφήτας, εὐαγγελιστάς τε καὶ ἀποστόλους, οἳ τὸν ἄνωθεν καὶ ἐξ οὐρανοῦ καὶ σωτήριον τῷ κόσμῳ βρύουσι λόγον, χορηγοῦντος αὐτοῖς τοῦ ἁγίου Πνεύματος ἅπασάν τε οὕτω κατευφραίνουσι τὴν ὑπ' οὐρανόν St. Cyril of Alex, "On the Orthodox Faith, 2, 1," PG 76, 1337.

[13] St. Ephrem, *Opera*, Rome, 1743, p. 41.

[14] St. Ambrose (cf. ch. 2, n. 2).

[15] "Atque haec propria et singularis Scripturarum virtus, a divino afflatu Spiritus Sancti profecta, ea est, quae oratori sacro auctoritatem addit, apostolicam praebet dicendi libertatem, nervosam victricemque tribuit eloquentiam. Quisquis enim divini verbi spiritum et robur eloquendo refert, ille, non loquitur in sermone tantum, sed et in virtute et in Spiritu Sancto et in plenitudine multa." *Providentissimus Deus*, EB 87; RSS, pp. 4–5.

cred Pages, written under the inspiration of the Spirit of God, are of themselves rich in original meaning; endowed with a divine power, they have their own value; adorned with heavenly beauty, they radiate of themselves light and splendor, provided they are so fully and accurately explained by the interpreter, that all the treasures of wisdom and prudence therein contained are brought to light.[16]

The *Constitution on the Sacred Liturgy* teaches that Christ is actively present in His word when it is read in the Church. The paragraph which contains this statement places the word in the series: sacrifice—Eucharist—sacraments—word—prayer. The *Constitution* then goes on to say of this series it has just enumerated that it is part of "that great work wherein God is perfectly glorified and men are sanctified." This sanctification is brought about by "signs that are perceptible to the senses, and is effected in a way which corresponds with each of these signs." The word is one of these signs; let us read the whole paragraph attentively.

To accomplish so great a work, Christ is always present in his Church, especially in her liturgical celebrations. He is present in the sacrifice of the Mass, not only in the person of his minister, "the same now offering, through the ministry of priests, who formerly offered himself on the cross," but especially under the eucharistic species. By his power, he is present in the sacraments, so that when a man baptizes it is really Christ himself who baptizes. He is present in his word, since it is he himself who speaks when the holy scriptures are read in the Church. He is present, lastly, when the Church prays and sings, for he promised: "Where two or three are gathered together in My name, there am I in the midst of them" (Mt 18:20).

Christ indeed always associates the Church with himself in this great work wherein God is perfectly glorified and men are sanctified. The Church is his beloved Bride who calls to her Lord, and through him offers worship to the Eternal Father.

Rightly, then, the liturgy is considered as an exercise of the priestly

---

[16] "Nec 'vivus sermo Dei et efficax et penetrabilior omni gladio ancipiti et pertingens usque ad divisionem animae ac spiritus, compagum quoque ac medullarum, et discretor cogitationum et intentionum cordis' (Heb 4:12), calamistris indiget, vel humana accommodatione, ut animos moveat ac percellat; ipsae enim Sacrae Paginae, Dei afflante Spiritu exaratae, per se nativo abundant sensu; divina virtute ditatae, per se valent; superno decore ornatae, per se lucent ac splendent, dummodo ab interprete tam integre et accurate explicentur, ut omnes thesauri sapientiae et prudentiae, quae in eis latent, in lucem proferantur." Divino afflante Spiritu, EB 553; RSS, p. 94.

office of Jesus Christ. In the liturgy, the sanctification of man is signified by signs perceptible to the senses, and is effected in a way which corresponds with each of these signs; in the liturgy, the whole public worship is performed by the mystical body of Jesus Christ, that is, by the head and his members.

From this it follows that every liturgical celebration, because it is an action of Christ the priest and of his body which is the Church, is a sacred action surpassing all others; no other action of the Church can equal its efficacy by the same title and to the same degree.[17]

By the ministry of the word they [the bishops] communicate God's power to those who believe unto salvation (cf. Rom 1:16), and through the sacraments, the regular and fruitful distribution of which they regulate by their authority, they sanctify the faithful.[18]

This series of texts is sufficient to indicate that we are dealing here with a traditional doctrine. It now remains for us to determine how we should understand the repeated testimonies of tradition in regard to the saving power of the word.

The word of God exercises its saving power as a word. It does not act by magic, as though it were some ancient execration text, or by some mysterious power of repetition as is attributed to certain magical formulas. A human word is endowed with a power which

---

[17] "Ad tantum vero opus perficiendum, Christus Ecclesiae suae semper adest, praesertim in actionibus liturgicis. Praesens adest in Missae Sacrificio cum in ministri persona, 'idem nunc offerens sacerdotum ministerio, qui seipsum tunc in cruce obtulit,' tum maxime sub speciebus eucharisticis. Praesens adest virtute sua in Sacramentis, ita ut cum aliquis baptizat, Christus ipse baptizet. Praesens adest in verbo suo, siquidem ipse loquitur dum sacrae Scripturae in Ecclesia leguntur. Praesens adest denique dum supplicat et psallit Ecclesia, ipse qui promisit: 'Ubi sunt duo vel tres congregati in nomine meo, ibi sum in medio eorum' (Mt 18:20).

"Reapse tanto in opere, quo Deus perfecte glorificatur, et homines sanctificantur, Christus Ecclesiam, sponsam suam dilectissimam, sibi semper consociat, quae Dominum suum invocat er per ipsum Aeterno Patri cultum tribuit.

"Merito igitur Liturgia habetur veluti Jesu Christi sacerdotalis muneris exercitatio, in qua per signa sensibilia significatur et modo singulis proprio efficitur sanctificatio hominis, et a mystico Jesu Christi Corpore, Capite nempe ejusque membris, integer cultus publicus exercetur.

"Proinde omnis liturgica celebratio, utpote opus Christi sacerdotis, ejusque Corporis, quod est Ecclesia, est actio sacra praecellenter, cujus efficacitatem eodem titulo eodemque gradu nulla alia actio Ecclesiae adaequat." Const., no. 7.

[18] Constitution of Vatican II, De Ecclesia, from the "unofficial Latin translation" The New York Times, November 23rd, 1964, p. 20.

it exercises precisely as a word, that is, when it is understood and accepted; even sometimes when it is knowingly rejected, it has a power by way of reaction. The divine word possesses a saving power which is operative when it is understood and accepted in faith; if it is rejected, then it still has power: that of passing judgment.

One indication that the word of God is the actual salvific activity of God can be seen in the fact that God's word leads to judgment. Judgment here has the biblical meaning of a decisive situation. The word of God is both judgment and grace, since it both reveals our state of sinfulness and offers us salvation in Christ. It produces a crisis since man must now decide whether or not to acknowledge his state of sin and accept Christ as his salvation (cf. Jn 12:31; Heb 4:12–13). This sort of decisive situation cannot be brought about by just any kind of truth, but only by an actual confrontation with God Himself which takes place in the word of God. And since the decision effected by the word of God must necessarily come to pass, this word itself is more than a mere statement about something; in the word of God there is present the grace of God, and, in a certain sense, God Himself.[19]

The modern custom of listening to the Epistle and Gospel being read out in a language which is unintelligible, may lead some to think that all this talk about the power of the word is a bit exaggerated, or it may foster the notion that the power has something to do with magic. But the situation in which we have found ourselves until recently is not the usual one. The word that I do not understand is not for me a word at all, but only sound, perhaps music; it does not have in me the proper effect of language. This is why the liturgical renewal being promoted by the conciliar con-

[19] "*Ein Kennzeichen dafür, dass das Wort Gottes aktuelles Heilshandeln Gottes ist, muss man darin sehen, dass das Wort in die Krisis, in das Gericht führt. Gericht hat hier die biblische Bedeutung einer gnadenhafte Entscheidungssituation. Das Wort Gottes ist Gericht und Gnade zugleich weil es zugleich unsere Sündigkeit aufdeckt und das Heil in Christus anbietet. Dadurch ensteht Krisis, weil der Mensch sich nun entscheiden muss, ob er seine Sündigkeit anergennt und Christus als sein Heil annimmt. (Jn 12:31; Heb 4:12–13). Diese Art von Entscheidungssituation kann für den Menschen nicht durch beliebige Wahrheiten herbeigeführt werden, sondern nur durch eine aktuelle Konfrontation mit Gott selbst, welche sich im Wort Gottes ereignet. Da Entscheidung durch das Wort Gottes notwendig wird, ist Wort Gottes mehr als ein Reden über etwas; in dem Wort Gottes wird Gottes Gnade und darin in gewisser Weise Gott selbst präsent.*" Volk, in Fries, Handbuch Theologische Grundbegriffe, vol. 2, p. 868.

stitution wishes to have the proclamation of the word of God in the vernacular so that it will be once again a true word in the Church.

We are dealing here with a supernatural power, one that must be received in faith. At the outset, the preaching of the Gospel may engender faith: "Faith is from hearing, and that hearing comes about by the word of Christ" (Rom 10:17); ". . . in Christ, by the Gospel, I fathered you" (1 Cor 4:15); this is the new creation called into being by the saving word. The Christian who already possesses the faith should listen to the word of God in an explicit attitude of faith. He should hear it as the word of God—for such it is—and then this word releases its energy in the hearts of those who believe. This attitude of faith, as something radical and total, as something derived from grace, gives rise to a new spiritual atmosphere in which the inspired word can resound to the fullness of its potentiality. Outside of such a context, the bible degenerates into an object of study, a source of distraction or delight, as though it were but a human word. The Scriptures cannot be read as though they were just another book, even a spiritual book. In the liturgical action, the atmosphere of faith and grace is created and then the word of God is proclaimed. In all rites, the proclamation of the word is preceded by a call to attention, meant to stir the people to an awareness in faith of what is going to take place; and at this point, the designation of Christians as "hearers" finds its fullest application.

The saving action of the Scriptures is not mediate, or parallel, or consequent in relation to the word. Some seem to think this way: Man hears the word of God, and this is a human act performed with a good intention, and at the same time God gives His grace. The grace comes immediately from God; the word is only the occasion of its being given. But such a theory is simply unacceptable: It denies that the word of God is an action of God; it refuses to accord to God the power of acting through His word. Such thinking, which we have met before when discussing the words of Christ, does not do justice to the many passages of Scripture in which the word bears witness to itself. The words of Jesus were not merely the occasion for an immediate and miraculous activity on the part of the Father; Christ really acted through His word. But the Scriptures are the word of Christ abiding in the Church.

Nor is it sufficient to say that the word of God operates mediately through the doctrine it conveys: The Scriptures provide me with instruction, and this instruction has an influence on my actions as a man and as a Christian. In the same way, for instance, I acquire a knowledge of doctrine from a treatise in theology, and this has its influence on my life. All this is true, but it is not enough. We cannot lower the word of God to the level of just one more theology manual. This point is crucial: It is not simply that the inspired word speaks about Christ; it is rather Christ Who speaks, and "with authority"; the text of the bible does not only speak about grace, it is itself an act of grace. The word of God is not only a font of truth, it is also a source of life. St. Thomas poses to himself this question:

. . . why is not every writing inspired, since according to Ambrose, "anything that is true, no matter by whom said, is from the Holy Spirit"? I answer that God works in two ways: He works immediately, and then the work is uniquely His own; and He also works through the mediation of inferior causes, such as the operations of nature. Thus, we read in Job (10:8): "Your hands, O Lord, have formed me," though this activity was accomplished by a natural operation. And so, with regard to man, God instructs the intellect, both immediately through the sacred writings, and mediately through other writings.[20]

(Notice that St. Thomas envisages the immediate activity of God as taking place through the sacred text, not parallel to it.)

Even less satisfactory is the view which holds that Scripture, or rather God, dispenses grace as a reward for having read the text: This would be to reduce reading the Bible to the level of any good work. Though the Spirit can give grace as He wills, His word is still objectively greater than any good work on the part of man, just as the Eucharist is objectively greater than any well-intentioned human activity. It seems strange, indeed, to maintain that the Spirit can confer as He wills except through the medium of His word

---

[20] "Sed dices: quomodo non alia omnis scriptura divinitus inspiratur, cum secundum Ambrosianum, omne verum a quocumque dicatur a Spiritu Sancto est? Dicundum est quod Deus dupliciter aliquid operatur, scilicet immediate, ut proprium opus, sicut miracula; aliquid mediantibus causis inferioribus, ut opera naturalia ut in Job (10:8), 'Manus tuae, Domine, fecerunt me . . .'; quae tamen fiunt operatione naturae. Et sic in homine instruit intellectum et immediate per sacras litteras, et mediate per alias scripturas." "Comm. on 2 Tim 3:16" (cf. n. 7).

(the burden of the proof for such a view rests with him who holds it).

The saving activity of the inspired word is not a sacrament: In a sacrament, in addition to the word, there is a thing or an action which concurs in making up the symbol. A sacrament, in its capacity of symbolic sign, really "does what it signifies." But on the other hand, the Scriptures are much more than a sacramental.

Semmelroth[21] distinguishes and unites the two activities in the following way: Christ effected salvation by His death and resurrection and by the preaching of His message. These two realities both derive their subsistence and divine quality from the same divine personality; they complement one another: The word, besides being an explanation, is an action, and the action is explained in the word. We can neither understand nor possess Christ if we divide these two elements of his life: action and word. These two realities are prolonged in the Church: Christ's action is contained in the sacrifice of the Mass and in the other sacraments which are centered in the Eucharist. The word of Christ is in the Scriptures, which have been confided to the Church and are proclaimed within her. Action and word still operate in unity: The word is also action when it is proclaimed or read; and action reveals its meaning in word. The union between these two elements in the liturgy is not something haphazard or arbitrary:

The two parts which, in a certain sense, go to make up the Mass, namely, the liturgy of the word and the Eucharistic liturgy, are so closely connected with each other that they form but one single act of worship.[22]

Our efforts to understand this doctrine of the saving power of the word can be greatly hindered by too "corporeal" an idea of grace and too ritualistic an idea of the sacraments. People insist a great deal on the fact that grace is a created entity which is given by God according to His generosity and our merit; but perhaps they

[21] O. Semmelroth, S.J., The Preaching Word, New York, 1965, esp. "God's Word and Man's Reply," pp. 55–71.

[22] "Duae partes e quibus Missa quodammodo constat, liturgia nempe verbi et eucharistica, tam arcte inter se coniunguntur, ut unum actum cultus efficiant. Sacra proinde Synodus vehementer hortatur animarum pastores ut, in catechesi tradenda, fideles sedulo doceant de integra Missa participanda, praesertim diebus dominicis et festis de praecepto." Const., no. 56.

neglect another aspect of grace, namely, that God is personal, and that grace is the basis of our friendship, of our "common life" with God. Karl Rahner has posed the question in terms of eternal glory:[23] In heaven, God does not communicate Himself through the medium of a created entity but directly and intimately. Grace, too, can be looked on as a mystery of communication and union. This is not to deny that the soul is really changed by grace, or to make of grace something purely extrinsic; on the contrary, it is to see that the change which is effected within the soul comes about through a participation in the life of God. Just as in a human dialogue, man turns to another person, so too, God turns toward us and speaks to us in an act of self-communication; and communication with God is grace: "Through the tongue of the prophets, we hear God speaking with us" (Chrysostom).

In His word, God gives us knowledge of Himself, introducing us into His mystery; and to know God is grace: "This is eternal life, to know You, the only true God, and Jesus Christ, Whom You have sent" (Jn 17:3). According to St. Gregory, "we know the heart of God in the words of God"; and St. Jerome says that "to be ignorant of the Scriptures is to know not Christ."

What we have said above is not intended to deny other aspects of grace, such as its reality as gift or merit; our intention has been to show the place of word in the work of salvation.[24]

In regard to the sacraments, the study of E. Schillebeeckx has served to highlight their character as an encounter with Christ:[25] They are an encounter which is less than that of heaven, since it takes place in signs and symbols; yet they are more intimate by far than that which is open to us naturally by inference and deduction. In this sense, the word is classified along with the sacraments without there begin an increase in their number. The parallelism Eucharist—Scripture, derives ultimately from Chapter 6 of St. John's Gospel.

Given the very nature of a word, it seems reasonable to admit

---

[23] Cf. *Theological Investigations*, vol. 1, 2nd ed., Baltimore, 1963, ch. 10, "Some Implications of the Scholastic Concept of Uncreated Grace," pp. 319–346.

[24] Cf. O. Schilling, *Das Wort Gottes im Alten Testament. Zur Diskussion um die Sakramentalität des Wortes Gottes*, Miscellanea Erfordiana, Leipzig, 1962.

[25] *Christ the Sacrament of the Encounter with God*, New York, 1963.

variations in intensity or concentration of salvific power; just as it is possible that the same word can have various degrees of effectiveness proportionate to the degree that it is understood, or according to the dispositions of the one receiving the word. Under this aspect of intensity, the Gospels hold a privileged and central position.

When Origen speaks of the "inspiring power" of the sacred text, he has no intention of defining "*theopneustos*," or of establishing its primary meaning in Second Timothy; he wishes only to describe a real quality of the inspired word:

Having received of His fullness, the prophets sang of that which they received of the fullness; and therefore, the sacred books breathe forth the fullness of the Spirit, and there is nothing in the prophets, the law, or the Gospel which has not descended from the fullness of the divine majesty. That is why the words of fullness found in the Scriptures are inspiring today. They are inspiring for those who have eyes to see what is heavenly, ears to hear what is divine, and nostrils able to detect the scent of fullness.[26]

THE POWER IN ACTION

The saving power of the Scriptures is a potentiality which must be actualized, and this actualization occurs in various contexts which are like so many concentric circles radiating out from the liturgy.

Liturgy. The central circle, which is proportionately more intense in its actualizing power, is the liturgy. This principle governed the use of Scripture in the Israelite community: Not only the Psalms, but many other texts besides had a liturgical function and were read in the context of the liturgy. In the early Christian community, the letters of St. Paul were read at the liturgy, as were the Gospels, and often the practical norm of canonicity was simply "those books which are read at the liturgy"; this explains why we find prohibitions against certain works being read at the liturgical assembly. During a time when the reading of the

---

[26] "Ex plenitudine ejus accipientes prophetae ea quae erant de plenitudine sumpta cecinerunt; et idcirco sacra volumina Spiritus plenitudinem spirant, nihilque est sive in prophetia, sive in lege, sive in Evangelio, sive in apostolo, quod non a plenitudine divinae majestatis descendat. Quamobrem spirant in Scripturis Sanctis hodieque plenitudinis verba. Spirant autem his qui habent et oculos ad videnda coelestia, et aures ad audienda divina, et nares ad ea quae sunt plenitudinis sentienda." "Homily on Jer 21, 2," PG 13, 536.

Scriptures was a rare practice among Catholics, the liturgy managed to preserve at least some measure of the traditional practice.

In the liturgy, the inspired word is read as a source of instruction and of grace. It is not a question simply of recalling what Christ said on one occasion, but of what He is saying now, speaking as one having authority and power: "Who spoke through the prophets," "Who is speaking now through the reader."

Christ is present in word, since it is he Himself who speaks when the holy scriptures are read in the Church.

In the liturgy, God speaks to his people and Christ is still proclaiming his gospel.[27]

The initial formula "At that time" can have the effect of reducing the reading to a mere historical remembrance, but it ought to be taken as an affirmation of the historical dimension of Christ Who, in His Incarnation and His speaking, assumed the limitations of time and space. It is not the memory of the word which "abides forever," but the word itself, because in the liturgical action the transcendent dimension of the historical event is made present once again.

From what we have said, it is easy to see the importance of the reading or proclamation of the word which takes place at the liturgy. We need only recall what was said in our discussion of the actualization and re-presentation of a literary work, which through a reader or a body of interpreters receives once again the fullness of the only type of existence possible to it.

We should apply here what we have said about the representation of a work before a public, and the integral "play" of complete community participation without a public. The reader lends his voice and his sensibilities to the mute notation on the page, and once again the word exists and is actual.

A reader must not hide himself behind a recitation which is frigid, impersonal, or "hieratic." There have been times when an attitude of sacred elevation was extremely effective; the reader was an impersonal herald. Nowadays, however, we prefer to have all the expressive possibilities of the original text re-presented in its actualization, so that in the voice of the reader there is a sort of new incarnation: "He is speaking through the reader." This means that

27 *Const.*, no. 7 (cf. n. 17), and no. 33 (cf. ch. 14, n. 13).

the readers must be well-trained and should, perhaps, be promoted to an order for the service of the liturgy. But even without this special ordination, the *Constitution on the Sacred Liturgy* declares expressly that readers fulfill a liturgical function (cf. no. 29).

An actor in the theatre commits his whole life to the literary text, to make it come alive on the stage and in the souls of his audience; and as he gives life to the text, he himself lives both spiritually and physically. So, too, a reader must commit himself to the text—without histrionics, imparting to it his own life in the service of the community. Then the text will become alive, and will impart in its turn a life greater than that of him who reads and of those who listen. "Consider carefully that which is written, that you may save yourselves and him who is the reader among you" (St. Clement).

The assembly must truly listen. So long as the liturgical readings were proclaimed in a language that was not understood, the best solution was to read the text simultaneously in a missal. But now that the readings are truly such, the situation is completely different. Let us imagine that there was some new bestseller which had achieved a great success, and all the members of the Russian reading club got together to enjoy the original. There they were, each one deep in his own arm chair reading a copy of the same book: We could not really call it a community activity, except accidentally in that they were all reading the same story. Something similar happens at the liturgy if those present, rather than listen to the reader, attend each one to his own missal. If the community is to act as such, then its activity must be centered on the same reality; there must be a real participation if there is to be union in the word. The word is one yet multiple, it is given to all and joins all together, causing them to share in the same life. And thus united in the passive activity of listening, the community passes to the "play" of song and prayer in which it expresses its response to the word by actualizing the word.

Often, this common prayer of the faithful will itself be an inspired word, a Psalm for instance. In this case, the actualization occurs in choral singing: A psalm written in the plural is only represented wholly when it is sung in common; when it is said privately, the adaptation is legitimate, but something of its full extent is limited. This inspired word possesses power as prayer: Christ is joined to us in this prayer in a very special way; He is praying with us and in us, and His prayer is efficacious:

He is present, lastly, when the Church prays and sings, for he promised: Where two or three are gathered together in my name, there am I in the midst of them" (Mt. 18:20).[28]

If someone were to say that this Psalm is written for us, he would not be missing the truth. For the divine words belong to us, and to the whole Church of God as gifts from God; they are read out loud at every assembly as spiritual food provided by the Spirit.[29]

Obviously, the liturgical reading of the text does not re-present it exactly as it was first composed; the text receives a new interpretation both from the fact that it is recited, and from the new context and combination of texts in which it finds itself. The context is not something peripheral to the work, some decorative addition; it is part of the re-presentation and affects the concrete meaning of the texts selected. Such a process in principle is not an infidelity to the text, but derives ultimately from the nature of a literary work—especially one that is inspired—which, as we have seen, cannot be exhausted by one re-presentation or translation.

We say that this is true "in principle"; we cannot expect a special divine assistance to protect the text from every error or exaggeration in interpretation. We know that there is no deformation in the essentials; in regard to the accidentals, there is a good deal of latitude, and each generation must seek a form of expression which is ever more faithful and more effective.

Homily. The second sphere pertains to the same context as the first and is intimately related to it: It is the liturgical homily.

Because the sermon is part of the liturgical service, the best place for it is to be indicated even in the rubrics, as far as the nature of the rite will allow; the ministry of preaching is to be fulfilled with exactitude and fidelity. The sermon, moreover, should draw its content mainly from scriptural and liturgical sources, and its character should be that of a proclamation of God's wonderful works in the history of salva-

---

[28] *Const.* no. 7 (cf. n. 17).

[29] Ἡμῖν οὖν γεγράφϑαι τὸν ψαλμὸν εἰπών τις, οὐκ ἂν ἁμάρτοι τῆς ἀληϑείας. Διὸ καὶ ἡμέτερά ἐστι τὰ ϑεῖα λόγια καὶ τῇ τοῦ Θεοῦ ἐκκλησίᾳ ὡς ϑεόπεμπτα δῶρα, καϑ' ἕκαστον σύλλογον ὑπαναγινώσκεται, οἷόν τις τροφὴ ψυχῶν χορηγουμένη διὰ τοῦ πνεύματος. St. Basil, "On Ps 59," PG 29, 464.

tion, the mystery of Christ, ever made present and active within us, especially in the celebration of the liturgy.[30]

By means of the homily, the mysteries of the faith and the guiding principles of the Christian life are expounded from the sacred text, during the course of the liturgical year; the homily, therefore, is to be highly esteemed as part of the liturgy itself; in fact, at those Masses which are celebrated with the assistance of the people on Sundays and feasts of obligation, it should not be omitted except for a serious reason.[31]

The homily should base itself on the sacred text and expound the mysteries of faith and the principles of the Christian life. For centuries, the homily was a form of living theology, dogmatic, moral, and ascetic. Rather than proofs it presented mysteries, rather than ethics it presented the Christian life. There are examples even in the sacred text of homiletic style: The Book of Deuteronomy presents Moses in the role of a northern Levite preaching to the people, and many passages in St. Paul's letters are paraenetic.

The homily must explain, that is, it must unfold for the people the riches contained in the inspired text; it must break the bread of the word, spreading out its treasures for all to contemplate.[32] The liturgical homily is an extension of the inspired word: The word increases in breadth and loses in concentration. We cannot maintain that whatever the priest says is the word of God in the strict sense of the term, but a homily should share in the nature of the inspired word. This means that a true homily participates somehow in the veracity and dynamism of the word of God, and it is another way of actualizing its power.

There is another type of instruction, which, though it is not a

---

[30] "*Locus aptior sermonis, utpote partis actionis liturgicae, prout ritus patitur, etiam in rubricis notetur; et fidelissime ac rite adimpleatur ministerium praedicationis. Haec vero imprimis ex fonte sacrae Scripturae et Liturgiae hauriatur, quasi annuntiatio mirabilium Dei in historia salutis seu mysterio Christi, quod in nobis praesens semper adest et operatur, praesertim in celebrationibus liturgicis.*" Const., no. 35:2.

[31] "*Homilia, qua per anni liturgici cursum ex textu sacro fidei mysteria et normae vitae christianae exponuntur, ut pars ipsius liturgiae valde commendatur; quinimmo in Missis quae diebus dominicis et festis de praecepto concurrente populo celebrantur, ne omittatur, nisi gravi de causa.*" Const., no. 52.

[32] Cf. *Divino afflante Spiritu*, esp. EB 553 and 566.

homily strictly so called, can fulfill an important function: We refer to an introductory explanation of the reading. The homily presupposes that the text was understood when it was read, and goes on from this point to expound the message. The introductory instruction starts from the fact that text itself is very imperfectly understood, and goes on to prepare the people to hear the reading profitably. There is nothing strange in such a procedure; many plays and operas take care to prepare their audiences to understand and share their message.

In our day, in many countries, the people have become strangers to the inspired word. In such a situation, they need to be introduced to the language of the Bible, to its style and to its world. An introduction of the type we have been describing would logically conclude with a reading of the sacred text: Such preparation could be an important feature of a Bible service. We have to set up a certain dialectic in order to penetrate the text; its schema would be either introduction→reading→commentary; or reading→homily →reading. In the liturgy itself, the proper form is proclamation→ homily; but special circumstances can dictate another form until the people are ready to profit fully from the traditional arrangement.

Bible Services. The inspired word can achieve actualization in a form of liturgy which is only mediately related to the Eucharistic sacrifice:

Bible services should be encouraged, especially on the vigils of the more solemn feasts, on some weekdays in Advent and Lent, and on Sundays and feast days. They are particularly to be commended in places where no priest is available; when this is so, a deacon or some other person authorized by the bishop should preside over the celebration.[33]

In order to be liturgical, and to actualize the word in the Christian community, these services must have some reference to the Eucharistic sacrifice; and thus they form another concentric circle

---

[33] "*Foveatur sacra Verbi Dei celebratio in solemniorum festorum pervigiliis, in aliquibus feriis Adventus et Quadragesimae, atque in dominicis et diebus festis, maxime in locis quae sacerdote carent: quo in casu celebrationem diaconus vel alius ab Episcopo delegatus dirigat.*" *Const.,* no. 35:4.

flowing out from this life center. Since they have the word as their specific object, such services can make use of reading, reciting, or re-presentation. There is ample room for an introduction and com-mentary, for a repetition of the reading, pauses for personal reflec-tion, etc. The greater liberty allowed in the manner in which the text is actualized can have many advantages both didactic and spir-itual, though we cannot automatically conclude that such proce-dures constitute the ideal of the Christian life: The high point of the Christian life is the Eucharist. But it is true that insofar as they make the word actual and cause people to participate in it, these services actualize the saving power of the word: Christ really speaks to His people, and just as in the Eucharistic blessing, so here, too, Christ really blesses His people.

Another concentric circle is formed by preaching done in the name of the Church. This should also draw its power from the inspired word. All Christian preaching centers on the mystery of Christ, that is, on revelation; and this revelation is contained in Scripture. Preaching should derive from the sacred text first in re-gard to the doctrine it proposes, second in regard to the language it uses, and third in regard to the power it dispenses.

Tradition has always recognized the value of placing rhetoric at the service of the word; many of the Fathers are prime examples of this. The use of eloquence to prepare a conversion is itself a sort of *"praeparatio evangelica"*; however, the power of Christian preach-ing does not reside precisely in the force of persuasion, but is con-tained within the inspired word.[34]

There are some who seem to consider preaching as nothing more than an exercise of eloquence: As a result of the artillery fire of arguments, we force the surrender of the will to God, and once the gates of liberty have been opened, God enters and acts immedi-ately with His grace. This makes of a sermon a purely human activ-ity. It is a battle of persuasion which prepares for grace, but which does not itself pertain to the sphere of grace. Such a thing is pos-sible, but it is not specifically Christian. When preaching really derives from the word of God and is an extension of it, then the preaching itself is an instrument of grace, because it actualizes the

[34] Cf. P. Duployé, *Rhétorique et Parole de Dieu,"* Paris, 1955.

saving power of the inspired word. In this sense, and only in this sense, can rhetoric and eloquence be considered a prolongation of the word of Christ.[35]

There is another concentric circle, which we have reserved for last, though not because we considered it to be peripheral or unimportant: We refer to the private reading of the Bible. Private does not mean independent; it has reference, rather, to that type of reading in which one's relation to community is not given expression, and in which the individual dimension of the personal search for God is accentuated. Such reading can never be completely private: The Christian has received the Bible from the Church (it would be a really beautiful liturgical ceremony if the head of a family or an individual Christian were actually to receive the sacred book during an assembly of the community). The fundamental fact makes every devout reading of the Bible a "Catholic action," one which finds its wellsprings within the community, and which can never lose its ecclesial dimension.

But we wish here to concentrate on the individual aspect of the reading: that kind of activity in which I go to my room, or to the Church, and open the Bible to read it by myself. Here, too, in secret, the inspired word begins to exist anew, God speaks once again, He reaches me with His word in order to save me: "Thus speaking, He looks for us" (St. Augustine).

The life of a good Christian is grafted on to that of Christ, and the Spirit dwells actively within him. When such a person reads the word of the Spirit, we cannot imagine that He Who inspired the text will withdraw or remain inactive. A real Christian does not, of course, exclude the teaching of the Church from his own private reading of the sacred text; rather, he approaches the inspired word with his Christian faith and formation, his Christian life and outlook; he possesses already within him a predisposition toward hearing the word of God and a connaturality with it. None of this dispenses him from diligent application and from the humility which is able to seek and accept advice, but it does provide him with a fundamental security. The Fathers constantly recommend this kind of personal reading:

[35] Cf. A. Wilder, *The Language of the Gospel*, New York, 1964, ch. 1, "The New Utterance."

Since you have the consolation of the divine writings, there is no need for me or for anyone else in order that you may know what is proper. You yourself have the counsel and guidance of the Holy Spirit to show you what to do [36]

But this is what has ruined everything, your thinking that the reading of Scripture is for monks only, when you need it more than they do. Those who are placed in the world, and who receive wounds every day, have the most need of medicine. So, far worse even than not reading the Scriptures is the idea that they are supererogatory. Such things were invented by the devil.[37]

And therefore, I ask that we do not approach the content of the Scriptures thoughtlessly, but rather read carefully what we find there, so that the fruit we gather may be profitable, and sometime later we may be able to receive in turn the virtue which pleases God.[38]

We should imitate sailors who arrive safely in port after a storm. Just lately freed from the tumult and roar of the waves, let us moor our souls in the reading of the Scriptures as in a quiet harbor. The Scriptures are a tranquil port, an impregnable wall, an unshakable tower, a glory which cannot be carried off, armor impregnable, unfailing cheer, constant delight, whatever good may be thought of, this you will find in the assembly of the divine Scriptures.[39]

---

[36] Ἔχουσα δὲ τὴν ἐκ τῶν Θείων Γραφῶν παράκλησιν, οὔτε ἡμῶν οὔτε ἄλλου τινὸς δεηθήσῃ πρὸς τὸ τὰ δέντα, συνορᾶν αὐτάρκη τὴν ἐκ τοῦ ἁγίου Πνεύματος ἔχουσα συμβουλίαν καὶ ὁδηγίαν πρὸς τὸ συμφέρον. St. Basil, "Letter 283," PG 32, 1020.

[37] Τοῦτο γάρ ἐστιν ὃ πάντα ἐλυμήνατο ὅτι ἐκείνοις (μοναχοῖς) μόνοις νομίζετε προσήκειν τὴν ἀνάγνωσιν τῶν Θείων Γραφῶν, πολλῷ πλέον ἐκείνων ὑμεῖς δεόμενοι. Τοῖς γὰρ ἐν μέσῳ στρεφομένοις καὶ καθ᾽ ἑκάστην ἡμέραν τραύματα δεχομένοις, τούτοις μάλιστα δεῖ φαρμάκων. Ὥστε τοῦ μὴ ἀναγινώσκειν πολλῷ χεῖρον τὸ καὶ περιττὸν εἶναι τὸ πρᾶγμα νομίζειν. Ταῦτα γὰρ σατανικῆς μελέτης τὰ ῥήματα. St. John Chrys., "Homily 2, 5 on Mt," PG 57, 30.

[38] Διὸ, παρακαλῶ, μὴ ἁπλῶς ἐπερχώμεθα τὰ ἐν ταῖς Θείαις Γραφαῖς κείμενα, ἀλλὰ μετὰ προσοχῆς ἀναγινώσκωμεν τά ἐγκείμενα, ἵνα τὴν ἐξ αὐτῶν ὠφέλειαν καρπούμενοι, ὀψὲ γοῦν ποτε τῆς κατὰ Θεὸν ἀρετῆς ἀντιλαβέσθαι δυνηθῶμεν. St. John Chrys., "Homily 21 on Gn," PG 53, 183.

[39] Τούτους (ναῦτας) δὴ ἡμεῖς μεμησώμεθα, καὶ τῆς πρώην ταραχῆς ἀπαλλαγέντες, καὶ τοῦ θορύβου, καὶ τῶν κυμάτων, ὥσπερ εἴς τινα λιμένα εὔδιον, τῶν Γραφῶν τὴν ἀνάγνωσιν τὴν ψυχὴν τὴν ἡμετέραν ὁρμίσωμεν. Καὶ γὰρ λιμὴν ἀκύμαντος, καὶ τεῖχος ἀρραγές, καὶ πύργος ἄσειστος, καὶ δόξα ἀναφαίρετος, καὶ ὅπλον ἄτρωτον, καὶ εὐθυμία ἀμάραντος, καὶ ἡδονὴ διηνεκής, καὶ πάντα ὅσα ἄν εἴποι τις καλὰ, τῶν Θείων Γραφῶν ἡ συνουσία. St. John Chrys., "Homily on Ps 48," PG 55, 513.

All of the instances we have discussed—liturgical reading, homily, Bible service, preaching, private reading—open out into the last circle in which the word resounds—meditation. Every human word possesses or creates a resonant space within the soul: "I have to think about that for a while," a word has impressed us deeply, or a poem imposes silence as it ends. "To ponder in one's heart" is to allow a word the tranquillity and space that it needs to resound in our souls so that it penetrates, reaching to the division of joints and marrow, seeping down into the depths of our soul. Sometimes a piece of music stays with us, echoing within us; unconsciously, we hear its ebb and flow, its themes return and combine anew; we treasure its sweetness and accept its insistence. There are times when, after having heard a piece of music, we want to hear no more; we wish only to be quiet and recollected.

The phrase is brief, yet its power great. . . . through tiny words the grace of the Spirit plants wisdom within those who are attentive; and sometimes one sentence provides those who receive it with nourishment sufficient for the whole journey of life.[40]

Such resonances are not, strictly speaking, repetitions, yet they are actualizations of the word.

Let us keep within our souls a space wherein the word of God can resound; as it echoes and returns, its grace will reach and touch us. As one word fully resounds, our soul expands and allows greater scope for melody. In this vast expanse which we find within us, God is present in His word. And then our soul receives another word, a word of song and praise and prayer; and the first word of God is answered by another. The answer reaches God somehow as it resounds within us and becomes our own. This is the dialogue of grace and of salvation; persons are united in a word which is divine and human. God has spoken our language in a human way, He has searched for us and found us; in order to find us, He has let us find Him in the mystery of His Word.

---

[40] Εἰ γὰρ καὶ βραχεῖα ἡ ῥῆσις, ἀλλὰ πολλὴ ἡ δύναμις. . . . ἡ δὲ τοῦ Πνεύματος χάρις οὐχ οὕτως, ἀλλὰ τοὐναντίον ἅπαν διὰ μικρῶν ῥημάτων πᾶσι τοῖς προσέχουσι φιλοσοφίαν ἐντίθησι: καὶ ἀρκεῖ ῥῆμα πολλάκις ἕν λαβόντας ἐντεῦθεν, πάσης τῆς ζωῆς ἔχειν ἐφόδιον. St. John Chrys., "Homily 1, 3 on the Statues," PG 49, 18.

Bibliography for Chapter 15

As was mentioned before, the bibliography given in Chapter 14 is relevant to the topic treated here. The fundamental work on the power of the word is that by O. Semmelroth, *The Preaching Word*, New York, 1965 (cf. the review of the original German by M. Zerwick in VD 40, 1962, pp. 153–157). The articles by Rahner and Semmelroth in *The Word*, compiled at the Canisianum, New York, 1964, also treats aspects of this question. There is also the book by H. Volk, *Zur Theologie des Wortes Gottes*, Münster, 1962.

In regard to the reading of Scripture, there is the work of C. Charlier, *The Christian Approach to the Bible*, Westminster, 1958; L. Bouyer's *The Meaning of Sacred Scripture*, Notre Dame, 1958; and the beautiful pamphlet by Pierre-Yves Emery, *La méditation de l'Écriture*, Taizé, as well as some interesting pages in Dom J. Leclercq, *The Love of Learning and the Desire for God*, New York, 1961. There are any number of articles and books which are designed to help in the reading of the sacred text: the articles in the periodical *The Bible Today* are excellent.

Appendix

A Résumé of the Dogmatic Section of Christian Pesch's
De Inspiratione Sacrae Scripturae, Numbers 373–636

I present here a *précis* of the dogmatic section of Pesch by way of
homage to his great work. His manual has been replaced by others in
most lecture rooms, but this is unfortunate. No one had or has at his
disposal the wealth of information, scriptural, patristic, and theological, that he had; and this not only in the historical section, but also in
the systematic analysis.

I hope that my act of homage will also be of use. Pesch offers us the
classical systematic treatment, and thus the synthesis of his work which
follows will serve to put my study in the larger context of the "*doctrina
communis,*" and to indicate those areas in which I have intended to
make a contribution.

It is true that many of Pesch's opinions were conditioned by the
historical situation in which he lived and are highly influenced by motives of an apologetic nature. As such, they are interesting for the light
they throw on that epoch. Nevertheless, many problems are posed
quite exactly and formulated with precision, and the author himself
offers us material for new solutions provided that we study it critically.
Then again, there are solutions proposed here which are just as valid
now as when they were first formulated.

I hope, then, that these pages will be of service to students. The
professor may make use of them as a basis for commentary, availing
himself of the work itself.

The synthesis which follows is an English translation of an outline
composed almost entirely of the words of the author himself, and relying for the most part on the italicized words in his text.

Christian Pesch, *On the Inspiration of Sacred Scripture*

PART II. DOGMATIC TREATISE

CHAPTER I. THE EXISTENCE OF INSPIRATION

Article I. The Testimony of Scripture

1. The Old Testament

The Law: Dt 34:10; Nm 12:6ff. The Psalmist (David): 2 K 23:1; Ps 45:2. The Prophets: The word "prophet" includes the notion of a man who is moved by God to speak, and who, in the name of God and not in his own, speaks to the people: Ex 7:1, 4:15–16; Jer 15:19, 1:9; 1 K 2:27; 9:6; Hos 9:7.

The prophets, so as to be able to be legates of God to men, receive into their intellects and wills the divine motion, by which they are made living instruments of God: 1 K 10:10, 19:20; 2 Chr 20:14; Ezr 3:12; 2 Chr 24:10; Za 7:12.

By reason of their more elevated knowledge, they are often called "seers": 1 S 3:1, 9:9, 11, 18, 19; Is 29:20, 30:10.

The motion of the will: Is 6:9; Jer 1:7.

Unwillingness to receive the words of the prophets is the same as rebellion against God: Jer 7:25; Ezr 3:7; Za 7:13.

In receiving divine influence, the prophets are not necessarily deprived of the use of the external senses, still less of the use of reason: Ex 4:10; Jer 1:6; Jon 1:3; 1 K 19:4, 10, 14. True and false prophets: 2 K 9:11; Jer 29:26; Hos 9:7; Ct 3:4. Special cases: Ezr 2:1; Dn 10:4; Nm 22ff.

God sometimes orders the prophets to write: Ex 17:14, 34:27; Is 8:1, 30:8, 34:16; Hb 2:2, 3; Dn 8:26, 12:4; Jer 36.

2. The New Testament

In the New Testament, the sacred books of the Old Testament are considered prophetic books: Mt 1:22, 2:5, 15, 17, 23; Lk 24:44.

A collection of sacred books, called the Scripture, was in existence: Jn 2:22, 10:35; Gal 3:22; Jn 5:39, 7:42; 1 Pt 2:6; Rom 3:10.

This was divided into "The Law," "The Prophets," and "The Psalms": Lk 24:44; Mt 5:17; Jn 10:34, 12:34; 1 Cor 14:21. Individual passages were also called "The Scripture": Jn 19:36; Mk 12:10; Lk 4:21; Acts 8:35; 2 Pt 3:16.

Sacred Scripture was endowed with supreme authority: Mt 4:14; Jn 10:34; Acts 15:15; Rom 1:17; 1 Pt 2:6. Individual passages were as well: Gal 3:16; Heb 8:8, 13; Jn 10:35; Acts 1:16; Lk 24:44; Mt 5:18.

The reason for this authoritativeness was that God spoke through the sacred writers as through the prophets: Mt 1:22, 2:15; Jn 5:45; Mt 22:31, 41.

And the apostles of Christ spoke in the same fashion: Acts 1:16, 2:30; Heb 4:4, 10:15; Gal 3:8.

Inspiration is explicitly taught: 2 Tim 3:14, 15, 16; 2 Pt 1:19.

Scholion 1. Is it possible to prove the divine inspiration of Scripture by means of the typical sense? —It is not proved, but confirmed. Types are such as they are set forth.

Scholion 2. Is it possible to prove the inspiration of the New Testament by means of Scripture? —Not of the whole of the New Testament.

Article II. The Testimony of Tradition

1. Practical

An argument cannot be found in the word "inspiration" alone.

The sacred books of Scripture were everywhere read and explained in the public liturgy; apocryphal books were forbidden.

The holy Fathers sought, with the greatest zeal, to discover the meaning of Scripture and to explain it to others.

The Gentiles, well aware of the honor in which the sacred books were held by the Christians, considered it a great triumph if they were able to elicit scriptural traditions from them by force.

2. Theoretical

The Fathers customarily speak of "the divine Scripture," by reason of the fact that its authors are prophets through whom God spoke to men. Scripture is the word of God; letters sent from God to men through prophets, the Scriptures are said to be written by the Holy Spirit.

The Scriptures must be held to be so inspired by God that He is their true and proper author: councils of Florence, Trent, Vatican I.

Chapter II. The Essence of Inspiration

Article I. What Must Not Be Confused with the Dogma of Inspiration

Article II. On Divine and Human Authorship

Article III. What Is Insufficient for Inspiration

Article IV. What Is Not Required for Inspiration

Article V. The Influence of God on the Intellect

Article VI. The Influence of God on the Will and Executive Faculties

Article I. What Must Not Be Confused with the Dogma of Inspiration

The question of the identity of the human authors of the individual sacred books cannot be answered by the doctrine of inspiration; neither does the judgment of the inspiration or non-inspiration of an individual book depend on the doctrine of inspiration.

Nor is it possible to determine, on the basis of the dogma of inspiration, whether a book attributed in our canon to one author may not perhaps have been composed by a number of authors, or reworded by some editor and enlarged by certain additions.

Moreover, no literary genre is excluded from the ambit of inspiration.

Still less can there be any question here of the preservation of the sacred text, or any question of the versions.

The only thing which is to be considered here is the inspirative influence by which God is made the author of the sacred books. Personal inspiration can and does have various species and degrees. The inspiration involved here is that which is equally shared by all the sacred books and which distinguishes them from all other books. It is, quite simply, the inspiration to write. This is a question of dogma which looks of itself to some universal concept, and seeks to define that essential note which makes all the sacred books, however different one from another, inspired.

Article II. On Divine and Human Authorship

There are some who distinguish between the human writers and the divine author. Since the human writers are authors, though, it became customary to speak of the primary author and the secondary authors.

God is the principal cause, while the sacred writer is an instrumental cause.

It may be asked how it is possible for the principal author to use secondary authors as instruments and still remain truly and properly the principal author.

The sacred writers are living, rational instruments.

To answer the question, recourse must be had to that extraordinary supernatural influence called charismatic.

God, in His wisdom and power, habitually makes use of creatures in such a way as not to suppress their nature and faculties, but rather to apply them to the task which He wishes done. God employs the sacred writers for the purpose of writing, inasmuch as they possess the faculties apt for producing the books He intends. God elevates and moves these faculties.

Article III. What Is Insufficient for Inspiration

Preservation from error is not enough: *contra* Chrismann, Jahn, others.

The subsequent approval of the Church is not enough. Nor is it enough that God by subsequent approbation render divinely inspired books which were composed solely as human works. Opinion of Lessius.

Insufficient also are: divine counsel, command, initial excitation to write and direction in execution, a general suggestion of the matter.

Still less sufficient is that personal inspiration, of which recent Protestants often speak, as of a particular kind of personal religious experience.

Article IV. What Is Not Required for Inspiration

Revelation, strictly speaking, does not enter into the formal concept of inspiration. On the other hand, the language of the inspired books, because and to the extent that it is affirmed by God, can be believed with divine faith.

A distinction must be made between revelation broadly speaking and revelation strictly speaking. A distinction must also be made between the revelation made to the hagiographers themselves and the revelation made to us, through the hagiographers, by God. It is certain that the hagiographers did not receive through divine revelation the knowledge of all those things of which they wrote. Furthermore, where there is question of treating in writing those things which could be learned by supernatural revelation alone, the hagiographers themselves need not have received that revelation.

The sense in which everything is inspired can be said to be revealed. *Contra* Bonaccorsi. God speaks to us immediately in sacred Scripture, because the words of Scripture are the immediate communications of God to us; therefore, all that is inspired is revealed to us.

Nothing, however, prevents a man from being inspired to write those things which he already knew, independently of any extraordinary divine influence, or even such things as were known to other men and may already have been written by them as purely human works.

But with regard to the subsequent inspiration itself, revelation is necessary.

It is not necessary for inspiration that the man write in an ecstatic state.

Nor is it required that God predetermine the writer to write in such a way as to destroy human liberty.

Article V. The Influence of God on the Intellect of the Hagiographer

When one already possessed of the necessary knowledge comes to write the book, he must have four qualifications: He must conceive in his mind the idea of the book, he must consider the mode of expression, he must have the will to write, he must put counsel into execution. These are distinct qualifications, separable from one another. Some sacred writers expressly affirm that they wrote their books in this fashion.

If God is to be the principal author of the book, he must be the principal agent of those things by which men become authors.

The idea of the book must exist principally in the divine mind and be derived from it to the human mind. The divine idea is the exemplary cause of the writing of the book; the divine influence on the mind of the man pertains to the order of efficient causality.

This action is the light of judgment by which the man puts together sentences in such a way as fully to express everything in the order intended by God.

And the object of the supernatural judgments? It is not precisely the knowledge already possessed by the man, but theoretical judgments, whether natural or supernatural as to object, are prerequisite.

God illumines the writer by a supernatural light, in virtue of which he judges those things and in that order to be written which God wills to be written, as God wills them to be written.

Scholion 1. Were the hagiographers conscious of the fact that they were inspired? —Not always.

Scholion 2. And was the Second Book of Maccabees taken from the books of Jason? —Certainly.

Article VI. Regarding the Influence of God on the Will and Executive Faculties of the Hagiographer; the Divine Assistance and the Transmission of the Books to the Church

Since God as principal author wishes that the man himself decide to write the book, a corresponding charismatic motion of the will is called for.

A double influence of God on the will of the writer must be acknowledged: One is moral, from which the practical judgments proceed; the other is physical.

On the point that it is not necessary for authorship that the writing be done by the physical operation of the author himself: 1 Pt 5:12; Rom 16:22; 1 Cor 16:21; 2 Th 2:2; Gal 6:11.

For God to be author and co-writer of the sacred books, it is not required that there be an immediate charismatic influence, physical as regards the executive or writing faculties and the actual writing itself. But divine assistance is required.

From this becomes evident the difference between sacred Scripture and conciliar or pontifical definitions: Divine assistance pertains to the latter only to the extent that they are infallibly proposed as revealed.

God, when He inspired the sacred books, intended that they be handed down to the Church in the name of God as the written word and as the source and rule of faith.

Conclusion. Definition and Degrees of Biblical Inspiration

Biblical inspiration is a charismatic illumination of the intellect, motion of the will, and divine assistance bestowed on the hagiographer for the purpose of writing those things, and only those things, which God, in His own name, wishes to be written and to be handed on to the Church.

The inspiration of the sacred writer, because it is a finite motion, can admit of degrees.

Degrees of inspiration are not to be distinguished among the inspired books themselves, as if one were more the word of God than another or have greater authority to command theological faith.

CHAPTER III. THE EXTENT OF INSPIRATION

Article I. Generally
Article II. Individual Expressions
Article III. Specific Words

Article I. The Extent of Inspiration to All Things Contained in Scripture

Restrictive opinions: Newman, Holden.
    The testimony of Scripture: 2 Tim 3:16.
    The testimony of the Fathers.
    The Fathers often discovered the most exalted meanings in the slightest phrases.

Article II. The Sense in which the Individual Expressions of Scripture Are the Words of God.

What God says is so, without doubt is so; but what God says is said by others, is not necessarily so.

Sometimes human expressions are involved which are approved or disapproved explicitly, either by God, by Christ, or by the hagiographers. In regard to these, we have the infallible judgment of God: Mt 16:16; Tit 1:12; Jn 11:50; Acts 17:28.

If a rather long passage is commended as true, that surely is true which is intended and affirmed by the passage as a whole; but each and every word which occurs in the passage is not necessarily true, where these have no necessary relationship to the principal intent: Jb 42:7, 42:3; Acts 6-7 (Stephen's discourse).

If certain men are praised in sacred Scripture for having done some good thing or even for having notably accomplished many deeds, it does not follow from that fact alone that all their words are said to have been true: Ex 1:19-20; Jud 10:12. Approval can be given without specific words: 2 Mac 7:18ff.

From those words which are related in historical fashion must be distinguished the words of imaginary persons which are employed, by the intention of the sacred writer, to represent certain teaching or opinions: Wis 2, 5:4.

Relation in the Bible of words said by others confers no canonical dignity on such words, but leaves to them that dignity which they have independently of the inspired writing: 2 Mac 1:15ff., 9:1ff.; Jn 9:31; Acts 5:34.

When the words of the apostles in their apostolic activity are set forth, their doctrine on matters of faith and morals must be believed, not because what they say has been written down by an inspired author, but because they received from Christ the gift of infallibility when exercising their apostolic task: Acts 20:25; 2 Tim 4:20; Acts 21:29. What holds true of the apostles holds true of the prophets: 2 K 7:1.

If angels are sent as envoys of God to announce certain things to men, their words are to be believed with divine faith: Lk 1:20; Acts 7:53; Gal 3:19.

If the hagiographer proposes a doctrine pertaining to faith and morals, God himself proposes this doctrine: Gal 5:2; 2 Cor 13:3; Sir 12:12.

Within the limits of those things which by divine law are licit and open to men, the sacred writer can give counsel in temporal as well as in spiritual matters. Through inspiration, God witnesses that this counsel is reasonable: 1 Cor 7:10.

In the historical books, the sacred writers sometimes relate what they themselves said. In virtue of inspiration, it is certain that they once said such things; but words once said are hardly made divine by the mere fact that they are narrated by a sacred writer: Ex 2.

If the hagiographer speaks vaguely or doubtfully, it is certain that God is neither doubtful nor ignorant, but affirms the doubt or even the ignorance of the hagiographer: 1 Cor 1:14; Acts 25:6; Jn 2:6.

The sacred writers often express the feeling they experienced while writing: Rom 1:11, 9:1; 2 Cor 6:11; Gal 1:6, 3:1, 4:19, 5:12. These are words of God by which God does not express His feelings, but by which He witnesses to the emotions which St. Paul had while writing under inspiration. These emotions were morally good.

Difficulty regarding curses. These put into words the law of God against the enemies of God; they are often prophetic; they invoke a sanction already promulgated by God.

Sometimes the hagiographers not only propose a doctrine, but also strengthen it by arguments. These arguments, since they are inspired by God, cannot be false and ineffectual. Arguments *ad hominem* are not excluded: 1 Cor 15.

New Testament writers frequently argue from the words of the Old Testament according to the Septuagint translation, and not according to the original text. Such an argument is not an argument from Scripture.

Another case is presented by the accommodation of the words of Scripture to mean something rightly expressed by the words themselves, even though they had, in their original context, another meaning: Rom 10:18; 2 Cor 8:14.

N*   395

Conclusion: Whatever things are said by the hagiographers are by that reason alone the words of God, for God bears witness to the truth and correctness of the individual expressions according to the sense intended by the hagiographers.

Article III. The Extent of Inspiration to the Individual Words of Scripture

The state of the question: Inspiration must be extended also to the very words themselves in some fashion. But how? A distinction is to be made between mental or formal words, imaginative words, external material words. Our question concerns the influence of God on the words of the imagination: How do they depend on charismatic influence?

Opinions: external dictation: orthodox Protestants; internal dictation: by which God would stir up individual images of individual words and would impel them to be written. Supernatural illumination for the apt expression of the matters involved.

Arguments: Ps 54:2; Jer 36:18. The prophetic formula "to speak the words of God." Certain of the letters of St. Paul (Heb, Cor): The ideas are St. Paul's, but the words and style are the secretary's. The hagiographers cite Scripture in somewhat changed words, in the style of Rom 9:33. Two variants of a single text can be found: 2 K 22 and Ps 18. There are variations in style as well as imperfections: 2 Cor 11:6; 2 Mac 15. Inspired words have perished: the Aramic version of St. Matthew; textual corruptions; versions . . . the Fathers sometimes make a distinction between words and meaning.

One recent explanation: God so supernaturally elevates and moves the whole man, as an instrument for writing, that He determines the book to be produced, with all its perfections and imperfections; and, since inspiration consists in this very elevation and motion, everything must be recognized as inspired which is produced by the writer, supernaturally elevated and moved.

The opinion of Pesch himself: Although it is psychologically impossible that the material execution be completely uninfluenced by the judgment, formed by a charismatically illumined and moved writer, of what is to be written, still there is no solid argument by which it can be proved that each and every material word of Scripture is determined in the individual by God; indeed, there are reasons which suggest that this is by no means the case.

Scholion: The opinion of Augustine on the special majesty of biblical rhetoric.

CHAPTER IV. THE INERRANCY OF SACRED SCRIPTURE

Article I. The Fact
Article II. The Allegorical Interpretation of the Fathers
Article III. Standards of Truth
Article IV. Physical Matters
Article V. History
Article VI. Myths and Legends
Article VII. The Fathers on History
Article VIII. Implicit Citations
Article IX. Popular Traditions

Article I. Sacred Scripture Is Immune from Errors

By the inerrancy of the sacred books is meant that property by reason of which whatever is taught in Scripture is true and utterly excludes all error.

Opinions: The ancients were unanimous on this point. Orthodox thinkers remain so. Rationalists reject the position. Some Catholics restrict it to religious matters.

Arguments: Jn 10:35; Acts 1:16; Lk 24:44; Mt 5:18. The Fathers. The theologians. The popes.

Article II. May Not the Patristic Argument for Inerrancy Be Weakened by the Allegorical Interpretations of the Fathers Themselves?

Objection: The Fathers of the Church either failed to see our difficulties or, if they saw them, hid behind an allegorical interpretation.

Response: The Fathers affirmed the principle of inerrancy not inductively, from ignorance, but dogmatically; those who held tenaciously to the literal sense held the same principle; they often explained metaphorically; but they always supposed a literal sense.

Article III. The Same Standard of Truth Is Not To Be Applied to All Parts of Scripture

Moral truth or veracity. Pseudonyms.

Logical truth: the conformity of what the hagiographers experienced and what they wrote with objective truth. The truth of history, of parable; fictional tales can be inspired. The truth of song in description or in prophecy; conditional predictions.

All the expressions of Scripture are certainly true, but according to that standard of truth which is appropriate to the genus of the individual books, be they historical, prophetic, poetic, or didactic.

397

The question of critical historiography must not be confused with this one. Is it possible that there pertain to the words of Sacred Scripture more truth than the hagiographers themselves understood and intended? Some say that whatever the sacred author did not will to say, God did not will to say. Pesch's reply is that the hagiographers did not perfectly understand all the things which God wished to express by their words. The testimony of the authors on this point: St. Augustine, St. Jerome, St. Thomas Aquinas, Suarez, Leo XIII.

Conclusion: There frequently underlies the words of Scripture a higher meaning than that which can be discovered by the common rules of interpretation, and this full breadth of meaning of the inspired words was not always grasped by the hagiographers themselves.

Article IV. The Relation of the Truth of Scripture to the Sciences

God gave Scripture to men for the purpose of furthering the way of salvation, and not for communicating secular instruction: 2 Tim 3:16–17.

A distinction must be made between that which is revealed *per se* (mysteries) and that which is revealed *per accidens* (history).

Whatever has been revealed, in the way in which it has been revealed, is the word of God, which the faithful may not deny. It is possible for that which has been revealed *per accidens* to be corrupted (numbers, e.g.). From the very fact that they can have a common object, a certain tension exists between the theologian and the natural scientist. St. Augustine, St. Thomas Aquinas, Leo XIII. But no contradiction is possible. Note the existence of popular or common speech, which goes by appearances.

Article V. The Difference between Physical Matters and Historical Matters

History as such either narrates facts or it is false. Yet it remains possible for the narrator to set forth fictitious material or to quote extraneous material.

1. Popular science speaks of things known to all; history does otherwise.

2. Nature does not pertain to salvation *per se*, whereas the history of salvation certainly does.

3. Many historical facts have been revealed and must be believed: the Creed.

Discussions of what is called "history according to appearances."

Sacred history is true with respect to extent: inasmuch as it does not tell all that was known to the hagiographers and others: Jn 21:25.

It is true with respect to manner: inasmuch as it uses indeterminate or summary expressions. It is true with respect to intent: inasmuch as the author's sole intention is to refer to what he has found in the sources.

The substance of sacred history is true; the manner of describing historical matters is that which was employed by the ancients, not that which is customary among moderns.

Article VI. Are There Myths or Legends in the Historical Books of Scripture?

Pesch means by this (he mentions no names) a narration which, under the guise of history, tells things which are substantially false. This is something essentially different from an historical allegory, which proposes abstract ideas in fictional narrative form. Texts of the Fathers.

Article VII. Did Some of the Fathers Teach that the Historical Narrations of Scripture Were Not Always Truly Historical?

Texts and discussion.

Article VIII. Implicit Citations from Sacred Scripture

The truth of the citation and the truth of the matter cited.

Explicit citations: Neh 7:4ff.; Jer 28:2ff. (reproving); Tim 1:12 (approving).

Implicit citations: 2 Chr 5:9, 8:8; 2 K 24:9 with 1 Chr 21:5; Gn 46:21 with 1 Chr 7:6; 1 Chr 2:3 with 4:1; 1 Chr 8:29 with 9:35; Ezr 2 with Neh 7; 1 Mac 3:39 with 2 Mac 8:9.

At times recourse is rather to be had to corruption of numbers.

Some are certaintly present, others not arbitrarily to be supposed; nor can the whole of the Old Testament be reduced to them.

Citations of the Old Testament in the New Testament according to the version of the Septuagint. Some consider the Septuagint to be inspired. Where the meaning is the same, there is no difficulty. Where the meaning is different.

Article IX. Popular Traditions

These are handed on orally, not by a canon; likewise, religious tradition, even revealed.

There is nothing to prevent the sacred authors of the Old Testament from drawing, among their sources, from what we would call popular traditions. But within popular tradition, truth is preserved and handed on in a way different from that proper to what is written according to artistic rules: poetically and concretely, by proverb and metaphor, on the basis of appearance and opinion; little by little it may come about that the true becomes mingled with what is false.

The sacred author can take what is true from these traditions, even retaining the popular style; but he cannot retain the false without disapproving of it.

CHAPTER V. THE MEANING OF SACRED SCRIPTURE

Article I. Literal Meaning

Article II. Typical Meaning

CHAPTER VI. THE CLARITY AND SUFFICIENCY OF SACRED SCRIPTURE

Article I. The Clarity of Scripture

Article II. The Sufficiency of Scripture

Article I. The Clarity of Scripture

The opinion of Protestants on the clarity of Scripture as a norm.

Certain Scriptural expressions are clear, while others are obscure.

The whole of Scripture, taken as a single book, must be called obscure and difficult rather than clear and easily understood: remoteness of cultural milieu, frequently unknown circumstances, mysteries, corruption of the text.

Why the Holy Spirit wished His books to be obscure: historical condition, variations among men; He demands the reader's coöperation and effort.

Article II. The Sufficiency of Scripture

Opinion of Protestants.

It is not adequate to prove its own authority.

Nor is it sufficient to prove that it has been preserved incorrupt.

Its insufficiency is due to the nature of those who had to be instructed: They neither knew how to read, nor did they know languages.

A *priori*, it is improbable that God, by giving men a book, would have imposed on all men the obligation of reading it and of gathering from it all that was necessary for salvation.

Christ provided in a better way for the preservation of revealed truth: Mt 28:18; Mk 16:16, 20; 2 Tim 1:13–14, 2:2; Tit 1:5, 7, 9. Patristic doctrine.

Christ instituted oral tradition as the principal and universal means of preserving and handing on revealed doctrine.

Scripture depends on tradition inasmuch as its authority is known from tradition.

The books of the New Testament infallibly assert the magisterium instituted by Christ.

Scripture, inasmuch as it declares that Christ instituted a living magisterium from which it was necessary to learn all truth, can rightly be said to be sufficient to show us the way of salvation.

Scripture depends on the Church inasmuch as only the infallible magisterium of the Church can make known the inspiration of the whole of Scripture.

Scripture sets down a rule of faith from which the Church cannot withdraw.

Further, Scripture was given to the magisterium of the Church that it might learn from Scripture what was to be taught learned and unlearned alike. Inasmuch as God willed to provide for the needs of the teaching Church by means of Scripture, Scripture is undoubtedly sufficient for the purpose intended by God.

Scripture is sufficient to demonstrate the dogmas which are contained in the Creed and which must be believed by all without exception.

Scripture is sufficient to resolve many controversies with those heretics who, along with Catholics, recognize the sacred books as inspired.

Scripture does not suffice to make all capable of rightly explaining it.

The Church does not bestow dignity on Scripture, but recognizes and affirms it.

The Church does not subject Scripture to herself, but interprets it.

The excellence of Scripture consists in its being formally the word of God.

CHAPTER VII. THE CRITERIA OF INSPIRATION

Article I. The Universal Criterion: Tradition
Article II. Internal Criteria
Article III. The Testimony of Scripture about Itself
Article IV. The Apostolate

Article I. The Universal Criterion of Inspiration Is Sacred Tradition

The testimonies of tradition.

From the nature of the thing: since it is a divine operation, not immediately perceptible.

Are only those books inspired which have been handed down in the canon?

What of those books already in existence in apostolic times and considered by some as inspired, but not received into the canon?

Have some inspired books perished? 1 Cor 5:9; Col 4:6.

Article II. What Internal Criteria Are of Value in Establishing the Fact of Inspiration?

According to Protestants: antiquity, majesty, efficacity, attacks, miracles.

Internal criteria are not sufficient; nonetheless, they are of worth in recommending Scripture.

Negative criteria: these are applied only with difficulty to Scripture.

Positive criteria: unity, inerrancy. These are valuable, but not sufficient to convince. Prophecies fulfilled. The authority with which it speaks. The "feel" of Scripture.

Article III. The Value of the Testimony of Scripture Regarding Its Inspiration

Once the Hebrew canon has been historically established, the testimony of the New Testament regarding the Old Testament becomes valuable. Similarly, the collection of Old Testament citations in the New Testament. But there is no mention in the New Testament of the following books: Ru, Ezr, Neh, Est, Ct, Ob, Na, Ct, Eccl.

The testimony of the New Testament is not a sufficient and universal criterion to establish the inspiration of the whole of the Old Testament, much less of the New Testament itself.

Article IV. May Not the Apostolate Be a Criterion of Inspiration?

It is a negative criterion by reason of time.

Opinions.

What tradition tells us.

Controversies.

Index of Names

Biblical References

413

411

Index of Subjects